The Sinews of
American Commerce

Credit—Man's Confidence in Man

THE SINEWS OF
AMERICAN COMMERCE

Hanover Square 1844

ROY A. FOULKE
MANAGER, SPECIALIZED REPORT DEPT.
DUN & BRADSTREET, Inc.

Published by
DUN &-BRADSTREET, Inc.
on the Occasion of its 100th Anniversary
1841 - 1941

THE BUSINESS widely known today as Dun & Bradstreet, Inc., The Mercantile Agency, was organized in 1841, a year of great economic and social crisis in America. During the intervening one hundred years from 1841 to 1941, the evolution in the technique of credit reporting has become a vital part of our national economy. Dun & Bradstreet, Inc., is now entering its second century of credit service to American industry, commerce, finance, and insurance, in the midst of a great world crisis.

THE SINEWS OF AMERICAN COMMERCE commemorates the one hundredth anniversary of the founding of this enterprise. Over years of peace and war, prosperity and adversity, inflation and deflation, the specialized activities of The Mercantile Agency have closely paralleled the expanding use of credit in the United States. This community of interest is expressed in the publication of this volume which is a study of the development of credit and credit institutions from the days of the earliest permanent settlement in America to the very present.

President

DUN & BRADSTREET, Inc.

Management Chronology
of The Mercantile Agency

LEWIS TAPPAN, *Proprietor* - - - -	1841-1847
LEWIS TAPPAN BENJAMIN DOUGLASS } *Partners* - - -	1847-1849
BENJAMIN DOUGLASS ARTHUR TAPPAN } *Partners* - - -	1849-1854
BENJAMIN DOUGLASS ROBERT G. DUN } *Partners* - - -	1854-1859
ROBERT G. DUN, *Proprietor* - - - -	1859-1900
ROBERT DUN DOUGLASS, *Executive Trustee*	1900-1931
ARCHIBALD W. FERGUSON, *General Manager*	1910-1931

In 1931 the R. G. Dun Corporation was organized to take over the business of R. G. Dun & Co., the style under which The Mercantile Agency was then being operated, and the National Credit Office, Inc. In 1933 the business of The Bradstreet Company, which had been founded in 1849 by John M. Bradstreet, was acquired and the present style of Dun & Bradstreet, Inc., was adopted. Arthur D. Whiteside has been the President of the corporation from 1931 to the present time.

Officers and Directors of
Dun & Bradstreet, Inc.

ARTHUR D. WHITESIDE - - - - -	*President*
CHARLES E. TERRELL - - - - -	*Vice-President*
ARCHIBALD W. FERGUSON	*Vice-President & Treasurer*
THURLOW W. CUNLIFFE - - - -	*Secretary*
ARTHUR GARRETT - - - -	*Assistant Treasurer*
D. DOUGLASS DEMAREST - - -	*Assistant Secretary*

Board of Directors

EDWIN G. BAETJER	KENNETH B. GORDON
CHARLES M. CLARK, JR.	WILLIAM GREENOUGH
THURLOW W. CUNLIFFE	FRANCIS N. IGLEHART
GEORGE C. CUTLER	LESLIE G. McDOUALL
KINGMAN DOUGLASS	JOHN S. TABER
ARCHIBALD W. FERGUSON	CHARLES E. TERRELL

ARTHUR D. WHITESIDE

☆ *Preface* ☆

Credit, as a vital medium of exchange, has had its greatest application in the constantly expanding economic life of democratic America. Here, on the shores of a virgin continent, this currency minted of faith, has contributed as never before in history to the dynamic conquest of a new land, to the unprecedented rapid development of its resources, and to the building of a national economy that is strong far beyond any early aspirations.

Metallic currency was scarce from the earliest days of the first colonial settlement until the discovery of our own immense treasuries of gold and silver in the far west in the nineteenth century. That very scarcity "conditioned" the colonial business mind to liberal terms of sale, and created the most favorable environment to demonstrate the indispensability of credit to commercial and industrial progress.

Outside of modest colonial pawnbroking activity, and the development of the fire insurance company in the middle of the eighteenth century with its extension of mortgage loans, early credit was virtually a product of the daily activity of mercantile business enterprises, of importers, of wholesalers, and of retailers. Just before the end of the Revolutionary War the first commercial bank made its appearance on the economic scene and additional specialization in the extension of credit took place. As the years went by, more and more specialization occurred until today, hundreds of thousands of commercial and industrial business enterprises, thousands of pawnbrokers, insurance companies, commercial banks and trust companies, mutual savings banks, building and loan associations, factors, title guarantee and mortgage companies, sales and discount finance companies, personal loan companies, credit unions, industrial banks, stock exchange commission houses, credit agencies of the Federal Government, and the Federal Government itself, are engaged, each in their own specialized way, in extending credit.

Credit has been called a commodity, a perishable currency, a right of action, and many other terms far more rhetorical and legal. It is in truth a power rather than a thing, for it generates an energy which society utilizes in the profitable exchange and distribution of goods. The credit dollar is a much more potent element of sales energy than the cash dollar as the credit transaction is often the *beginning of a long and profitable relationship. It is the credit dollar upon which sustained relationships are built, and around which such human attributes as confidence, courage, and ability revolve.*

The gathering, the analysis, and the dissemination of credit information over the past one hundred years in America for and in behalf of the hundreds of thousands of commercial, industrial, financial, and insurance business enterprises of all kinds and sizes, have been quietly performed by that little known type of organization which has come to be characterized as the mercantile credit agency. The performance of these functions requires the services of thousands of skilled men and women employed by hundreds of mercantile credit agencies serving specialized trades and territories, as well as those which operate nationally. The credit reporter who carries on the basic work of the mercantile credit agency and the credit executive in the business enterprise, are the ever watchful eyes in the traffic tower which control the flow of exchange through the infinite channels of modern commerce, industry, and finance.

The purpose of this volume has been to gather the early facts and the folklore, the history and the evolution of American credit over the years from James Towne and Plimoth when business relationships were limited and simple, to the very present when they are infinitely more complicated; to examine the experiments and experiences with practical credit principles in our formative years; to part and to comb the complicated skeins of credit in modern commerce and to follow them to their sources; to consider the original and epoch making contributions of the pioneer credit reporters. Here is what we might call a credit interpretation of American economic life, a historical study of the intangible force which has made the wheels of economic, social, and political life go round. Credit is truly the sinews of commerce.

☆

The footnotes to the text are used only when references are made to original material such as unpublished handwritten letterbooks, ledgers, journals of business enterprises, and minutes of corporations from early colonial days to comparatively recent years, and to specialized studies which have appeared in periodicals. All published volumes from which material has been helpfully gleaned are listed in the bibliography at the end of each chapter.

July, 1941   R. A. F.

CONTENTS

Part Four · Evolution of The Mercantile Agency

Illustrations

PART ONE

☆

Credit Migrates to America

*I*N 1583, Sir Humphrey Gilbert personally paid all expenses to equip and to supply an expedition of five vessels with two hundred and fifty men, to make a permanent settlement on the island of Newfoundland. The ships sailed across the ocean from England, the adventurers disembarked, a colony was set up. . . . and then all traces of that settlement mysteriously disappeared like a pebble dropped in the middle of the Pacific Ocean.

From 1584 to 1587, Sir Walter Raleigh financed three expeditions, likewise entirely out of his own pocket, to the island of Roanoke off the coast of North Carolina. The third and last of these expeditions was confidently expected to become a permanent colony in the New World. Like the earlier attempt of Gilbert, however, this settlement mysteriously disappeared and has provided another of the great enigmas of American colonial history. After these three costly, personal, experiences, even Raleigh with his wealth and great influence, decided that the expenses entailed in planting a permanent colony in America were too great for one individual to bear.

Then came the first permanent English settlement at James Towne in Virginia, and the second at Plimoth in Massachusetts. Why and how they were financed are related in the following pages.

I ❋ First Two Business Ventures in the Colonies

ON SATURDAY, the twentieth of December in the "yeere" 1606, a fleet of three little vessels, the *Sarah Constant* of one hundred tons burden, the *Goodspead* of about forty tons, and the *Discovery,* a little pinnace of twenty tons, set "saile" from London, England, on a voyage across a broad watery expanse which has since become known as the Atlantic Ocean. Because "the winds continued contrarie so long," and "wee suffered great stormes" as the honorable gentleman, George Percy, the eighth son of Henry, eighth Earl of Northumberland, wrote in an unofficial diary of this memorable trip, the three little ships were unable to get out of sight of the English coast for six long "weekes."

An ocean crossing which may now be made on a luxury liner in four days with all of the comforts of home is far from the long drawn out trial of physical endurance that it was in the days of King James I. An early seventeenth century vessel was simply a hold built out of stout timbers, and covered by a deck. The hold was partly filled with sand ballast which then provided the floor. There were no dining rooms, lounge rooms, cocktail bars, gymnasiums, or highly polished kitchens. Each passenger not only brought along his own food but he did his own cooking at a fireplace built on the sand with a chimney running up through the deck. John Winthrop, the first governor of the Massachusetts Bay Colony, in his early *History of New England,* recorded the business propensity of "one Taylor, of Linne" who brought a milch cow with him when he crossed from England in 1640, and "sold the milk to the passengers for 2d the quart."

3

The hold was the abiding place of the passengers, but it also served as the storeroom for the supplies and the passengers' belongings. There were no private staterooms; the hold, in fact, was simply one large room as long and as wide as the ship. The officers and the crew lived in crowded quarters on the deck. These voyages were so long and so strenuous, and the food consisting of bread, salt meats, fish, beer, and strong drinks, was so monotonous and so meager, that deaths generally occurred. This little fleet heading southwestward carried one hundred and twenty men, no women and no children, and fifteen actually died before the shore of Virginia was sighted.

Captain Christopher Newport, who commanded the fleet, led the way around Spain and Portugal and then southwest through the old passage with the trade winds he trusted and knew so well. It was the route which had been developed by the Spaniards out of the experiences of many decades, as the shortest and the most favorable to the wide expanse of their settlements in the West Indies, on the mainland of South America, and in Central America. So Captain Newport, unacquainted with what later was to become known as the "great circle route" of the airway age, went the longest way 'round by the Canaries, southwest to the Windward Islands, northwest to Dominica and Guadaloupe, past Montserrat and Nevis to the Virgin Isles, and then northwest again to reach the mainland of the North American continent.

James Towne Settled as an Investment

It was "about foure a clocke in the morning" on the twenty-sixth day of April in the year 1607, over four months from the time they had set "saile" from London, that these three little ships, with the one hundred and five soldiers of fortune, who were still alive and only too anxious to trod again on dry land, were driven into the magnificent "Bay of Chesupioc directly, without any let or hinderance." This group of men had been duly commissioned to make the first permanent English settlement at James Towne, to explore the neighboring country, to convert the Indians to Christianity, to grow the crops, and of the greatest importance of all, to find profitable mines of precious silver and gold, similar to those which the Spaniards had long ago discovered and were actively exploiting at this time in Mexico and in Peru.

That expedition was a great adventure in the sense that adventuring is going thousands of miles away from home, from relatives and friends, from scenes and environments to which one has been long accustomed, from security into the vast unknown. In fact, the members of that first, memorable, permanent English colony in America were termed "adventurers" in the early records; however, those at home who had invested funds in the venture were also termed adventurers by Lord De-la-warre as they had "adventured" their money. It was an age of very refined and delicate distinctions.

The adventure of settling in America was to mean primitive hardships, unbearable heat, unwholesome water, disease, fighting for one's life, and the slow stark ebbing of life in the face of dwindling food supplies and vacillating Indian tribes, now very friendly, now cunningly hostile. It was to mean excitement in which lives were to be lost. It was to mean starvation and discouragement, with the probability that many would never again see the friendly chalk cliffs of Dover. This was particularly true in the early years of the colony, when there was such a complete failure to provide adequate food supplies, and to realize that wealth in the form of precious metals was not located along the North Atlantic seacoast awaiting exploration and the conquering European, as the early Spaniards had found it so easily in the land far to the south.

"The Treasurer and Company of Adventurers and Planters of the City of London for the first Colony in Virginia," or as the enterprise came to be known, "The London Company," received its charter dated the 10th of April, 1606, from King James I, commissioning it to establish the colony of Virginia, and it was pursuant to this charter that the three little ships set "saile" in the latter part of that year. Virginia, as the name was used in this highly descriptive title, included the entire Atlantic shore of North America as far north as the Hudson River.

This charter was granted to Sir Thomas Gates, Sir George Somers, Edward-Maria Wingfield, Thomas Hanham, Raleigh Gilbert, William Parker, George Popham, and "divers others," merchants, traders, and landed gentlemen. They knew no more about America than the typical, present-day investor knows about the oversea interests of any large American corporation with ramified international interests, in which he is a stockholder. Moreover, these early seventeenth century shareholders expected a profit from their investment just as present-day stockholders expect dividends from their investments. The shares in the London Company were originally sold to two hundred and three investors at twelve and one-half pounds each; a number which was materially increased at subsequent reorganizations. Thirteen of these original shareholders were also investors in the Muscovy Company that had a monopoly of the trade with Russia, and one hundred and sixteen were investors in the more successful East India Company. Quick profits and large profits were the order of the day and age. Here, however, was a dubious financial speculation if ever there was one.

This first permanent English settlement is of deep and peculiar interest to us because it was absolutely and fundamentally a business venture, a matter of investing money to earn a financial return. The James Towne settlement was the plantation of the London Company in the sense that the Company founded it and exercised jurisdiction over it. The London Company owned the land; it owned the equipment; it had property rights for a stipulated number of years in the labor of the settlers whom it sent over. The Company provided taskmasters; it fed and clothed the laborers; and it owned the produce resulting from their labor. In the present-day sense, the James Towne settlement was an industrial branch of the London Company whose headquarters were in England, rather than a compact political community.

Capital Accumulation in Great Britain

The sixteenth and the seventeenth centuries were years of capital accumulation in Great Britain. During the early part of this period, capital was represented largely by extensive real estate holdings on which sheep could be raised for their wool, the transition period between mediæval feudalism and the profit system in England. During the third quarter of the sixteenth century, capital was invested to an increasing extent in the machinery of commerce; that is, in ships and in merchandise to be carried to all parts of the known world for sale and for trade. In that process, the trading-voyages of many of the English, as Brooks Adams so carefully makes the basis of English economic development, were almost instinctively united with privateering and with the profitable slave trade by such well-known characters of English history as Drake, Hawkins, and Raleigh, men who combined a predatory martial and commercial temperament.

England changed in the sixteenth century from a country predominantly agricultural and commercially dependent upon Italy, the Hanse towns, and the Lowlands, receiving all of its finer manufactures from abroad, with little foreign shipping and overseas trade, to a country whose naval supremacy was acknowledged and whose merchant fleet rivalled that of the older commercial nations. As more and more capital became available from the exploitation of the Spaniards, it went into ships, shipping, and more merchandise for foreign trade.

There were no manufacturing industries comprised of substantial business enterprises in which money could be invested. Strange as it may now seem, when Queen Elizabeth died in 1603, and left behind her three thousand splendid dresses, the English nation did not hold a foot of land outside of the British Isles although it had all of the potentialities of a great modern state, a restless poor population, growing wealth, and the remnants of a declining social order.

Conquests by Spain Set the Fashion

The strongest, wealthiest, and most important nation in Europe at this very time was Spain, not England. Before the establishment of the first permanent English settlement at James Towne, the Spanish empire in opulent South and Central America and the fertile West Indies had existed for almost a century. By 1574, approximately one-third of a century before Captaine Newport had set "saile" from London, the Spanish settlers in America numbered 152,500. In addition to Spain and these extensive New World colonies, the Spanish sovereign was also the ruler of Germany, of Austria, of Flanders, and of several of the Italian states.

The Spaniards had found the world's richest silver mine at Potosi in 1545. It was the steady flow of this precious metal from the New World which provided the wealth to maintain dominance over a commercially expanding Europe down to the defeat of the Invincible Armada. If the Spaniards could find silver and gold so easily in Mexico and Peru, the English could do likewise in Virginia. It was far-fetched reasoning and expectation from our enlightened viewpoint, but it must be realized that the descriptions of the natural resources of this hemisphere were based largely upon a misleading idea of the geographical extent of the profitable exploits of the Spanish conquerors and explorers in Central and South America. These exploits were the most profitable of their kind in all of the pages of history.

Emphasis on the Precious Metals

At this time, increases in the home stocks of silver and gold were considered absolute wealth in all of the chancelleries of Europe, a theory which held for the two entire centuries preceding the publication of

Adam Smith's revolutionary *Wealth of Nations* in 1776. Exports must exceed imports, it was meticulously reasoned, in order to provide a favorable balance of trade which would then be paid in imported silver and gold.

The high value then attributed to the precious metals accounts largely for this conception of trade. Coin benefited the landed interests by raising the value of estates. Minted money enabled property owners to acquire a permanent, yet flexible, form of wealth, as commodities deteriorated and could not easily be hoarded because of their bulk. Merchants acquired fluid capital for use either at home and abroad. Artisans who largely manufactured one commodity were becoming dependent upon coin as the means of buying and selling. And in the days before the Bank of England was chartered, specie provided a far more reliable currency than the private instruments of credit.

So, we find during this period, that the English merchants who might have invested their surplus funds in large-scale manufacturing industries, if such a form of investment had been known at the time, gladly furnished the funds for exploration and colonization as profit-making ventures, particularly where the return was confidently expected to be in the direct form of the precious metals.

Investors Obtained No Dividends

In June, 1607, when Captaine Newport set "saile" homeward from Virginia, he had stowed away in his cabin a few handfuls of glittering yellow ore, now popularly known as "fool's gold." When he reached England he carefully turned his find over to the London Company. Here was real wealth. Ships now could sail to Virginia with supplies and return like the Spanish galleons loaded with treasures. The "adventurers" who had risked their investments would be wealthy, as wealthy as the maharajahs of India. But alas, the chemists reported with long faces that the glittering yellow ore was nothing but iron pyrites and worth not a penny!

This profit-seeking, economic interpretation of the first perma-nent English settlement in America is emphasized by the fact that the colony was hardly one year old, when the investors who had furnished the funds to plant the colony in expectation of immediate large profits, threatened to forsake the settlers amid their tremendous difficulties including actual starvation, as "banished men" if cargoes of goods worth

£2,000 were not immediately forthcoming. By this time the colony was in a terrible state. Many of the settlers had actually died. There was nothing to send as a return cargo except timber, so the entire community spent months in felling trees and in trimming logs for that homeward shipment of goods. There was no silver. There was no gold.

The lack of profits brought about a serious financial situation to the Company in England. When the shares in the venture had been sold, only a portion of the capital had been requested. A substantial number of the investors had counted upon their immediate profits to meet their second instalments. Consequently many of the original investors refused to pay the second instalment, and even more, the third instalment; so, whereas £52,624 was subscribed in stock from 1609 to 1619, only £36,624 was actually paid in. A pound sterling at this time, had a value between $20 and $25 in our modern currency.

The financial condition of the Company as early as 1610 was a serious problem. In the absence of working capital, Sir Thomas Smith borrowed against these unpaid subscriptions to keep the business alive and to finance follow-up voyages to Virginia. In 1612, the Company received the privilege of conducting lotteries to secure additional working funds. These lotteries yielded great profits; they were spoken of thereafter "as the real and substantial food" by which the Virginia settlement was actually nourished. In fact, until March, 1621 when the license to conduct lotteries was withdrawn by King James I, lotteries not only provided the funds to sustain a losing venture, but the very means of keeping the distant settlers alive.

Men of great wealth and political power were behind the organization and the management of the London Company. Sir Thomas Smith, the greatest merchant of his day was Treasurer until 1619 when he was succeeded by the statesman, Sir Edwin Sandys. Smith had been accused of mismanagement, as the Company had failed to show profits and no dividends had been forthcoming, especially at the very time when the East India Company was returning handsome profits to its investors. Under the Sandys' succeeding régime, however, the business likewise failed to produce profits. Operating costs continued to mount with no material offset in the form of income. America with its relatively sparse settlement of primitive natives was a far different country than populous India with its ancient teeming civilization.

In 1621, the Company was virtually bankrupt but like many business enterprises of today that are extended financially, it managed to drag along, year after year. No matter how embarrassed a business enterprise might be financially, it is impossible to anticipate when it might drop into the chasm of failures; like the old model automobile, it can always travel a few miles more. In 1624, the charter of the London Company was finally annulled, and the colony became a royal province administered directly under the authority of the king. During those intervening years, from the time when the three little vessels had set "saile" from London, approximately £150,000 had been sunk in this single unprofitable venture.

The tremendous difficulties in planting a colony thousands of miles westward and then supporting it with the costly transportation of requisite food, guns, ammunition, farming equipment, tools, cattle, and household goods, had not been quite so enchanting, quite so successful, or quite so profitable as raiding the Spanish main, carrying slaves, or trading with distant India. Gold and silver is where one finds it, but very little has ever been found in Virginia.

Plimoth Settlement Financed by a Loan

On the 6th day of September, 1620 a little more than thirteen years after the colonization of James Towne as a business venture, the *Mayflower,* a three-masted, double-deck vessel of one hundred and eighty tons put to sea from Plimoth, England, for Virginia, where those on board had obtained permission from the London Company to land and to plant a second colony. When this little vessel actually put to sea, it was only after three years of the most arduous negotiations, beginning in December, 1617 when the initial request had been forwarded from Leyden, Holland, signed by the greater part of the Pilgrim congregation, asking permission to settle in America. Discouragement followed discouragement, including the dissension in the management of the London Company because of the unprofitable operations, but finally through the influence of Sir Edwin Sandys, who had now become the Treasurer, the privilege to plant another colony in Virginia was finally obtained.

After this privilege had been secured, however, one more negotiation of fully as great importance, had to be entered into and completed. The Pilgrims had very little capital; their earnings in Holland barely furnished a living as the craftsmen's guilds had not permitted them to do well-paid work. Funds were needed in those days fully as

Whereas _Henry Earle of Huntingdon_ hath paid in ready mony to Sir _Thomas Smith_ knight, Treasurer of _Virginia_, the summe of _Fortye Lownds_ • • • • • • • • • • for his aduentures towards the said voiage. It is agreed, that for the same, he the said _Earle of Huntingdon_ his heires, executors, administrators or assignes, shall haue ratably according to his aduenture, his full part of all such lands, tenements and hereditaments, as shall from time to time bee there recouered, planted, and inhabited. And of such Mines and Mineralles of Golde, Siluer, and other mettals or treasure, Pearles, Precious stones, or any kinde of wares or Marchandizes, commodities or profits whatsoeuer, which shall be obtained or gotten in the said voiage, according to the portion of money by him imployed to that vse, in as ample maner as any other Aduenturer therein shall receiue for the like summe. Written this _fourth_ of _august_ ⁓ _Anno Domini_ 1610

Edward May

"Bill of Adventure," Acknowledging Payment for a Share Interest in The London Company

much as today, to uproot a band of settlers from one country where they had lived for twelve years, to transport them far across an ocean to an unknown virtual wilderness, and to furnish the primitive household utensils, farming implements, handy tools, seeds, clothing, food, supplies, arms, and ammunition, needed to develop livelihoods and to protect themselves.

The question of raising additional funds which together with their accumulated meager savings would be sufficient for this purpose, was not quite so difficult as it might seem at first glance. Capital accumulation had by this time created a class of wealthy merchants and traders in London and Liverpool who were looking for ways and means of putting their "surplus" funds to work, just as representatives of American investment banking firms were looking for ways and means of putting American capital to work, prior to 1929 in Argentine, Australia, Brazil, China, Peru, and Greece.

Thomas Weston, a merchant of London, had heard rumors of the negotiations which were being carried on with the London Company. The Pilgrims were hard-working, sober, industrious, God-fearing characters, men who lived up to their word, and the extension of a modest amount of credit to such a group of conscientious individuals looked like an unusually safe and profitable opportunity for making a loan. Weston made a trip from London to Leyden, especially to interview "Mr. Robinson and other of the cheefe of them," as Bradford laboriously wrote in his early history of the Plimoth Plantation. After this meeting, Weston, with his associates, were so satisfied with the opportunity for profits and the safety of what money they would put out, that they offered to furnish the necessary funds to finance the Pilgrims on their contemplated voyage across the ocean.

Terms of Original Loan Were Heavy

The agreement, which was finally drawn up between them, provided that the entire company of one hundred and one emigrants would constitute a partnership responsible to the London merchants who were backing the venture "for all credit advanced and to be advanced," credit to hire a ship to carry them to a new land, and to purchase all necessary supplies to get settled there. As guarantee to the investors who were furnishing the requisite credit, the entire body of emigrants bound themselves under the terms of an agreement to work for a period of seven years, to place their produce into a common warehouse and to receive their subsistence out of the common store, a temporary communistic arrangement for the good of the entire body.

At the end of the seven years there would be a settlement. The services of each emigrant would be rated as a capital of £10. For every £10 of property he brought with him he would receive an additional share. All profits would be reserved for the seven years, when the entire amount, and all houses and land, gardens and fields, would be divided among the shareholders according to their respective interests. A London merchant, who had advanced £100 would receive tenfold more than the penniless emigrant for his entire service of the seven years. That equation certainly gives an early relationship between the value of capital and labor!

After weathering many cross winds and the usual autumnal storms, the Pilgrims found themselves in sight of land on November 6, 1620, but far to the north of the territory where they had obtained permission to settle. The cold season was advanced and the place for the settlement had to be chosen. Week after week they searched the coast for a satisfactory harbor, amid snow and hail and rain, with illness rampant, and food supplies running low. Finally, on December 21, they made their historic landing at Plimoth, the entire country being "full of woods and thickets," and presenting "a wild and savage line."

Unlike the soldiers of fortune who had settled at James Towne and who were mostly gentlemen, yeomen, and merchants, and whose primary interest had been the discovery of precious metals, the settlers at Plimoth were petty farmers, laborers, and artisans, who had been forced to learn difficult trades in Holland, where they eked out a precarious livelihood after fleeing from England. They were accustomed to hard work and they were planning a permanent settlement for the rest of their natural lives. Their interests were in building durable homes, growing crops for food, trading for furs with Indians, and cutting timber for shipment to England.

The original loan, we have seen, was for a seven-year period and the settlers were to lead a kind of communistic existence, with all produce put into a common storehouse. In 1623, however, the communistic arrangement was modified; a parcel of land was assigned for use to every family so that it could raise its own food, "for the young men that were most able and fitte for labour and service did repine that they should spend their time and streingth to worke for other men's wives and children, with out any recompense."

Terms of Loan Revamped and Extended

In 1626, after the passage of six of the original seven years for which the initial credit had been granted, Izaack Allerton was sent to England to negotiate a final settlement with the London merchants for the funds advanced and not repaid up to that time. The new agreement provided that the Pilgrims who were still indebted to the extent of £1,800 would repay this amount at the rate of £200 yearly "on the west side of ye Royall Exchaing in London . . . . on ye feast of St. Migchell," the first payment to be made in 1628. So, instead of dividing the assets in accordance with the terms of the original agreement, the Pilgrims worked out an arrangement whereby they were to obtain title to all of the possessions in the colony for the sum of £1,800 to be paid in nine equal yearly instalments, that is, with annual instalments of £200 each, running up to, and including the year, 1637.

This agreement, however, was not the end of the financing arrangements. In addition to the £1,800 owed to their London backers, there were outstanding other obligations "aboute some £600." These total obligations were nominal when compared with the staggering losses of the London Company but the amount was substantial to men who had spent their entire lives on the bare margin of existence, sufficiently so, to give concern to William Bradford, Miles Standish, William Brewster, John Alden, Thomas Prence, Edward Winslow, John Howland, and Izaack Allerton, as to how they could be discharged.

Trading Agreement in Behalf of the Colony

It was now finally decided that these particular men should form a general partnership in behalf of the entire colony, to trade in colonial and English merchandise with the hope and expectation of earning sufficient profits to retire these debts. Allerton was sent to England for this purpose and there he concluded an arrangement with three of the London backers, James Sherley, a goldsmith, John Beauchamp, a salter, and Richard Andrews, a shipowner, who agreed to become partners in the trading agreement. Sherley, Beauchamp, and Andrews would purchase merchandise in England for the account of the group; shoes, cotton and woolen cloth, linens, bedticks, blankets, salt, spikes, nails, tools, pistols, muskets, powder, and shot, which would then be sold by the Plimoth partners to the settlers, traded with the Indians, or with the European fishermen on their annual voyages to the fishing banks off

Newfoundland and Nova Scotia; and, in turn, would receive and sell for the account of the Plimoth partners, all shipments from the colony, primarily beaver, bear, mink, fox, and otter furs, fish, and timber.

Unfortunately this trading agreement did not turn out as planned. First of all, the English partners undertook certain speculations without the knowledge and the approval of the colonists, such as sending ships from England to fish along the fishing banks, ventures which turned out to be extremely unprofitable. Second, over the years, the English partners disagreed among themselves, and unbeknown to the colonists, Sherley kept the proceeds of the sale of later shipments for his own personal account. Third, the records were so poorly and incompletely kept both in England and in Plimoth that a reconciliation of accounts became more and more difficult.

Final Arrangements for Settlement of the Loan

Disputes about these matters were carried on year after year. Finally in 1641, James Sherley, who was getting well along his allotment of years, appointed two close friends who were residents in Massachusetts, to represent his interest in trying to come to some adjustment on these long-standing obligations. The final agreement—it was now twenty-one years since the *Mayflower* had sailed from England—recounted that the Pilgrim partners were still indebted to the three English partners for £1,200; of this sum £400 would be paid as soon as releases would come from the English partners, and the remaining £800 in yearly instalments of £200 each. Under this arrangement, it took the Pilgrim fathers until 1645, twenty-five long years, and not the originally anticipated, biblical seven, to repay their merchant-backers, who had assisted the original venture by the modest extension of credit.

So, we see that the settlement at James Towne was financed by a chartered organization, the London Company, solely as a profit-making piece of business, just as a modern corporation might undertake a venture in Chile, in South Africa, or in Cuba, to earn a profit. The settlement at Plimoth, on the other hand, was financed on credit, initially by a loan for seven years with a participating profit feature. This loan was extended for the sole purpose of making profits by wealthy London merchants, and the Pilgrims were indebted to certain of these particular merchants, not for seven, but for a continuous period of twenty-five long years.

Bibliographical References to Chapter One

ADAMS, BROOKS, *The Law of Civilization and Decay;* New York, 1898.

BEARD, CHARLES A. and MARY R., *The Rise of American Civilization;* 1927, Edition of 1936, New York.

BRADFORD, GOVERNOR WILLIAM, *History of Plimoth Plantation.* Original manuscript history of Plymouth written in the years preceding 1647; Boston, 1898.

BROWN, ALEXANDER, *The Genesis of the United States;* New York, 1890.

BRUCE, PHILIP ALEXANDER, *Economic History of Virginia in the Seventeenth Century;* Two Volumes, New York, 1895.

GRAS, N. S. B., and LARSON, HENRIETTA M., *Casebook in American Business History;* New York, 1939.

NETTELS, CURTIS P., *The Roots of American Civilization;* New York, 1938.

PERCY, MASTER GEORGE, *Observations gathered out of a Discourse of the Plantation of the Southerne Colonie in Virginia by the English, 1606.* The original manuscript is not preserved, and what has come down to us is an abridgment published for the first time in 1625 by Samuel Purchas. Reprinted in *Narratives of Early Virginia, 1606-1625,* edited by Lyon Gardiner Tyler; New York, 1907.

PHILLIPS, ULRICH B., *Plantation and Frontier Documents: 1649-1863;* Volume I of "A Documentary History of American Industrial Society;" Cleveland, 1909.

SMITH, CAPTAIN JOHN, *A True Relation of such occurrences and accidents of noate as hath hapned in Virginia since the first planting of that Collony, which is now resident in the South part thereof, till the last returne from thence;* London, England, 1608. Copy in the library of the New York Historical Society.

WINTHROP, JOHN, *The History of New England from 1630 to 1649;* a two-volume record of the Massachusetts Bay Colony kept over the early years of the Colony by the first Governor, edited by James Savage; Boston, 1853.

WOODWARD, W. E., *A New American History;* New York, 1938.

PART TWO

☆ ☆

Credit in the Colonies

A SUBSTANTIAL portion of the domestic trade and foreign commerce of the colonies was carried on by the exchange of one product for other products. The "other products" might be commodities specified by law to be legal mediums of exchange, raw materials or manufactured merchandise used in primitive barter, the metallic currencies of foreign countries, inflated paper money of the several colonies, credit instruments such as bills of exchange, promissory notes, and open book accounts.

Barter was the most common method of carrying on trade and commerce throughout most of this era, and depreciated paper money the most widely used during the Revolutionary War. All of the above mentioned "other products," however, were used simultaneously during the entire colonial period.

Mediums of exchange whether actual commodities, metallic currency, paper money, bills of exchange, promissory notes, or open book accounts, are all expressions of credit. The receiver must have confidence that the unit of exchange will provide a familiar standard; if wampum, tobacco, pork, or handmade nails, of a recognized quality; if metallic currency, in the amount and fineness of the metallic content of the currency, itself, and of the government which coined it; if paper money, of the faith of the government or the organization which issued it; if bills of exchange or promissory notes, of the signers of the instruments; and if open book accounts, of the debtor.

II * From Wampum to "Continental" Paper Currency

WHEN the early colonists sailed from England, they took sufficient victuals with them to care for their needs, not only on the high seas, but also for an extended period after their arrival and settlement. The soil in a new land had to be prepared carefully, the seeds planted, and the crops cultivated before they could be harvested. The way of nature is bountiful but slow. The James Towne expedition sighted land on April 26, 1607, but Captaine Newport did not start his return voyage to England until June 22, almost two months later, and by that time substantial inroads had been made upon the initial stocks of the settlers' precious provisions.

In the earliest description of the happenings at this first permanent English settlement on the new continent, published in London in 1608 by John Smith, he wrote that the "plantation" had provisions on hand only "for thirteen or fourteen weeks" when Captaine Newport headed his ships away from the verdant shores of Virginia. By September 10, forty-six of the adventuring settlers had died from illness and the lack of nourishment. He continued lucidly but quaintly, "Onely of Sturgion wee had great store, whereon our men would so greedily surfet, as it cost manye their lives."

Finally, when their victuals were "within eighteene dayes spent," twenty-eight year old John Smith with youthful, sweeping, self-possession staved off utter and complete famine by taking a short trip "to the mouth of the river, to Kegquouhtan, an Indian Towne, to trade for Corne." Eskimos might have an unsatisfied craving for gum

19

drops, but the Indians who were living at Kegquouhtan at this time were naïvely attracted by "blew" beads, little scraps of polished copper, bells, pins, needles, glasses, and hatchets, all of which had fortunately been included in the first outward cargo, and which Smith now skill-fully and artfully traded for bushels of the staple golden grain of the new land, Indian corn.

Just as the Pilgrims had been about to sail from England, a difference of opinion had arisen with Thomas Weston who insisted that somewhat more onerous terms with greater security, be given to him and to his close associates for their advances of credit, than those which had been so carefully discussed and so meticulously set down in the original agreement between them. Because the Pilgrims would not agree to the suggested change, Weston refused to advance an additional £100 needed, Bradford explained, "to clear things at their going away," and the little group of hardy wanderers, "were forst to selle of some of their provisions to stop this gape, which was some three or four score firkins of butter which commoditie they might best spare."

Unfortunately, the settlers at James Towne with their greater interest in searching for the precious metals, failed to realize the immediate and absolute necessity of cultivating large crops. They planted a little wheat, a few patches of pumpkins, potatoes, and some melon, but hardly enough to sustain an entire colony of young, hardy adventurers. Additional provisions and supplies, they felt assured, would be sent over by the London Company to protect and to develop the substantial monetary investment which was already at stake. But, as it disastrously turned out, they were unable to depend upon adequate food supplies from England, and moreover, when such shipments were made they were often damaged, destroyed, lost, or even consumed en route. "There was no talke, no hope, no worke, but dig gold, wash gold, refine gold, load gold."

The Pilgrims Trade with the Indians

The Pilgrims, on the other hand, took life more seriously; they were planting a permanent colony where they would spend the rest of their earthly lives. Their dwindling food supplies were augmented with fish, clams, and fowl, and then diligently stretched until the auspicious harvest which provided the occasion for that first historic Thanksgiving. The crops raised during this season, the elders then carefully estimated, would be sufficient for the needs of the entire colony for no longer than approximately six months. Wheat grains and pea seeds which had been transported with the utmost care from England, had been planted and painstakingly cultivated, but for some unexplained reason, these two crops turned out to be almost worthless during this first crucial season. Food supplies dropped lower and lower, until late in the summer of 1622, each person was receiving an allotment of but one-quarter of a pound of bread a day, watchfully doled out by Governor Bradford. Butter which they had sold "at their going away" was the least of their vital needs.

Unlike the more worldly, profit-seeking, management of the London Company, who had so practically arranged the first cargo for the James Towne settlers, the Pilgrims had failed to bring along "blew" beads, pieces of bright copper, bells, pins, needles, glasses, or extra hatchets, articles which could have been used in trade with the more friendly Wampanoag Indians of the north for precious corn. In one of those coincidences which so often changes the course of history, it now happened that the English ship *Discovery,* trading southward along the coast toward Virginia under one Captain Jons, sailed into the Plimoth harbor just at this particular time of solemn and dramatic need. With Captain Jons, the settlers now engaged in primitive barter, trading beaver skins for English beads and knives, more welcome under the circumstances than all of the jewels of the Arabian nights, so that "they were fitte againe to trade for beaver and other things," and by "other things" Governor Bradford meant nourishing food, principally golden grains of Indian corn.

Origin of American Commerce

From these earliest days, commerce with the Indians was thus essential to the actual existence of the colonial settlements, commerce which would provide the very sustenance of life. No credit was involved in these business dealings. It was primitive, age-old, simple trade. The settlers had to barter for the corn which they needed. Fortunately they could exchange primeval *objets d'art* for indispensable, nutritious, life-sustaining food.

As the colonies grew in population and spread in area, the commerce with the Indians grew to immense proportions, developing into the exchange of beads, hatchets, knives, muskets, ammunition, blankets, coats, biscuits, and most important of all, of wampum, for beaver, otter, mink, bear, raccoon, and fox furs and skins. Until 1646, beaver was to be the greatest single item of export from the colonies to Europe. In this early, primitive, and basic barter with the Indians is found the origin of the present tremendous domestic and foreign commerce of these United States. How simple the origins really are of most of our complicated modern business institutions!

Later, fish destined to provide the great basis for the mightiest of the New England industries, and still later rum, were to succeed furs as the most important single items of foreign commerce. And over the entire period of the colonial years, timber and timber products in the form of ships, masts and spars for the British royal navy, staves out of which barrels could be made by sugar shippers in the West Indies and wine merchants in the Portuguese and Spanish Islands, pitch, tar, rosin, turpentine, potash, tobacco, and rice were to be important, staple items of export.

Wampum the First Colonial Money

At the present time, the United States is the gold reservoir of the world. In addition to unprecedented metallic wealth of our own, billions of dollars in gold have been entrusted to our care by sovereign nations and by foreigners whose current political and economic outlooks are as unsettled as the shifting sands of the desert. In June, 1940 we held 73.6 per cent of the gold reserves of the fifty-two, important central banks and governments in the world for which figures periodically were made available.*

The daily statement of the United States Treasury as of December 31, 1940 showed this greatest stock of the precious yellow metal in all history, amounted to the colossal figure of $21,994,000,000. One of the great, fundamental problems of economics and of politics, when the present World War becomes material for far-seeing philosophers, will be what to do with this tremendous stock of gold, as most of the nations of the world will be practically stripped of the metal which has provided the traditional standard of monetary currency and the basis for settling international balances. Already this unusual situation has brought about more than a mild reversion to primitive barter in international commerce.

Our everyday, domestic trade is carried on with copper coins, nickel coins, silver coins, and paper money of many kinds and descrip-

---

* *Federal Reserve Bulletin*, December, 1940, Volume 26, Number 12, p. 1328.

tions (except "gold certificates"), United States notes, Federal Reserve notes, Federal Reserve bank notes, National bank notes, and silver certificates. To support these various issues of paper money we have accumulated this immense amount of gold bullion and a collateral supply of silver bullion. Our stock of gold bullion finally became so imposing that the Treasury Department in 1936 constructed what has been widely described as an impregnable storage fortress to hold this precious metal at Fort Knox, Kentucky, and in 1938 one for silver at historic West Point, New York.

Primitive Colonial Economic Life

With such a variety of everyday coins and paper money, with such tremendous reserves of gold and silver, is it any wonder that it is difficult for us, today, to picture an early society on this continent consisting of a few hundred, and then a few thousand of Europeans who were attempting to live and to carry on a growing commerce with the natives, among themselves, with Europe, and with the West Indies, with practically no metallic currency? In fact, the keynote of our entire colonial economic history is found in the scarcity of metallic currency, and in the constant series of expedients and experiments by which the colonists attempted to solve this basic economic dilemma. What a basic economic dilemma it proved to be over the years! The problem was to the colonists what the puzzle of unemployment has been and is to us, in our own day.

The seventeenth and eighteenth centuries comprised a continuous period of primitive life on this continent. No other word adequately describes it. There was only one way to pay for the necessary supplies of manufactured equipment, implements, tools, merchandise, and goods, which were so greatly needed and constantly imported from Europe. Furs, lumber, lumber products, tobacco, rice, and later, fish and rum, had to be shipped in payment. The lumber, lumber products, tobacco, rice, and later, the fish from the fishing banks, and the rum, were provided by the actual labor of the colonists, themselves.

To obtain the furs, which was by far the outstanding single item of export in the early years of New England and New Netherlands, something had to be given to the Indians in exchange, as the animals were trapped almost entirely by the natives and the skins brought to the early settlements and trading posts. The most important article used in this early exchange with the Indians was nothing more or less

than the native aboriginal jewelry, Indian wampum. Today we think
of wampum as comprising picturesque museum pieces; three hundred
years ago it was cash, the one prime, absolute, medium of exchange
used to carry on colonial, domestic trade.

Early Use and Importance of Wampum

Wampum was the name given to black and white beads made
from the whorls of periwinkle shells in which holes were bored with
stone drills, the beads then being strung on fibres of hemp, on tendons
taken from the forest meat, or embroidered on pieces of deerskin to
form girdles or belts as ornaments and charms. Like all primitive races,
the Indians were congenitally superstitious. Each shell cylinder was
about one-eighth of an inch in diameter and approximately one-quarter
of an inch long. To bore these cylinders with a primitive stone drill
was the work of a deft artisan, who must then polish them on stones
"in a weary round of labor." All early accounts of the colonies agree
that the finished product had a unique degree of elegance.

The enterprising Dutch, at this time, the brilliant commercial
nation of Europe, were the first to appreciate the indigenous economic
use of wampum as token money in their trade with the Indians
on Long Island. Here, it is said, the finest wampum was produced.
In March, 1627 Isaak de Rasier, Secretary of the Dutch settlement of
New Netherlands, sailed into Plimoth harbor in the bark, *Nassau,* to
negotiate a friendly trade treaty with Governor Bradford. In that cargo
there happened to be wampum valued at approximately £50 which
de Rasier now exchanged with the Plimoth settlers. These beads subsequently were taken north to the Plimoth trading post on the Kennebec
River, and here they moved as slowly as ice skates in Brazil, until the
news of the existence of the wampum reached the ears of the interior
Indians. Then a spontaneous and effective demand for wampum arose
and expanded, year after year, until it was in use as everyday monetary
currency in every colony.

As long as beaver was the most important single item of export,
wampum maintained its basic intrinsic value, but that value constantly
fluctuated with the European market price for beaver. These fluctuations are clearly evidenced by the contemporary legislation of the
various colonies. About 1630, for example, Roger Williams wrote that
wampum was quoted at approximately three beads for a penny, and in
the same year, Massachusetts made it legal tender at six beads for a

penny for any sum under twelve pence, and in 1641, for any sum of £10 or less.

By 1645, the inventories of deceased colonists commonly contained items of wampum, and, strange as it may now seem to us, frequently there was mention of no other money. Judgments of the courts were made payable in wampum. The Dutch had hardly any other effective currency for the smaller sums, and as late as 1662, practically all of the revenue in New Netherlands was actually paid in wampum and in beaver skins.

Decline in the Use of Wampum

Wampum reached its height in real value about 1646. After that date, it began to decline for three fundamental reasons. The price of beaver skins, with which it was so closely related, fell in England, and as a result, the value of wampum dropped in the colonies. The white man, with imported steel drills, was able to manufacture the beads more rapidly than the Indians, and soon there was an "over-issue" of the money, an over-issue similar to that of German marks after the first World War but the final black-out was not quite so complete. Finally, counterfeiting began; the natural black beads were worth double the white ones, and shrewd colonists with an ever-present eye on the profit-motive began to dye the white beads!

All of the New England colonies had withdrawn the legal tender quality from wampum by 1662. It remained in circulation in smaller transactions, and continued to circulate in the more remote, interior districts of New England and as far south as the Potomac River until the beginning of the eighteenth century. In spite of its disadvantages, wampum served as a universal currency in the colonies for practically three-quarters of a century, and during most of that time it was readily exchangeable for merchandise, labor, and taxes. Frequently there was no other currency. It was the first widely used unit of credit, and the first widely used medium of trade in the colonies.

Commodity Money in the Colonies

At the same time that wampum was being used so extensively, other commodities also began to appear as mediums of exchange. If, today, we had few or no metallic coins in circulation, and no sound paper money as everyday currency, we would try similar ingenious expedients. A means for carrying on commerce has always been developed by the aggressive members of society. In fact, it has been explained that during the summer of 1931, in the early years of the Great Depression, when Benjamin Stringham was on the road from Idaho to Salt Lake City with several automobile truck-loads of potatoes, he conceived the idea of exchanging his surplus products directly for other commodities in the temporary, local, absence of actual money.* This movement of simple barter and exchange developed into what has since become widely known in the West and Middle-West as self-help organizations.†

Products Used as Currency in Northern Colonies

In 1631, just three hundred years before Benjamin Stringham drove his trucks loaded with potatoes into Salt Lake City, the colony of Massachusetts ordered that "corne shall pass for payment of all debts at the usual rate it is sold for, except money or beaver be expressly named." The colonies generally voted from year to year the rates at which certain specified products would be received into the public treasury in payment of taxes, and in this way, an attempt was made to control prices. Wheat in 1640, for example, was made current at six shillings a bushel in Massachusetts, rye and barley at five shillings, and peas at six. In 1662, Rhode Island made beef, pork, and peas, receivable not at a fixed rate, but at their market prices. In 1674, Rhode Island made wool at twelve pence per pound, a standard of value. In comparison with most other commodities, wool represented a fundamental improvement as it had an imperishable quality. Pennsylvania, in 1683, made flax at eight pence a pound, and hemp at four pence a pound, current for the payment of debts.

The fact that commodities could be used as money under local colonial laws did not, and could not determine their actual commercial values. The value of surplus produce, and the surplus could only be used in the export trade, was determined by foreign market conditions, and legislate as they would, the colonists could not maintain values on these commodities higher than they would bring when sold abroad, less transportation costs. That would seem to be almost an economic axiom. Great Britain had a similar experience in attempting to maintain

* "Barter and Exchange Movement in Utah," in *Monthly Labor Review*, March 1933, Volume 36, Number 3, p. 451, pub. by U. S. Dept. of Labor. † *Monthly Labor Review*, December 1939, Volume 49, Number 6, pp. 1335-1347.

the price of rubber by restricting production under the Stevenson Rubber Restriction Plan in the Malay peninsula in 1922-1928, and we have had a little familiarity in this line of economic experimentation in recent years, with wheat, cotton, and silver. Values of basic raw products are determined by world markets, not by legislation.

It was soon discovered that when commodities which were not uniform in quality, and very few were uniform in quality, were used extensively as colonial money, taxes and other debts often would be settled by payment with the poorer specimens. The commodities used as money were the staples of each region. Most farmers raised them and so doing "operated mints." The temptation was too great not to put the poorer quality into circulation. As a result of this instinctive economic behavior, righteous Massachusetts in 1658 issued an order that no man should attempt to discharge his taxes with "lank" cattle.

Other disadvantages also showed themselves; the cost of transporting produce with which taxes were paid from different parts of the Massachusetts colony to Boston amounted to about ten per cent of the entire receipts, and an additional loss of approximately five per cent was incurred through shrinkage and deterioration. The treasury, moreover, had to be relieved from time to time of redundant merchandise by placing it on the market at the current price, which incidentally and generally would be somewhat below the legally accepted rate. Meat and grain had to be guarded against deterioration. New York finally solved this particular problem by ordering that pork and beef accepted as money would be valued by the barrel and would be "well repacked by the sworn packer" of the province. Here was a kind of a modern meat-packing inspection system.

Most commodities used as money were large in bulk in relation to their value. Wheat and tobacco worth five shillings often weighed as much as sixty pounds. Naturally it was rather difficult to use these commodities in everyday trade; payments of any appreciable size required a conveyance to move them. One could not very well carry a pound sterling's worth of wheat, or pork, or wool in his pocket.

In this economic setting, it was natural that a variety of products, in addition to the commodities specified by respective colonies as money, would be used to pay the costs of education. One student, later president of Harvard College, settled his bill in 1649 with "an old cow," and the accounts of the construction of the first college building include an entry, "Received a goat 30s plantation of Watertown rate, which died."

27

Products Used as Currency in Southern Colonies

Other staple products were utilized as substitutes for the scarce metallic money in the Southern colonies. Of these products, tobacco was the most important. Tobacco was used as currency in Virginia for almost two centuries beginning about 1619, and in Maryland for a century and a half. Houses, furniture, food, farm implements, and cattle were actually valued and sold for so many pounds of tobacco. In the latter part of the seventeenth century, for example, the personal estate of Cornelius Lloyd was valued at 131,044 pounds of tobacco.

Like corn, wheat, and cattle in New England, tobacco fluctuated greatly in value; as the production of tobacco increased, its value depreciated, and persons who had wages payable to them in so many pounds of tobacco found themselves with a shrinking purchasing power. Tobacco, moreover, was not a uniform product, and like cattle, the quality might range from the best to worthless trash. In fact, if one may place reliance upon current radio programs, the same degree of variation exist today; tobacco may be mild or strong, kind or unkind to your throat, with considerable nicotine or little, depending upon the soil where it is grown, the leaves which are selected for curing, the curing process, and whether or not it is toasted, or treated with health giving ultra-violet rays! Maryland in 1698, found it necessary to legislate against the fraud of packing trash in hogsheads which contained good tobacco only on the top. Virginia found it necessary to do likewise in 1705.

An innovation of considerable significance took place in 1713 when a Virginia tobacco act provided for an early type of warehouse receipt. Planters were directed to bring their tobacco to public warehouses where it would be tested, weighed and stored. The planter then received in exchange, certificates called tobacco notes. These notes stated the amount and the quality of the tobacco deposited, and constituted the planter's title to the tobacco. The notes were freely transferable and were used in place of actual tobacco for all payments in the colony. The last holder acquired the right to remove and sell the tobacco covered by the note.

South Carolina in 1687, made corn legal currency at two shillings a bushel, English peas at three shillings six pence a bushel, and pork at twenty shillings a hundred weight. In this colony, however, rice became the principal medium of exchange. The assembly made rice receivable for taxes in 1719, "to be delivered in good barrels upon the bay at Charleston." Rice went into circulation as money chiefly in the form of rice orders or certificates, similar to the tobacco notes in Virginia, at the rate of thirty shillings for one hundred pounds of rice.

All of these commodities naturally had fluctuating market values. The laws of most of the colonies, however, made them legal tender at a fixed rate. In South Carolina, for example, where corn was one of several legal commodities, it passed at two shillings a bushel. The invariable practice was to value these commodities for public payment at legal prices which would be higher than the prevailing market prices. Shortly after the act of 1687, it was found in South Carolina that the money prices of the commodities used as currencies, were actually three times their sterling values.

Necessity the Mother of Ingenuity

During the colonial years, many commodities in addition to those already mentioned, were authorized and used as money in the payment of public and private debts, oats, bacon, dried fish, tallow, butter, cheese, sugar, brandy, whisky, and even musket balls. New Hampshire always in need of European manufactured commodities, and with little direct foreign commerce, passed what was probably the most original act in 1693, requiring that vessels not owned in the province pay for each ton, a duty of eighteen pence in money or one pound of powder. When the need for powder subsequently increased, the law was modified requiring payment in powder, alone. Necessity was certainly the mother of ingenuity in developing mediums of exchange for paying taxes and for carrying on domestic trade. In the current interpretation of legislation, this would mean only one thing, government regimentation, the regulation of prices.

It was impossible to collect money for taxes from settlers who had no money. Primitive substitutes, crude as they were, had to be created to assist in the economic foundation of a new free society where trade was being developed and nourished in spite of all natural handicaps and difficulties.

The use of commodity money differed somewhat from simple barter insofar as the colonial assemblies enacted legislation providing that the specified products would be received in payment of taxes and all other public debts. The enumerated commodities then served as actual money. They were paid by the colony to its creditors; their use in all public transactions was compulsory. Consequently they differed in legal standing from all other commodities which were bartered in private trading transactions. There existed a sustained demand for commodity money commensurate with the fiscal needs of the colonial government, and so, any individual would accept a designated product with the assurance that he would be able to dispose of it in the payment of taxes. Ordinarily, if a Virginian received tobacco in payment of a debt, he did so, not with the purpose of using the tobacco himself, but of making other purchases with it.

Similar situations actually exist in widely different parts of the world today. Salt is currently used as a medium of exchange in Abyssinia; brick tea in Siberia, Turkestan, Mongolia and Tibet; black and white shells in the Solomon Islands; round flat stones from twelve inches to twelve feet in diameter, something like colonial millstones, in the island of Yap; while during and after the first World War, oilcloth, wood, porcelain, and leather currency were in widespread use in Germany, and iron money in Belgium, Italy, Russia, and Germany. After all, what we generally think is our highly delicate, modern economy is not so very far removed from these natural economic experiments of our own early colonial days.

Scarcity of Metallic Currency

There were no gold or silver mines in the English colonies. In fact, the only colonial mines of any kind, and they were worked very little at the time, produced copper in Connecticut, lead in Virginia, and iron ore in Connecticut, northern New Jersey and eastern Pennsylvania. In his action-filled novel, *Drums Along the Mohawk,* Walter D. Edmonds painted a vivid picture of a war prison developed out of the copper mine at Simsbury, Connecticut, where British sympathizers were interned during the Revolutionary War. The prison was seventy feet below the open air! As late as the Revolution, our tremendous natural wealth of industrial metals was virtually unexploited. Consequently the only way for the colonists to obtain gold and silver specie was to import it in exchange for other commodities, or to receive it in payment as carriers for English commerce on the high seas.

The colonists, for the most part, were people of little or no means, and they brought very little money along with them; what little they occasionally did bring, was speedily sent back to England in payment for articles of luxury, necessary tools, and supplies, such as agricultural implements, plows, hardware, muskets, ammunition, shot, household utensils, crockery, blankets, shoes, and glassware. Even when the balance of trade with England or with the West Indies was favorable to a particular trader, the final settlement of the indebtedness was more likely to be in needed merchandise than in metallic coins.

The obvious method of attempting to meet this very natural but unfortunate predicament, and the one which has been tried in similar circumstances in all ages and in all parts of the world, was by the simple prohibition of the export of metallic money. Here was an early attempt at economic discipline. A Massachusetts law of 1654 forbade the exportation of coin, except a sum not over twenty shillings for traveling expenses, upon pain of forfeiture of the offender's entire estate. In 1697, another act was passed liberalizing the amount a person could carry out of the province to not more than £5 for his necessary expenses. New York, Virginia, and Maryland at one time or another also tried this radical expedient. These laws, however, were allergic to the interests of the mother country and the influence of the Crown stood staunchly in the way of enforcing such "left-wing" legislation.

This same technique of attempting to retain control of metallic money and of bullion is in wide and spectacular use today. Since July, 1931 German citizens have been unable to take reichsmarks out of the country; since September, 1931 Italian citizens have not been allowed to export lira. In September, 1939 the export of capital was forbidden by France except when special permits were secured through the Central Bureau of Exchange. Similar war restrictions have been made effective in Great Britain and even in neighboring Canada. From both of these countries, travelers may take out only enough money to cover "necessary expenses." In fact the bullion and exchange restrictions of the countries of the world today are about as complicated as Einstein's theory of relativity. Moreover, there are infinite variations from country to country in these restrictions.

West Indies the Source of Silver Currency

As the foreign commerce of the colonies developed, trade increased with the many islands in the West Indies, with the Canary Islands, with Madeira, with Portugal, and with Spain which controlled the great silver mines in Mexico and Peru. Because of the very extensive trade between the West Indies and the Spanish Main, most of the islands in the Caribbean Sea were well supplied with Spanish coins. Specie from this source now crept into the colonies partly through the regular channels of foreign trade and partly through the half-piratical operations of buccaneers or privateers who preyed upon the rich Spanish commerce. By the end of the last quarter of the seventeenth century, commerce with the West Indies was of such considerable importance that it was the principal source of "hard money."

Most of the coins which circulated in the colonies were thus Spanish and Portuguese rather than English, the Spanish silver dollar or "piece of eight," Seville, Peru, and Pillar pieces of eight, pistoles, doubloons, ducatoons, crusadoes, guineas, Johannes, and Lyon dollars. It was no automatic simple task to reduce such a heterogeneous variety of monetary units to a common standard, especially when these coins differed considerably in weight and fineness, and the original mint errors had been magnified by the universal practice of clipping and sweating, which was not difficult with the rude stampings of that period. By the middle of the seventeenth century, it has been authoritatively estimated, the coins in circulation in the colonies had lost about one-fourth of their original weight.

A mint was finally established in Massachusetts in 1652 to bring order out of the prevailing currency chaos. This mint produced three-penny pieces, six-penny pieces, and the famous pine-tree shillings. In 1684, the mint was closed by the British government on the theory that coinage was solely a royal prerogative. The mint had been established while the king was in exile and England was being ruled as a Commonwealth by Cromwell. It functioned for thirty-two years, but all of the coins produced were stamped with the identical date of 1652. This was the first and last attempt of any of the colonies to provide their own metallic currency.

The First "Devaluation"

Partly because of its low metallic content, and partly to attract more specie by a favorable estimation, the colonies vied with each other in raising the valuation of the coin mostly in use, the Spanish silver dollar of eight reals, aptly known as "pieces of eight"* in *Treasure Island* and all other popular "pirate literature." This mighty coin was the original of our American dollar. While a standard piece of eight with seventeen and one-half pennyweight of silver had a mint value

* Pieces of eight were often cut into pie-shaped segments to be used as smaller coins. It was from a pie-shaped piece of one-quarter of this coin, representing "two reals" that we obtained our colloquial expression of "two bits."

of four shillings, six pence in English silver coin, the rate was generally made five shillings in the early life of the colonies for convenience.

The colonists kept their accounts in English monetary terms* of pounds, shillings, and pence, even though few English coins were in circulation. In fact, it was a common practice of American merchants for twenty years after the adoption of the dollar unit by Congress in 1792, to keep their books in pounds, shillings, and pence, and to have an extra blank column in their ledgers where they converted their first entries into dollars and cents at their leisure.

The value of a piece of eight accordingly was expressed in shillings and pence. In 1652, Massachusetts raised the valuation of a piece of eight to slightly under six shillings; a little later Virginia increased the value to over six; New York went up to six shillings nine pence in 1676; Massachusetts to six shillings eight pence in 1682; and Pennsylvania followed in 1707 with a valuation of seven shillings six pence. In 1701, the colonial legal value given to a pennyweight of silver in a standard piece of eight ranged from 3.42 pence in Virginia to 5.6 pence in Pennsylvania and West New Jersey. The legal value of the identical coin varied by 34.5 per cent in the different colonies, quite an unnatural and abnormal discrepancy.

The English government finally attempted to introduce order into this confusion, and in 1704, the Board of Trade prepared a royal proclamation fixing the maximum value of a standard piece of eight, at six shillings. This proclamation aimed to lower the accepted rate in South Carolina, Pennsylvania, New England, and New York, while it permitted, although it did not require, the raising of the value of a piece of eight in Virginia and Maryland. The proclamation, however, contained no provision for its own enforcement, and accordingly the Northern colonies and South Carolina ignored it with perfect immunity. In the two colonies of Virginia and Maryland, strong royal governors prevented its violation.

The objects sought by the colonists in establishing the legal rates of metallic coins above their sterling value were twofold: one was to attract "hard" currency from other regions where lower rates prevailed, and perhaps to induce the hearty pirates to bring their booty in; the other was the age-old belief of the debtor class that inflation in the guise of an arbitrary higher value of legal tender would provide cheap money.

* The account books of Joseph Rhoads 1st and 2nd, of Philadelphia, predecessors of the existing J. E. Rhoads & Sons, Philadelphia, Pa., and Wilmington, Del., were carried in English currency down through the year of 1809. Occasional receipts in dollars and cents in the years immediately preceding 1809 were converted into pounds, shillings, and pence. This concern was started in 1702 as a tanner of leather. It is the third oldest concern in the country that has remained continuously in the hands of the same family.

It would seem somewhat more than a mere coincidence that the pirates were most active during the years when the assemblies were raising the legal value of foreign coin; moreover, the colonies most guilty of harboring pirates placed the highest value upon the particular coin which the pirates had in their possession. While piracy flourished, Boston, Philadelphia, New York, and Charleston obtained their largest stocks of silver and gold.

Colonial laws which placed legal valuations on pieces of eight, also defined this coin as current lawful money. As most private contracts, and all public payments called for the tender of current lawful money, any act which raised the legal value of pieces of eight meant that a debtor could liquidate an obligation by paying fewer coins. Here was the first American precedent for the "devaluation" of the dollar. Unfortuately there is no information available regarding the exact amount of coin in circulation during this interesting period. Some colonies were more fortunate than others and the quantity in circulation in each region varied considerably from year to year, but at no time was there a sufficient supply for the reasonable needs of domestic trade, foreign commerce, and public business.

Certain colonies such as New Hampshire and Connecticut managed to get along with practically no metallic currency. As soon as coins arrived in these two colonies in payment for the sale of ships, timber, and timber products which were the primary exports, the money was re-shipped out in payment for merchandise obtained from England or from the other colonies. Rhode Island with a more active trading and carrying business procured a larger supply of coins, but even here it was almost as difficult to retain any reasonable amount in local circulation as the money was generally re-shipped to Boston, New York, and Philadelphia in payment for merchandise. In turn, it was sent by the merchants at those more important trading centers to England, to reduce balances due to the creditors there.

Simultaneous Use of Different Mediums of Exchange

New York, Pennsylvania, and Massachusetts at times had more "hard" coin than the other colonies, but only at certain times. For many years after 1700 there was a distinct shortage, probably due to the suppression of the pirates who had left large supplies of silver at their more friendly ports of call, and only light mutilated pieces were in circulation. Maryland and Virginia had very little specie; South Carolina, at times, seemed to be much better off, because she was nearest to the Spanish colony in Florida where silver was plentiful.

The use of commodity money and small quantities of metallic currency of various kinds at the same time, presented many natural inconveniences to domestic commerce. Prices differed according to the medium of exchange which one used at the time; namely, country pay, money, pay as money, and "trusting." For instance, in New Haven around 1700 "country pay" was represented by grain, pork, and beef at the prices set by the General Court that year. The General Court was the early name for the local colonial assembly. "Money" was represented by pieces of eight, pine-tree shillings, silver coins of the various kinds already mentioned, and if the amount was small, by wampum. "Pay as money" was represented by provisions at prices one-third less than those set by the General Court. "Trusting" was the result of an individual bargain between the merchant and the buyer in the extension of credit.

There were no fixed prices in wholesale trade or in retail shops; the price arrived at for each sale was the result of haggling between the salesman and the customer just as the price of a second-hand automobile is arrived at today. Not until around 1815 did Arthur Tappan start to revolutionize the wholesale and retail dry goods trade in New York City by using the one-price system, a unique innovation which A. T. Stewart, the pioneer modern merchandiser successfully carried forward in his larger retail store on Broadway, New York City, following 1837.

Beginning of Paper Money

John Winthrop, Jr., the first governor of Connecticut, was a son of John Winthrop, the first governor of the Massachusetts Bay Colony. He is known to have carried on extensive correspondence with friends in the Royal Society in England, the "brains trust" of their day, in which he elaborated upon an approach to paper currency. This was a great step in the seventeenth century economy of trade as paper currency was unknown at the time. Winthrop apparently had obtained some idea about such a medium of exchange from a pamphlet, *Key to Wealth, Or, A New Way for Improving Trade,* by William Potter, published in London in 1650, as a copy of this treatise appeared in that part of his library which was bequeathed by a lineal descendant, Francis B. Winthrop, Esq., to the New York Society Library in 1812.

In this treatise, the author explained that to "multiply the decayed Trade of this Land" and by "this Land" he meant England, a new supply of gold or silver was essential, but in this absence he advocated an unprecedented and unknown type of currency, paper money bearing no interest, secured not by gold or silver but by other "sufficient" assets, mostly real estate. This hypothetical paper currency would be accepted, according to the author's unique plan, by an increasing number of merchants who would prominently display a flag or sign outside of their places of business, as an indication that they would accept the unexampled currency at its face value. It was, however, many years after Winthrop's early correspondence with his friends across the ocean, and under far less theoretical circumstances, that paper currency made its initial appearance on this continent.

First Issue of Colonial Paper Currency

The first of the four wars between the English and the French for the possession of the great colonial empires, known in the colonies as King William's War, broke out in 1689. As a result of the initial success of the French and Indians in raiding and destroying Schenectady in New York, Salmon Falls in New Hampshire, and Fort Loyal (now Portland, Maine), in Massachusetts, the Northern colonies sent delegates to a meeting in New York in May, 1690 to make plans for unified defense and retaliatory action. New York and Connecticut were to raise an army and attack Montreal by way of Lake Champlain. Massachusetts was to prepare and to send a naval force against the towering French stronghold of Quebec.

In carrying out her part of these plans, Massachusetts prepared the most pretentious military and naval expedition which had been organized in the colonies up to that time. A fleet of thirty-four ships set sail on the 9th day of August, 1690 under the leadership of the thirty-nine year old Sir William Phipps, the energetic, orphan colonist who had already risen to wealth and an English title, and who had just returned laden with booty from the capture of Port Royal in Acadia. If Quebec could be captured, the French power in America would be broken.

After groping its way slowly up the St. Lawrence River, the fleet arrived before the massive cliff of Quebec on the 16th day of October. The Massachusetts men landed and laid siege to the town. Instead of immediate and overwhelming success, expected from the recent experience at Port Royal, the expedition gradually turned into a dismal, hopeless failure. Quebec held out. Winter approached with its bleak cold weather, its snow and ice and hail. Disease and discouragement spread among the colonists as they seemed unable to make any impression upon the powerful French stronghold. Finally, it was decided to break camp. The men boarded their ships, and the entire fleet sailed out into the Gulf of St. Lawrence, around Nova Scotia, and then southwestward, back to Boston.

This expedition had entailed great expense. Ships has been purchased and hired. Cannons, muskets, powder, and shot had been acquired. Food supplies had been purchased. Equipment for sailing the seas, and then besieging the enemy, had been bought. The men, the sailors and the soldiers, had to be paid. That failure cost Massachusetts no less than £50,000 and stately Quebec was not to be conquered until many years later.

It had been fully anticipated that the entire cost of this expedition would be defrayed from the proceeds of the victory. To the victors would belong the spoils! Utter failure, debts, unpaid soldiers, and threats of mutiny at Boston now called forth an extraordinary and unexpected measure, the first issuance of paper money. With an exhausted treasury, Massachusetts issued, in December, 1690 its first paper currency to pay the soldiers and the sailors who had returned unsuccessful and penniless from Quebec, and to discharge the many other debts incurred in provisioning, arming, and organizing that extensive, but unfortunate and ineffective expedition. The experiment was not only the origin of paper money in America, but the origin in the entire British Empire.

The first issue of colonial paper currency amounted to £7,000. This sum, however, proved insufficient for its purpose and within a few months was increased to £40,000. The currency was printed in denominations ranging from five shillings to five pounds. It was paid out during the last month of 1690, and during the entire year of 1691. On each piece of currency was printed the promise of the Government reading, "This indented Bill of . . . . Shillings, due from the Massachusetts Colony to the Possessor, shall be in value equal to money, and shall be accordingly accepted by the Treasurer, and Receivers subordinate to him in all publick payments, and for any stock at any time in the Treasury." It was soon learned, however, that this simple printed promise would not maintain value. The best of intentions has never been sufficient to make paper money equal in value to actual metallic currency. The experiment had to be tried in order to be learned, and then it had to be tried over and over again in one colony after another.

The General Court of Massachusetts now proceeded to support the credit of the outstanding paper currency by an act in 1692, which provided that the bills would be made legal tender and receivable for public taxes at a premium of five per cent over silver, and at the same time secured by public taxes and other revenues. This measure was successful in keeping the paper money on a par with specie for about fifteen years. It was a natural, logical, and practical experiment. It worked until political expediency became more important than the soundness of the finance of colonial Massachusetts.

These bills passed from hand to hand, and served the actual purpose of specie currency so long as there was a reasonable prospect of their ultimate redemption. The early issues were payable in one year and so were virtually non-interest bearing certificates of indebtedness, much like present day treasury warrants which are issued in anticipation of taxes. In 1704, however, the time for redemption was extended to two years; in 1707 to three years; in 1709 to four years; in 1710 to five years; in 1711 to six years; later to thirteen years. William Douglass, one of the early colonial economists thoughtfully analyzed these postponements in 1740, "Thus unnaturally, instead of providing for Posterity, they proceeded to involve them in Debt." What a powerful moral there is in that simple quotation! The delay in redemption became a habit and finally weakened the willingness of the legislature of the colony to pass effective taxation laws even for current expenditures.

Paper Currency in Colonial Massachusetts

Queen Anne's War began in 1701. At the end of 1702 the paper money outstanding in the colony of Massachusetts had been reduced to £5,000. The expenses of this second great colonial war between the English and the French, now increased the outstanding obligations year by year, until at the end of 1708, the paper currency re-issued over the promise of the colony of Massachusetts amounted to £43,000. In 1709, a second issue of paper money, this time for £30,000, was provided to meet the rapidly growing military and naval expenses largely incidental to another calamitous expedition against the powerful French fortifications at Quebec.

As the volume of paper currency grew larger, its daily current value now grew less and less. An inexorable economic law was be-

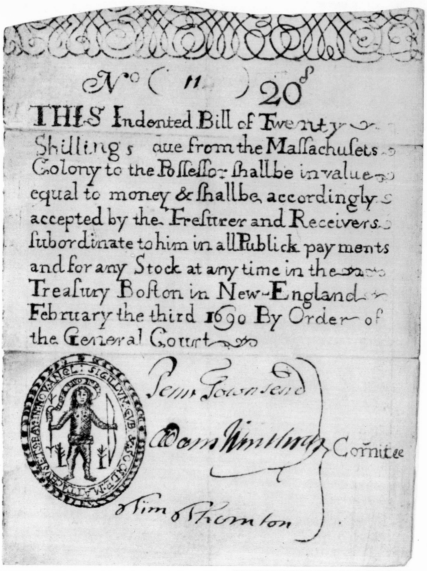

Early Paper Currency in America

ginning to make itself felt. By 1714, it was estimated that a total of £194,950 in paper currency had been issued in the Massachusetts colony, alone. Province bills, as this paper money came to be known, were now at a discount of thirty per cent, and as they depreciated they drove out what little metallic money had remained in circulation. At the same time prices rose in terms of the depreciated paper currency. When the Boston town-house was erected in 1712, carpenters received five shillings a day, all in cash. In 1739, they received twelve shillings a day in paper, equal to two-thirds of their former wages, and even this amount was further reduced by obliging them to take one-half in shop goods at twenty-five per cent or more advance above the money price.

In 1745 King George's War broke out. To take the place of Port Royal in Acadia which had been retained by the English at the end of Queen Anne's War, the French had constructed what was widely considered to be an impregnable fortress on Cape Breton Island and had named it Louisburg. The New England colonies now massed their strength against this single, powerful stronghold. An army of four thousand men was raised, more of a mob than an army, and sailed under the command of William Pepperrell, the rich merchant of Kittery, Maine. The expedition surprised Louisburg, insufficiently garrisoned and supplied. A British fleet in the nearby waters kept French reinforcements from reaching the beleaguered fort, and after a siege of forty days, Louisburg surrendered.

By this time, the credit of Massachusetts was so low that the colony could float no more paper money. The ordinary circulating medium had broken down entirely. There was a general and complete lack of confidence in the financial policy of the colony. In need of more money, Massachusetts now resorted to the universal means of raising funds when all other methods are hopeless, a lottery. Only £7,500 was obtained!

The reimbursement of Massachusetts for its expenses in this successful, epic expedition and siege against Louisburg was now suggested and agitated by the colonists and by their lobbyists in England. In 1746, vouchers were submitted to the English cabinet showing actual expenditures of £261,700. After three years of investigation and discussion, the English Parliament, in 1749, voted to repay Massachusetts for the actual expenses incurred in the campaign. The sum of £183,649, 2s. 7½d. sterling, or 650,000 ounces of silver and ten tons of copper were remitted to the Massachusetts Bay Colony, but on the one condition that the outstanding paper currency would be redeemed. Due to the difference in valuation between English and colonial currency, this sum was about equal to £244,866 "lawful money" in Massachusetts. Here was far more metallic currency than Massachusetts had ever possessed at one time, a tremendous mass of "hard" coin for the colonial era.

The transfer of this immense sum to the three London representatives of the Massachusetts Bay Colony was made by a draft upon the Bank of England. With it the representatives purchased Spanish silver pieces of eight and English copper coins of one-half pence and farthings. In September, 1749 the inhabitants of Boston, little accustomed to the use of metallic money, saw two hundred and seventeen chests full of Spanish dollars, and one hundred casks of coined copper taken off the good ship *Molyneaux,* loaded on seventeen trucks, and dragged up King Street to the treasury office.

Until June 3, 1751 the treasurer of the colony redeemed outstanding paper currency at the following rates: for every forty-five shillings in old tenor bills, one piece of eight; for every eleven shillings and three pence in the middle tenor and new tenor bills, one piece of eight. There had been three issues of currency with different values; as the early issue sank lower and lower, a new issue had come out at a higher stated value. The six commissioners redeemed £50,705 in the old tenor, £38,431 in the middle, and £1,703,099 in the new tenor.

The motive for the non-payment of these bills, until England came to the rescue, was not outright repudiation. It was generally said to have been a matter of necessity and of patriotism; we have heard somewhat similar reasons for the tremendous increases in the debt of the Federal Government in recent years. Both situations, although separated by two hundred years or more, have the same basis in human experience, the political fear of laying heavy taxes to pay for a greater portion, or all, of current expenses. It was a very simple political, but unsound, economic expedient.

Paper Currencies in the Other Colonies

Frontier struggles forced the Carolinas, as it had Massachusetts, to issue paper money. Wars are always letting loose new and unseen forces. The first issue in South Carolina took place in 1703, and was used to liquidate the indebtedness arising from the St. Augustine expedition. The subsequent acts of both North Carolina and South Carolina now pled the exigencies of Indian Wars as the reason for emitting additional paper currency.

The Canadian expeditions and the accompanying requisitions on the Northern colonies for necessary money and supplies started the colonies of New Hampshire, New York, Connecticut, New Jersey, and Rhode Island on their more or less hectic paper money careers in 1709 and in 1710.

Conditions were probably the most deplorable in Rhode Island where there seemed to have been absolutely no check upon the issue of fiat currency; even the neighboring colonies complained about Rhode Island paper money which finally fell to four per cent of its face value, and legislated against it. In the Middle colonies the situation was never so oppressive, due to the stubborn resistance of the governors to this short-circuit method of liquidating obligations. The depreciation of paper money was about twenty-five per cent in New York, Pennsylvania, and New Jersey. Approximately the same depreciation took place in Delaware, Maryland, and Virginia, but in the Carolinas the monetary situation was more onerous than in any of the colonies except Rhode Island, depreciation finally taking away nine-tenths of the value of the bills. Maryland issued no paper currency until 1734, Delaware until 1739, Virginia until 1755, and Georgia until 1760.

The evils of depreciation were greatest in the New England colonies, partly because the experiment started in the North and was carried out with a unique degree of conscientious thoroughness, and partly because of the confusion with the various "bank" issues which are explained in the following chapter.

At the same time that Massachusetts received its reimbursements for its expenses of the successful Louisburg expedition from Great Britain, the other colonies which had incurred similar expenses were likewise repaid. The amounts received by the other colonies, however, were so small in comparison to the volume of their outstanding paper money that it was impossible to arrange any redemption programs, Connecticut received £28,864 English pounds sterling, New Hampshire £16,355, and Rhode Island but £332.

Colonial Paper Currency Filled a Need

Ingenuity seemed to have been exhausted in devising variations to the colonial issues of paper currency. "There were interest-bearing notes, some of which were legal tender, while others were not; there were non-interest-bearing notes, some of which were legal tender for future obligations but not past debts; some were legal tender for all purposes, and others not legal tender between private persons, but receivable for public payments. In some instances funds arising from certain sources of taxation were pledged for the redemption of the notes, in others not. In some cases they were payable on demand; in others, at some future time. Sometimes they were issued by committees, and sometimes by a specially designated official." A merchant in the course of a single day might be offered as payment, many currencies of several different colonies, each with a different current value.

Of all the numerous issues of paper money, not one was redeemed in conformity with the promises of the colonies. In spite of the disadvantages, early colonial paper money seems to have met a very real and acute need, namely, the lack of a sufficient quantity of metallic coin to serve adequately as a medium of exchange. Commodity money, used during the seventeenth century, was hardly suited to the requirements of the expanding commerce of the eighteenth century. The innovation of paper money was more adapted to the growing domestic trade, and had it not been abused, or had the economic basis been better understood, it could have served the colonists more advantageously. Even with all of the abuses and disadvantages, it found defenders among the ablest men of the colonial period.

Benjamin Franklin, in 1729, at the tender age of twenty-three, was perfectly willing to solve this fundamental economic problem of his day and age, in a pamphlet, *A Modest Inquiry into the Nature and Necessity of Paper Money*. Thirty-eight years later, in 1767, when he had become the most eminent individual in all of the colonies, and when acting as the resident agent of the colony of Pennsylvania in England, he prepared a report on the *Vindication of the Provincial Paper-Money System* which became widely known and read. This report contained the following interesting views:

Pennsylvania, before it made any paper money, was totally stript of its gold and silver; though they had, from time to time, like the neighboring colonies, agreed to take gold and silver coin at higher and higher nominal values, in hopes of drawing money into, and retaining it for the internal uses of, the province. . . . The difficulties for want of cash were accordingly very great, the chief part of the trade being carried on by the extremely inconvenient method of barter; when, in 1723, paper money was first made there, which gave new life to business, promoted greatly the settlement of new lands (by lending small sums to beginners on easy interest, to be repaid by instalments), whereby the province has so greatly increased its inhabitants, that the export from hence thither is now more than tenfold what it then was; and, by their trade with foreign colonies, they have been able to obtain great quantities of gold and silver, to remit hither in return for the manufacturers of this country. New York and New Jersey have also increased greatly during the same period, with the use of paper money; so that it does not appear to be of the ruinous nature ascribed to it.

Notwithstanding these views, orthodox for the day, Dr. Franklin as he came to be known, was one of the few men who later raised his voice against the issuance of inconvertible paper currency to finance the Revolutionary War.

"Continental" Paper Money

Colonial left-wing experimentations with paper money came to one grand climax during the Revolutionary War. When the British soldiers clashed with the minute-men at Lexington, the colonies had no supplies of arms, no equipment, no ammunition, or the money with which to purchase them, or to pay the soldiers. Under these circumstances, the first task which presented itself was to provide the necessary financial resources, the proverbial sinews of war. There were only three ways for raising necessary funds, the issuance of paper currency, increased taxation, or borrowing either at home or abroad. The Continental Congress resorted to all three of these methods but the issuance of paper currency was their chief reliance.

The Continental Congress was an emergency body, with little authority and no compelling power for the collection of taxes; it could not commandeer property at the beginning of the war lest it turn people against the American cause, and it could not borrow adequate funds from the wealthy. Should Great Britain win, all of the obligations of the colonists would be repudiated just as the obligations of the Confederate States were later repudiated after the Civil War. For this reason, foreign capitalists and investors were not particularly attracted to the risk of making loans to the Continental Congress as profit ventures. The chance of ultimate repayment was just a trifle too remote.

The States had no common currency, either paper or metallic; there were no banks in existence that could extend credit; and the existing supply of foreign coins in circulation was rather nominal. The only previous experience which the colonists had in raising funds was in the issuance of negotiable promissory notes in the form of paper money. That experience was as complete as it was disastrous. Yet, once again they resorted to printed currency in the face of hardships associated with earlier colonial emissions. As is so often the case in history, it was simply and solely a matter of expediency.

In June, 1775 almost with the beginning of hostilities, Congress authorized the first issue of paper money amounting to $2,000,000. When this issue was provided, it was confidently believed by the members of the Continental Congress that the debt thus created would be promptly redeemed without loss to anyone. It was to be a temporary measure! By the end of 1776, $25,000,000 of notes had been put into circulation and depreciation amounted to thirty per cent. By the end of 1777, $38,000,000 of "Continental" paper money had been issued and the depreciation had risen to approximately seventy per cent.

Forty-two emissions of paper currency were authorized by November 29, 1779 for a total of $241,552,780 and $191,500,000 had actually been issued. The Continental Congress finally became alarmed at its own action and limited the amount of paper currency to be placed in actual circulation to $200,000,000. This measure is somewhat reminiscent of the more recent action of the 75th Congress in passing legislation in May, 1938 after ten years of high-powered spending, restricting the Federal debt to the fairly respectable sum of $45,000,000,000, and then, of the 77th Congress in raising the limit in February, 1941 to $65,000,000,000.

Paper currency of $160,000,000 had been issued prior to September 3, 1779 and by that time, the States had provided no more than $3,000,000 in tax money for its redemption. Moreover, the States had issued their own paper money. State and "Continental" currencies now circulated side by side, each affecting the value of the other. Since the aggregate of all kinds of paper money was greatly in excess of reasonable needs for a medium of exchange, the paper currencies depreciated early and rapidly, and the prices of all commodities and services rose correspondingly.

By the latter part of 1779, the entire currency system had broken down hopelessly. Money without credit is no money. This the delegates to the Continental Congress learned when paper currency became almost worthless. Tavern keepers took down their signs and refused to entertain passing strangers. In a letter to Elbridge Gerry written from Braintree, Massachusetts, John Adams described the situation, "I find the same perplexities here that we felt at Yorktown, a general inclination among the people to barter, and as general an aversion to dealing in paper money of any denomination. . . ." Trade, when it did not revert to primitive barter, became mere chance.

In this predicament, Congress in October, 1779 requested the States to furnish, not money to purchase supplies but the actual supplies such as corn, wheat, flour, hay, and oats for the armies in the field. It must be kept in mind that the Continental Congress had absolutely no authority over the States; recommendations for raising funds could be made but not enforced; tax-gatherers could not be appointed and sent forth with arbitrary instructions and power to collect taxes as in the ancient days of Rome! With thirteen sovereign States, the situation was beyond any sound, intelligent, reasonable approach. The colonists were throwing off allegiance to Great Britain ostensibly because she assumed the right to lay taxes without their consent, and there was no disposition to substitute a strong central government for Great Britain at this preliminary stage of our national history.

"A wagon-load of money," George Washington freely wrote, "will scarcely purchase a wagon-load of provisions." Finally the General Court of Massachusetts passed a "Tender Act," enabling debtors to turn over to the sheriff of their own county, at appraisal, any cattle, grain, deal boards, or other produce, in payment of debts. This process completed the circle of transmutation from currency into no currency.

The merchants now began to look to France, to Spain, and to Holland for loans which would bring in specie, just as Finland in January and February, 1940 hoped for loans from abroad to purchase airplanes. Between 1777 and 1783, France extended loans of $6,352,500, Holland $1,304,000 and Spain $174,017 in addition to which France made outright gifts of $2,107,000 and Spain of $181,500. Most of these funds were disbursed in Europe for the purchase of necessary supplies to carry on the war.

When the outstanding "Continental" paper money was limited to $200,000,000, a paper dollar was worth between one and two cents in specie. This tremendous depreciation, the fact that loans had been obtained abroad, and the fact that some metallic money was getting into circulation through purchases by the British and French troops, finally led to a decision to retire the "Continental" bills from circulation. On March 18, 1780 the Continental Congress enacted legislation to the effect that the States should collect taxes and use the money to redeem the outstanding bills at the rate of forty paper dollars for one silver dollar. If a taxpayer was assessed a tax of one silver dollar, he could pay forty dollars in "Continental" bills which would then be destroyed. Eventually $120,000,000 of the "Continental" paper currency was retired by this process, leaving $71,500,000 in circulation.

After 1781, the remaining bills depreciated to the vanishing point but remained a medium for speculators who hoped, that in the not too

far distant future, they would be redeemed by Congress. About $6,000,-
000 of the outstanding $71,500,000 was subscribed for bonds under the
Funding Act of 1790, at the rate of one hundred to one and the balance
was lost, destroyed, or retained as souvenirs. "Not worth a Continental"
has remained to this day a term for utter worthlessness.

The bills which had been issued simultaneously by the States
consisted of both paper currency and interest-bearing treasury notes,
an aggregate of $250,000,000. The only security behind most of these
obligations was the credit of the respective States, many of which would
not even levy taxes for the redemption of their own currency. Depreciation was about on a par with "Continental" currency. After 1780,
the paper money of the States was drawn in as tax money at various
rates of depreciation, in Georgia and Virginia, for example, at $1,000
paper to $1.00 silver; in North Carolina at 800 to 1; in New York 128
to 1; in Maryland 40 to 1. By this process, the indebtedness of the
States represented by paper currency was largely effaced by the end
of the war, the depreciation having served as a forced means of obtaining credit from everyone.

The first draft of the Federal Constitution provided that Congress
be given the right "to emit bills on the credit of the United States."
As a result of the disastrous experience with "Continental" paper money,
the Constitutional Convention, by a vote of nine States to two, struck out
this clause, after a debate which showed it was the consensus of opinion
that the Federal Government should be prohibited from issuing these
particular instruments of credit.

This opinion was unquestioned during the lifetime of the men
who witnessed the adoption of the Federal Constitution. Daniel
Webster in 1836, explained this viewpoint in the United States Senate,
"Most unquestionably there is no legal tender and there can be no legal
tender in this country, under the authority of this Government or any
other, but gold and silver. . . ." For seventy-five years no suggestion
of the existence of such a power to make paper a legal tender can be
found in the legislative history of the country. In the dark hours of
the Civil War, however, legal tender paper was issued by Congress;
and, twenty years later, the Supreme Court in the case of Juilliard
v. Greeman* reversed the action of the Constitutional Convention by
declaring such paper currency constitutional even in times of peace.

* Legal Tender Case, 110 U. S. 421; 4 S. Ct., 122; 28 U. S. (L. ed.) 204; (1884).

Bibliographical References to Chapter Two

BANCROFT, GEORGE, *History of the Colonization of the United States;* Two Volumes, New York, 1885.

BEARD, MIRIAM, *A History of the Business Man;* New York, 1938.

BOGART, ERNEST LUDLOW, *Economic History of the American People;* 1930, Edition of 1935, New York.

BOLLES, ALBERT S., *The Financial History of the United States, 1774-1789;* New York, 1880.

BOOTH, MARY L., *History of the City of New York from its Earliest Settlement to the Present Time;* New York, 1866.

BULLOCK, CHARLES J., *The Finances of the United States from 1775 to 1789 with Especial Reference to the Budget;* Madison, Wis., 1895.

CLARK, VICTOR S., *History of Manufactures in the United States, 1607-1860;* 1929 Edition, New York.

COLWELL, STEPHEN, *The Ways and Means of Payment, a Full Analysis of the Credit System with its Various Modes of Adjustment;* Philadelphia, 1859.

DAVIS, ANDREW McFARLAND, *Currency and Banking in the Province of the Massachusetts Bay;* Two Parts, New York, 1901.

DEWEY, DAVIS RICH, *Financial History of the United States;* 1902, Second Edition 1903, New York.

DOUGLASS, WILLIAM, *A Discourse Concerning the Currencies of the British Plantations in America;* Boston, 1740.

FRANKLIN, BENJAMIN, *The Works of Benjamin Franklin;* Twelve Volumes, compiled and edited by John Bigelow, Volume IV, New York, 1904.

KIRKLAND, EDWARD C., *A History of American Economic Life;* 1932, Edition of 1939, New York.

LAMB, MRS. MARTHA J., *History of the City of New York—Its Origin, Rise, and Progress;* Two Volumes, New York, 1877.

NETTELS, CURTIS P., *The Money Supply of the American Colonies Before 1720;* Madison, Wis., 1934.

OSGOOD, HERBERT L., *The American Colonies in the Eighteenth Century;* Volume III, New York, 1924.

POTTER, WILLIAM, *The Key to Wealth, Or, A New Way for Improving Trade;* published in London, England, 1650. A copy in the New York Library Society.

TAPPAN, LEWIS, *The Life of Arthur Tappan;* New York, 1870.

WEEDEN, WILLIAM B., *Economic and Social History of New England, 1620-1789;* Two Volumes, Boston, 1890.

Volumes Previously Cited

BRADFORD, GOVERNOR WILLIAM, *History of Plimoth Plantation.* Original
manuscript history of Plymouth written in the years preceding 1647;
Boston, 1898.

BRUCE, PHILIP ALEXANDER, *Economic History of Virginia in the Seventeenth
Century;* Two Volumes, New York, 1895.

SMITH, CAPTAIN JOHN, *A True Relation of such occurrences and accidents of
noate as hath hapned in Virginia since the first planting of that
Collony, which is now resident in the South part thereof, till the
last returne from thence;* London, England, 1608.

WINTHROP, JOHN, *The History of New England from 1630 to 1649;* a two-
volume record of the Massachusetts Bay Colony kept over the early
years of the Colony by the first Governor, edited by James Savage;
Boston, 1853.

III ☆ Evolution of Credit in the Colonies

*D*URING the period which comprised our colonial life, from 1607 when Captaine Christopher Newport sailed his fleet of three little ships into the "Bay of Chesupioc," to 1776 when the Declaration of Independence was announced to the world by the Continental Congress, four commercial practices developed from the evolving economic environment which are of peculiar credit interest to us. First, a decreasing but at all times a substantial portion of our domestic trade was carried on by means of primitive, crude barter; second, credit was extended and concessions were made by local settlements and by the colonies direct to enterprising individuals to assist them in starting certain types of business enterprises vitally needed in a new country; third, credit terms were gradually developed in the domestic sale of merchandise; and fourth, colonial importers obtained very substantial credit on liberal terms from distant English factors, exporters, and merchant-bankers. Each of these four developments was but a manifestation of the natural adjustments of a new, energetic, growing society to a steadily expanding, commercial horizon.

The economic history of the thirteen colonies is fundamentally a fascinating story of experimentation after experimentation to find a better medium of exchange, until the ultimate washout with the "Continental" currency during the Revolutionary War. What a perfect washout that turned out to be! France added a similar chapter to the history of currencies a few years later in the complete repudiation of outstanding assignats and mandats in 1797, and then with the mild exception

49

of Confederate paper money during the Civil War, the world patiently awaited the debacle of Germany in 1923, when the mark was succeeded by the rentenmark at the unheard ratio of 1 to 1,000,000,000,000 to provide the most spectacular example of all currency depreciation.

Transactions by Barter

From the earliest days in colonial life, barter on a large scale became the accepted means of trade. Where credit was not customarily extended, something had to be given in exchange for a desired article or commodity, and in the void resulting at times from the nominal, and always, from an inadequate supply of metallic currency, that something was some other commodity, product, or service. Through the seventeenth and eighteenth centuries, provisions and home products, such as wheat, rye, barley, corn, tobacco, beef, pork, rice, yarn, nails hammered out at the fireplace during the long evenings in the Winter, and the infinite variety of similar products mentioned in the preceding chapter, furnished the very lifeblood of colonial domestic commerce. These products when given in exchange for some other commodity or service came to be known colloquially as "country pay."

An historian, learned in the economic lore of these very early days, described a typical situation, "A clapboard house in Essex County, Mass. with three chimneys was sold for £45 in corn and cattle." Then he explained more generally, "It was common to barter a cow for clothing and family supplies." As early as 1634, the Massachusetts Bay settlers were exchanging "sack, strong waters, linen cloth and other commodities" with the Dutch at New Netherlands for sheep, brass pieces, sugar, and beaver skins. In 1642, a few years before the Pilgrims had liquidated their indebtedness in England, a Dutch ship of three hundred tons arrived from the West Indies laden with salt which was exchanged for plank and pipe staves. A "pipe" was an enlarged cask used to store and to transport wine.

Colonial Ships Sold by Barter

Local colonial records show that as early as 1661, a ship was built at Gloucester "68 ft. in the keel, 23 ft. broad from outside to outside, 91.2 ft. long in the hold under the beam, 'Two decks, forecastle, quarter deck.' The great cabin was 6 ft. high." This ship was sold at £3.5s per ton of which £150 was payable in muscovado sugar deliverable in Barbados. Contracts for the construction of colonial ships, and all New England was as tremendous a shipbuilding area throughout the colonial period as Michigan is of automobiles today, seldom called for payment in cash because there was so little metallic currency in actual circulation. On the very eve of the Revolutionary War, more people in Maine and in New Hampshire were actually engaged in shipping and shipbuilding than in agriculture.

These ships were not large; they ranged from twenty to three hundred tons burden but they sailed the watery highways of the known world. Over the entire spread of the colonial years, it was customary to build ships for colonial, English, and West Indian operators and to be paid in such various produce as English manufactured goods, spikes, rope, and fishing equipment, sugar, molasses and wines, or part in cash, and part in these commodities.

Many years later, for example in 1741, Samuel Moggandge of Newburyport contracted to build a vessel for the Boston merchant firm of Cummings and Harris, with the buyers to furnish "all the iron-work, nails, pitch, tar, turp. & oakium." Cummings and Harris agreed to pay partly in cash and partly in a long list of carefully specified goods. This complicated and somewhat ambiguous barter agreement called for the following: "£300 in Cash, £300 by orders on good shops in Boston, two thirds money; four hundred pds. by orders up the river for tim! & plank, ten bbls. flour, 50 pds. weight of loaf sugar, one Bagg of cotton wool, one hund. bushels of corn in the Spring; one hhd. of Rum, 100 weight of cheese; the remaining part to be drawn out of the said Cummings and Harris' shop: the whole am't of price for vessel £3000 lawful money" [Old Tenor].

The average burden of ships constructed in Massachusetts, up to 1721, was only sixty-two tons. They were small, not because of any inability on the part of the shipwrights to construct larger vessels, but, because of the ever present hazards of commerce throughout the sixteenth and seventeenth centuries. The toll of shipping taken by storms, wrecks, pirates, privateers, and accidents was so high that the cautious ship-owner with an alert weather-eye on the diversity of his investments, preferred to place his money in several small vessels rather than in a few large ones, just as the cautious investor today spreads his investments in many different securities in a variety of lines of business. Fishing boats and vessels built for the New England trade ranged in size from ten to thirty tons, ketches used in the West Indian trade averaged about sixty-eight tons, and the ships sold to English merchants, many of them after they had carried one cargo to England, averaged only one hundred and two tons. With these small vessels, however, the colonists built up their extensive, very profitable foreign commerce.

The Country General Store

How do you imagine you would be received in this day and age, if you should walk into a furniture store, and after placing an order for a comfortable overstuffed chair and a friendly looking divan, you should offer so many bushels of wheat or rye or corn in full payment; or how do you imagine you would be regarded if you should place an order for a new Ford convertible sedan and agree to pay with a certain number of barrels of cider, 10 proof, to be delivered over the following three months; or suppose you should drive up to a gasoline service station, ask for ten gallons of ethyl gasoline and instead of tendering a five dollar bill which would call for change in legal tender, you should offer a few choice pumpkins just picked from the vine in full payment?

Big business, measured in the millions of dollars could never have been developed on the basis of barter. Department stores would never have come into existence; neither would specialized finance companies, nor the large corporations producing durable consumer goods such as automobiles, electric refrigerators, vacuum cleaners and electric washing machines, products which must obtain large and steady national distribution in order to be manufactured in line production at low costs.

In a small way, however, that is exactly what occurred in the origin of that great American democratic institution, the country general store with its friendly, worn chairs and its near-by cracker barrels. Only in its middle age, however, did the country store acquire its pot-bellied stove around which the neighbors could gather to discuss the political questions of the day. The early stores were heated by old-fashioned fireplaces. The invention of the first American stove was the creation of the versatile Benjamin Franklin in 1742, and the pot-bellied stove did not arrive until many years later.

To these early, country, general stores came the surplus products of the surrounding colonial farmers, grain, cheese, butter, potash, eggs, feathers, household manufactures such as yarn, and the ever needed home-made nails. The values of these products were credited by the merchant to his customers in terms of money. When they made purchases of European goods such as imported dress-goods, crockery, glassware, powder, shot, bar iron, or West India wares such as molasses, sugar, and salt, the accounts were debited. In this simple, everyday way practically all of the early transactions of the country general store were carried on by barter, but with a money terminology. When a debit existed, the obligation was a debt of honor and scrupulously repaid. The storekeeper in turn, resold or bartered the produce he collected, to the wholesale merchant or merchants in the nearby city from whom he purchased his stock in trade.

Such a wholesale merchant was the successful Thomas Hancock, the uncle of John Hancock, of signature fame. Young John Hancock was taken into his uncle's home when a boy of seven, educated at the Latin School and at Harvard, then brought into his uncle's establishment, first as a clerk, and in 1763, as an equal partner. In 1764, he inherited the major part of Thomas Hancock's fortune, quite reasonably estimated "about £70,000" and one of the largest accumulated in colonial Massachusetts. Records of this wholesale business from 1755 to 1762 show among other products, the sale of knives, combs, handkerchiefs, necklaces, reams of paper, and bolts of cloth to country stores, for which there were received in payment such products as wheat, rye, oats, barley, and potatoes. The ordinary terms of sale extended to retail shopkeepers and country stores called for payment at the end of six, nine, or twelve months, with interest at six per cent per annum on overdue balances.* Accounts, however, were usually balanced only at the end of extended periods, which often ran on year after year.

Barter was the means of trade not only of the country general store. As late as 1768, an advertisement in a weekly newspaper indicated that trade was being carried on extensively in a colonial center as large as New York City by barter. At that time Philadelphia was the largest city in the colonies. New York and Boston were running neck and neck for second place, each with a population between 20,000 and 25,000. This interesting advertisement read as follows:

Ten Eyck and Seamen, Have entered into the noted Flour Store, lately kept by Mr. John Abeel near Coenties Market, where they follow the same Business; they have generally by them for Sale, the best of fine middling and common Flour; they have also to dispose of either Wholesale or Retail, Rum, Molasses, Tea, Pepper, Coffee, Chocolate, Alspice, ground and unground Ginger, Snuff, Copperas, Indigo, Brimstone, Loaf and Lump Sugar, Muscovado, do. by the Hogshead, Barrel or less Quantity; also a few Pipes of choice old Teneriff Wines, by the Pipe, Quarter Cask, or five Gallons, etc. etc. most kinds of Country Produce will be taken in Payment for

---

* "Thomas Hancock, Colonial Merchant" by Edward Edelman in the *Journal of Economic and Business History,* November, 1928, Volume 1, Number 1.

the same: *It will often suit them to exchange Flour for many of the above Articles, which will make a considerable Easement to the Purchaser thereof, and will answer their Ends as well as Cash, as they must pay Cash for such Articles.**

Foreign Trade by Barter

The early foreign commerce of the colonial traders was largely carried on in this very same way. John Winthrop, Sr., kept a careful record, as early as 1633, of the ships which sailed from Massachusetts to Virginia with furs and fish. The fish were generally exchanged for tobacco, the most desired of all colonial products, the tobacco and the furs then being carried to England where they were sold or used in barter for English merchandise. New England skippers often sailed with cargoes of dried and salt fish and home manufactures to southern ports, where they exchanged these products for red oak staves to be used in making barrels for sugar, for rice, and for meat. Then they would head for the West Indies where these southern products would be readily bartered for rum, molasses, sugar, ginger, logwood, and other tropical products, which would be brought home as the basis for another round of trade.

Other New England and New York merchants developed this triangle trade from the opposite end. Ships laden with foodstuffs, horses, lumber, and lumber products would sail direct to the West Indies or to the Bay of Honduras. These products would be bartered for cotton at St. Thomas and Surinam, lime-juice, fustick, and redwood from Curacao, sugar, spices, and drugs from other Caribbean islands. On the homeward voyage, the ship might call at Charleston for rice and indigo, and all of these products then shipped to the London market from a northern port.

The commerce with the islands of the West Indies was most substantial during the entire colonial period; it was only exceeded by the direct trade with England. In many of these voyages to the Caribbean Sea home products were actually peddled from one port to another in search of the best possible trades. John Van Cortlandt, who carried on an active import and export business from New York City, sent his brig *Matty*, for example, in the four years 1765, 1766, 1767, and 1768 on several voyages to the West Indies. The master invariably was instructed to sail direct to Barbados, Montserrat, or Nevis, but if the particular

* *The New York Gazette and Weekly Mercury*, Monday, September 26, 1768, p. 3. This advertisement appeared in eight following, but not successive numbers of this weekly newspaper, up to, and including December 12, 1768.

market to which he headed was "lo" then he was to "proceed down" to the Leeward or Windward Islands. The typical instructions then read, "Dispose of your Cargo for the best price you Can & bring back the Proceeds in Good Sugar," and sometimes in rum.*

The captain of a larger vessel might sail to Spain, to Portugal, or to England, and exchange his cargo for the products of those countries. At London he might pick up woodenware, pewter, iron pots, kettles, frying pans, spades, axes, hammers, dishes, ship iron, cordage, paint, knives, firearms, and ammunition for which there was always a sustained demand at home. In later years, there developed the tremendous three cornered trade with Africa and the West Indies; the vessels would leave port with New England rum which would be bartered for slaves on the Gold Coast; the slaves would be carried to the West Indies and exchanged for molasses; and the molasses then would be brought home to be used in the distillation of more rum. What fortunes were made out of this trade, not only in the colonies, but also in England!

Foreign trade by barter, however, probably reached its apogee in the great China trading voyages sent out by the redoubtable John Jacob Astor after we had become a nation, in the years from 1816 to 1825. These ships would sail from New York loaded with blankets, cutlery, muskets, lead, iron, rum, and gin, touching first at the Hawaiian Islands where part of the cargo would be exchanged for sandalwood, which, however, would still have to be cut. From the Hawaiian Islands the course would be set for the North Pacific where part of the remaining original cargo would be exchanged with the Russians for seal skins and the fur of sea-otters, then southward to trade with the natives in the vicinity of the Columbia River and along the coast of California.

By this time, the original cargo would have been pretty well disposed of, and the captain would return to the Hawaiian Islands where he would pick up the sandalwood which had been cut in the meantime. The course would now be set for Canton. The sandalwood, and the furs obtained from the Russians, would be bartered at Canton for teas, silks, nankeens, chinaware, sugar, and spices. Back the ship would sail to the Hawaiian Islands where part of this cargo would now be sold, on to New Archangel where part would be bartered with the Russians, and then southward to California where the remaining Chinese products would be exchanged with the Spaniards for more seal skins, sea-otter furs, silver and pearl-shell. Once again, the captain would head for the Hawaiian Islands where more sandalwood would be stored, and

* *Letter Book of John Van Cortlandt, 1762-1769,* pp. 127, 136, 146, 152, 168, 195, 215. (New York Public Library)

then away for a second visit to Canton. The entire cargo would be bartered for Chinese goods, but this time the vessel would head for the home port of New York. Three to four years might have elapsed from the time the ship had originally sailed from New York, and practically all of this complicated trade would have been carried on by barter, the exchange of merchandise for merchandise.

Barter in the World of Today

International commerce in recent years has not been so far removed from the routine of the Middle Ages and from our own colonial era. Barter again is with us in a big way, this time being carried on not by individuals but by governments, even by the two greatest capitalistic countries in the world. On June 29, 1939 the Senate ratified a treaty between the United States and Great Britain providing for the exchange of no less than 600,000 bales of cotton for 95,000 tons of British rubber, each valued at approximately $30,000,000.

In fact, for eighteen months prior to the outbreak of the present World War, hardly a week went by in which mention of some barter deal between foreign governments was not reported in the press. The German Reich was a party to more of these actual and contemplated deals than any other country, Italy second, and then a scattering among other nations. Germany, for example, was exchanging machinery for expropriated oil with Mexico; rolling stock for beef and wheat with Argentine; pipes and copper sulphate for bananas from American shippers in Honduras; barbed wire, nails, automobiles, Diesel trucks, and pharmaceutical products for cotton, coffee, cottonseed oil, rubber, hides, and cabinet wood with Nicaragua. With no surplus gold, in fact, with a dolefully inadequate supply to support its own currency, with domestic policies which reduced and reduced international trade, with stringent exchange restrictions, the only way Germany could pay for needed raw materials in the world market was to barter for them, commodity for commodity. The exact terms of the now historic treaty of 1939 between Germany and Soviet Russia are still unknown but it is no secret that Germany expected Russian oil, wheat, cotton, fodder and manganese in exchange for German industrial machinery and arms.

The same situation prevailed, but to a less exaggerated degree, when Italy exchanged silk and rayon for Mexican oil, when Bolivia bartered petroleum for Uruguayan wheat, and when Brazil exchanged sugar for Chilian nitrates.

Tremendous progress has been made in the appreciation of the laws of economic life over the past two hundred years, but in this one respect, the business world has traveled the circle and is back with the primitive of primitives, the very dawn of civilization. Barter again has become an important basis of international commerce.

Loans by Settlements and Colonies

Strange as it may seem, the precedent of extending loans by governmental agencies, which has been so characteristic of our business life during the past eight years, goes back to the very early days of colonial New England. The first loans of this nature were made by the local settlements to assist individuals in setting up new industries for which there were great need in a new land, industries to provide the necessities of a simple life. Colonial loans were also made to individuals against real estate, and finally, innumerable lotteries were authorized and drawn for somewhat similar purposes.

Need for Skilled Artisans

The greatest, single initial need of a colonial settlement was for a muscular, efficient blacksmith. He, it was who made or repaired hoes, rakes, shovels, firearms, locks, hinges, cooking utensils, harness, fireplace tools, hammers, and everyday hardware. The common metal tools of the day were largely made by blacksmiths in the seventeenth century. In 1635, the town of Lynn, "settled John Deacon, blacksmith, and afterwards allotted to him twenty acres of land." In 1658, Haverhill gave a house and land to John Johnson, blacksmith, at a cost of £20, which was raised by subscriptions from twenty persons. Colonial life could hardly flow along without the blacksmith's " . . . large and sinewy hands, and the muscles of his brawny arms." He was more important in the daily life of the colonist than the modern gasoline station is on a lonely Arizona desert road today.

The broadsides published as early as 1610, by the London Company in England, to obtain emigrants for James Towne especially sought artisans such as skilled blacksmiths, coopers, carpenters, shipwrights, turners, brickmakers, bakers, weavers, shoemakers, and sawyers. In a circular issued in January, 1611, such men were solicitously asked to "repaire to the house of Sir Thomas Smith in Philpot lane in London before the end of this present moneth of Januarie, the number not full, they shall be entertained for the Voyage, upon such termes as their qualitie and fitnesse shall deserve." As the London Company, until it became a royal province in 1624, held property rights for seven years in the labor of the settlers whom it sent over, it was somewhat less successful in settling skilled workmen than the towns of New England which offered greater tangible inducements.

In 1638, the town of Salem was asked by the General Court of Massachusetts to loan £30 to the glass men, presumably to assist them in starting a glass factory, and to deduct the amount from its next colony tax. Gradually it became a common, natural practice for towns to make money grants to assist in the erection of mills, sometimes in the form of an outright gift, or as it was called, "a bonus," and sometimes in the form of a loan. The town of Newbury, for instance, in 1645, gave £20 to the builder of its first grist-mill. Salem loaned John Wareing £5 in 1685 to pay his spinners.

Rhode Island in 1725 extended credit of £500 to William Borden, at interest and upon security, to assist him in establishing his sailcloth mill. Three years later the colony made him an additional loan of £3,000 without interest but upon additional security, to enlarge his factory, but on the condition that he would manufacture one hundred and fifty bolts of duck per year. This particular loan was continued eighteen years, quite a respectable long-term loan. Massachusetts loaned £800 to Joseph Plaisted in 1735 "to be repaid in small instalments," to enable him to erect and to equip a plant to manufacture potash. The town of Woodbridge, New Jersey, gave £30 in 1770 to the builder of its first grist-mill.

Pennsylvania likewise granted aid either in the form of loans or of subcriptions to "societies and companies of manufacturers." Some of the early loans were for particularly worthy and ambitious, if far-fetched projects, such as the credit of £1,000 extended to the Philosophical Society in 1770 to encourage silk-culture. Pennsylvania, in 1786, now a State, loaned Whitehead Humphries £300, for five years, without interest but upon double security, to assist him in starting the manufacture of steel. Two years later, £200 was loaned to John Hewson, without interest but upon "sufficient security," to enable him to extend his calico-printing business.

Over the entire colonial period the mercantile economic policy of England was based on the theory that the colonies should be subordinate to British industrial needs. The colonies were to supply raw materials and commodities such as lumber and lumber products, masts for the royal navy, naval stores such as potash, turpentine, tar, pitch and resin, fish from the fishing banks, and tobacco. In return, they were to purchase increasing quantities of English manufactured goods. This policy would build up a profitable carrying trade for the British ships, make England less dependent upon the Northern European countries for lumber products, and bring increased trade and profits to British industry.

Thus, while industries favorable to England were to be built up, those which would provide competition to English merchandise, were virtually prohibited. Such an inclusive economic policy could not be completely enforced, especially after the Northern colonies put larger and larger fleets upon the high seas, but the policy was so effective that colonial manufacturing carried on prior to the Revolutionary War in competitive fields, was of limited and only local significance.

Bank Note Currency Without Banks

In 1714, another economic innovation saw the light of day, an experiment which placed a new type of credit into.the hands of the colonists. Massachusetts issued her first "bank" of £50,000. "Issuing a bank" may seem peculiar in our day and age, but only because of the checkered evolution which has taken place in the connotation of the word "bank." These particular early colonial banks under no consideration should be confused with our modern commercial, savings, or industrial banks.

A little over two hundred years ago, a "bank" was nothing more or less than "a batch of paper currency." It had no permanent place of business, no corporate existence, no vice-presidents, no tellers, no fancy grilles to intrigue depositors, no credit investigators or credit departments, no particular attraction to colonial precursors of Jesse James. It did not receive deposits, make discounts, nor negotiate checks or drafts. These particular issues of paper currency were distinguished from all other paper currency, issued first by Massachusetts in 1690, and then by the other colonies during the succeeding years, by the simple fact that they were intended as loans of public credit to individual borrowers against mortgages on personally owned real estate. They were in the nature of elementary land banks which made credit available to the owners of land, the credit being in the form of negotiable paper currency which could immediately be put into circulation.

The first "bank" was repayable by the colonists who were fortunate enough through influence to obtain credit in this original way, one-fifth of the principal each year with interest at five per cent per annum. Similar issues took place in Massachusetts in 1716, 1721, and 1728, bringing the total amount of these specialized bills to £260,000. This currency circulated side by side with the ordinary colonial paper money. Many of the loans, were extended and extended, in some cases remaining unpaid for more than thirty years.

Rhode Island issued its first "bank" of £40,000 in 1715. This issue of paper currency was loaned on mortgages for ten years, also at five per cent interest. The "banks" then followed in rapid order in Rhode Island until the ninth was made in this one colony in 1750. The real estate offered as security was supposed to be double the value of the loan. Under existing New York State Laws, savings banks today are restricted in making loans on improved and unencumbered real property to 60 per cent of the appraised value, or 66 2/3 per cent if residential property. These restrictions, however, do not apply to loans insured by the Federal Housing Administration.

The colony of New Hampshire "issued" similar "banks" for eleven and twenty-three years at varying rates of interest. Pennsylvania "issued banks" for twelve years at five per cent per annum but limited the loans conservatively to £200 to one person. Every colony except Virginia issued these particular loan bills. Land was, of course, the most common form of wealth and while logical in theory, it was an impractical security for an issue of notes, as wealth in such a form could not very easily be converted into cash for the redemption of an issue. The experiment, however, went on and on.

Whereas the loans from the first local settlements to assist in the establishment of essential industries were the forerunner of the present day operations of the Reconstruction Finance Corporation, these early so-called issues of "banks" were the forerunners of the lending activity of the Home Owners' Loan Corporation. As Will Durant emphasizes in *The Life of Greece*, there is really nothing new today, no matter how radical, how original the politician becomes. All of our current economic, social, and political problems agitated the brilliant and turbulent life of ancient Hellas over two thousand years ago.

The very same thing may be said about our colonial days. Colonial politicians had no great difficulties in determining economic policies which would involve losses. That was really a simple matter! The Home Owners' Loan Corporation likewise in February, 1940 announced that it had taken losses on foreclosed property of $78,000,000 and the final aggregate loss, according to a study of the corporation, might "eventually more than triple" this amount. On December 31, 1940 its capital stock of $200,000,000 had a recognizable deficit of $85,489,334!

Colonial Lotteries

The medieval custom of raising funds by lotteries also provided money for establishing and fostering occasional new colonial industries. More often, however, lotteries were used for relieving manufacturers who had unfortunately lost their property by fire. Little could be done in colonial days to stop a blaze started by a casual spark, as there was no fire fighting equipment outside of an occasional inexperienced volunteer fire company, and no responsible fire insurance company until *The Philadelphia Contributionship* was founded in 1752. Catastrophic fires were an ever present hazard, due to the general use of open fire places for heating.

When the glass works at Germantown, Massachusetts, for example, burned in 1756, the legislature allowed the owners to raise £1,250 by a lottery. Rhode Island, in 1758, granted the privilege of operating a lottery to H. Chapman, of Newport, to compensate him for the loss by fire of his distillery, soap house, cooper's ship, joiner's shop, and other property. In 1772, the same colony granted a lottery to Griffin Green, whose forge at Coventry had been destroyed by fire. Two years later, Jeremiah Hopkins of Coventry, was allowed to operate a lottery for $200, to enable him to equip a gun shop. Even Harvard College in 1773, when only thirty-six bachelor of arts degrees were awarded, received financial assistance from a lottery.

In 1776, a lottery was operated under a resolution of the Continental Congress to provide funds for the army but with very little success. Lotteries continued to be used after the Revolutionary War but to a decreasing extent and often with very little profit. Connecticut, for example, allowed William Cundall, in 1787, to set up a lottery to promote his woolen factory. The prizes were to equal the price of the tickets, less three per cent for expenses, but were to be payable in woolens manufactured by the undertaker. In 1790, the same State granted the privilege of operating a lottery to the Hartford Woolen Factory, the proceeds to be used for the purchase of new machinery.

Probably the most prominent use of the lottery after the War for Independence and up to about 1800, was as a supplementary aid in raising funds to complete toll bridges, toll roads, and toll canals, three types of business activity in which considerable money was then being invested. Funds were obtained in 1792 in this manner to assist in the construction of three bridges in New Jersey including the Passaic bridge which was 492 feet long and the Hackensack bridge 980 feet long, and during the same year, in developing the seven mile toll road between Norwich and New London in Connecticut. In 1795, several lotteries were operated to obtain funds to complete the canal from the Santee River to the Cooper River in South Carolina, in 1796 to help along the work on the South Hadley Falls Canal in Massachusetts, and to complete a toll bridge at Portland, Maine. Four years later the promoters of the Amoskeag Canal in New Hampshire obtained assistance in the same way.

The poor results from many of the lotteries of this later period was due to the initial development of the corporation as a more flexible unit of business activity. Shares of stock, now coming into existence, were offering many of the advantages of speculation without the principal disadvantage of complete loss inherent in all except a very limited number of the lottery tickets.

After the adoption of the Federal Constitution, the regulation of lotteries became subject to State laws. They were made illegal by New York and Massachusetts in 1833. Other States followed, and after Congress prohibited the use of the mails for lottery purposes in 1890, the last authorized lottery, the famous Louisiana State Lottery, which had been operated by a private company under a franchise which brought in approximately $40,000 to the State each year, transferred its operations to Honduras were it finally went out of existence around 1915. Various forms of illegal lotteries have continued in the larger cities, the most important being the so-called "policy rackets" which pay on the terminal number of daily bank clearings, and which District Attorney Thomas E. Dewey so successfully prosecuted in 1938 in New York City.

Early Extension of Domestic Credit

The earliest colonial records of the seventeenth century show occasional instances of credit extended to the Indians. We have seen that in the first years of both the James Towne and Plimoth settlements, corn was obtained by barter with the natives when food was scarce and famine was abroad. The Indians customarily raised large quantities of corn but occasionally in succeeding years when their supplies ran low due to poor crops, they purchased corn on credit from the colonists, particularly from the Dutch in New York and from the English in Massachusetts. The credit terms provided for payment in beaver skins during the following year.

The extension of credit between colonists originally took the form of loans of such products as food, seed, powder or shot, from one neighbor to another in anticipation of the next crop. Similar credit has always been granted liberally on the frontier. A settler in real need, facing identical problems of protection and of providing livelihoods for his growing family, has never had to go farther than the door of his nearest neighbor for assistance. Such loans assumed the character of duty. No questions of financial responsibility were ever raised.

As commerce developed between colonial merchants, bills of exchange and promissory notes became the customary credit instruments. They took the place of the modern check which did not come into existence until many years later in the early development of deposit banking. Domestic bills of exchange throughout the colonial era were generally payable three, five, or ten days after sight. Because of the extensive varieties of paper money in circulation, it was customary to state the specific currency desired in the bill of exchange, whether sterling, the particular currency of a particular colony, or specie. In modern times, bills of exchange are usually negotiated through a commercial bank, but prior to 1782 there were no banks. These instruments accordingly were endorsed and passed from merchant to merchant as our present day checks are sometimes passed, until presented for final payment or credit. Promissory notes, especially when signed by men of property, likewise, often passed from hand to hand for several months, all the time serving as real currency.

Unique Types of Early Credit

One of the very earliest pieces of colonial legislation regarding the extension of credit was concerned with the vagrant ways of seafaring men while in port, a matter which annoyed the Puritan shipmasters. In 1682, an act of the General Court of Massachusetts forbade all seamen to purchase anything on "trust." This legislation was enacted, however not because excessive risks or losses were assumed in extending credit to seamen, but because a seaman, like any debtor, might be placed in a debtor's prison if he failed to meet his obligations, and that was particularly calamitous to a Puritan captain who was anxious and ready to sail only to find a member of his crew was unavailable.

There were few bridges until the colonies became more thickly settled. If one wanted to cross a river he was ferried by a nearby settler who added a little to his income by such services. There is an interesting record that the usual charge for being ferried about this time between Newburyport and Salisbury, Massachusetts, was two-pence for a man, and sixpence for "great cattle and horses." Apparently personal credit was granted occasionally to those favorably known to the ferryman, as the charge, that is, the use of credit, called for one penny apiece extra.

Credit for postage was allowed to accumulate at the general office in Boston as a convenience to responsible individuals. When they failed to settle their postal obligations promptly, they were informed by advertisements, as early as 1712 "that on Monday or Tuesday next without fail, they would repair to the Post Office, and Pay the same, where attendance shall be giv'n every day from 8 in the Morning to 12, and from two to six in the afternoon."* Advertisements, however, gradually became more emphatic, finally warning debtors to settle their bills, or their privilege "of charging" would be cut off. This practice continued for many years, as a typical bill for postage between Boston and Newport, Rhode Island as late as 1772 was reproduced in the well-known volume, *Commerce of Rhode Island.*

Early Lack of Uniform Credit Terms

The mention of exact terms of sale in the early colonial records, were few and far between, possibly because there were no customary terms. Credit probably was extended for one month, three months, nine months, or twelve months, depending upon mutual understanding in the absence of established trade customs. Most of the early transactions were barter, or "trusting" because of friendship or neighborliness.

An account which John Hull, the most successful general merchant of the day in Boston, rendered to John Winthrop, Jr., covering transactions during the latter part of 1660, showed that Hull had sold eight bushels of wheat received from Winthrop on "three months tyme" in order "to get 4s 3d, or else could have had but 4s in money for it." The selling price depended upon the terms of payment, the credit for three months costing the purchaser three pence per bushel. This ac-

* *Boston News Letter*, Monday, December 15 to Monday, December 22, 1712, Number 453, p. 2.

count showed a final balance of £1.9.6 due to Hull, apparently from the fact that Hull was selling imported merchandise to his customers and buying farm produce from them at the same time.

The ledger of Stephanus Van Cortlandt, the well known merchant who was also twice Mayor of New York City, disclosed accounts from customers running on and on, for periods up to five years. Mathew Clarkson, for example, opened an account on October 18, 1695 by the purchase of "sundry" articles for £1.01.0. From that day until sometime in 1700, fifty-seven items were charged with only one credit offset, represented by wheat delivered in 1699 and valued at £13.16.0. At the time of Van Cortlandt's death in 1701, the balance owing after more than five years of charges, amounted to £62.6.4.

A less extensive account consisting of twenty-two items stood in the name of one Francis Vincent. This particular account was opened on August 16, 1695 and increased steadily without a single payment to a total of £31.6.10 in 1701. In that year, after five years of credit in increasing amounts, the full debt was discharged by a note of one Corbitt for £20, and the payment of £11.6.10 probably in cash, although the ledger contains no mention of the exact form of the payment.* Many other accounts during these years showed running credit for two, three, four, and five years, in some cases with occasional credits in produce or cash, in other cases, with no offset until the account was paid in full, and in still others, with no payments when entries ceased at the time of the proprietor's death.

Joseph Rhoads of Philadelphia had many accounts where the sales of tanned hides were offset from month to month by the delivery of such products as "ruff leather," "sheepe skins," "calfeskin," hides of goats, horses, hogs and dogs, oats, buckwheat, bark, and potatoes. Many of these accounts ran on, year after year, with a balance due to Rhoads even after the receipt of one "calfeskin" as an opening credit. In a rare instance a "demande" note was taken; as early as 1728 there is recorded in the account book such a note for "fourteen pounds Eghtten chillings and sespence."†

Similar running transactions were carried on by Boston merchants. Messrs. Tidmarsh & Appleton made purchases every few days of such varied products as fish, turpentine, salt, stockings, wine, tar, and Spanish iron, and also borrowed sums of money up to £755 from wealthy James Bowdoin. On the other hand, this firm made occasional sales of

---

* *Ledger of Stephanus Van Cortlandt of New York, 1695-1701,* pp. 8, 50, 66, 150, 195. (New York Historical Society)
† *Account Book of Joseph Rhoads, 1st, about 1723-1740.* (J. E. Rhoads & Sons, Wilmington, Delaware.)

"nailes," "bundles of Hemp," Spanish iron, turpentine and "tarr" to James Bowdoin simultaneously, but in somewhat larger amounts. Aggregate transactions beginning with an entry on June 21, 1728, "To Balance due to James Bowdoin accompt This Day Settled" of £838.5.9 and ending January 12, 1729, amounted to the substantial sum of £8,977.4.7. The account was balanced on this last date probably by the payment of £544.17.7 in cash to James Bowdoin although there is no specific mention whether the final credit of this account was in cash, merchandise or a note.*

Credit References and Credit Information

About 1728, twenty-two year old Benjamin Franklin organized the Junto, a club initially composed of eleven members who met at a tavern in Philadelphia every Friday evening to discuss subjects of humane, secular, and practical interest. Twenty-four queries, covering the wide range of Franklin's inquiring young mind, were discussed at each of these meetings. Two of the subjects, Carl Van Doren points out in his recent book, *Benjamin Franklin,* show Franklin's alert interest regarding rumored, as well as exact credit information concerning local business enterprises. The first of these two queries was: "Hath any citizen in your knowledge failed in business lately, and what have you heard of the cause?" Such information was particularly pertinent to one who was wondering about human and natural phenomena. The second query was: "Have you lately heard of any citizen's thriving well, and by what means? . . . ." Information of this character represented very practical new business ammunition for an aggressive, adaptable salesman in a newly established and growing printing business.

Colonial merchants were known to give credit information to one another regarding desirable customers in the West Indies. John Rindge, the successful shipbuilder and ship operator of Portsmouth wrote a letter in 1730 to Messrs. Knight & Fairchild, his agent at Barbados, volunteering to assist them. This letter contained a sentence to this effect, "I shall make it my business to recommend my friends to your house if it will be agreeable."†

Occasionally a prospective colonial buyer on credit would offer references regarding his own reliability and responsibility. Thos. Benedict of Norwalk, Connecticut, for example, in 1752 wrote Daniel

* *C. E. French Collection of Colonial Papers, 1701-1740.* (Massachusetts Historical Society)
† *Letter Book of John Rindge, 1728-1731.* (Massachusetts Historical Society)

Henchman, a colonial bookseller of Boston. Henchman's daughter, Lydia, became the wife of the successful merchant, Thomas Hancock. Benedict wrote in a manner so typical of the period with no punctuation, "I have occasion of some Books in your way and should be very glad of them if it will sute you to Credit me till some time next Summer and which I am Sensible you will be willing to do if you can be satisfied that you will get your money then and for your Farther satisfaction as to my Character I Refer you to Messrs Green & Walker Merch^ts in Boston & the Bearer hereof Capt Daniel Ketchum."* Unfortunately there is no record as to whether the information obtained from these two early credit references was sufficiently favorable, and whether or not the order was filled, and then duly paid!

Wholesale merchants knew their nearby customers personally, and arrived at their own independent decision as to the amount of credit to be granted, just as wholesalers do today. However, when certain importers and wholesalers developed large businesses and began to sell outside of their immediate circles, recommendations of prospective customers, which was the earliest form of credit information, became quite essential. A letter from Philip Cuyler, a successful New York merchant, to one Martin Dewey in 1759 illustrates this development. "I Should Esteem it a verry Singular favour," he wrote, "if you woud Take the Trouble to Recommend to me Such Persons your Neighbours who are Dealears that you Look on to be Good men whom you may assure they Shall be Treated on the Best Terms as I have made it my Determind Resolution to Sell my Goods So Low as will Induce all Persons to Deal with me who Study their Interest and I will Give nine months Credit at the Expiration of wch Time I will Take their Lawfull money or Good Bills of Exchange in Payment."†

Similar requests for credit information are scattered here and there in the letter books (these books contained pen and ink copies of colonial business correspondence long before the days of typewriters) of many of the colonial merchants as their only source of credit information was from customers, friends, and relatives. In a letter written by John Scott, Jr., of Charleston, South Carolina, to Christopher Champlin of Newport, Rhode Island, in 1765 appeared the interesting sentence, "As for Mr. Jos. Atkinson, he is a man lately come from England to set up the Tallow Chandlering business, but quite a stranger to me." Apparently Champlin had been seeking credit information. Inquiries were occasionally made regarding the financial con-

* *Daniel Henchman, A Colonial Bookseller*, by William T. Baxter. A pamphlet reprinted from The Essex Institute Historical Collection, Salem, Mass., 1934. † *Letter Book of Philip Cuyler, 1755-1760.* (New York Public Library)

dition of a debtor, but very quietly, so as not to arouse any general suspicion. Such a report was made by William Samuel Johnson of Stratford, Connecticut, to one James McEvers. The information encompassed in that investigation is certainly a realistic credit report: "I have known Mr. Kuler two or three years. He is a person of a very shrewd turn, of capacity enough but I apprehend not very much acquainted with Trade, and his character for Integrity I have very little opinion of. He is possessed of what you call New England Artifice, and sly cunning in great perfection. I have made all the inquiry concerning his Circumstances that I could since I received your Letter but cannot yet learn anything particular."

Henry Lloyd of Boston, who carried on a large scale business, gave similar indications of being careful of his credits. In 1765, he wrote Thomas Smith of Philadelphia, "As there is a prospect of my being Commissioned by M͟r David Beveridge of your City to purchase him a Vessell here I take the Liberty of asking you whether you think I shall be safe in advancing the greater part of the money for him, as I am entirely unacquainted with his Circumstances."*

Twelve Months Become Customary Credit Terms

By the time the eighteenth century came around it had become quite customary for the importer-wholesaler in the seaport cities and towns to extend credit for approximately twelve months to his retail customers, shopkeepers, storekeepers, and country general stores. Credit terms of one year seem to have been required as obligations often could be retired only after the following crop season. Business relationships, customs, and habits were becoming established as the population expanded, and the volume of foreign and domestic trade increased. In 1737, Peter Faneuil, the active young merchant who built and gave Faneuil Hall to Boston, wrote to M. Miguel Pacheco da Silva, London, that he had sold imported goods "at 12 & 15 Months Credit & if I can get paid for them in two Years time I shall account myself well of."†

The security of long outstanding debts like those of Stephanus Van Cortlandt and Peter Faneuil does not seem to have caused much uneasiness. Thomas Fitch, a successful importer of Boston, likewise, was undisturbed by the goodness of much of the indebtedness he was forced to allow, although inconvenienced by the long waits for settlements. In

* *Letter Book of Henry Lloyd, 1765-1767.* (Baker Library, Harvard Graduate School of Business Administration)
† *Letter Book of Peter Faneuil, 1737-1739.* (Baker Library, Harvard Graduate School of Business Administration)

1724, he wrote to an English supplier: "So soon as Ere I receive payment for ye Cloths I shall be glad to make Yo returns, but tho' the men are good I sold them to yet they nere pay me in less yn 12 months and sometimes take longer time wch is ye Common Course of Credit given here." In 1748, John Swift who carried on a moderate sized importing business at Philadelphia wrote his uncle, John White of London, that he had not been attracted by country store business, "I have had little dealings with any of the Country Store Keepers, I never took any pains to get acquainted with any of them, because I did not care to give the Credit that they generally require."*

The original ledgers and account books of colonial merchants which have been preserved, unfortunately contain little mention of selling terms. The accounts generally run on and on with credit extended year after year, and with offsets more in the form of "country pay" than metallic currency, or paper money. The letter books of the same merchants contain numerous mention of terms of sale.

Gerard G. Beekman, a merchant of New York wrote to Messrs. Gideon & John Waton in 1757 that it was not in his "Power to Point Out any one article that Will Command Cash at any tolerable Proffit, for it is a Custom w! Our Merchant to give from 6 to 12 m? Credit for all kinds of Dry goods."† In the following year, William Wilson of Philadelphia stated in a letter to a London merchant that dry goods were sold on credit for six to twelve months, as an explanation why it was necessary for him to have the same credit. In 1766, John Hancock emphasized these same terms in a letter to Messrs. Harrison & Barnard, London, ". . . . send me no more [merchandise] unless you can give me one year's credit, as I have to give the same here."

Three Reasons for Long Credit Terms

Shopkeepers who lacked "country pay" or ready money, were oftentimes quite willing to purchase merchandise at a higher price if payment could be put off into the future. There is every indication that this quality of the human mind is just as prominent in the twentieth century. During the entire colonial period, there were no fixed definite prices as is customary in business today. Individual prices were determined at the time of each sale by the bargaining powers of the buyer and the seller. Every transaction was a horse sale! John Van

* Letter Book of John Swift, 1747-1751. (Historical Society of Pennsylvania)
† Letter Book of Gerard G. Beekman, 1752-1770. (New York Historical Society)

Cortlandt of New York, more than one hundred years after the time of John Hull, explained in 1767 to a correspondent in the West Indies that a higher price could be obtained by selling on credit: "I am sorry your Rum and Sugar Came to So low a Market I made the most of it I could I sold all the Rum on a Credit in order to Git the Best Price I Could and am not in Cash for any part of the Cargo Yet. . . . I got a penny a Gallon more for your Rum than the Markett price, by Giving Credit here."*

The difference between a cash price and a credit price, when the latter was the higher, was not all profit, for interest charges had to be included in carrying an account to maturity. Philip Cuyler explained to a prospective customer in 1755, that "my price is at 150 per Cent for a 12 m° Credit, 140 per Cent for 3 Months,"† a difference of 10 per cent for nine months' credit.

The successful firm of Baynton & Wharton of Philadelphia emphasized the same policy to their Halifax factor in 1761: "From looking over the prices of ye Goods you sold at Hallifax," they wrote, "we are in hopes of gaining 10 or 15 per ct. . . . But we must deduct near 12 Mo. Interest from our supposed proffitt." Even if the difference in price was more than enough to cover the interest charge, there often remained the uncertainty as to whether settlement would be made promptly when the account became due. What was the credit standing of the customer? Would he be able to pay the bill when it matured on the longer terms? Would the account need to be extended? There have always been and there still are today recognized disadvantages to be considered when merchandise is sold on long terms in order to attract somewhat higher prices.

Importers and wholesale merchants were frequently forced by competition to accommodate colonial shopkeepers and storekeepers with generous grants of credit in order that they might be on even terms with their competitors. Otherwise they could hardly expect to hold their customers. Finally, in an effort to obtain new business, the merchant again found himself obliged to offer liberal credit terms in order to attract the trade of other houses. Terms of sale, as well as the product itself, have always been strong competitive instruments.

Collection Difficulties

One of the most persistent worries of the colonial wholesale merchant was how to secure the fairly punctual settlement of accounts

---

* *Letter Book of John Van Cortlandt, 1762-1769,* p. 165. (New York Public Library)
† *Letter Book of Philip Cuyler, 1755-1760.* (New York Public Library)

owed to him by his retail store customers. The steps which he took to protect or to secure his over-due accounts show both the inherent difficulties in the colonial situation, and the inter-connection between credit conditions within the colonies and the credit relations between colonial and English merchants. In some cases, debts were absolutely lost and nothing remained to be done except to charge them off the books. On the whole, however, it seems that most of the accounts which were owed to colonial merchants were sooner or later liquidated, either in part or in whole. The distress was caused by the uncertainty as to when the obligations would be paid.

The perpetual problem of the scarcity of an adequate medium of exchange was responsible for many of these difficulties. Creditors very frequently were unable to collect from their debtors simply because sufficient cash was not in circulation. Thomas Moffatt of Boston summed up the situation in somewhat of a rambling but enlightening letter in 1715, "As for Trade here with us it's at psent at a very low Ebb mostly for want of a medium of Exg to carry it on, ye Sil— money being all sent out of ye country to make returnes for England, & ye Bills of Creditt of ye Provence not being sufficient to carry on half of our Trade with any Creditt or Satisfaction so yt of all ye English factories we under-goe (I believe) ye greatest ill conveniences of any for unless its goods yts very much in demand, hardly any will fetch money down unless sold for ye 1st cost, & there is very few commodities yt ye country products but we must pay money down for, wch is no small hardshipp on us."

This condition persisted throughout the eighteenth century. Depreciated paper currency with different values in the different colonies made the problem more and more difficult. If paper money was unacceptable and hard money obtainable in small quantities, or not at all, the debtor was left helpless, unless he could persuade his creditor to accept raw materials, "country pay" in lieu of cash. Under these handicaps, it was not unusual for a wholesaler to accept a cargo of some salable commodity, sell the merchandise on commission, and apply the proceeds to the existing debt. This was quite similar to the relations between the city wholesaler and the country general store.

The colonial merchant who was not prepared to proceed at law against his delinquent debtors, and who on the other hand, was not disposed to stand idly by and make no effort to collect his outstanding accounts, usually sought to bring moral pressure to bear on his debtors. He would point out the unreasonableness of a situation which kept him out of his money for months and even years. Baynton & Wharton, for example, wrote in 1761 to a debtor of their "inexpressible regret" at having received neither remittances or letters from him in spite of solemn assurances that remittances would be forthcoming. "If you ever had any Friendship for us," they lamented, "or conceive yourself under any Obligations to us, we in the earnest Manner desire that you wou'd in some degree make up for our great disappointment by exerting yourself to the utmost to remit us fully by September." Interspersed with pleadings for settlements of this nature, were hints that patience was well-nigh exhausted and that other tactics would shortly be pursued.

Thomas Fitch, the Boston merchant, reminded a delinquent correspondent in 1732 that his debt was of three and a half years' standing. "I have waited Year after Year," he wrote, "to have recd Payment but You have wholly neglected to Pay it or any part thereof which is both unreasonable & intollerable. If therefore You now without delay send me down the sd Sum of 174.10.7 You'll do well thereby to save Your self the further trouble which otherwise I shall be under an unavoidable necessity of giving You my friend to whom the goods belonged being quite out of patience with You & me about it."

Up to the very days of the War for Independence, colonial merchants complained to their creditors in England that they were forced by circumstances to sell their goods on long credit. The complaint was meant to explain why remittances to England were slow and irregular and why it was absolutely necessary that the colonial merchants, in turn, have extensive credit from English factors, exporters, and merchant-bankers.

Organization of Colonial Business

Business enterprises during the entire colonial era were proprietorships or partnerships. Even in England there were very few commercial corporations outside of the privileged and monopolistic enterprises which engaged in foreign trade such as the *East India Company,* the *Muscovy Company,* the *Hudson's Bay Company,* and the *Royal African Company,* against all of which there was considerable prejudice in the colonies. Very little manufacturing was carried on outside of ship-building and what little there was, represented small scale business, far removed from the industrialization of our time which calls for tremendous investments in factories, machinery, transportation systems, and power plants. Business was largely commerce and trade, importing, exporting, wholesaling, and retailing.

Two of the wealthiest and most important merchants in New York City just prior to the Revolution, Philip Livingston and Robert Murray, had no partners. The larger businesses, however, were generally partnerships. Of the members of the New York Chamber of Commerce in 1755, sixty-one carried on business in association with others and forty-three were independent.

The predominance of partnerships produced an effect of discontinuity in business activity which seems unusual to us today with the common use of the corporate form, as partnerships were formed and dissolved with equal facility. Some associations lasted a few months, others many years. In case of dissolution the outstanding liabilities as well as the assets were divided among the partners. While membership in a firm probably meant that the principal time and effort of an individual was devoted in behalf of that enterprise, it did not hinder a partner from engaging in other business ventures, which to some extent took the place of present day outside investments. When sending for merchandise abroad, a distinction was often made between goods purchased for the firm and those for "own account." Joint individual ventures were also undertaken on the side, in which capital and goods of several persons were united in a single project. Active merchants and speculators like Robert Morris and William Duer were engaged in so many ventures at one time that it is probable they had difficulty in understanding or knowing their own financial condition.

Moreover, in colonial merchandising there was very little specialization. Retailers existed as a separate class and handled all kinds of merchandise. "Merchants," however, were distinguished by the fact that they had a "store" or warehouse in contrast to a "shop" and imported their own goods in bulk. Many of the "merchants" sold both at wholesale and retail.

Credit from English Factors and Exporters

We have seen how the Pilgrims obtained credit from their London "backers" to purchase necessary supplies of food, clothing, seeds, muskets, and ammunition, before sailing from England. During the following six years, that is, up to 1626, when Izaack Allerton made his trip to London to negotiate the "first" settlement, clapboard, dried fish, beaver, bear, mink, fox, and otter furs were sent to England as credits to their account, and products essential to the colonists which the English backers purchased and shipped to Plimoth such as cattle, powder, shot, seeds, hoes, woolen cloth, shoes, and leather goods, were debited to the account. At all times there was a running balance for which Governor Bradford and his associates were indebted. This was the typical arrangement between English factors, exporters, and merchant-bankers on the one hand, and American importer-wholesalers on the other hand, during the entire colonial era.

Credit Information on Colonial Concerns

The English merchant had no way that approached modern facilities for ascertaining the credit standing of a concern in the colonies when he contemplated the extension of credit. There was absolutely no credit service to which he might refer for information. Colonial merchants were almost three thousand miles away. English firms were, indeed, much better known to colonial merchants by repute than the smaller colonial concerns to the English. Some information regarding credit standing could occasionally be obtained from other English houses, just as an American concern today may often obtain information regarding a prospective customer in Havana, Rio de Janeiro, or Buenos Aires, from other American exporters, but the main reliance had to be placed upon the opinions of the English merchant's own customers in the colonies.

When a request for a connection was received by an English merchant from a colonial importer, a reasonable degree of care seems to have been exercised in investigating the applicant's character and standing. Generally the English exporter would write one or several nearby customers in the colonies, and through them obtain information regarding the local reputation of the applicant. Such credit investigations took time, three months at the very least, and if an order for merchandise had already been received, it would often have been quite inexpedient to hold up the shipment pending the receipt of the replies.

Under these circumstances it was not unusual for the English merchant to take "a chance" and make the shipment, if moderate in amount, before the investigation was completed. This is what Henry Cruger, Jr., of Bristol, England, did in 1766 and then wrote Aaron Lopez of Newport, Rhode Island, "I must, Dear Sir, make use of your Friendship to favour me in the most Private and Expeditious Manner what your opinion is of Mr. Robert Crooke of your place. I am sensible how delicate a thing it is either to ask or grant a favour of this sort, but these are occurrences that will happen in Trade. my reason for this enquiry is that I have sent Mr. Crooke out by way of New York a pretty large Cargo of Goods, without knowing any thing of his Circumstances therefore must trepass upon your Goodness for your Private Opinion of him which shall be kept by me as in unviolate Secret."

The extension of credit to merchants who came recommended by colonial correspondents was another matter. In 1759, Philip Cuyler placed his first order for merchandise with Elias Bland of London. In that letter he then went on, "Should any Doubts arise in Your Breast Respecting my Honesty or Capacity to Reimburse You be Pleased to have Refference to Your other Correspondents here [in the colonies] as well as to Messrs Champion & Hayley of Your City."* When young Jonathan Jackson started in business in Newburyport in 1765, he obtained a letter of reference from one James Griffin which he mailed to Messrs Devonsheir & Reeves of Bristol, England, with whom he accordingly placed an early order for merchandise.

Aggressive English merchants asked their good colonial customers to influence their friends, if they could, to remit orders, and even, at times, sent representatives from England to the colonial commercial cities to drum up trade. Thomas Wharton of Philadelphia wrote to John Waddell, New York, in 1756 introducing Godfrey Leacocke "from Hallifax in England, sent by a firm in Liverpool to Recommend such Persons As he thought proper to their Friendship & Trade."†

English Merchants Used as Bankers

It became quite customary for colonial importers to use English merchants as bankers. There were no international banking houses to supply the financial machinery needed for transferring funds between the colonies and England or the continent. A few of the English houses like the firm of Peach & Pierce of Bristol, David Barclay & Sons of London, Clay, Midgely & Co. of Liverpool, and Lascelles & Maxwell of London, were actually private bankers as well as factors and wholesale dry-goods houses. Many of the important international banking firms of the nineteenth century developed out of earlier importing and exporting businesses, the subsequent specialization in finance merely representing the expansion in this division of their early activity. Since

---

* *Letter Book of Philip Cuyler, 1755-1760.* (New York Public Library)
† *Letter Book of Thomas Wharton, 1752-1759.* (Historical Society of Pennsylvania)

there were no strictly financial institutions in the colonies to facilitate the transfer of funds, each colonial merchant tended to be his own banker, and at the same time occasionally furnished banking facilities for his friends and the general public.

When he wished to transmit a certain sum to a party in England, either for himself or for some other person, the colonial merchant, drew a bill of exchange on his principal English correspondent, and sent it to the payee in England, or sold it to the person in the colonies who wished to transfer the money. The merchant in England "accepted" the bill when it was presented, paid it when it fell due, and then debited the amount on the colonial merchant's account.

The supposition underlying these transactions was that the colonial merchant had credits with his English correspondent ample enough to cover his drawings. His drafts ordinarily were drawn upon the merchant in England to whom he sent his principal shipments of raw materials and other remittances, and with whom he kept his primary account. Not infrequently, however, when the colonial merchant thought he had a reasonable credit balance in England, the books would show an actual debit, or the existing credit might be too small to meet any extensive drafts. Any further drafts, therefore, left him in debt to his merchant-banker.

At other times, the colonial importing merchant actually overdrew his account when he was well aware that his balance was not equal to the strain of additional drafts. Such drawings were not due to careless indifference; rather they were caused by the merchant's lack of capital or inability to collect his outstanding domestic accounts. To have allowed the difficulty of collecting his local accounts to have interfered with his orders for merchandise from England would have meant a serious loss in trade. English houses made it a consistent practice to accept and to pay these drafts as part of their credit program, even in those cases where colonists had failed to notify them.

Confronted with this situation, the colonial merchant was naturally driven to take the line of least resistance. He bought on extended credit terms from his principal English correspondent and also drew bills of exchange on him—though he might lack adequate resources to meet them—with which he paid for goods purchased from other English houses. He might be concerned over his credit standing in the colonies and sometimes give prior attention to his debt here, either by postponing remittances to England or by overdrawing his account in order to support his credit standing at home.

Colonial Merchants Made Free Use of Credit

A consideration of the factors involved in the extension of colonial credit must not lose sight of a fundamental aspect in the credit relationships between colonial and English merchants. The need for capital with which to expand business and to develop home resources was almost unlimited, and the colonial merchant not only put his own earnings to work as new capital, but by drawing drafts he also found a method of obtaining extensive, and we might say involuntary, loans of capital from his English creditors.

Credit was being extended to colonial merchants in generous and increasing amounts by 1737, and on terms which the English merchants made earnest efforts to have observed. In that year Peter Faneuil advised M. Miguel Pacheco da Silva, London, not to expect payment for recent shipments "in less than 12 or 18 m°."* The usual terms were credit for nine or twelve months from the date of the invoice, during which period no interest was charged. After the designated period had elapsed, interest was customarily charged at the rate of five per cent per annum on the amount past due.

In 1755, Thomas Willing of Philadelphia, who was one of the most important merchants immediately prior to the Revolutionary War and one of the outstanding financiers after the War, wrote John Perks, Bristol, England, for merchandise, "such as are sold . . . on 12 mo^s. Credit."† Gerard G. Beekman wrote a brother located in London in 1760 regarding his New York "neighbor Franklin who has his goods from McEdmond Jenney of your place at 9 months Credit."§

William Stead of London in a letter to Christopher Champlin of Newport, Rhode Island, in 1762 regarding past due balances, emphasized the fact that sales had been "charg'd at 12 Months Creditt, which is now upwards of 3 years standing," so "that you cannot blame me for asking for the Ballance; for had much rather be paid at the time agreed on than have any Interest to charge which is no sort of satisfaction to us at this time. . . ." Two years later the firm of Champion and Hayley of London wrote Champlin, "Our time of Creditt with all our Friends in America is 9 Months from the date of their Invoices." When the English merchant asked for "punctual remittances," he ordinarily had reference to payment within this credit period and before interest charges took effect.

* *Letter Book of Peter Faneuil, 1737-1739.* (Baker Library, Harvard Graduate School of Business Administration)
† *Letter Book of Thomas Willing, 1754-1761.* (Historical Society of Pennsylvania)
§ *Letter Book of Gerard G. Beekman, 1752-1770.* (New York Historical Society)

The firm of Jackson & Bromfield located in Newburyport, Massachusetts, placed an order in 1766 with Tappenden & Hanbey of London. That credit for twelve months was the typical terms would seem evident by the sentence, "We shall expect 12 Months Credit for these & all other goods we may write for hereafter." A letter written a few months later by the same firm to George Kippen & Son of Glasgow, carried the same impression, " . . . . we understand. . . . your term of Credit is 12 M?ᵒˢ & we think it most for our Interest to take it." Some English concerns, however, such as Stephen Apthorp of Bristol, were using terms of nine months, and during 1774, the firm of Lane, Son & Fraser, London, probably the leader among those specializing in trade with colonial importing-wholesalers, was using credit terms of eight months. Twelve months, however, seem to have become the most customarily used terms of sale.

This credit period seems long in our day, but analysis shows that the length of time for which the colonial merchant enjoyed the benefits of these customary terms, was considerably less than nine or twelve months. The invoice, for example, was dated in England at the time the goods were loaded for shipment. Approximately two months were required to deliver the goods to their destination, even if they went by a direct route. Delays in loading and unloading were frequent, and in many cases shipments had to be transferred before they reached their destination. Another six weeks or two months were required in sending a remittance back to England. Out of the total credit period granted, approximately four months, more or less, were lost in the course of shipping the goods and returning the remittance. Not only did the colonial merchant need time in which to pay the cost of the merchandise, but he generally had to sell the goods on extended credit terms, himself. The credit period which was granted to the importer-wholesaler was, therefore, not as extended as appears at first sight; and it is little wonder that when slumps and hard times afflicted the colonial business world, the merchants should have found it difficult to keep strictly within the terms.

One of the well known business houses of New York City just prior to the Revolutionary War was John & Henry Cruger. This house transacted an extensive business with the help of foreign branches managed by the sons of Henry, John Harris Cruger on the island of Jamaica, Telemon at Curacao, Nicholas at St. Croix, and Henry, Jr., at Bristol, England. One of the larger accounts of Henry, Jr. was Aaron Lopez of Newport, Rhode Island, and a considerable portion of the cor-

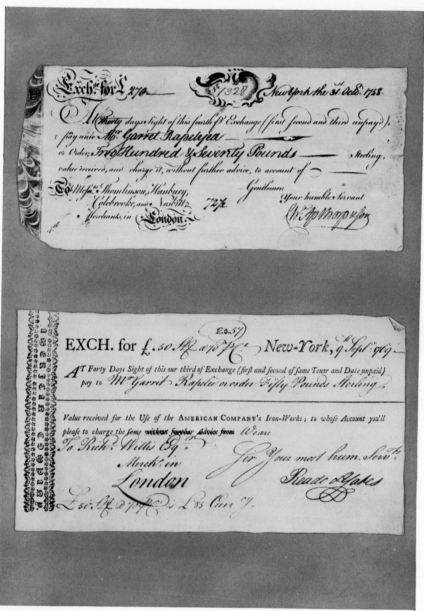

Colonial Bills of Exchange Drawn on London

respondence between these two men from 1765 to 1772 has been preserved and published. Lopez became more and more indebted to Cruger until his account in April, 1766 amounted to the very substantial sum of £10,760.9.8. As it grew larger, Cruger became more and more worried. His own liabilities increased as he was unable to collect from Lopez; he became unable to sleep, and finally he began to wonder if he, himself, would not become bankrupt before Lopez would appreciably reduce the account.

Under these circumstances Cruger wrote to Lopez in October, 1768: "I throw myself into the Bosom of your Justice and Benevolence, whether it will glow with an ardent Desire to show me a *Preference* to those of your Correspondents in London, whose Stars have been more propitious, Time will discover—their funds and resources compar'd to mine are inexhaustible. . . ." This correspondence seemed to have had no effect to cause Lopez to send either remittances or consignments of goods to Cruger to be applied on his account. In July, 1769 Cruger wrote with a little more emphasis: "the Cord of Friendship and Indulgence is strained so tight, that it must absolutely break, unless greatly relaxed by a considerable Consignment next Fall." By May, 1771 the balance had been brought down to £4,047.9.1, and in July, 1772 it amounted only to £2,452.15.11, exclusive of interest. Cruger was still pleading eloquently with his delinquent correspondent for a final settlement of the account. "Do, good Sir!," he wrote, "contrive to pay me off this fatal balance."

It is evident that English merchants did grant liberal credits and in most cases they did it willingly. Their letters frequently carried declarations of their readiness to meet overdrafts, and to ship goods on credit within reasonable limits. Moreover, extending liberal credit was, within limits, one way of getting business; new customers were attracted by it. It was also a means of holding trade already won. On the other hand, when once a colonial merchant was deeply in debt, as in the case of Aaron Lopez, his English creditor could not afford to drop him and lose the debt. In order to help the colonist back on his feet, the English house was obliged to continue the extension of credit.

Difficulties in Keeping Accounts Clear

Whether he needed cash to buy raw materials or funds with which to keep his stores well-stocked, it was the colonial merchant's over-drafts which accounted for a good portion of his indebtedness.

This overdrawing was not always intentional; often it was accidental. The explanation of these chance over-drafts is found in the fact that it was the general practice of English merchants to send formal statements of account to their colonial customers only once a year. In the interval between the receipt of such statements, the colonial merchant had to depend upon his own records and memoranda and on such information as his English merchant sent him, for his estimate of the condition of his account. With careful figuring, it was possible for him to approximate his true condition. But even under the most favorable circumstances it was difficult to arrive at a fair approximation, and the divergences between the colonial merchant's estimates of his balance and the actual facts often were considerable.

These discrepancies were attributable, in part, to the time which elapsed before the merchant in the colonies could learn exactly what credit was being placed to his account by the sale of his shipments. When his merchandise left the colonial docks, he heard no more of it for at least three to four months if it went to England or the continent, and for several weeks if it went to the West Indies. His next information would be a letter informing him that the vessel had docked. That letter had, perhaps, been sent as soon as the ship had arrived and before the goods had been sold. Market conditions and prices were always fluctuating, and it was therefore a matter of guesswork to estimate the net proceeds of the shipment. To the colonial merchant, however, a shipment was the equivalent of a deposit in his favor, something to be drawn against. Since his need for funds seldom abated, he often drew against the proceeds of the shipment, before he knew what the cargo had actually netted him.

Other factors added to the colonial merchant's uncertainty concerning the exact condition of his account. He could never be sure of the cost of the goods which he ordered and which would be charged to his account in England. With fluctuating market prices, the amount which he expected to pay might not be the price for which he would be charged some weeks or months later when the order was filled. In other cases orders for goods, which were not handled by the colonist's principal merchant, were paid for by having the seller draw a bill directly on the colonial merchant's account in England. The colonist, under these circumstances, could not know until several months later how much his order cost, or how much his account had been debited.

John Hancock, who had become the most prominent colonial merchant just prior to the Revolutionary War, found himself in this exact predicament. From the time of his uncle's death in August, 1764 he continually wrote to Messrs. Harrison & Barnard at London, his principal English correspondent, stating that he wished a detailed statement of his account so that he might know how he stood. In almost every letter for two years he confessed that he did not know how much he owed to them, and when he finally received the statement with interest charges aggregating £216.3.1 he was quite overwhelmed.

Foreign Trade of the Northern Colonies

The Northern colonies received the same kind of merchandise as the Southern colonies from England, but in the upper area, the merchandise went first to a seaport center such as Boston, Newport, Philadelphia, or New York. An unfavorable paper balance confronted these centers because of their extensive imports. They consumed, however, only part of the imported merchandise, the remainder being distributed largely to local shopkeepers in nearby communities and to country general retail stores.

With their fleets of home built and home owned vessels, the Northerners also carried on extensive trade with Nova Scotia, Newfoundland, Southern Europe, Africa, the Wine Islands, the West Indies, the Spanish colonies, and the other English colonies. In most of this trade, the balance favored the Northern trader who received in payment, the local commodities of those countries and colonies, some metallic currency, and bills of exchange drawn on London merchants, which he immediately remitted to England as a credit to his account.

Geographically, Boston enjoyed the favored position to carry on foreign trade. It had the best approach to Newfoundland where fish, European goods, some coin, and bills of exchange drawn on English houses, could be obtained. It was the logical trading center to supply the needs of fishermen who sailed from Salem and Marblehead to fish off eastern New England and Nova Scotia. It could market New Hampshire lumber and forest products in the Southern colonies, and foodstuffs such as wheat, oats, rye, flour, and bread from the Middle colonies in the West Indies. Its location made it a natural stopping-off place for ships bound to the colonies from England or from southern Europe, so it naturally became the distributing center of European merchandise, and the rendezvous of ships sailing under convoy from the Northern colonies during the French and Indian Wars.

The importance of New England shipping is easily realized by the fact that in 1715, Boston merchants owned practically all of the bottoms engaged in their Newfoundland trade and had established stores or maintained resident factors there. The supplies from New England arrived in the Summer and were exchanged partly for fish which was then re-shipped from Boston in the trade with the Catholic countries of southern Europe, or bartered on the spot with trading vessels from England, Ireland and southern Europe for wines, brandy, linen, Spanish iron, coins, and bills of exchange. The remainder of the supplies would be left with a resident factor who sold on credit to the settlers and to their servants during the Winter. The indebted settlers pledged the catch of the next season for payment.

By far the most important trade of the northern colonies, after the trade with England, was that with the British West Indies of Jamaica and Barbados, and the foreign sugar colonies, Surinam, St. Thomas, Guadeloupe and Martinique. New England exported fish, lumber, horses, provisions, and candles, while New York exported wheat, bread, flour, lumber, and horses. The principal commodities returned were molasses, rum, and sugar, and of less importance, indigo, fustic, ginger, lime juice, lignum vitae, and cotton-wool. Of most economic importance was the fact that exports exceeded imports, and the excess was obtained in Spanish silver coins, as described in the preceding chapter, and in those always desired bills of exchange drawn on English merchants and factors by the West Indies debtors.

Foreign Trade of the Southern Colonies

After 1619, England's interest in American commerce revolved primarily around the tobacco exports of two colonies, Virginia and Maryland. Prior to that time England purchased most of her requirements of tobacco from Spain, a trade to which the London merchants strenuously objected because it failed to afford employment for their vessels or to require the need of their marketing services. It was said in 1620, that the purchase of Spanish tobacco drained the kingdom yearly of £120,000 of metallic currency, and was one of the chief causes of the scarcity of gold and silver coin in England. This situation was gradually changed by the steady increase in the size of the southern tobacco crop.

About half of the southern exports, primarily tobacco, was consigned to London agents who sold on commission. The commission charge varied somewhat but more generally was 2½ per cent, based not on the colonial price of the product, but upon the English wholesale price, which included freight and customs. This made a tremendous difference as tobacco which sold for 1¾ pence in the colonies, sold for 10 to 11½ pence per pound wholesale in England. The proceeds were then used to purchase supplies ordered by the colonial tobacco grower, and for this service, another commission was charged, generally 2½ per cent.

Gradually many of the planters in the South became indebted to their English agents as the tobacco and complementary exports failed to equal the value of the slaves, the servants, and the imported merchandise. The indebtedness of many of the southern planters eventually reached substantial proportions and ran on from one generation to another. In this way many plantations became mortgaged to English creditors, interest being added from year to year. Once a planter became indebted to this extent, he was forced to consign his next crop to his merchant-creditor to pay past obligations and to obtain new supplies. The English merchant then was in a position to exploit the planter by charging high interest rates on the existing debt, and by sending inferior supplies at excessive prices.

Colonial and English Merchants, 1765–1776

On February 27, 1765 the Stamp Act passed Parliament. Merchants in New York, Massachusetts, Rhode Island, and Pennsylvania agreed to import no more merchandise from Great Britain, to countermand orders already given, and to make no payments to English creditors until the act was repealed. Rich, as well as poor dressed in homespun, and ate no lamb to save the wool.

Petitions began to pour into Parliament from the merchants of London, Bristol, Liverpool, Manchester, and Glasgow. One of the leading London exporters to the American trade, Barlow Trecothick testified before a committee of Parliament in February, 1766 that the American debts to merchants in these five cities amounted to more than £4,450,000. Laborers in Manchester, Nottingham, and Leeds lost employment. Merchants of Glasgow complained that they were threatened with absolute ruin as their trade was principally with the American colonies. The kingdom was alarmed by this economic resistance to a political act, as England and the colonies after 159 years of association, had become one closely knit economic system.

The Stamp Act was repealed by Parliament in 1766. In its place came the Townshend Act of 1767 imposing import duties on five varieties of glass, sixty-seven grades of paper, red and white lead, painters' colors, and tea. All of these articles were British manufactures, except tea, which was handled by the greatest British monopoly of the time, the *East India Company*. Now came a second non-importation agreement. The merchants in nine of the colonies, under the leadership of New England and New York, agreed to boycott all English merchandise except a few necessities such as coal, shot, and fishing tackle. Exports from Great Britain to New England dropped from £430,807 in 1768 to £223,696 in 1769, for New York from £490,674 to £75,931, and for all of the colonies from £2,157,218 to £1,336,122. The demand for the repeal of this legislation which was ruining British trade, inciting resistance in the colonies, and failing to produce the anticipated revenue, was made by English merchants. Parliament proceeded to the partial repeal of the measure.

Then came the Boston Tea Party, and in retaliation, the passage by Parliament of the five "intolerable acts." The first Continental Congress was now called and met at Philadelphia on September 5, 1774. Unanimously the delegates agreed to a third non-importation agreement, resolving that after December 1, 1774, "there should be no importation into British America from Great Britain or Ireland, or from any other place," of British merchandise. Subsequently the measure was turned into an embargo by a resolution "that from and after September 10, 1775, the exportation of all merchandise and every commodity whatsoever [except tobacco and rice] to Great Britain, Ireland, and the West Indies ought to cease, unless the grievances of America are redressed before that time." Imports from Great Britain now fell from £2,590,437 in 1774 to £196,162 in 1775, and then to £55,415 in 1776.

In the meantime English merchants, manufacturers, and exporters were galvanized into action for the third time. They had watched indifferently while Parliament had passed the coercive acts in 1774, but now there was a sudden realization that their greatest export market was closing to them. For months systematic propaganda was carried on to convince the ministry that the acts of 1774 should be repealed. This time, however, the ministry was adamant. The resolutions of the Continental Congress were answered by declaring Massachusetts to be a state of siege, by sending additional troops to America, and later, by forbidding New England and then the other colonies from trading with any part of the world except Great Britain and the British West Indies. Before this legislation became effective, the Revolutionary War was well under way.

Bibliographical References to Chapter Three

Brown, Abram English, *John Hancock, His Book;* Boston, 1898.

Commerce of Rhode Island, 1726-1774; Massachusetts Historical Society Collections, Seventh Series, Volume IX, Boston, 1914.

Davis, Joseph Stancliffe, *Essays in the Earlier History of American Corporations,* Two Volumes; Cambridge, 1917.

East, Robert A., *Business Enterprise in the American Revolutionary Era;* New York, 1938.

Harrington, Virginia D., *The New York Merchant on the Eve of the Revolution;* New York, 1935.

Massachusetts Historical Society, Volume VII, Fourth Series; Boston, 1865.

Porter, Kenneth Wiggins, *John Jacob Astor, Business Man;* Two Volumes, Cambridge, 1931.

Porter, Kenneth Wiggins, *The Jacksons and the Lees;* Two Volumes, Cambridge, 1937.

Schlesinger, Arthur Meier, *The Colonial Merchants and the American Revolution;* 1918, New Edition 1939, New York.

White, Andrew Dickson, *Fiat Money Inflation in France;* 1896, Reprinted in 1933, New York.

Williamson, Arthur Shellburn, *Credit Relations between Colonial and English Merchants in the Eighteenth Century;* an unpublished manuscript on file in the Library of the State University of Iowa, 1927.

Volumes Previously Cited

Bogart, Ernest Ludlow, *Economic History of the American People;* 1930, Edition of 1935, New York.

Brown, Alexander, *The Genesis of the United States;* New York, 1890.

Bruce, Philip Alexander, *Economic History of Virginia in the Seventeenth Century;* Two Volumes, New York, 1895.

Clark, Victor S., *History of Manufactures in the United States, 1607-1860;* 1929 Edition, New York.

Kirkland, Edward C., *A History of American Economic Life;* 1932, Edition of 1939, New York.

Nettels, Curtis P., *The Money Supply of the American Colonies Before 1720;* Madison, Wis., 1934.

Nettels, Curtis P., *The Roots of American Civilization;* New York, 1938.

Weeden, William B., *Economic and Social History of New England, 1620-1789;* Two Volumes, Boston, 1890.

PART THREE

☆　☆　☆

Credit in the United States

*D*URING *the early years of our national life, credit was represented largely by the sale of merchandise on terms of twelve months. During the first third of the nineteenth century the customary terms of sale used in mercantile circles were reduced from twelve months to six months, and during the Civil War, more drastically to thirty and sixty days.*

In the meantime, along with the gradual development in industry and commerce, came specialization in the extension of credit. Our money economy became a credit economy, and in that process many new types of financial institutions were evolved to supplement the extensive use of mercantile credit. Among these institutions were pawnbrokers, insurance companies, commercial banks and trust companies, mutual savings banks, building and loan associations, factors, title guarantee and mortgage companies, personal loan companies, credit unions, industrial banking companies, sales and discount finance companies, Stock Exchange commission firms.

The records of the beginnings of each of these credit institutions up to the present time when the Federal Government through its many recently-created, lending agencies has also become a powerful social and economic influence through the medium of credit, are described in the following three chapters.

IV ✫ Early Credit Institutions, 1776=1841

AT the time that the port of Boston was closed in 1774 in retaliation for the "Boston Tea Party" and General Thomas Gage was made somewhat of an impromptu local dictator, capital had been accumulated to the point where a class of wealthy individuals were living partly or wholly from their incomes on loans. Phineas Bond, a Philadelphia lawyer, for example, in 1776 had £1,792 outstanding in mortgage obligations and notes. The estate of Cadwallader Colden who had been Lieutenant-Governor of New York at the time of the Stamp Act, listed loans due from seventy-three persons in 1776. The estates of the wife of Sampson Blowers, the Boston loyalist attorney who defended the British soldiers charged with murder as a result of the "Boston massacre," and of Thomas Hutchinson, the last loyal Governor of Massachusetts, who had inherited considerable wealth from his colonial merchant father, were well-known fortunes of the day with large outstanding loans.

In an advertisement which appeared in consecutive numbers of a New York newspaper as early as May 8, 1769, Hendrick Oudenarde, broker, among other services, offered to lend money. This advertisement read, "MONEY upon Interest, on approved security, not less sums than £100. Also Money upon bottomry."* In a second somewhat more persistent advertisement of one John Coghill Knapp, attorney-at-law, appeared a similar brief paragraph, "Cash often to be had on approval, real, or personal security; to discount good bonds, bills, or

* *New-York Chronicle*, May 8, 1769 to June 6, 1769.

notes, and on bottomry."* Such loans, and the ability to make loans, were evidence of the gradual accumulation of surplus wealth which had become quite impressive in the larger trading cities along the Atlantic seacoast. It was also evidence of the broadening basis for the extension of both long and short term credit.

Although the active merchants in Virginia were fewer than in the trading centers in the northern colonies, the debts which the southerners freely incurred were enormous. The more extravagant scale of living on the southern plantations involved the extended use of credit obtained from English exporters, factors, and merchant-bankers. The system of marketing through English commission agents led the tobacco planters ever deeper and deeper into debt. With Shavian irony, Thomas Jefferson testified, "These debts had become hereditary from father to son for many generations, so that the planters were a species of property annexed to certain mercantile houses in London."

Credit During the Revolutionary War

At the eve of the Revolutionary War, the American tobacco crop was worth nearly as much to Great Britain as all other exports of the mainland colonies. Not until 1803 was the value of exported tobacco exceeded by that of cotton. Here was a sound basis for credit and the French lost little time after the outbreak of the war to exploit it. The first loan to the thirteen struggling colonies was made by the French tobacco "Farmers General" in 1777. Tobacco now became of fundamental importance as the foreign credits obtained by its sale in Europe were used to pay for powder, shot, muskets, blankets, goods, and supplies purchased abroad for the army. The sale of tobacco was the primary means of obtaining foreign exchange throughout the war.

Confiscation of Colonial Land

As soon as the Revolution developed into the war for independence, title to the immense amount of ungranted lands, held in the name of the King, was taken over by the respective States. Early in the struggle, many of the large land-holding loyalists moved into Canada, or returned to England, providing an opportunity for local legislative bodies to break up the great feudal estates which had been established in several of the colonies. New Hampshire, for example, confiscated

* *Ibid.*, May 8, 1769 to July 13-20, 1769.

twenty-nine estates, including the immense holdings of Governor John Wentworth. Massachusetts took the property of all who fought against the United States, including that of Sir William Pepperrell (the grandson and inheritor of the great fortune of William Pepperrell who commanded the Louisburg expedition) which stretched for thirty miles along the coast of Maine.

New York confiscated the estates of fifty-five loyalists including the vast Philipse manor of three hundred square miles, the 50,000-acre manor of Sir John Johnson, and the holdings of James De Lancey, Roger Morris, John T. Kemp, and Beverly Robinson. Pennsylvania prepared a black list of four hundred and ninety loyalists, and confiscated the immense estate of the Penn family, valued at £1,000,000, but subsequently granted the Penns £130,000 "in remembrance of the enterprising spirit of the founder and of the expectations and dependence of his descendants." Virginia seized the great estate of Lord Thomas Fairfax, and Georgia that of Sir James Wright.

Here were transfers of great wealth in land, and as such, the basis for credit and speculation. In our entire colonial and early national economic history, land was the greatest measure of wealth. After the Revolutionary War, vast tracts could be purchased with nominal down payments and the balance payable over the years. Speculation in land reached large proportions with Robert Morris, William Duer, James Wilson, later a Justice of the United States Supreme Court, Silas Deane mentioned in the preceding chapter, William Bingham of Philadelphia, the wealthiest merchant in the colonies after the war, Timothy Pickering, and Dutch financiers, well up in the front.

After the peace of Paris, five thousand loyalists asked the British government to recompense them for the loss of their colonial property which they valued at £10,000,000. The British settled these claims by actually making awards which totalled £3,292,452. Quit-rents which had cost the colonists $100,000 a year, and the two bulwarks of a native landed aristocracy, entails and primogeniture, were completely abolished.

Decrease in Foreign Commerce

The fermenting influence of war involves an expansion in activity along the entire economic front and that activity, in turn, necessitates an expansion in the use of credit. The outstanding evidence of the increased need and use of credit during the French and Indian Wars was the virtually uncontrolled expansion in the issuance of paper money which meant forced credit from all inhabitants who had occasion to handle the colonial currency. Simultaneously large amounts of credit were extended by colonial merchants to the British government, by providing equipment and provisions to the British forces in the colonies on extended terms of sale. During the Revolutionary War, the outstanding evidence of the greater use of credit again appeared in the form of involuntary loans obtained by forcing great amounts of depreciating paper currency into circulation. At the same time there took place an upward spurt in domestic commercial activity, something like the unprecedented expansion in the airplane and machine tool industries in the United States as soon as war blared forth in 1939.

The almost immediate loss of the entire British market in 1775 which had been the primary outlet for colonial products, disrupted all foreign commerce. This disruption was of great practical import because the large amounts of outstanding obligations due by colonial importer-wholesalers to the English exporters, factors, and merchant-bankers, were immediately frozen. To take the place of British commerce, trade now developed rapidly and directly with merchants in Sweden, Holland, France, Spain, and the Dutch West Indies, in a way which could never have taken place while the colonies were restricted by British legislation in carrying on their foreign commerce directly with Great Britain and the British colonies.

Merchants Liquidate English Debts

Although all debts of American merchants to English exporters, factors, and merchant-bankers were automatically frozen at the outbreak of hostilities, certain of the larger American importers, with native shrewdness, found ways and means of making remittances to England to reduce their outstanding obligations. Christopher Champlin of Newport, Rhode Island, for instance, instructed his correspondent in Lisbon to remit 200$ to George Hayley of London in 1776.

Arrangements for remittances in behalf of the well-known firm of Jackson, Tracy & Tracy of Newburyport were a little more complicated. This firm and its members, individually, operated one of the largest fleets of privateers on the high seas during most of the war. Prizes taken near the British Isles were sent to Bilbao, and after condemnation by a prize court, were sold by the firm's correspondent there, José Gardoqui & Sons. From these credits, José Gardoqui & Sons were instructed in a letter dated August 20, 1778, ". . . . to remit to

Mess.rs Lane Son & Fraser of London seven hundred Pounds sterling & to Mess.rs Cruger & Mallard of Bristol Three hundred & twenty Pounds sterling desiring them respectively to pass the same to the Credit of our Account w.th them—& to advise you & us respectively of their receipt of such Remittances—we wish you to make these Remittances immediately & to advise us of your having done it. . . ." War or no war, a means was found with Yankee ingenuity to liquidate existing debts.

Arise of "Continental" Houses

Before the Revolutionary War, big business in foreign commerce generally on credit terms of twelve months, which were often renewed or extended, was carried on primarily with the British merchants. Foreign commerce, but in much smaller proportions, was developed with other countries as soon as the war cut off this trade, but big business was now short-circuited into domestic trade. The mainspring of American economic development has been the ever present desire to earn profits, and the urge continued to function throughout our first Revolution. War or no war, conflict or no conflict, merchandise was bought and sold, principally for cash or on short credit terms.

Credit cannot exist without confidence in the security of property, even during a war, and in the recognized disposition of the purchaser of a commodity to pay for it at the appointed time. No man parts with his property unless he believes an equivalent will be returned. No man accepts a note, a check, or a draft, in payment for his commodities or services unless he believes that the credit instrument received, will be duly honored and paid. The existence of a system of credit is indicative that the people, comprising a community, believe that their neighbors are honest and will pay the debts which they freely contract.

The place of English exporters, factors, and merchant-bankers was now taken partly by continental European houses such as the John de Neufville & Son, and Daniel Crommelin & Sons, both of Amsterdam, José Gardoqui & Sons of Bilbao, and Berthon Brothers of Lisbon. John de Neufville & Son began to receive cargoes from many prominent Boston merchants and, in turn, shipped merchandise back to them. In some way, this firm gradually became widely acquainted with or known to American merchants in every important port from New Hampshire to Virginia. In the two years, 1780 and 1781, they sent sixteen ships to the States, engaging particularly in the valuable tobacco trade with merchants of Alexandria in Virginia.

Pick-up in Domestic Commerce

A majority of the successful merchants in the three most important New England cities of Boston, Salem, and Newport were conservative loyalists. In his historical novel, *Oliver Wiswell,* Kenneth Roberts
clearly pictures the size and the importance of this loyalist population in
Massachusetts. New York had somewhat fewer loyalists, and Philadelphia even less. Their businesses generally, though not entirely, were
broken, and their estates in many cases were confiscated as they fled into
exile. A new order of men came forward to handle the commerce
under the changed conditions of an embryonic nation, newcomers who
were springing up with aggressiveness, eagerness, will to power, and
will to get ahead, especially during a period of domestic turmoil.

Inter-colonial trade expanded because of the absolute necessity
of providing provisions, arms, ammunition, clothing, horses, wagons,
and supplies to the Continental armies, and food, clothing, and supplies
to the populations in the urban centers. Boston continued to obtain
flour from New York and the Chesapeake Bay; Rhode Island obtained
provisions for military use from Pennsylvania and Virginia; the forces
in Virginia obtained beef and pork from the Carolinas; the northern
Continental troops secured beef from Massachusetts and Connecticut,
and cereals from Pennsylvania and the upper part of the Hudson River.
The activity of furnishing wagons, forage, tents, cordage, canteens,
timber, kettles, oats, nails, weapons, ammunition, oxen, and horses for
military use became large scale business just as the production of bomb-
ing and fighting planes, cruisers and destroyers, tanks, motor trucks,
machine guns, rifles, and ammunition shells is essential in war today.

When New York City was taken by the British in 1776, overland
traffic between upper New York State and New England assumed large
proportions. Caravans of as many as two hundred teams might go
from Boston to Hartford to Claverack to Rheinbeck on the Hudson,
or from Springfield to Hartford to Newburg on the Hudson carrying
tents, clothing, salt, wheat, beef and pork. Railroads were still to be
created in the industrial world of the dim future.

This concentrated traffic across Connecticut offered war trading
opportunities which were fully realized by Jeremiah Wadsworth of
Hartford, and his close associates, Oliver Phelps, Israel Chapin, Julius
Deming, Epaphroditus Champion, and Barnabas Deane. Hartford
developed into one of the most important financial, trading, and produce
collecting centers because it was on these routes and because it appeared

to be safe from attack. Jeremiah Wadsworth, who became the most important capitalist after the war, obtained his financial impetus by furnishing supplies to the Continental army and to the French forces. Before the war he had little capital. After the war he was immensely wealthy. Here was one of the early, great American opportunists.

A moderate portion of the necessary military supplies was purchased with specie during the first year of the war, but as hostilities continued, a steadily increasing proportion was paid with depreciating Continental paper money. At the same time "waggon loads" of counterfeit currency were struck off in the British garrisons and sent into the country around New York City and on Long Island. During the latter years of the war, some purchases of provisions and supplies were paid by Continental Loan Office certificates. These certificates, if issued today, would be known as government bonds. Occasionally, however, a seller would accept only cash for some very essential commodity. Blair McClenachan, for example, frequently sold substantial amounts of powder and lead, usually imported from St. Eustatius, to the Commissary of Military Stores. On one occasion, the shrewd McClenachan and his partner, John Holker refused to deliver a cargo of lead until it was actually paid for, cash on the barrel-head, as Congress already owed Holker for clothing. They were taking no further chances!

During these war years, domestic trade was carried on with depreciating paper currency and terms of sale changed radically. No longer was it the practice, nor could it very well have been the practice, to give credit for twelve months. All merchants were now money-holders, and purchases were generally made for cash or on very short terms. No-one was anxious to hold "Continental" bills any more than the Germans were anxious to hoard marks in 1923.

Financial Difficulties of the Continental Army

Colonel Hugh Hughes was Assistant Quartermaster General of the Continental Army from May, 1776 to December, 1781. While at New York City in June, 1776 he ordered one Mr. Thomas Cheesman, "to hasten, as soon as possible to Staten Island, Elizabeth Town, Raway, Newark etc. and at each of those Places, contract (as cheap as you can) for as much good Suitable Ship Timber and two Inch Plank as Mr Benjamin Eyre shall judge necessary for building Six Gondolas or Row Gallies. . . . In like Manner you will purchase, or contract for, four Hundred suitable Knees for such Batteaux as were built by Mr. Sheaf.

... You will also purchase, or contract for, at as reasonable a Rate as they can be got, three Thousand Pieces of Scantling."* Here is a typical army order of the first year of the Revolutionary War, instructions to obtain supplies but absolutely no word regarding terms of purchase.

Occasionally an allusion to terms appeared in the records of the quartermaster's department under some unusual circumstance during the first two years of the war. The customary arrangement was for local committees to see that supplies were provided, the seller being given a receipt to be paid some time in the future, possibly when the war was ended, or given loan certificates. In a letter to Peter De Haven in July, 1776 Colonel Hughes ordered "five Thousand Canteens" and "three Thousand Pails," urging the utmost speed as "there is not anything of greater importance to an Army than Canteens at this Drowthy Season." In this letter Colonel Hughes did mention payment for some previous supplies, "Col. Moylan desires that you would apply for the Ballance of your Account, when you rec^d the other Part, and it will be paid." This financial correspondence was early in the war and depreciation in the paper money had hardly started. In succeeding years no-one would be requested to send in his account. Eleven days after the date of this letter, Colonel Hughes did, in one instance, confirm an agreement to pay cash for hay in a letter to John Lloyd, Esqr, ". . . I mean to fulfill the Agreement I made with you for your Hay; if it be such as I like, and you described; which was to give six Shillings per C^{wt} for it, when delivered here."

As the years went by, it became increasingly difficult to finance the war, to pay the soldiers, to obtain food, supplies, and ammunition at home and abroad, and the only expedient was the constant issuance of more and more paper money. By November, 1780 the difficulties attendant to the operations of the quartermaster's department were brought out most emphatically in a letter written by the Assistant District Quartermaster at Albany, Major Quackenbush, to Colonel Hughes, "Money, Money, Money I want. . . . I am very happy to hear you have set out with Money, I long much to see you with Money, I beg you will not forget to fill your Saddlebags with Money, before you leave Fisk Kill." The need for money and credit to obtain necessary equipment and supplies had become quite intense.

A short time later, in January, 1781 Colonel Hughes carefully admonished Major Quackenbush in a postscript to a letter, "In future you will avoid engaging to pay the whole of your Contracts, by any

* Letter Book of Colonel Hugh Hughes; April, 1776 to Sept. 1776. (New York Historical Society)

assigned Day or Time, or you will embarrass yourself and the Service, remember you may engage to Pay a Part out of the first you receive, without Injury to yourself or the Department—What I have said on the Subject of not engaging to pay at a certain time, is on the Supposition of your not being in Cash—Otherwise you may use your own Prudence." Apparently Major Quackenbush was not making his limited resources stretch as far as his superior officer thought he should. In February, Colonel Hughes wrote in the same vein, again from Fisk Kill, "You must not pay so great a part of your Contracts as you have done. The Office here don't pay more than a 4$\underline{th}$ or 8$\underline{th}$ and give Specie Certificates for the Residue. We shall not keep the Great Wheel in Motion, if we don't observe the greatest Frugality in our Expenditures."[*]

By this time, the difficulties due to the lack of cash and credit were by no means confined to the headquarters at Fisk Kill, or to the district office at Albany. Also in February, 1781, Colonel Jabez Hatch, District Quartermaster for Massachusetts elaborated on his difficulties in a message to Colonel Hughes, "In answer to your request to purchase twenty Tons of Oakum & Junk, I imagine it can be procured, at least the latter Article, had I the Cash to purchase it, such is the State of Public Credit in this Quarter, that I cannot obtain Credit on Public Account for the smallest Sum, this is partly owing to the Department being involved in Debt by Col. Chase, whom I succeeded.—I suppose not less than two Millions of Dollars, in the old Emission, are due for Forage, Wood, Transportation &c. which is very unfavorable to my Transacting Business upon Credit." In April, Colonel Hatch again reiterated his difficulties to Colonel Hughes, "The great Demands upon me in this Quarter, and the want of Cash, prevents my doing Business, as nothing can be procured on Credit."[†]

Even the headquarters at Fisk Kill were in the same condition. In March, 1781, Colonel Hughes wrote to Major Carthy, Assistant District Quartermaster at West Point, "Forage you shall have whenever it comes in. We are trying every Expedient to procure it. If I could but fix a Time for Payment I believe nearly sufficient might be had; but that I cannot without risking my Character, which I shall not do, till I see Ways and Means to fulfil my Engagements."[§]

David Wolfe, Assistant District Quartermaster at Claverack, New York had similar difficulties in carrying on without funds. Early in July, 1781 he placed this situation before Colonel Hughes, "The Teams

[*] *Letter Book of Major Quackenbush, Assistant District Quartermaster for Albany, N. Y.; Oct. 1780-April 1782.*
[†] *Letter Book of Colonel Jabez Hatch, District Quartermaster for State of Massachusetts; Oct. 1780-Sept. 1781.*
[§] *Letter Book of Major Daniel Carthy, Assistant District Quartermaster for West Point; Oct. 1780-April, 1782.*
(New York Historical Society)

& Guard arrived here destitute of Provisions, Forage or Cash; I supplied them with some Flour, as per Return: No Forage could be procured here without Cash. The Teams proceeded on for Fisk Kill, but how they will reach it without Money, being Strangers in this Quarter, and the Public Credit quite exhausted, I can't imagine. . . . Can assure it is almost impossible to do any thing here without Cash at this time. I beg you will send me a supply of that Essential Article as soon as in your Power." On July 30, 1781 Colonel Hughes replied from Fisk Kill to this letter, as he had already replied to so many other Assistant District Quartermasters who were performing miracles with little or no money or credit. "The want of Cash is a common Calamity. We have not a farthing of any kind, even to Keep the Expresses, and yet they do go by some means or other. . . . We labour under many Disadvantages that you are a stranger to, I well know, yet I don't wish to cheapen your services. . . . I have not had nor rec^d any Money since I saw you.— Whenever any arrives you shall have a Part, if it is large enough to divide, or worth the Expense.—"*

Oakum and tar were in constant demand by the quartermaster's department to be used in the construction and the repair of boats. It was absolutely necessary to have a minimum supply on hand at all times. In this predicament, Colonel Hughes in August, 1781 gave unusual assurance to Major Quackenbush at Albany that purchases of tar, but only tar, made on terms of three months credit would be promptly taken care of, "If you can procure as much Tar on Credit, as you pay for, or twice as much, you may, engaging Payment in hard Cash at the Expiration of three Months from the Time of Purchase, which you shall be enabled to fulfill, at least, I have the Q.M. General's word for the discharge of it, and no Doubt of the Performance."

The situation at Albany had become very serious by October, 1781. Major Quackenbush finally exploded in a letter to Colonel Hughes, "For God's sake let me have some money or I must quit this place we have nothing new since the last Express to your Quarter—I have not a Lock of Hay nor bushel of Grain of any sort nor Credit to get any." In a philosophic reply of great understanding written in November, Colonel Hughes held out no hope, "You talk of Money—The very Idea appears Chimerical—We have none, nor have we had. . . . Whoever expected to go swimmingly through this War, with his Pockets full of Cash, fairly obtained, reckoned without his Host.—No Nation that we

* *Letters of Colonel Hugh Hughes to and from Claverack, N. Y., Nov. 1780-April 1782.* (New York Historical Society)

read of, ever paid as they went, much less can one just emerging, and whose resources are not, nor cannot all be called forth, or organized till after the Contest, do it, which too few Consider."*

In December, 1781 David Wolfe was wondering how to purchase or hire sleighs to carry salt from Claverack to Fisk Kill. He put the problem up to Colonel Hughes, "I have this moment forwarded Capt Pynchons Letter—Twenty eight Sleigh's will be wanted to transport the Salt, in case it must be forwarded by land as to the mode of procuring them, without Cash, I know of none very Eligible or that can be rely'd on.—The People are weary of serving the Publick, many of them despair of ever receiving any compensation & seem determined to do nothing more on Credit—However if a price & certain time be fixed (Bona fide) for the Payment, three or four months hence—Or the amount discounted from their Specie Tax, I make no doubt but Sleigh's sufficient could be easily procured." How true it was then, and still is today, that credit is confidence in the ability of an individual, an institution, or a nation to meet his or its obligations on time.

Leaders in Business Activity

It seems to have been no unusual occurrence for an officer in the army or a prominent delegate to the Continental Congress to have been a partner in a business enterprise which carried on extensive and profitable business relations with Continental and State troops. Even at this early date in our national history, there existed a rather close, coincident relationship between political influence and profitable business.

The preeminent business man of the Revolutionary period was Robert Morris of Philadelphia. While acting as the "financier of the Revolution," he was a partner in the well-known firm of Willing & Morris that obtained profitable commission contracts from the Secret Committee of the Continental Congress (Morris actually became chairman in 1775 succeeding Willing); with the energetic Silas Deane of Wethersfield, Connecticut, he organized an international commercial, and later, land-speculating group which is said to have included Conrad Gérard, a future French minister to America, M. le Rey de Chaumont, a French government contractor, M. Ferdinand Grand, a banker of Paris, Sir George Grand, a broker of Amsterdam, and Thomas Walpole, a member of the English Parliament. This group purchased supplies

* Letter Book of Major Quackenbush, Assistant District Quartermaster for Albany; Oct. 1780-April 1782. (New York Historical Society)

for America and also carried on extensive side-line profitable activities such as purchasing prize ships taken by American privateers, which were then re-purchased by Deane for Congress.

The business associates of Morris grew steadily in number as he took advantage of every commercial opportunity. His extensive foreign connections not only enabled him to contract and to furnish Congressional supplies but also to secure private merchandise, some of which he sold to other governmental purchasing agents. He carried on business relations with other firms in all of the colonies.

Probably the second most important business man of this period was William Duer of New York. Early in the war Duer became known to Washington who engaged him on confidential activities. With John Jay and four others, he was named in 1776 on the secret "Committee for Correspondence" to detect and to defeat conspiracies. Subsequently he became a prominent and energetic delegate to the Continental Congress. As one of the inner circle associated with men of prominence, he was early asked to provide teams, food, powder, planks for bridges, and masts and spars for Continental frigates, axes, and other essential supplies for troops. In April, 1782 soon after the establishment of the contract system, Duer went vigorously into the profitable business of furnishing supplies to the troops, work which continued for several years after the war. In many of his activities he had as associates, Robert Morris, Jeremiah Wadsworth, and Silas Deane. Duer's career was even more spectacular than that of Robert Morris. Finally, in 1792 he was sentenced to a debtor's prison and there he died seven years later, a hopeless and negligible figure.

In 1775, Jeremiah Wadsworth became commissary of supplies for Connecticut, and late in the same year, he began to make purchases for the Continental troops, subsequently becoming Commissary General until December, 1779. In this capacity he made extensive purchases of clothing, grain, pork, beef, medical supplies, and received and paid out large sums of money. After he resigned as Commissary General, he formed the partnership of Wadsworth & Carter. In May, 1780 this partnership obtained desirable contracts to furnish supplies to the French army under Count Rochambeau, contracts which were extremely profitable. These contracts were of so much importance that the firm secured resident representatives in Providence and Newport, and traveling representatives in Connecticut and Massachusetts, men who purchased and contracted for necessary quantities of hay, straw, oats, rye, flour, soap, candles, beans, whiskey, wood, horses, and cattle.

These purchases were paid for by the firm of Wadsworth & Carter one-third in "hard" money and two-thirds in "Continental" paper money. In a letter to one Thomas Burr, Esq., dated November 3, 1780, Wadsworth outlined the above terms and remarked that on these purchases he would request credit for only fifteen days, "... if absolutely necessary, I would try to pay half in hard [money], but this will be difficult as Bills sell very low for hard cash. ... I settle my accounts once in fifteen days." With business being transacted on depreciated paper currency, terms had shortened very considerably. Wadsworth handled the firm's business from Hartford while Carter was out rounding up supplies. They wrote each other every few days, Wadsworth numbering his letters consecutively so that if any were lost, the fact would immediately become known. In this correspondence the terms of one-third coin and two-thirds paper money were discussed several times. Wadsworth with more business acumen than Carter insisted that one-third "hard" cash was absolutely essential for "if we push the paper Money too hard our whole business fails, cattle will be scarce and dear very soon. . . ."* In other words, if sufficient "hard" money was not offered, more and more farmers would refuse to sell their produce. In November, 1780 Continental money at Hartford was quoted seventy-two paper dollars for one silver dollar!

The "hard" cash was turned over to Wadsworth & Carter by the French, or obtained by selling bills of exchange drawn on the French government and cashed by Thomas Lloyd Halsey in Boston, John Chaloner in Philadelphia, and sometimes by the firm of Wadsworth & Carter, itself. These bills eventually would find their way to France for collection through American houses like those of Richard Harrison at Cadiz, or Elkanah Watson at Nantes, or foreign merchant-bankers such as José Gardoqui & Sons of Bilbao, or Daniel Crommelin & Sons of Amsterdam. In 1783, these bills were being paid by France twelve months after they fell due, not very prompt payment.

Developments in Mercantile Credit

Prior to the Revolutionary War, the colonies had been included within the commercial network of the British Empire. Now, after the treaty of Paris, they were orphans. Trade which had grown up with Spain, Portugal, France, Holland, and their possessions in the West Indies and in South America during the struggle for independence

* *Letterbook of Wadsworth & Carter, Oct. 7, 1780 to April 2, 1781.* (Connecticut Historical Society)

continued, but there was a natural urge for importers to revert back to old friends and established suppliers in Great Britain and the British West Indies. Established trade relations with British merchants on liberal credit terms of twelve months had been built up over a century and a half. Moreover, certain English merchandise, such as hardware and woolens, was in demand as no other country produced them so well, or so cheaply. Colonial trade had been extremely profitable to the English merchants, and they, on their part, were merely awaiting peace to extend long-term credit again, which was so essential in carrying on commerce with business men in a developing country.

Re-Opening of Commerce with Britain

The merchants in the thirteen States were hungry for European manufactured merchandise and luxuries at the end of the war, and as usually occurs when the demand is unnatural, heavy orders were placed and the market was soon overstocked. In the Autumn of 1784, the stores and warehouses of the importing houses and commission merchants were overflowing with European goods. By the Summer of 1785, the sale of merchandise had slowed up, retail shopkeepers and country general stores were having difficulty in paying for their purchases, and the more responsible importer-wholesalers were making every effort to extend their debts in Britain.

The means of payment with which the merchants had settled for British goods or West India sugar and molasses during the colonial period were now partly lacking. They continued to export tobacco, rice, fish, lumber, and forest products, but the specie, and the bills of exchange which previously to the Revolutionary War had been obtained from the West Indies and from southern Europe, were now largely missing. Under these circumstances, the only course was to export all available specie. It has been estimated that in the three years following the treaty of Paris at least £1,260,000 in coin went to Britain. Even this amount was insufficient to pay for all of the purchases, and colonial importers remained heavily in debt to their foreign creditors.

Political difficulties aggravated this commercial condition. Great Britain placed prohibitory duties on many American products, and made plans to replace the provision trade of the United States with that of Canada and of the British West Indies. All trade between the British colonies and the mother country, and between the British colonies themselves, were forbidden except to British vessels. Particularly injurious to American traders was the exclusion of our vessels from the British colonies in North America and in the West Indies with which a large volume of profitable commerce had been built up. Retaliation naturally took place. Massachusetts, New Hampshire, and Rhode Island, taking a page from the example of Great Britain, passed navigation acts forbidding exports in British ships.

This situation became more and more aggravated as individual States enacted restricting legislation. During the years from 1780 to 1789, Pennsylvania enacted fifteen tariff acts; Virginia, twelve; Massachusetts, New York, and Maryland, each seven; Connecticut, six; and the other States a smaller number. More tariff acts were passed by the thirteen States than by any equal number of European nations in the same number of years, following the first World War.

While the acts of the Southern States were chiefly for revenue, the tariffs of the Middle and the New England States were dictated by motives of protection and retaliation for the loss of the lucrative West India trade. The States could not agree among themselves and the duties varied from five per cent to one hundred per cent. At the same time, some States were admitting identical goods, free of duty. British merchandise naturally entered through the free or the cheapest ports. Finally, the States began to make commercial war upon one another, and to enact tariff laws excluding each other's products. When New York placed high duties on British imports, Connecticut and New Jersey attracted this trade by lowering their duties. New York then retaliated by taxing the products of those States when brought to New York City. The situation became as involved as international politics.

At the same time, the mechanics of domestic trade became just as involved and as uncertain as foreign trade. One historian wrote regarding this difficult period: "The machinery for exchanging property creaked in every joint, because the whole system of finance was ill-adjusted." States repudiated their debts; merchants over-imported merchandise when duties were favorable, debtors found difficulty in paying, and the courts could not find means to enforce payment. In this unfortunate situation, merchants took whatever movable property they could obtain, then took mortgages as additional protection. "The distress was beyond comprehension."

In this emergency the legislatures of the States now did two things. In the first place, they passed stay laws or moratoria, suspending the right of creditors to collect debts for a certain period; and in the second place, seven of the States reverted to the issuance of paper money to take the place of the vanishing specie. Only New Hampshire, Massachusetts, Connecticut, Delaware, Maryland, and Virginia, in which the wealthy merchants or the planters controlled the legislative bodies, were able to resist the demands of the farmers and debtor classes for "cheap" money. It was no wonder that debtors sought an avenue of escape from their burdens, for imprisonment for debt was common; the prisons were filthy and unsanitary; and the processes of the courts were expensive.

The difficulties in carrying on trade resulted in the ruin of many of the struggling manufacturers which had sprung up during the Revolutionary War. The cheaper English products, imported in large quantities and sold at auction (a practice which was extensively used at this time in the distribution of all kinds of imported merchandise) at low prices or on long credit, brought many domestic concerns to bankruptcy. Measured by the size and number of our twentieth century corporations these concerns were small and few; there were no great factories, but the distress in the cities was sufficiently serious at the time.

Under these trying circumstances, a memorable convention met at Annapolis in 1786 to discuss methods of enabling Congress to regulate the all important problem of commerce. This body was the forerunner of the greater convention which assembled in Philadelphia in 1787. Commerce, or the lack of regulated commerce, was the impelling necessity which now forced the States into the formation of a more consolidated national government. Bad finance, unpaid public debts, soldiers suffering for their pay, national discredit—all affected the popular mind—but none quite so much as the broken and dwindling trade.

Credit Information

In June, 1783, George Washington on disbanding the Continental Army, addressed a letter to the governors of the thirteen States. Washington intended this letter as his final testament to the American people, never dreaming that nearly fifteen years afterwards, he would deliver another farewell address. The subject of this letter was the need of forming a national government, of solidifying the success of arms and of guaranteeing the future, but along with the politics of that message was a brief description in general terms of our tremendous national wealth, a description even truer, as the intervening years have shown, than the writer could possibly have realized. "The citizens of America," Washington wrote, "are the sole lords and proprietors of a vast tract of continent, comprehending all the various soils and climates of the world, and abounding in all the necessaries and conveniences of life." Out of such a territory, trade had to develop at an increasing pace with a constantly expanding application and knowledge of credit.

The greatest single source of credit throughout the economic history of the world has been the trade of commercial and industrial business enterprises; the credit extended by one business concern to another, and by retail merchants to the consumer. Credit references were offered by buyers of merchandise, credit recommendations were sent by one merchant to another, and dunning letters mailed in the years following the Revolutionary War, just as in the colonial days. Trade slowed up during the war, an intermission occurred while supplies of all kinds were being provided for the army, and then the earlier established trade customs and habits reappeared.

In 1792, for example, Samuel Greenhouse of Fredericksburg wrote a letter to Matthew Carey, the prominent protectionist, printer and book-seller of Philadelphia, ordering several volumes. In that letter he carefully offered references which could be consulted regarding his character, "I now take the Liberty of writing to you for a few Books which am requested to get from Philadelphia. Your acquaintance with me is too slight to render you safe in Sending the Books without a greater certainty of having the Money remitted for them I therefore recommend you to Mr Randolph Atto Genl. I. Wm Barnes in third Street =Those Gentlemen can give you satisfactory Information of who I am & wether I shall probably be punctual in making my Remittance for these or any other Books which I may hereafter be in want of."[*]

Franklin & Doty, importers and commission merchants of New York City wrote in April, 1793 to one George Watson in England, "By the recommendation of our mutual Friends, Franklin Robinson & Co., we take the liberty of enclosing thee an order for tin plates, which thou wilt please to execute on the best terms in thy power."[†] Similar letters were written to a number of other houses in Great Britain in 1792, 1793, and 1794. The recommendations and the credit information given by Franklin Robinson & Co regarding Franklin & Doty, apparently was all that was necessary for this firm to obtain credit in England for their reasonable mercantile needs.

Toward the end of the eighteenth century, one of the most important commission houses in New York City was Goold & Co., composed of Edward Goold and his son, Charles D. Goold. This firm sold

[*] *Letter Book of Lea & Febiger, 1787-1794.* (Historical Society of Pennsylvania)
[†] *Letter Book of Franklin & Doty, and Thomas Franklin, 1791-1809.* (New York Historical Society)

the merchandise sent to New York City by many prominent New England merchants of the day, well-known importers of Boston, Portsmouth, Newburyport, Salem, and Beverly. Merchandise of all kinds was handled on a commission basis, but for the risk of the shipper. In 1797, the firm wrote to one of its prominent correspondents, Samuel Gray, "We also hand you an Abstract of the Sales of the *John's* Cargo for your information and one of the Sherry wine as far as we have proceeded from which you will see that we are still in advance for you tho it will not be long before further payments will be made on the *John's*. Tho' there never has been a much more Critical time that we have had to do with and these Sales are not inconsiderable We have great pleasure in saying there is not a bad or dubious Debt amongst the whole."[*] Apparently Goold & Co., made some study of the responsibilities of the dealers to whom they extended liberal credit in behalf of the New England importers, and they were justly proud of the fact that they had been able to discriminate between the sound and the unsound credit risk.

In 1809, John Hamilton of Philadelphia wrote a letter to Messr. H. Purkitt & Son of Boston recommending one Daniel Smith for credit. "The principal purpose of this letter" he said "was to acknowledge your attention and to beg leave to introduce a friend of mine to your acquaintance, who deals also in fish, Mr. Daniel Smith. I think any contracts he makes you will find him punctual, I believe he will address you by this mail."[†] James Wier of Lexington, Kentucky, in answer to an inquiry from Hicks, Jenkins & Company of New York City in 1816, replied that Robert Worth was "a steady, honest, upright man." He possessed some property and his father was a wealthy farmer. Wier believed Worth would do his best to fulfill any engagements entered into in the East.

Letter books of this period also contained occasional requests for credit information, written from one merchant to another. In 1825, for example, Hamilton & Hood of Philadelphia requested some confidential advice from Messrs Gifford & Gourlay in New York City, "This morning we have heard that our friend P. W. Engs has got into some difficulty in his business, he is in our debt about 450 Dolls—but will not be at maturity till the 3/6 of Dec! — we only ask how far this report is true, & if in your Judgment we could do anything by going on we hope this report be as it may that you will keep it to yourselves please drop us a line on this Subject in confidence stating to us the real situation of P. W. Engs as far as you know." This request had a typically modern

* *Letter Book of Goold & Co., 1797-1798.* (New York Public Library)
† *Letter Book of John Hamilton, 1809-1813.* (Historical Society of Pennsylvania)

tone. In the following year Hamilton & Hood wrote E. F. Chambers, Esqʳ, of Washington apparently in answer to a request for a little helpful credit information, "Your enquire about Wᵐ Warner and John Wardell, we do not know such a person as John Wardell—Wᵐ Warner has left this City for some year & lives in Wilmington he is not in business, & has lately taken the benefit of the act of Insolvency, he had a brother John who Died in the Havanna."*

Trade by Barter

The account book of Nathanial Littleton Savage, one of the landed and commercial aristocrats of Virginia during and immediately after the Revolutionary War, indicated that he customarily accepted a variety of farm products in the settlement of his accounts just as Thomas Hancock had done at Boston a little earlier. Wheat and oats, peas, brandy, codfish, tobacco, pork, lamb, cotton cloth, and in one case, a "Bay Mare at £110 paper value," were received over the years from 1776 to 1784, to offset purchases of groceries by, and loans made to local settlers. Rent was credited by gallons of oysters, and in one account, twelve newly made chairs at four shillings each were received from James Finch, carpenter, to settle a loan of £2.8.0. Like so many colonial business transactions, a substantial portion of these accounts ran on year after year before any partial or complete attempts at settlement were made.† Barter continued in a big way as a means of commerce and trade, particularly in the country districts.

Hollingsworth Johnson & Co. of Richmond wrote in a letter to Robert Gamble of Staunton in 1786, "This acknowledges the Recᵗ of 215 Grey Deer Skins and 44 Red which will be placed to your Credit." A little later in the same year this firm wrote Thomas C. Minor of Louisa, "The Tobacco mentioned is at your Credit in our Books."§ Barter was the natural means of trade where the population was predominantly rural. In 1800 there were only twelve cities in the United States with a population in excess of five thousand, and these cities contained less than four per cent of the total inhabitants of the country.

In 1802, F. A. Michaux, a member of the Society of National History of Paris, arrived at Charleston, sailed to New York, and then made an extended trip through the States of Ohio, Kentucky, and Tennessee, and back to Charleston in North Carolina under the auspices

* *Letter Book of Hamilton & Hood, 1824-1837.* (Historical Society of Pennsylvania)
† *Account Book of Nathanial L. Savage, 1768-1785,* pp. 19, 27, 42, 43, 54, 55, 56, 67. (New York Public Library)
§ *Letter Book of Hollingsworth Johnson & Co., 1786-1788.* (Historical Society of Pennsylvania)

of the French Minister of the Interior, principally to observe the state of agriculture and the natural produce of that territory. Observations regarding commerce were also carefully noted. In the record of that trip which was published under the title, *Travels to the West of the Alleghany Mountains,* Michaux pointed out that barter was quite the customary means of trade. When he reached the town of Carlisle in Pennsylvania, he wrote that the storekeepers purchased and bartered with the "country people for the produce of their farms, which they afterwards send off to the sea-port towns for exportation." At Morgantown in western South Carolina, the inhabitants came for twenty miles around to "purchase mercery and jewellery goods from England, or give in exchange a part of their produce, which consists chiefly of dried ham, butter, tallow, bear and stag skins, and ginsing, which they bring from the mountains."

Thomas Ashe, Esq., an Englishman made an extensive trip across the Alleghany Mountains, in 1806, then down the Ohio and the Mississippi Rivers to New Orleans. When no farther west than Erie, in Pennsylvania, he discovered the scarcity of money and the extent to which barter provided the everyday means for trade. "I do not conceive," he wrote, "that I assert too much, though it may be surprising to you, in saying, that the entire business of these waters is conducted without the use of money." Storekeepers in the larger towns bartered manufactured goods for "flour, corn, salt, cyder, apples, live hogs, bacon, glass, earthenware, &c. . . . The storekeepers make two annual collections of these commodities; send them down the rivers to New Orleans; and there receive an immense profit in Spanish dollars, or bills on Philadelphia at a short date." They then sail from New Orleans to Philadelphia or Baltimore where they purchase "British and West India goods of all kinds; send them by waggons over the mountains to their stores in the western country, where they always keep clerks; and again make their distributions and collections; descend the waters; and return by the same circuitous mountainous route, of at least 5650 miles." Ashe had ridden "an excellent horse to the head of the waters" at Erie and having no further use for the animal, as he was going down the Alleghany River in a boat, proposed to sell him to the highest bidder. He was offered in exchange, salt, flour, hogs, land, cast iron salt pans, Indian corn, whiskey,—in short, everything except what he wanted—money.

As early as 1817, thirteen thousand wagons travelled to Pittsburgh from Philadelphia and Baltimore loaded with merchandise. The shortest distance between Philadelphia and Pittsburgh was two hundred and forty miles. The prevailing freight rate was $7.50 per hundred pounds, so high that low priced goods could not bear the transportation costs. Conestoga wagons made the trip in sixteen days, going from twelve to twenty miles a day.

The active New York firm of Lambert Brothers, commission merchants and wholesalers, had $860 Kentucky money to their credit with a distant Kentucky merchant. This currency was so depreciated in value that the firm used the term "barter" when suggesting to George Johnson, Esq., the debtor, that he purchase local produce with it. This interesting letter written in October, 1823 read as follows, "We have not yet rec^d the avails of the $860 Kentuckey Money & presume you find difficulty in disposing of it. It would be difficult to sell it here at any rate. If you cannot sell it at 50% discount you had best hold on to it—perhaps it may be bartered away with the Kentuckey Merchts or boat men for whiskey, Flour or Tobacco or we should have no objection to vest it in the cheapest Cotton as you judge best."*

About 1828, Philadelphia held first place among the seaboard cities in supplying merchandise to traders in the western country across the Alleghany Mountains. Kentucky and Tennessee were nearer to Philadelphia than to New York. St. Louis was the principal wholesale center in what was then the real far West, a position gained by her relatively early development as the center of the valuable fur trade. New York was just beginning to challenge Philadelphia as a result of the opening of the Erie Canal in 1825. Freight rates were to tumble as low as one-tenth of what they had been prior to the opening of the canal.

Two interesting volumes containing 1,939 pages, and filled with pertinent information regarding American industry, were printed in 1833 by order of the House of Representatives under the impressive title, *Documents Relative to the Manufactures in the United States Collected and Transmitted to the House of Representatives, in Compliance with a Resolution of Jan. 18, 1832, by the Secretary of the Treasury.* Commissioners had been appointed by the Secretary of the Treasury in the eleven States in which most of the manufacturing was carried on at the time, Maine, Massachusetts, New Hampshire, Vermont, Rhode Island, Connecticut, New York, New Jersey, Pennsylvania, Delaware, and Ohio, to obtain "facts and information" regarding "the manufactures of wool, cotton, hemp, iron, sugar, and such other articles" as were manufactured to considerable extent in the United States. This extensive information was sought as a basis for Congressional tariff legislation.

* *Letter Book of Lambert Brothers, 1822-1829,* p. 159. (Baker Library, Harvard Graduate School of Business Administration)

A list of very detailed and pertinent questions, generally containing from thirty-five to forty items, was mailed or delivered personally by the Commissioners in each of these States, to the manufacturers of the enumerated products, and to manufacturers of a large number of other products. Many manufacturers failed to return the questionnaire with the answers, and many replied partially, but on the other hand, the fact that it took 1,939 pages of small type to publish the replies which were obtained, indicated that the survey was probably the most detailed, industrial study, made up to 1832 in the United States.

Among the questions asked every manufacturer was one of peculiar credit interest. This question read: "Whether the manufacture is sold by the manufacturer for cash? and, if on credit, at what credit? if bartered, for what?" This survey was conducted five years before the panic of 1837, a period of industrial expansion when there were very few really important industrial enterprises in the country; more a period of youthful, manufacturing development.

Specific terms of sales were reported by 324 manufacturers who gave exact answers to this particular question. In addition to these 324 specific replies, 64 manufacturers reported that their sales were made on credit without stating any terms, 57 that their output was sold for cash, and 18 that their entire output was bartered for local agricultural produce such as beef, pork, grain, corn, tobacco, potatoes, and other necessary items such as coal, wool, and hides used in the manufacturing processes. That barter was still, in 1832, an essential technique of trade was evidenced by the fact that, in addition to the 18 concerns whose entire output was disposed in this way, 148 manufacturers, or in the aggregate, 36 per cent of those replying, reported that some portion of their production, generally one-quarter to one-half, was disposed of by barter. The lack of an adequate supply of a sound medium of exchange, as throughout the entire colonial period, exerted a powerful daily influence on commerce and industry.

The machinery of credit and exchange was still rudimentary and only laboriously keeping pace with the growing business demands of the country. Cargoes of western iron or cordate were traded directly for cargoes of logwood, cotton, and sugar at New Orleans. New England manufacturers exchanged cloth with Boston and Providence merchants for wool and cotton. Mills paid their operatives with store orders, or with cloth, or iron. The factories at Waltham and Lowell, organized after the second war with England, were probably the very first to pay employees regularly in currency but this example spread slowly.

Terms of Sale

In the years immediately following the Revolutionary War, credit terms extended by the importer-wholesaler to retail storekeepers and to shopkeepers, particularly those in the interior, generally reverted back to the colonial terms of twelve months. American importers were offered the customary twelve months credit by wide-awake English exporters. Typical of this revision to the earlier colonial terms is the situation disclosed in a letter written by the firm of Franklin & Doty, New York City, to John Hoyland of Sheffield, England, in February, 1793. "We have concluded not to forward a bill [of exchange] with this order but for thee to ship them on 12 m⁰ Cʳ as thou hast formerly done to the late house of Seaman & Franklin."* The firm of Seaman & Franklin had been succeeded in 1792 by Franklin & Doty.

Shorter terms were occasionally used but they were generally renewed, so that for all practical purposes, terms of six months often became twelve, eighteen, and twenty-four months, depending upon the financial responsibility of the buyer, and his ability to acquire a medium of exchange with which to liquidate his obligations. Lewis Ogden of New York City, who had been a delegate to the Provincial Congress in 1776, and had served on its committee to draft a constitution, found himself in this position. In October, 1789, he wrote letters to many of his customers, Robert McClallen, Messʳˢ Jouncy & Given, Messʳˢ Barnett & Ogden, Mʳ Charles Churchill, Messʳˢ Peter R. Livingston & Moncrieffe Livingston, Mʳ Egbert Van Schaick, and Messʳˢ John & James Stoutenburgh, requesting immediate reimbursement for past due obligations. Typical of these letters was the one written to Robert McClallen, in which Ogden said, "You will oblige us in recollecting that when we supplied you with Goods last Fall, we were particular in mentioning that we shou'd expect Punctual Payment in six months, and that we cou'd deal with no one upon any other Terms of Credit, as the Inconveniency to us in making our Remittances wou'd be greater than any profits arising from the sale of our Goods. The small Payments we have rec " we're sorry to observe bear but a small Proportion to the amount of the Debt, as you also will see by the A/C inclosed. We must therefore earnestly request that the Ballance be discharged in the course of this Fall, as it will not be in our power longer to protract the time of payment."† These letters were written not when obligations fell due at the end of six months, but approximately one year after the sale of the merchandise.

* *Letter Book of Franklin & Doty, and Thomas Franklin, 1791-1809.* (New York Historical Society)
† *Letter Book of Lewis Ogden, 1787-1798.* (New York Public Library)

When Michaux reached Lexington, Kentucky, in 1802, he found the same twelve months' terms. "It is an easy thing," Michaux wrote, "for merchants to make their fortunes; in the first place, they usually have a twelve-months' credit from the houses at Philadelphia and Baltimore. . . ." T. M. Harris wrote similarly in the volume, *The Journal of a Tour into the Territory Northwest of the Alleghany Mountains,* published in 1805, "The merchants here, as well as those of the western county, receive their goods from Philadelphia and Baltimore; but a small part of the trade being given to New-York and Alexandria. The terms of credit are generally from nine to twelve months."

Henry B. Fearon, an Englishman who made a tour of the United States in 1817, in behalf of a group of his fellow countrymen who were considering a substantial investment in western real estate, stopped at Cincinnati. Fearon wrote regarding Cincinnati merchants, "The credit which they receive at Philadelphia is from six to seven months, but they can seldom pay at the specified time, and are then charged 7 per cent interest." At this time the "first-rate" retail shops according to the same author, were selling half of their merchandise on credit terms which ranged from six to eighteen months.

The terms of sale used by importers varied somewhat, depending upon the product sold or the arrangements made in a specific sale. Joseph Lee, Jr., of Boston, for example, wrote William Hogden of Alexandria, Va., in 1801 regarding commerce between the two ports, ". . . . the prices of the Articles of Flour, Corn, & Tobacco, I have annexed they sold on a Credit of 60, 90, or 120 Days more or less according to circumstances." In 1817, Henry Lee, a well-known importer of Boston, was selling gin on terms of four months. He admonished the firm of Perit & Cabot of Philadelphia who apparently was handling his merchandise at that port, "I prefer Grocers to speculators, and don't give beyond 4 Months." During the same year, Lee was using terms of ten months in the sale of saltpetre. He explained, "I have made a contract through Messrs Perit & Cabot of Philadelphia with Messrs Dupont & Co. Powder makers for Two hundred thousand pounds of Saltpetre to be delivered in Eighteen Months from 11th July 1817 to be paid for in approved notes at 10 Months Credit from date of delivery. . . ."

Terms of sale were becoming slightly varied. Lambert Brothers in New York City wrote to one of their suppliers in 1823 that they would like to effect the sale of the "balance of saws on hand" on "3, 6, 9 & 12 mos or even 6, 9 & 12 mos" or even 9 & 12 months terms.*

* *Letter Book of Lambert Brothers, 1822-1829.* (Baker Library, Harvard Graduate School of Business Administration)

An analysis of the survey of manufacturing plants conducted in
1832 by eleven State Commissioners in behalf of the Secretary of the
Treasury, as already mentioned, indicated that 324 industrial concerns
were using credit terms of sales in New England and the North Atlantic States. A summary disclosed the use of the following twenty-seven
credit terms or combinations of credit terms, and the number of
manufacturers using each:

Terms		Number
2-3	Months	1
2-4	"	4
2-4-6	"	1
2-6	"	5
3	"	21
3-4	"	4
3-6	"	14
3-6-9	"	1
3-9	"	1
3-12	"	2
4	"	24
4½	"	3
4-6	"	29
4-6-8	"	2
4-8	"	1
4-12	"	1
6	"	119
6-8	"	31
6-9	"	10
6-9-12	"	2
6-12	"	8
6-24	"	1
7	"	4
8	"	14
9	"	6
9-12	"	1
12	"	14
Total		324

Of the 324 returns to this interesting question, 119 or 36.7 per cent
were using terms of six months. The next most popular term of sale
was from six to eight months used by 31 manufacturers, third was from
four to six months used by 29, and fourth was four months used by 24
concerns. The tabulation of the number of manufacturers that sold
on six months terms, alone, or on six months terms along with shorter

or longer terms, amounted to 223 concerns, or 68.8 per cent of the total. Clearly a quiet evolution had occurred in the terms of sale used in the distribution of merchandise. As industrial plants had been started in New England and the North Atlantic States, terms had been shortened so that six months had become the most popular and widely used terms for extending mercantile credit.

In 1838, Henry C. Carey, the son of Matthew Carey of Philadelphia, from whom Samuel Greenhouse of Fredericksburg had sought credit for the purchase of books in 1792, set down the following observations regarding the existing credit system of the United States:

There are few circumstances connected with the American Union more worthy of remark than the credit system, which extends itself over the whole of their vast territory. The traders of Missouri and Arkansas—of Mississippi and Alabama—of Illinois and Michigan—distant 1,000, 1,500, or 2,000 miles and returning but once in 12 or 18 months, are supplied with merchandise on credit, and the small difference charged in consideration thereof is evidence of the punctuality with which they fulfill their engagements. Those traders give credit to the farmer, the planter, and the small storekeeper, who in turn grant it to the labourer, and the charge that is made therefor is exceedingly small.

During this period, discount terms seem to have been quoted occasionally in domestic trade. In a volume regarding the principles of trade, commerce, and banking, published in 1838 by B. F. Foster, there were included fifteen examples showing how invoices should be prepared. Eleven out of fourteen examples concerned with the sale of dry goods, indicated that the merchandise sold by wholesaler distributors to retail shopkeepers was sold without discount terms; three examples, however, showed a five per cent discount for cash payment. One problem relating to the sale of 250 pounds of cochineal quoted a discount of one and one-half per cent for cash.

Early Years of Pawnbroking

Second in time of origination only to the practices of mercantile enterprises in extending credit, came the ancient pawnbroker. The technique of the pawnbroker is as old as the earliest historical chronicle, and although the records often disclosed grasping characters in this historic rôle, pawnbrokers down through the ages often provided credit when available from no other source. As early as 1657 pawnbroking was known in New York City. In the *Minutes of the Court of Burgomasters and Schepens,* appeared information indicating that it was not unusual for early Dutch settlers to use funds obtained by pawning goods "in drinking and jovial company." At this early date in American history, the pawnbrokers were the "tapsters and tavernkeepers." These enlightening early minutes read:

Daily complaints are made to the Honorable Magistrates of this city of Amsterdam in N.[ew] N.[etherlands] against the many tapsters and tavernkeepers, who to keep their business going detain such persons, as for their own sake and advantage would better attend to their occupations and protect their families honorable with God's help, but cannot make up their minds to it, because of the pleasures they find in drinking and jovial company by which they not only spend their daily earnings, but also when out of money pawn the goods serving to the necessities of their families and thereby obtain the means of continuing their usual drinking bouts. ¶ Their Honors, the Burgomasters and Schepens, to obviate this evil therefore forbid all tapsters and tavernkeepers to receive in pawn any goods, of whatever nature they may be, such as clothing, furniture or the like, and to sell drinks therefor under the penalty of 25 fl. the first time, of 50 fl. the second time with a suspension of their business for 6 weeks and for the third offence closure of the place and restitution of the pawned property.

In 1782, immediately after the organization of the Bank of North America, in which he played such a vital part, Robert Morris wrote that he had been informed usury was being practised at Philadelphia, that where loans were absolutely necessary, interest at five per cent per month was obtained even when pledges "were lodged for repayment," and that before the organization of the bank, the lenders actually obtained ten per cent per month and upwards. These transactions, even in the light of the high charges of the day, seem to have taken on attributes of high pressure pawnbroking.

Pawnbroking Arose from Used Clothing Business

Unlike all other types of loans, the pawnbroker takes no note or promise to pay from the borrower. The essence of pawnbroking rests on the legal doctrine that his claim extends solely against the property pledged. This technique of extending credit was not specifically authorized by statutes in any of the colonies, but was carried on openly with high interest charges by virtue of the recognition in common law of the pawnbroker's right to make a storage charge. Although the practice of pledging personal property for loans extended back into our early colonial days, it is probable that as a recognized business activity, pawnbroking was not followed much earlier than 1800. Prior to that date the practice of pawning was perhaps generally confined to isolated requests for loans from neighbors or from business acquaintances, with the exception of situations somewhat similar to those which came to the attention of the early Dutch Burgomasters and Schepens. The lack of a class of urban wage-earners would hardly have provided an economic basis for pawnbroking much earlier.

At the beginning of the nineteenth century, there were a number of dealers in second-hand goods, principally clothing, in New York, Boston, and Philadelphia, who gradually drifted into the money-lending business. They were accustomed to appraise the value of used merchandise. Most of these individuals were emigrants from those European countries where pawnbroking had been a profitable business activity for centuries, and so had realized its unique possibilities in the important growing cities of the new land. Customers found it more advantageous to borrow from the second-hand dealer on the articles they had purchased from him, rather than to resell the merchandise in the regular course of trade, since the charge for the loan would be less than the cost of replacing the property.

Early Regulations of Pawnbrokers

The necessity of regulation finally became more and more evident as the lender was inclined to take increasing advantage of the borrower, making high charges and allowing a very limited time to the pawner in which to redeem his property. The first mention of pawnbrokers in the *Minutes of the Common Council* of New York City occurred on June 3, 1805, when "Alderman Drake and Mr. Hopkins were appointed a Committee to enquire into the propriety of passing a law to regulate pawn brokers." On February 13, 1809, the Common Council received a presentment from "the grand inquest of the city and county" complaining that "the great number of Pawnbrokers and the unrestrained manner in which they conduct themselves" had become a source of serious and alarming mischief.

A little over three years later, on July 13, 1812, the Common Council of New York City, passed the first ordinance in the United States regulating pawnbroking. The pawnbroker was permitted to charge twenty-five per cent per annum on any loan of $25 or less, and seven per cent per annum on any loan exceeding $25. After an article had been in his possession for one year, the pawnbroker had the right to sell it at public auction, provided a notice was published in an authorized newspaper for twelve days giving the time and the place of the

City of New York, ss.

Be it Remembered, That
on the *31.* day of *May* ——— in the year of our
Lord, one thousand eight hundred and *seventeen* before me,
JACOB RADCLIFF, Esq. *Mayor of the said City, personally ap-*
peared *Mathew Mygatt* ——————— *of the*
Third *Ward, and* *Joseph Houston* ——— *of*
the *third* *Ward, and* *Thomas Hapson* ———
of the *fourth* *Ward of the said City, and acknowledged them-*
selves, jointly and severally, to be indebted to the Mayor, Aldermen,
and Commonalty of the City of New-York, in the sum of Five Hundred
Dollars, *lawful money of the said state, to be levied of their goods*
and chattels, lands and tenements, for the use of the said Mayor,
Aldermen, and Commonalty, if failure shall be made in the perform-
ance of the condition following:

Whereas, *the said* *Mathew Mygatt* ——— *hath*
on this day obtained a LICENSE *as a* PAWN-BROKER, *and dealer in the pur-*
chase or sale of Second-Hand Furniture, Metals or Clothes.

Now *the condition of this Recognizance is such, That if the said* *Mathew*
Mygatt ——————— *shall, during the time that he shall hold the*
said License, observe and comply in all respects with the ordinance of the Mayor,
Aldermen, and Commonalty of the said City, entitled, "*a Law to regulate Pawn-*
Brokers, and dealers in the purchase or sale of Second-Hand Furniture, Metals,
or Clothes," *and such further ordinances as may be made in the premises, then this*
Recognizance to be void, or else to remain in full force.

Taken

Mathew Mygatt

Early Pawnbroker's License, New York City

sale. The rate for loans in excess of $25 was so low that the business could not be operated profitably under the law. As a result, higher rates were charged notwithstanding this ordinance by some pawnbrokers, while others would remain within the letter of the law by making several loans, each on a different article, for $25 each. These legal rates remained in force in New York City until 1883, a period of seventy-one years, when a State law was enacted providing for charges at the rate of three per cent per month for the first six months on loans of $100 or less, and two per cent per month thereafter.

Early Surveys of Pawnbroking

The *First Annual Report of the Society for the Prevention of Pauperism in the City of New York* published in 1818, contained surveys of existing institutions contributing to pauperism and, among them was listed the pawnbroker. The establishments of pawnbrokers in this report were "considered as very unfavorable to the independence and welfare of the middling and inferior classes." The report seriously continued, "The artifices which are often practiced to deceive the expectations of those who are induced, through actual distress or by positive allurement, to trust their goods at these places, not to mention the facilities which they afford to the commission of theft, and the encouragement they give to a dependence on stratagem and cunning, rather than on profits of honest industry, fairly entitle them, in the opinion of the Committee, to a place among causes of poverty."

Apparently, as the result of this report, an ordinance was passed by the Common Council in 1819 providing that pawnbrokers be "regularly licensed by the mayor of the City of New York, and bonds entered into, in the penal sum of five hundred dollars, with two suretees, to obey and perform the exactions of the statute." In the *Second Annual Report of the Society for the Prevention of Pauperism*, which was made in 1820, the first mention is made of the number of active pawnbrokers in New York City, "Ten persons are now licensed and under legal obligations. . . . Each pawnbroker's books must contain a description of the articles pawned, the amount of money thereon borrowed, with the name of the pawner, and the rate of interest received."

At this period pawnbrokers customarily advertised their services in newspapers. The expressions used in these advertisements were quaint and distinctive. Typical of them is the following announcement of the opening of a branch office which appeared in 1827:

MONEY TO LEND—John I. Hart, Licensed Pawn Broker, No. 540 Pearl, corner of Elm-street, respectfully acquaints the public, that in addition to the above old establishment, he has opened a *Branch of Accommodation* at No. 87 Catherine, corner Cheapside-street, where loans, in money, may be had on liberal terms, in large or small sums, on gold and silver watches, silver plate, jewelry, dry goods, wearing apparel, household furniture, and all kinds of merchandise. ☞ Goods taken by the package.*

Unpublished records regarding pawnbroking developed by Samuel W. Levine in his early research contain a copy of a Document No. XLV, which was presented to the Board of Assistants of New York City on December 30, 1831. This document disclosed that in 1828 an ordinance had been passed by the Common Council requiring that separate licenses be obtained to conduct a pawnbroking business and to act as a dealer in second-hand articles. In 1823 there had been eight licenses in New York City to carry on both operations; in 1824, eleven; in 1825, sixteen; in 1826, forty-four; and in 1827, thirty-nine. In 1828, when these two types of operations were separated there were only nine licensed pawnbrokers, and in the three years, 1829, 1830, and 1831, there were twelve. At this time the greater number of all loans was for less than one dollar and "of the whole, twelve-fifteenths" were "in sums less than one dollar and fifty cents."

Matthew Carey in a volume published in 1830, *Public Charities of Philadelphia,* quoted detailed records kept by the New York pawnbrokers for the year 1828 showing that 149,890 articles had been pawned by 71,576 persons. Slightly over one-half of these pledges represented articles of men's and women's clothing, while slightly less than one quarter represented watches, table silver, rings, and jewelry.

Early Pawnbrokers

The earliest pawnbroker of record and not a particularly high-minded type was one John S. Sommer of New York City. Sommer carried on his operations before the first regulations were passed by the Common Council. In 1804, he kept a clothing store and did some money lending at 31 Catherine Street. Some time later he moved to 13 Chatham Street. In 1816, a recommendation was made by a committee of the Common Council that his license not be renewed as he had been making charges which ranged from sixty per cent to sixty-five per cent per annum, instead of the seven per cent allowed by the New York City ordinance of 1812 on loans in excess of $25.

* *New York Inquirer,* Tuesday morning, January 9, 1827.

A petition made to the Common Council of New York City in 1818 by a group of pawnbrokers, to reduce the license fee from $50 at which it had been established several years earlier, was signed by ten individuals, all of whom presumably were licensed pawnbrokers at the time, Catherine Dermott, Margaret Bell, Samuel Mayo, John Gray, James Trivett, Josh. Chapman, George Smith, Joseph Laymon, Leonard Bell, and Thomas Whyme. Of additional interest, is the assertion in this petition that more pawnbrokers were carrying on their operations in the city without having taken out licenses than those who had paid the yearly $50 fee. On this basis there would have been over twenty active pawnbrokers in New York City in 1818.

At this time the pawnbroking business was fully as active in Philadelphia and Boston, both important centers with relatively large laboring populations. In 1823, the first act relating to pawnbroking was passed by the Pennsylvania legislature placing the business under the regulation of cities and district corporations. *The Philadelphia Directory* of 1828 contained a full page advertisement of one Stephen Blatchford, a pawnbroker whose business, according to the advertisement, had been established in 1819. In addition to the usual loans on watches, silver plate, and jewelry, this advertisement carried an interesting footnote to the effect that advances would also be "made on New Carriages, Gigs, Dearborns, &c., &c.," the "Dearborns" being light carriages.

William Simpson, Inc.

The oldest pawnbrokerage house in active operation today is William Simpson, Inc., of New York City. About 1822, William Simpson arrived from Barrowdale, Cumberland County, England. It is believed that he had been a silversmith in his home country, a profession which often acted as pawnbrokers in England. For some unknown reason he assumed the name of Walter Stevenson when he arrived in this country. He started in business as a pawnbroker at 23 Chatham Street (now Park Row), New York City, some years later took in a brother, Thomas Simpson, as a partner, and was eminently successful. On May 11, 1840, when this firm took out a new bond for $500, the active partners who signed the bond were Walter Stevenson, Thos. Simpson and John M. Davies.

At the death of Walter Stevenson in 1847 the business was acquired by his brother, Thomas Simpson, and subsequently by a younger relative whose exact connection is now unknown, John B.

Simpson. Around 1890, control was acquired by William Simpson, a nephew of John B. Simpson. Successful operations were continued under the personal direction of William Simpson until 1916, and then by his son, William, Jr., until the business was incorporated in 1925 under the existing style of *William Simpson, Inc*. This enterprise has been operated only from three locations and today at 91 Park Row is located only a short distance from the original office in 1822.

This concern carried on a typical pawnbrokerage business as described in the preceding pages. Loans were made at the rates determined by city ordinances on clothing, diamonds, jewelry, silverware, and other objects upon which loans were customarily granted from time to time. By 1900, loans on clothing had been eliminated by this firm with the exception of advances on Paisley shawls. Since 1905 loans have been made only on diamonds, jewelry, and silverware.

R. Simpson & Co., Inc.

The second oldest pawnbrokerage house in the country is *R. Simpson & Co., Inc.* This enterprise was started in 1827 by Robert Simpson, who is believed to have been a brother of Walter Stevenson. It was originally located at 195 Bowery, New York City. Operations were carried on at this location until 1897, when the headquarters were moved to 133 West 42nd Street, New York City. Here the business is operated today. Robert Simpson died in 1884 and the business was inherited by Thomas Simpson, a nephew who had come from Barrowdale, England, in 1862. In 1918, the business was incorporated under the laws of the State of New York. It is now controlled by the two active sons of Thomas, namely, Robert C. and Thomas B. Simpson.

Third Oldest Pawnbroker

What pawnbrokerage house is the third oldest is somewhat of a mystery due to the lack of basic records. It is generally believed that *M. & S. Fridenberg,* a firm which operated in Philadelphia until August, 1940, was started in 1832. Mone Fridenberg who arrived at Philadelphia from Portugal in 1830, started this business as a partnership with Solomon Isaacs Prout, who had emigrated from Amsterdam in 1828. Because of the unusually stringent laws enacted by the Pennsylvania legislature in 1940, *M. & S. Fridenberg* discontinued operations in Pennsylvania. At the time this concern ceased making loans in Philadelphia it was in the hands of the fifth generation of one of the founders. No exact records are available giving the opening date but the *Philadelphia City Directory* of 1840 showed Mone Fridenberg to have been established in the pawnshop business at that time.

Early Insurance Companies

Because of the outstanding importance of colonial shipping, marine insurance was the first type of insurance to be widely used in the colonies. As early as 1721, one John Copson advertised in Philadelphia his intention of opening a marine insurance office, but if he actually opened the office, it was soon abandoned as no record exists of its activity. In 1724, Joseph Marion, a notary public, trained as a clerk, copyist, and "accountant," opened an insurance office in Boston which he operated for twenty-four years. This office served as a meeting place for merchants desiring marine insurance, and for wealthy individuals who made it a practice to underwrite the insurance offered on any ship and its cargo for a particular voyage. Few individuals would underwrite more than £200 on a single bottom or cargo, and frequently as little as £50. Boston, Philadelphia, and New York were the great, colonial, shipping centers and it was at these points that marine insurance early took root.

Not until marine and fire insurance companies were organized did insurance underwriting involve the creation of a modest fund to cover any emergency. When such funds were created, it was necessary to find some avenue of investment on which a reasonable return could be earned. Out of this situation arose the practice on the part of the early underwriting organizations of extending loans secured by mortgages, a practice which proved sufficiently profitable and conservative to act as a precedent for mutual savings banks when they came into existence during the second decade of the nineteenth century. Here was the third type of credit institution to become operative in America.

The first fire insurance company to be organized in the colonies was the *Friendly Society* of Charleston, South Carolina. This concern was organized in 1736 for mutual fire protection. Operations were carried on successfully for four years when a conflagration which destroyed some three hundred houses wrecked the treasury and the concern dropped out of existence. Then the scene shifted to the very important, commercial city of brotherly love. It is something of a

coincidence that the two oldest mutual, and the two oldest stock fire insurance companies in existence in 1941 were started in Philadelphia.

The Philadelphia Contributionship

On March 25, 1752 a group of prominent business men, foremost
among whom was Benjamin Franklin, organized *The Philadelphia
Contributionship for the Insurance of Houses from Loss by Fire*. This
enterprise has had a continuous existence since that date. On February
20, 1768 when the concern had been established sixteen years, a charter
was granted by James Hamilton, Lieutenant-Governor of the Province
of Pennsylvania, and confirmed by King George III of England.

The paid-in capital of this enterprise, and the premiums paid
for insurance, were immediately used to make mortgage loans. As
early as July 11, 1752, less than four months after its organization, an
application was received for a loan of £500 from John Bailey to be
secured by a corner house and lot at Front and Chestnut Streets, Philadelphia, and by ground rent. After careful consideration the board
granted the loan on September 22, 1752, but not to the full extent of
£500; it was made for £300 for one year with interest at the rate of
six per cent per annum. This loan was renewed at successive maturity
dates and finally repaid on March 27, 1759.

The second application for a mortgage loan was received from
Ulrick Sherrick on April 3, 1753 for £200 to £300 to be secured by three
hundred acres of land in Lancaster County. Four days later the board
granted the loan for £200. This obligation was repaid June 1, 1759.

The third loan was sought on February 5, 1754 by William
Maugridge for £200 to be secured by a plantation in Berks County
consisting of an undisclosed number of acres of land. This loan was
granted in May, 1754. The early records regarding this transaction contained an interesting clause, "The Board being informed that Benjamin
Franklin will engage that the interest shall be punctually paid. . . ."*
indicating that the loan was granted at least partially on the word or
the responsibility of Benjamin Franklin. This obligation remained
outstanding much longer than either of the first two loans; it was not
liquidated until March 25, 1769, a period of almost fifteen years.

It was the policy of the management up to the year 1810, to restrict
the investment of all surplus funds to mortgage loans. The assets
shown by successive balance sheets in the early *Minute Books* disclose

* These loans appear in *The Minute Book of the Directors of The Philadelphia Contributionship, 1752-1769.*

only cash, accrued interest, and mortgages. On March 25, 1793 the balance sheet had total assets of £16,640 consisting of these three items. Beginning with July 5, 1810, funds were invested at various times during that year in a total of thirteen shares of stock in the first Bank of the United States at an aggregate cost of $7,771.97. In 1811, funds were invested in the stock of the Bank of North America, and in 1817 in the stock of the Schuylkill Navigation Co., which had been organized in 1815 to make a navigable waterway from Philadelphia to the headwaters of the Schuylkill River. During the first fifty-eight years of its existence, the only investments of *The Philadelphia Contributionship* represented the extension of credit secured by mortgages, and in the succeeding years throughout the nineteenth century, this practice was the principal, if not the sole means of investing surplus funds.

The Mutual Assurance Company

The second oldest, existing, mutual fire insurance company arose from the decision of *The Philadelphia Contributionship,* after thirty-two years of operation, not to insure or reinsure houses having trees nearby, even at a higher rate. In September, 1784, forty men, many of whom were members of the older company, and who wanted both insurance and green trees, now proceeded to organize this new enterprise under the name of *The Mutual Assurance Company for Insuring Houses from Loss by Fire,* in Philadelphia. This company has since been popularly and widely known as "The Green Tree." In February, 1786, after operating seventeen months, a charter was obtained. Prior to 1801, fire insurance companies generally issued policies to cover a period of seven years. In that year *The Mutual Assurance Company* issued the first perpetual insurance policy in America, one deposit covering the premium in full for the life of a building.

The early financial policy of this concern was naturally similar to the policy with which the official staff was familiar, the utilization of surplus funds to make mortgage loans. The application for the first loan was received within seven months after the date of organization. At the monthly meeting of the trustees held at the Indian King tavern on Wednesday, April 13, 1785, it was "agreed to let Mr. Matthew Clarkson have £300 on interest." The second loan was made to Isaac Gray for £200 on May 11, 1785. The third loan was made to John Phillips (Barber), a negro for £75, and the fourth to Christlieb Bartling for £200; these two loans being voted on June 8, 1785. All were mortgage loans, all bore interest at the customary rate of six per cent per annum, and all carried no specific maturity date.

The loan of £300 to Matthew Clarkson was paid in May, 1797, when a new loan of £500 was granted to Matthew Clarkson and Michael Hilleages. This mortgage in turn, was liquidated in full by the administrators of the estates of these two men in April, 1806. The loan of £200 to Isaac Gray, which covered a house and plantation, was paid in February, 1793, when James Strawbridge purchased the property and took out a mortgage for £300. The loan to John Phillips was foreclosed in 1788 when Phillips was unable to pay. The loan of £200 to Christlieb Bartling which was on his home "in Cherry Street, between Fifth & Sixth Street" and on a nearby lot, was paid in full sometime between September, 1793 and July, 1795.

In 1791, funds were invested for the first time in assets other than in mortgage loans. At three different times during this year stock was purchased in the Bank of North America, one share on March 10, for £153.15.0, one share on August 11, for £165.0.0 and one share on September 23, also for £165.0.0. Investing funds in stocks was an innovation and the management experimented very conservatively. Not until nineteen years after this example had been set by *The Mutual Assurance Company* did *The Philadelphia Contributionship* make its initial investment in securities. The second investment, other than in mortgage loans, was made by *The Mutual Assurance Company* in May, 1793 and consisted of the purchase of $1,900 par value six per cent bonds of the United States for £590.15.3 ($1,575.37). In May, 1794, two shares of stock in the Bank of Pennsylvania were acquired for $870.*

On September 25, 1841, after fifty-seven years of continuous successful operations the greater part of the assets of *The Mutual Assurance Company* continued to be invested in mortgage loans. Total assets amounted to $392,443.28, and of this sum, forty-one mortgage loans contributed $252,675.73 or 64.4 per cent, investments in stocks and bonds $82,411.74, two houses, one of which was used as an office $40,789.21, and cash of $16,566.60.

Insurance Company of North America

The *Insurance Company of North America,* the oldest stock fire and marine insurance company, was organized as an association in November, 1792 to take over the assets and to carry on the insurance

---

* Typewritten copy of *Minute Book No. 1, The Mutual Assurance Company,* September 29, 1784, to April 9, 1794.

business of *The Universal Tontine*. This concern had been speculatively organized during the preceding March to underwrite fire and marine insurance. In 1794, the business was incorporated by the State of Pennsylvania. When the accounts of *The Universal Tontine* were settled in May, 1793, a "Bal. of Doll $3571\frac{13}{100}$" was transferred to the credit of the *Insurance Company of North America*. Along with this cash, the insurance company acquired \$17,491 six per cent bonds of the United States, \$11,230.88 three per cent bonds of the United States, \$3,603.85 deferred bonds of the United States, and fifty-seven full shares of stock in the first Bank of the United States.* The deferred bonds represented securities issued according to the funding act of 1790, which bore no interest until the year 1800. In June, 1793 the board of directors voted to subscribe for fifty shares of stock in the Bank of Pennsylvania.

One provision of the original charter restricted the investment of funds to "securities for or evidences of debts due by the United States, or in the stock of the Bank of Pennsylvania, or of the Bank of the United States, or of the Bank of North America, or of the Schuylkill and Delaware Canal Company, or of the Schuylkill and Susquehanna Company, or of the Lancaster and Philadelphia Turnpike Company, or of any other company that now is or hereafter may be incorporated by the State, in such manner, and in such sums, as the President and Directors of the said company may judge proper." A supplementary provision of the charter provided specific restrictions for making loans; money could be loaned "upon bottomry and respondentia," popular bases for short term credit at that time.

Bottomry according to maritime law was an instrument by which a ship was pledged as security for a loan. *Respondentia* represented a process by which a ship-owner would borrow funds upon the security of a vessel's cargo, agreeing to pay within a stipulated period of time, such as twenty-four months, or sixty days after the return of the vessel. The original sum together with a substantial increment, usually twenty-four per cent, was paid for the use of the money, but if the vessel and cargo were lost, then no payment was made either on the principal or the increment. These loans were widely used forms of credit in the eighteenth century and well into the nineteenth century.

The first loan made by the *Insurance Company of North America* was, however, of a very different character. It was in the nature of an ordinary note receivable accepted in July, 1793, in payment "for Premiums to New Orleans" and was "payable in Four & one half months."

* *Directors' Minute Book, Number 1, Insurance Company of North America, 1792-1803,* p. 86.

These terms were materially shorter than the customary twelve months which were being extended in mercantile circles, but nevertheless, this transaction represented a unique type of credit for an underwriter. The board of directors had every confidence in the reliability and in the financial means of the owner of the insured ship.

The second loan was in the nature of the acceptance of notes for the sale of a ship. The good ship, *Industry* which had stranded, had been salvaged by the *Insurance Company of North America*. The board in July, 1793 agreed to sell this vessel, "the Purchaser to pay the Expences & Repairs done since her Arrival in Port" for "approved Notes, one half payable in two months, and the other in four." Apparently the insurance company, early in its career, salvaged wrecked vessels, made repairs, and then sold them at auction to the highest bidder or at a private sale. The *Minute Book,* in August, 1793 revealed the owner-ship of a second vessel in a resolution which read, "Resolved, That the Sloop *Washington* be advertised for Sale at Public Auction on Wednes-day next, at Sixty Days Credit, for approved notes."

The third type of loan was voted by the board in April, 1794, "On motion, Resolved, that six Thousand Dollars be lent to Mr. Stephen Kingston on his giving good Security by Bond or Notes, to the Satis-faction of the Committee of the Week, to repay the same with Interest in twelve months from the Date." At the same meeting it was agreed to lend George Meade $3,000 on the same terms as the loan to Kingston, but one week later the amount of the loan to be granted to Meade was raised to $4,000. No mention was made in the *Minute Book* as to what collateral, if any, was pledged to secure these two loans.

In November, 1794, an application for a loan was received from (Robert) Morris & Nicholson. This request took place about two weeks after Morris had obtained a mortgage loan of $30,000 from the *Insurance Company of the State of Pennsylvania*. On December 1, 1794 the board agreed to make the loan for three years provided adequate security was given. The records in the *Minute Book* now become a little vague, but it would seem as though $73,080, a sum more than twice as large as the original request, was advanced to Robert Morris to purchase stock in the Bank of Pennsylvania, and in addition to this entire block of bank stock which was now taken by the insurance company as collateral, Morris executed a mortgage covering what was known as the "Morris-ville Estate," as additional security. Morris subsequently was unable to meet the interest on this loan, and title to the "Morrisville Estate" was acquired by the *Insurance Company of North America*. In 1798

the estate was sold to Thomas Fitzsimons. Fitzsimons likewise de-
faulted in the payment of his interest, and upon request, executed "a
Deed for 65,000 acres of Land in Georgia" as security "for premiums
due by him and for which Judgment had been obtained."[*]

Insurance Company of the State of Pennsylvania

The *Insurance Company of the State of Pennsylvania,* the second
oldest stock fire and marine insurance company, was chartered in April,
1794 and has had a continuous operating existence since that time.

The very first investment by this corporation represented the purchase of $80,000 six per cent bonds of the United States, made on
October 20, 1794, at a cost of $80,266.67. On the following day, a letter
was presented to the board from Robert Morris proposing to borrow
$80,000 upon "Mortgage, etc.," Two days later, applications for loans
on mortgages were also received from John Wilcocks and the very
wealthy merchant, William Bingham. After consideration of the various
proposals, the board of directors agreed to extend a loan of $30,000 to
John Wilcocks for one year from October 30, 1794, the loan to be secured
by a first mortgage, and a loan of $20,000 to William Bingham. Both of
these loans were still outstanding for the respective amounts on January
1, 1801. The records indicate that Wilcocks used his borrowed money
to purchase the land pledged to secure the mortgage from no other than
Robert Morris. This double-pass was probably one more means being
used by Morris to raise cash at a time when his heavy liabilities were
becoming ever more pressing.

On October 31, 1794, a loan not of $80,000 for which he had
originally applied, but of $30,000 for one year, secured by "a Mortgage
Bond & warrant" was also made to this self same Robert Morris. The
amount of this loan was reduced substantially below the application,
probably because Morris was carrying on successful negotiations at this
identical time, to obtain a larger sum than he had originally sought
from the *Insurance Company of North America.* The land covered
by this mortgage was the "plantation called the Hills, and a Mill and
Plantation in Montgomery County."[†]

As a result of the great variety of his interests and speculative
activities following the Revolutionary War, interests in shipping, merchandising, road building, canal building, banking, and insurance, the

[*] *Ibid.,* pp. 80, 99, 110-118, 131, 154, 181-182, 190-192, 303.
[†] *Directors' Minute Book, Number 1, Insurance Company of the State of Pennsylvania, 1794-1803,* pp. 16-40.

financial affairs of Robert Morris were becoming more and more involved about this time. As soon as the *Insurance Company of North America* and the *Insurance Company of the State of Pennsylvania* were organized and ready for business, Morris arrived at their doorsteps to utilize such substantial portions of their funds as he was able to borrow. On October 28, 1795, Morris was given notice by the *Insurance Company of the State of Pennsylvania*, that interest for one year was due on this mortgage loan. Under date of November 4, 1795, the *Minute Book* contained a record that "he had taken no notice thereof" and "It was resolved that the Secretary inform Mr. Morris that unless the Interest be immediately paid the mortgage will be foreclosed without Delay." Morris was unable to solve his financial difficulties and was finally imprisoned for debt in 1798, four years after this particular mortgage loan was granted, when sixty-four years of age.

In March, 1799 the property of Robert Morris pledged for this loan was advertised for sale by the sheriff for the payment of the mortgage of $30,000 and $4,275 accrued unpaid interest. Two months later, Henry Pratt purchased a part of the estate, paying the purchase price in notes of one Paul Siemens which he presumably endorsed, the notes running for two and four months. Apparently the obligation of Robert Morris to the insurance company had been endorsed or guaranteed by the responsible firm of Reed & Forde, as in November, 1799, they made arrangements to reimburse the insurance company for the difference between the $34,275 due, and the amount received from the sale of part of the estate to Henry Pratt.

Reed & Forde was a prominent Philadelphia firm of the day, engaging in foreign commerce both on their own account and on commission; they owned and operated their own ships captained by members of their own families; they engaged in many kinds of financial operations, and in buying and selling western lands. They loaned money to well known individuals such as Edmund Randolph and Robert Morris, and they sold bank stock to George Washington who later complained that the price had been too high.*

The only available records of the *Insurance Company of the State of Pennsylvania* for the first few years of its existence are contained in the first Directors' *Minute Book*. The early cash books and ledgers have disappeared over the intervening years. The first *Minute Book* contained no information that this company, like the *Insurance*

---

* "Reed and Forde—Merchant Adventurers in Philadelphia," by Arthur P. Whitaker in *The Pennsylvania Magazine of History and Biography*, Volume LXI, Number 3; July, 1937.

Company of North America, salvaged ships and sold them on short terms. There are indications, however, that quite a few claims for lost ships were made in the early years of its existence, and it would seem as though the company must have salvaged some of these vessels in the normal course of efficient operations. It is possible that salvaged ships were sold for cash, or that they were sold on note terms and the facts not recorded in the minutes, as such sales were considered more or less routine transactions.

Some short term credit was extended for other purposes. When vessels or cargoes were lost, the company occasionally granted loans to owners, with interest, pending the settlement of the claims. Notes receivable were also accepted for the payment of premiums. In fact, a regular schedule existed by which notes for three months covering insurance premiums were acceptable when a vessel sailed from one port in the United States to another, to the West Indies, to British ports in North America, or to the Spanish colonies; for six months when to or from any port in Europe or on this side of the Cape of Good Hope; and for twelve months when to or from any port beyond the Cape of Good Hope. A discount of six per cent was allowed for cash payment.*

Early Growth in Insurance Companies

From these transactions, it is clear that the early fire and marine insurance companies were basic institutions of credit. The early loans of *The Philadelphia Contributionship* and *The Mutual Assurance Company* were confined to short-term loans secured by mortgages. The *Insurance Company of North America,* and the *Insurance Company of the State of Pennsylvania,* in addition to mortgage loans, extended short-term credit on promissory notes in the normal course of operations for many other purposes. The use of promissory notes was far more extensive during the entire colonial period and the early years of our national existence than today, due to the need of longer credit and the lack of an adequate supply of monetary currency.

By 1800, thirty-three charters had been issued by the various States to incorporate insurance companies. Fifteen had been issued in New England, seven by New York and Pennsylvania, and eleven by the three southern States of Maryland, Virginia, and South Carolina. By this time only two branches of the insurance business were of any considerable importance, marine and fire, and most of the companies

* *Ibid.,* pp. 20-22, 55, 85, 91.

handled insurance of both types. Marine insurance expanded with the growing commerce, and fire insurance, although much less widespread, became more and more vital as the population increased and crowded into towns and cities. Life insurance was occasionally underwritten by the marine and the fire companies, but only as a casual, incidental, and little understood type of insurance.

Development of Bank Credit

There were no bankers in the modern sense in the colonies; such functions of banking as were carried on, having been handled by wealthy merchants like Thomas Hancock, his nephew John Hancock, and Nathaniel L. Savage. The prominent merchants in the seacoast cities accepted deposits in a small way, made loans, and issued drafts on their correspondents in other trading centers in the colonies and overseas. They granted loans and credit to friends for travel and for general accommodation. They sold bills of exchange, which served the purpose of modern letters of credit, drawn on foreign merchant correspondents located principally in England. They were in the true meaning of the term, merchant-bankers.

Typical Colonial Bankers

Thomas Hancock, for example, wrote a letter in June, 1760 to His Excel? Thoss Pownall Esq͞r, Governor of Massachusetts when he sailed from Boston to London to accept the appointment as Governor of South Carolina, "Your Excellency having Lodged in my Hands in Province Securities the Sum of Four Thousand Four Hundred & Sixty five pounds, ten shillings & one penny in Lawfull Money upon Interest on your own accoᵗᵗ and risque as List Deliver'd your Excellency Sign'd by me. Whenever you may have occasion to Draw for said Money in part or for the whole, your Bills shall be punctually paid. Please always to give notice before you Draw that I may have time to Exchange the Notes into Cash."*

Nathaniel L. Savage carried on somewhat similar banking functions along with his extensive mercantile operations in Virginia. Savage's *Account Book* (1768-85) contained somewhat "over one hundred accounts, representing a territory which extended from the Atlantic

* *Letter Book of Thomas Hancock, 1750-1762.* (Baker Library, Harvard Graduate School of Business Administration)

Ocean to Frederick and Shenandoah Counties, seventeen counties being specifically named, and others doubtless included, and many of these accounts partake of the nature of loans." A substantial proportion of these loans were made in 1775 or a year or two earlier. Most of the loans were not repaid until the close of the Revolutionary War. One of the largest loans "was £3,116 which was borrowed in 1773 by Carter Braxton, and which, in 1783, after certain credits had been deducted, amounted to £3,175.15. . . . In 1775 Colonel John Randolph and Colonel Archibald Cary gave their joint bond for £100, about £20 of which was paid by Cary in 1782, and the balance due was paid by Edmund Randolph in 1784, the year of John Randolph's death. In 1775, Colonel Thomas Nelson gave his sterling bond on interest for £236 16s., which after including 33 1/3 per cent for difference of exchange amounted in 1784 to £451 15s. 8d."*

Wealthy merchants and individuals who made loans, gradually discontinued operations as a result of the steady depreciation in Continental and State currencies during the Revolutionary War. Loans and currency depreciation have never gone amicably hand in hand. The risk of loss to the lender is about on a par with the possibility of harm when swimming in shark infested waters.

Organization of the Bank of North America

A distinctive feature of post Revolutionary War business activity was the development of the corporation. Today the institution of the corporation is about as common as depreciated currency was in the Revolutionary period, but when the treaty of peace was signed at Paris, the corporation as a unit of business activity was hardly known. Like Bushnell's early submarine it was in process of evolution. During the entire colonial period only one-half dozen American business charters had been granted; only eleven were issued in the United States between 1781 and 1785, of which two were banks; twenty-two between 1786 and 1790, and one hundred and fourteen between 1791 and 1795.

The first important corporation to receive a charter from the Continental Congress was the *Bank of North America,* Philadelphia, organized late in 1781 by Robert Morris while the Revolutionary War was in process. Here was the fourth type of credit institution. This bank received a perpetual charter eight years before George Washington

* "A Typical Business Man of the Revolutionary Era," by Susie M. Ames, published in *Journal of Economic and Business History,* Volume III, Number 3, May, 1931, pp. 419-420.

was elected President of the United States. The permitted capitalization was immense for the times, no less than $10,000,000 divided into shares with a par value of $400 each. Public subscriptions came in pitifully slow; only by the greatest exertion was $70,000 secured from private subscribers, probably because the final outlook for the settlement of the war was still somewhat clouded. These were the shares purchased by *The Mutual Assurance Company* in 1791 when that concern made its first outside investment.

When a frigate arrived in Boston from France in 1781 bearing $470,000 in specie as a loan to the struggling colonies, Robert Morris, then the Superintendent of Finance, subscribed $254,000 of this sum for stock in this new institution in behalf of the Continental Congress. The government became the principal stockholder. Jeremiah Wadsworth received subscriptions in Hartford to the stock, and at the same time, purchased one hundred and four shares for his own account to become the largest single stockholder after the government.

Thomas Willing was elected president and Tench Francis was appointed cashier. Willing was a well-known Philadelphia business man who, prior to the Revolutionary War had been an importer-wholesaler, insurance underwriter, and a partner of the redoubtable Robert Morris in the firm of Willing & Morris. Operations were begun with a total staff of six persons and the ledgers were kept in Mexican dollars and ninetieth parts thereof, not a very auspicious start. This institution was, however, the third incorporated commercial bank in the world, having been preceded only by the Riksbank in Sweden, and the Bank of England in London. It was the first incorporated bank in the New World and although the United States was desperately poor in terms of specie, it is interesting to realize that the *Bank of North America* improved upon the experience of its old world predecessors by beginning its corporate life with actual coin on hand.

The bank promptly loaned the funds paid in by the government for capital stock. The doors opened for business on January 7, 1782 and on April 1, 1782 the Treasury of the United States was indebted to the bank for $300,000, and on July 1 for $400,000. Business was picking up! When the directors asked Morris to reduce this obligation he sold $200,000 of the stock owned by the government, mostly to Holland bankers, and used the proceeds to reduce the loan. By July 1, 1783 the remaining holdings of the government had been sold and in six months the debt had been entirely discharged. Although the bank was beset by many difficulties in its early days, it was financially profitable from the outset. Profits for the first half year netted four and one-half per cent, and dividends for 1783 averaged fourteen per cent.

By 1786, nearly one-half of the capital stock was owned by five wealthy individuals, Robert Morris, John Swanwick, and William Bingham of Philadelphia, and Jeremiah Wadsworth and John Carter of Hartford. John Swanwick had become a partner in Willing & Morris in 1783. William Bingham was the extremely wealthy merchant of Philadelphia who was prominent for many years in the commercial life of the nation. Jeremiah Wadsworth and John Carter comprised the Hartford firm of Wadsworth & Carter, that we have seen, acquired profitable contracts to supply the French forces in America. Together the five men owned 464 of the outstanding 1,000 shares.

The apparent success of the *Bank of North America** in granting credit profitably and safely, led to agitation for the organization of similar institutions elsewhere, Portsmouth in New Hampshire, Providence, Richmond, and Charleston. The next two banks, however, were organized in 1784 in New York and Boston, the *Bank of New York* in New York City, and the *Massachusetts Bank* in Boston.

The Bank of New York

The *Bank of New York* formally commenced operations on June 9, 1784 and for seven years did business under articles of association drawn up by Alexander Hamilton. On March 21, 1791 it was incorporated under the laws of the State of New York with an authorized capital of $900,000 divided into shares of $500 each, and with a paid-in capital of $318,250. Here was the second organized bank in the United States. The charter conservatively and paternalistically provided that debts of the bank were not to exceed three times the amount of the "capital subscribed," that property was not to be held except for purposes necessary to banking (what an anomaly that would have been considered in the years immediately prior to 1929!), and the bank was not to buy and sell stocks.

The by-laws of the *Bank of New York* adopted May 19, 1791, shortly after its incorporation, provided that discounts "shall be made at the rate of seven per centum per annum" and that all bills and notes offered for discount shall be delivered to the bank on Monday or Wed-

* This venerable banking institution was consolidated with the *Commercial Trust Co.*, Philadelphia in 1923 to form the *Bank of North America and Trust Company*. This institution, in turn, merged in 1929 with the *Pennsylvania Company for Insurance on Lives and Granting Annuities*, Philadelphia. In this process, the *Pennsylvania Company for Insurance on Lives and Granting Annuities* inherited the oldest continuous bank account in the country, that of *John T. Lewis & Brothers Company*, manufacturers of paint, which was opened with the *Bank of North America* in 1782, and is still active in 1941.

nesday. The loans would be considered by the directors on Tuesday or Thursday and be made known on the following day. Apparently a full day was needed to make the credit investigation and consider the information! The by-laws also provided that discounts could not be made for a longer period than thirty days but "that three days of grace" would "be allowed." On March 1, 1792 the discount rate was reduced to six per cent per annum, and by August a loan of $35,000 secured by bonds of the United States government was made to the *Society for establishing useful Manufacturers,* of Paterson, New Jersey at five per cent per annum. This concern, according to Alexander Hamilton's plans was to be the great integrated manufacturing enterprise of the new nation. Although the early loans were not supposed to run for more than thirty days, loans for four months and longer were being approved by 1794 to the Federal Government.*

Jeremiah Wadsworth was the second president, but only for one year. By 1796, the business of the bank had so increased that a more desirable location was needed and accordingly the house and lot on the corner of Wall and William Streets were purchased from William Constable for £11,000 New York currency. Here the bank has remained ever since and here it is in active, successful operation today.

The Massachusetts Bank in Boston

The *Massachusetts Bank* obtained its charter from the State legislature on February 7, 1784. Here was the third bank to be organized in the United States. The authorized capital was $300,000 consisting of 600 shares with a par value of $500 each, of which $253,500 was paid in when the institution opened its doors on July 5, 1784. A substantial part of the capital was furnished by six Bostonians, of whom the most important was a retired merchant handling his investments, William Phillips of the family which founded the two academies, one at Andover and the other at Exeter.

The money received in payment of shares, and the funds accepted as deposits, were the various kinds in common circulation at the time, the respective values of which were often uncertain. The varieties included Portuguese johanneses, half johanneses and moidores; Spanish doubloons, pistoles and pistareens; British guineas, half crowns and shillings; French Louis d'or and Mexican dollars. The acceptance of this variety of coin resulted in a subtle decision that a depositor be per-

---

* *Minute Book of Board of Directors of the Bank of New York, May 2, 1791 to April 4, 1831.*

mitted to withdraw the same kind of money that he had deposited!

None of the six gentlemen whose name appeared on the original charter had first-hand knowledge about operating a bank. Orville and Wilbur Wright must have been up against a similar situation when they flew the first airplane. So, almost the first act of the organization committee was to write Thomas Willing, president of the *Bank of North America* in Philadelphia, asking how to establish a bank, and how in his experience, a bank should be operated. Willing replied at great length in a letter, even going so far as to supply the Boston gentlemen with their "Laws," and "Rules and Regulations."

The bank was organized as a profit making venture by investing capitalists and retired merchants with surplus funds to invest in its stock. With that incentive, however, there seems to have been a desire to free the Boston importers from the rich merchants of London to whom they were continually and substantially indebted. If local loans and discounts could be obtained, the Boston importers would need less credit in London and they would naturally be in a better bargaining position when placing orders for merchandise. No longer would it be necessary for them to place their principal orders with the trading house to which they had previously been largely indebted.

Originally the bank was thought of as an institution which would accept deposits but would not emphasize this function. In fact, in its early years, the bank would accept no deposit less than $300, and it would pay no check less than $100 unless drawn to close an account. From 1786 to 1791, a charge was made for keeping money on deposit.

The procedure of granting loans appears strange in comparison with our present day methods. The smallest loan was limited to $100 and the maximum to $3,000. A loan might be granted upon a single name if secured by deposited collateral, either in the form of merchandise or securities; or it might be made upon personal credit of two persons of "ample property." If the former, the loan might run for sixty days; if the latter, only for thirty days. Here, at last, was a market for commercial paper in Boston, and Boston in 1790 was the third largest city in the United States with a population of 18,328. The charge was uniformly six per cent per annum in the form of a discount.

In 1790, the management decided that no discount was to be made for less than $300, and in 1807, to loan not over $70,000 to one person as promisor or endorser. With the continuation of the need of currency as a medium of exchange which was so widespread throughout the colonial period, the bank proceeded to issue its own notes. Many of the early banks which were subsequently organized, unlike the *Massachusetts Bank** had no function except to put their own notes into circulation. The *Massachusetts Bank* began its career by issuing notes of $1.00 to $100, including denominations of $1.50, $2.50, $3.50, and $4.50. After 1792 no notes were issued for less than $5.00.

First Bank of the United States

After the organization of the *Massachusetts Bank,* seven years elapsed before another commercial banking institution opened its doors. The development of commercial banking was slow as the functions of banking continued to be performed by the larger mercantile houses, just as lawyers continued to be consultants on bookkeeping problems after the first firm of accountants was organized in the United States in 1883. The customers of important mercantile houses had bank deposits in the form of their credit balances. On his balance, the customer would draw bills of exchange, which took the place of our modern checks. With the customary long terms, which were often renewed and extended in the sale of merchandise, the importer-wholesaler virtually extended banking credit, especially when interest was charged if an account remained unpaid after maturity.

Ten years after the organization of the *Bank of North America,* banking was still a strange, a little understood activity in our mercantile world. As the early banks operated profitably, capital was gradually drawn into this new field as it is into any new profitable field whether it be in the development of canals, railroads, public utilities, or the manufacture of automobiles or airplanes.

The fourth bank to be organized was the first *Bank of the United States,* located at Philadelphia. This institution obtained its charter from Congress on February 25, 1791. On July 4, 1791, $10,000,000 of stock was placed on sale of which $2,000,000 was taken by the Federal Government to be paid in ten equal annual instalments. Here was a continuation by the national government, almost as soon as it was organized, of that early colonial policy of extending credit to assist in the organization of business enterprises.

The organization of the bank was not completed until December 5, 1791 when the doors were opened for business. For the first time, the *Bank of North America* now had a rival in its own city and that rival had a capital ten times as large as the older institution. Moreover,

---

* In 1903 the bank was merged with the *First National Bank of Boston*, and the now historic name, the *Massachusetts Bank*, relinquished in favor of the homonymic title, the *First National Bank of Boston*.

Thomas Willing resigned as president of the *Bank of North America* to become president of the *Bank of the United States.* A feeling arose in some quarters that the national bank with its tremendous capital would now absorb the three banks already established and prevent the organization of others. However, nothing of the kind happened. The organization of other banks was not discouraged, indicating the need for even more banking credit and showing the ability of the young country to supply the capital.

The operating schedule, like that of the *Bank of New York,* provided that all bills or notes be offered for discount on Mondays or Wednesdays, the discounts settled on Tuesdays and Thursdays, and the results made known on the succeeding days. Branches were opened in Boston, New York, Charleston, and Baltimore in 1792 with boards of directors consisting of local merchants and capitalists, and subsequently in four other cities.

The five thousand shares of stock of $400 par value each, owned by the Federal Government were sold over the years from 1796 to 1802 at a very considerable profit, the last 2,220 shares bringing $580 per share in 1802. The profit on the sale of the entire five thousand shares was no less than $671,800 in addition to which regular dividends averaging 8 13/14 per cent per annum had been received. A substantial block of this stock was purchased by Baring Brothers & Company, at the time, the strongest merchant-banking firm in England, and from them acquired years later by Stephen Girard of Philadelphia.

For twenty years the first *Bank of the United States* furnished a supply of sound paper money to carry on commerce; acted as the fiscal agent of the Federal Government by collecting, transferring, disbursing, and caring for its funds; and provided banking facilities for commercial transactions. Its paper money went into general circulation throughout the country at par. By a majority of only one in each house, Congress refused to renew the charter when it expired in 1811. At this time 18,000 of the 25,000 outstanding shares of stock were owned in Europe. As foreign stockholders could not vote, the bank was controlled from an operating viewpoint, by the stockholders in the United States owning 7,000 shares. When the charter expired, Stephen Girard of Philadelphia, then the most successful merchant and the wealthiest man in the country, was the largest single stockholder.

The bank building with its equipment was now purchased by Stephen Girard who opened his own private banking house for business in May, 1812 as *Stephen Girard's Bank* with many of the officers and employees of the old bank, and with a capital of $1,200,000. This private bank continued in active operation until the death of Girard on December 26, 1831 when the trustees named in his will took possession and liquidated its affairs. Among the assets were 6,321 shares of stock in the second *Bank of the United States,* then valued at $664,715.

Growth in Banking to 1841

The primary functions of commercial banks and trust companies today, are to receive deposits and to extend credit. The early banks were banks of discount, that is, they extended credit by discounting promissory notes. They were not important as depositories, except for governmental funds. In these early years the funds which were loaned came from the capital of the bank and from the circulating notes which it issued, rather than from the credits provided by depositors.

In 1841, for example, the 784 commercial banks had outstanding loans and discounts of $386,487,000 but aggregate deposits only amounted to $64,890,000. The money loaned was provided by capital of $313,-609,000 and by circulating notes of $107,290,000. By 1841, deposit banking had made a little progress in Boston and somewhat greater progress in New York. A financial statement of the *Massachusetts Bank* in September, 1841, showed that its loans amounted to $971,803.97, and its deposits were only $200,059.08. The funds for its loans were provided largely by its capital of $800,000, its surplus of $42,237.45, and its circulating notes of $91,746. The *Bank of New York,* however, had apparently developed the practice of crediting loans to deposits which would then be subject to withdrawal by check. In October, 1841 the New York institution had outstanding loans of $1,672,279.80. Its deposits amounted to $1,279,340.17 and more nearly approximated the loans than was the case with the *Massachusetts Bank.*

In other words, the business man at this stage in the development of commercial banking, did not think of banks in connection with deposits, except possibly in New York City. A bank meant a place to discount his notes. For his discounted promissory notes or trade acceptances he received bank notes, that is, actual currency which he took away with him and put into circulation, not a credit to his deposit account which he would draw upon as needed.

In 1790, there were but three banks in existence. By 1800 there were twenty-eight with aggregate paid in capital of $21,300,000, and in 1811, when Congress refused to re-charter the first *Bank of the United*

States, eighty-eight with aggregate capital of $42,600,000. As industry and commerce expanded, as our population grew, and as the frontier moved steadily westward, the opportunity broadened for the profitable operation of this new type of economic organization which was to take over from the early merchant, that part of his wide activity which represented the lending of money.

With the first *Bank of the United States* no longer in existence, the field was left free for State banking and the opportunity was seized. Between 1811 and 1816 the number of banks increased from eighty-eight to two hundred and forty-six. There was little experience to guide either the legislatures that had the power of incorporation, or the bank managers who were to experiment in this new field. Many banks were organized with absolutely no restrictions. Between 1812 and 1817 the circulation of all bank notes increased from $45,000,000 to $100,000,000.

There were also problems of remittance. The mails were notoriously unsafe. To overcome this predicament, it was not uncommon to send paper money in two different mails. A merchant would cut the bills in halves and mail one-half of each bill at one time, and the other parts by a following mail. If one mail was lost, it was still possible to get the halves redeemed by the bank of issue. James Wier of Lexington, Kentucky followed this practice in March, 1817 when he sent three hundred dollars in paper money to Philadelphia.

By 1820 there were 307 State banks with a capital of $102,100,000, by 1829, 329 with total capital of $110,100,000. In the meantime the second *Bank of the United States* had been organized and was operating on a capital of $35,000,000. The number of commercial banks now went steadily upward every year and in 1837 there were 788 banks operating on a capital of $290,800,000, with aggregate loans of $525,-100,000 and total note circulation of $149,200,000. These figures of loans and circulation represented the greatest amount of bank credit in use up to that time in the history of the United States and were indicative of the increasing volume of commercial business and land speculation which involved the extensive use of credit. The number of banks increased to 901 in 1840 and then dropped to 784 in 1841.

Mutual Savings Banks

The mutual savings bank was the fifth credit institution to become operative in the United States. The first mutual savings bank in America was *The Philadelphia Saving Fund Society* which began business December 2, 1816. The second was the *Provident Institution for Savings,* Boston, which obtained its charter from the General Court of Massachusetts only eleven days later, December 13, 1816. The Boston institution was the first savings bank to be incorporated. The Philadelphia society operated for a little over two years as a voluntary association, without a charter, and without any formal sanction from the State legislature.

The idea of organizing *The Philadelphia Saving Fund Society* was originated by Condy Raquet, at the time, president of the *Pennsylvania Life Insurance Company;* and of the *Provident Institution for Savings* by James Savage, Sr. A public notice issued February 19, 1817 by *The Philadelphia Saving Fund Society* said that "the object of the institution is to aid and assist the poorer and middling classes of society in putting their money out to advantage." Both Raquet and Savage frankly characterized savings banks as "benevolent institutions" or "charity." In fact, the expenses of organizing these early institutions were freely borne by men interested in the movement. These expenses were not large as *The Philadelphia Saving Fund Society,* for many years, was open for business only two days in each week, Monday morning from 9 to 11 o'clock to accept deposits, and Thursday at the same hours for withdrawals.

In the early years of the nineteenth century, farming was the major industry of the country. Farmers, however, were not in "the humble walks of life," nor were they of the "poorer and middling classes." The farmer was thrifty but his thrift did not express itself through deposits of money. "He used his gains, instead, to buy more livestock or more land. His ideal for the prosperous farmer, was one whose acres were extensive, whose buildings were sufficient and in good condition, whose livestock were numerous, and whose children were numerous too." For him the rainy day was never very rainy, and as a safeguard against it, "the farmer had his fodder in the barn, his vegetables in the cellar, his meat in the smoke-house, and his children. . . . It was not until the farmer had ceased to be the most numerous factor in the population, that the day for savings banks arrived." Our credit economy expanded with the growth in urban population.

Over the years the functions of savings banks have become to receive money, to repay it with interest, and to invest the amount which is kept on deposit with the exception of so much as is needed for current expenses, cash reserves, and to meet the ordinary demands of depositors. In mutual savings banks there are no stockholders looking for divi-

ADDRESS

OF

The Philadelphia Saving Fund Society.

TO THE PUBLIC.

TO promote economy and the practice of saving amongst the poor and laboring classes of the community—to assist them in the accumulation of property that they may possess the means of support during sickness or old age—and to render them in a great degree independent of the bounty of others—is a duty incumbent upon all, who by their services or advice have it in their power to effect so desirable an end. Of the charitable Institutions that have had for their object, the amelioration of the human condition, none perhaps deserve higher commendation, than those which, under the title of *Provident Societies* or *Saving Banks*, have lately been established throughout the kingdom of Great Britain. Their design is to afford a secure and profitable mode of investment *for small sums* [returnable at the will of the depositor on a short notice] to mechanics, tradesmen, laborers, servants *and others*, who have no friends competent or sufficiently interested in their welfare, to advise and assist them, in the care and employment of their earnings, and who frequently, from a total ignorance of the accumulating power of money, neglect to provide beyond the wants of the day. To such individuals, we say, these associations hold out the offer of *disinterested friendly services*, and whilst they do so, they pledge the names and characters of those who conduct them, that the confidence which they invite, shall never be violated by mismanagement.

In imitation of those laudable establishments, a number of the Citizens of Philadelphia have associated for similar objects, and aware that without the co-operation of the great body of the community, the benefits of the Institution will not be so widely dispensed as they are capable of being—they respectfully solicit the attention of the public to the following Plan of their Association. If masters would communicate it to their servants, and manufacturers, mechanics and tradesmen to their workmen, a knowledge of the existence of the institution and of its beneficial objects, would soon be circulated far and wide, and its effects could not fail to be visible in the conduct and morals of many.

A pamphlet will soon be published for *gratuitous distribution*, which will contain some short tables of the amount which will be produced in a certain number of years, from the weekly or monthly savings of certain small amounts, and it is hoped that those into whose hands it may fall, will use every endeavor to make the contents of it known to those who they think can be benefitted by the information. It will be observed that the plan of this association differs in one respect from some of those established in England. In the latter a *specific interest* is not allowed, but in place thereof, such interest is calculated as will be produced from the Government Stocks, at the days upon which deposits are made, and the depositor has at his risk the occasional fluctuations. To avoid such uncertainty, as well as to facilitate the calculation of interest, which upon small amounts would be exceedingly laborious, it has in this Institution been deemed most advisable to stipulate the rate of interest whereby all may derive a *certain and similar revenue*. This rate has been fixed at *near five per cent.* which is the most that, taking into consideration the interest on Public Securities, the expenses of the establishment, and the risk of fluctuation in prices, can prudently be allowed. Still, however, should the profits of the business exceed the necessary expenditures, their amount will be divided every three years, amongst the depositors who have remained such during the preceding year.

With this exposition of its views, the Society presents to the Public the following articles of Association, in the confident expectation that its motives may be properly estimated, and that it may meet with the general support of the community.

The office of the Society, *which first commenced its operations by the receipt of deposits on Monday the 2d inst.* will be open every *Monday* morning from 9 to 11 o'clock for the deposit of money, and on every *Thursday* during the same hours, for the payment of such sums as may be withdrawn, at No. 22, south Sixth-street, between Market and Chesnut-streets.

OFFICERS OF THE SOCIETY.

President—Andrew Bayard.

Managers—Samuel Archer, Richard Bache, Charles N. Bancker, Clement C. Biddle, Samuel Breck, John Brown, (N. L.) Turner Camac, Israel Cope, Reuben Haines, Thomas Hale, Henry Hollingsworth, Samuel Humphreys, Adam Konigmacher, John M'Crea, John Moore, Israel W. Morris, Richard Peters, jr. Condy Raguet, William Schlatter, James Schott, Samuel Spackman, John C. Stocker John Strawbridge, Roberts Vaux.

Secretary and Treasurer—George Billington.

Trustees—The President and Cashier of the Bank of the United States.

FROM THE FREEMAN'S JOURNAL AND PHILADELPHIA MERCANTILE ADVERTISER, DECEMBER 13, 1816, COURTESY OF THE MERCANTILE LIBRARY, PHILADELPHIA

Address on the Formation of the Philadelphia Saving Fund Society

dends. All returns on investments, after paying unavoidable expenses, theoretically go to the benefit of the depositors.

The Philadelphia Saving Fund Society

The Philadelphia Saving Fund Society operated as an association from December 2, 1816 to March 31, 1819 when its assets were transferred to a corporation. The charter obtained from the State legislature contained two unusual provisions; first, deposits could not be accepted from any one individual in excess of $500 in any one year, and, second, aggregate deposits of the society were limited to $300,000. These two provisions may seem peculiar restrictions with our background of modern deposit banking, but it must be remembered that the legislature was making economic and financial history, and that it was groping in the dark for a policy.

In an age when there were limited securities in which funds could be invested conservatively, such a policy may be easily understood. This era preceded the days of railroad, industrial, and public utility stocks and bonds. The corporation was just becoming the important vehicle of business operations. In 1826, the limitation on aggregate deposits was raised to $600,000, in 1828 to $1,100,000, in 1833 to $1,500,000, and finally in 1851, all such restrictions were removed.

The amount of annual deposits by individuals, limited to $500 in the original charter was reduced to $200 in 1828, apparently on the initiative of the State legislature. The limit of $200 remained effective until 1869, when it was returned to $500. The limitation stood at this figure until June, 1922 when the limit for yearly deposits was raised to $2,500 and total deposits to $15,000. The initial practice of having the office open to depositors for a few hours only on two days each week continued until 1865, although over these years, the number of hours and the part of the day were changed from time to time. Since 1865, the bank has been open every business day but at varying hours and times of the day.

The problem of investing the deposits, with no precedent, was the basic problem of operating the society successfully. In the Articles of Association adopted on December 4, 1816, investments were limited after great discussion to "Government Securities or other Substantial Public Stocks." Apparently "other Substantial Public Stocks" was to include all securities considered worthy by the investment committee. On February 2, 1818, however, this characterization was changed to "any public stock or substantial security on real estate," in order to widen the scope of investments.

Up to 1818, investments of the society had been limited to obligations of the United States and of the city of Philadelphia. The very first investment was made on December 17, 1816 in $450 United States six per cent bonds, purchased at a premium of one per cent. The entire investments of the society then continued to be made in six per cent bonds of the Federal Government for the first sixteen months of its existence. As a result of the change in policy in February, 1818, funds were now put out on long term credit, that is, on mortgage loans. The first mortgage loan was granted on April 1, 1818, and was for $7,000. This loan was granted to William Strickland and was secured by a mortgage on two lots and a house on Walnut Street, west of Eleventh Street, Philadelphia. No street number is mentioned in the recorded instrument. The loan was extended for two years and apparently was renewed as it was not paid until January 15, 1822.

The second loan was made to "The Mayor, Aldermen and Citizens of Philadelphia on June 4, 1818 and was to mature at the end of seven years, on June 3, 1825. The face amount of the loan was $2,300 but the loan was discounted for $1,444.53, the interest to accumulate so that the full principal would fall due at maturity." On June 3, 1825 the loan was paid by cash of $2,300.

The third loan was the purchase of an $8,000 mortgage already outstanding from one John McCrea. The purchase was made in three payments, $3,800 on June 23, $1,000 on June 29, and $3,040 on July 2, 1818, a total of $7,840 for the $8,000 mortgage. This mortgage had been given by John Wharton to John McCrea on January 26, 1818 and covered a three story brick building and lot, "situated on the South side of Chestnut Street between Delaware, 12th and 13th Streets at the distance of 172 feet Eastward from the East side of the said 13th Street in the said City." On April 27, 1861 when the mortgage had been reduced to $5,500 it was assigned to *The Philadelphia Contributionship;* in January, 1867 to Matthew Hurzinga Messchert, attorney at law; and in January, 1868 to the *Insurance Company of North America.* On January 30, 1879, sixty-one years after the mortgage was taken out, it was paid in full.

On March 4, 1822 the investment policy was again liberalized, this time by the authorization to make loans on security. The first collateral loan of this nature was extended on March 25, 1822 secured by shares of stock in the second Bank of the United States. Subsequently this type of credit, secured by collateral with ample margin became an important source of earnings, but not to the same extent as it was used by the *Provident Institution for Savings.*

When the assets of the Association were transferred to the Corporation on March 31, 1819, they consisted of United States six per cent bonds $9,218.79; mortgages $35,075.36; city loan $1,573.34; and cash $1,250.66, a total of $47,118.15. In a period of slightly more than one year, mortgages had become, by far, the largest asset.

On occasions, second mortgages were taken and apparently title to certain of this property was acquired under default. The following interesting statement exemplifying this experience appeared in the report of January 1841: "It is gratifying to be able to add that of the whole amount of mortgages held by this Society from its establishment to the present hour, namely, $1,857,761.76, not one cent of principal has been lost. In one instance, however, interest for about seven years was lost, owing to the Society having as far back as the year 1818 taken a second mortgage." Since May 6, 1835 it has been the policy to lend only on mortgages where there has been no prior encumbrance.

Provident Institution for Savings, Boston

The printed notice, by which the *Provident Institution for Savings* invited the public, on February 19, 1817 to use its service, pointed out the special attractiveness of its facilities for seamen. When savings banks were later organized at Newburyport and Salem this same emphasis was used. Seamen received this unusual consideration due to the fact that shipping was the first industry in New England to develop a numerous employee class. Long before Boston had any important factory population, there had developed an employee class among the men who went to sea, and who worked at ship-building and rope making. They were the most appropriate body in the world to need early savings banks. Thus it was within shipping and its allied industries that savings banks found their early welcome, and it was not by chance that the first three savings banks in Massachusetts, the *Provident Institution for Savings,* in Boston, the *Salem Savings Bank* organized in 1818 in Salem, and the *Institution for Savings in Newburyport and its Vicinity* organized in 1820; and the first savings bank in Rhode Island, the *Savings Bank of Newport* organized in Newport in 1819, were located in places where shipping was active and where seamen and shipyard mechanics comprised a representative part of the population.

Deposits as small as one dollar were accepted by the *Provident Institution for Savings* but in its early years no interest was credited until five dollars were accumulated. A limit of $1,000 was set for an account. Moreover, no deposit would be received at one time in excess of $100 except in the case of seamen who wished to deposit their wages. One of the most unusual of the early decisions was to the effect that as soon as an account amounted to $100 or more, the bank could compel the depositor to take at its withdrawal, either some stock which the bank owned at current value, or cash, at the option of the bank. Moreover, a depositor did not have the right to withdraw money at pleasure. He could withdraw funds only on semi-annual dates. This practice was soon liberalized and the right to withdraw was increased to quarterly dates. Even then the depositor had to give notice one week in advance so that the bank would be fully prepared to acquire the funds.

According to article 7 of the by-laws of the bank, "The money deposited shall be invested either in the stocks [bonds] of the United States, or of this State [Massachusetts], or in the capital of some of the banks within the town of Boston, or in that of the National Bank, or in private securities, at the discretion of the Trustees, &c., and no Trustee or officer shall ever be a borrower." Before operations actually started a standing committee was substituted for the Trustees, and after January, 1821, the funds were handled by the Board of Investments.*

The method which this standing committee employed to utilize the deposits was very different from the initial policy of the trustees of *The Philadelphia Saving Fund Society*. On the very day on which its doors were opened for business, February 19, 1817, an account was opened with the Manufacturers' & Mechanics' Bank, Boston with a deposit of $1,109. On March 5, 1817 an account was opened with the New England Bank, also of Boston, with a deposit of $2,262. In July, 1818, an account was started with the Massachusetts Bank, the following year with the Suffolk Bank, and in 1820 with the Union Bank.†

Interest was credited by these commercial banks on the balances of the *Provident Institution for Savings* at the rate of six per cent per annum. The first credits appeared in the *Treasurer's Journal,* on July 12, 1817 when $243.60 interest was received from the Manufacturers' & Mechanics' Bank and the New England Bank. The accounts grew rapidly and as they grew, interest increased. At all times the funds were available. Here was the most conservative of banking operations.

* *Trustees' Records, Provident Institution for Savings, 1816-1916;* pp. 2, 7, 23.
† *Treasurer's Ledger, Provident Institution for Savings, Feb. 19, 1817-1824;* pp. 7, 8, 14, 16, 30, 56.

No change was made in this policy for over two years. Earnings consisted solely of bank interest. The first innovation occurred on December 1, 1819 when a loan (apparently unsecured) was made to the Massachusetts General Hospital for sixty days with interest. Then followed a series of loans to individuals secured by the pledge of collateral. On December 8, 1819 a loan of $4,000 was made to Asher Adams, broker. The records merely state that collateral was received as security, no mention being made of the specific collateral which was pledged. Five days later a loan of $3,600 was made to I. F. Dennison for three months secured by $4,000 six per cent United States bonds. On September 25, 1820 a high point was reached when a loan of $100,000 was made to William Gray, Esq., of Boston for twelve months at five per cent interest secured by 1,110 shares of stock in the second Bank of the United States with a ten per cent margin.*

The third use of deposited funds did not take place until September 20, 1820 when the bank made its first purchase of government securities, $20,000 United States bonds, loan of 1820, bearing interest at the rate of five per cent per annum and purchased for $20,300.

A statement of the assets of the *Provident Institution for Savings* was made up for the consideration of the Board of Investments as of February 24, 1821. This statement showed cash of $200,238.21 on deposit at interest with the Manufacturers' & Mechanics' Bank and the Union Bank; $20,000 in United States five per cent bonds; and $187,000 representing thirteen loans to eleven different borrowers, ranging from $500 to $100,000 made at five, five and one-quarter, five and one-half, and six per cent rates of interest. Most of these loans were to run for one year and all were secured by United States bonds, stock in the second Bank of the United States, of the Suffolk Bank, and of the State Bank, except three loans, one of $15,000 to the Treasurer of Suffolk County, one of $5,000 to Harvard College, and one of $12,000 to the Massachusetts General Hospital.

Unlike *The Philadelphia Saving Fund Society* which early in its history made mortgage loans, the *Provident Institution for Savings* seemed to have no early interest in this form of investment for savings. Not until February 22, 1837, twenty years after its organization was the first mortgage loan extended, a loan of $4,500 to Henry K. Hancock secured by property on Washington Street, Boston, for four years at six per cent per annum. The second mortgage loan was made in the following month, on March 31, 1837 to Dr. John Ware for $26,000 also

* *Treasurer's Journal, Provident Institution for Savings, October 27, 1819 to January 9, 1822; pp. 104-151.*

at six per cent per annum. No mention was made in the records of the Board of Investments of the maturity of this loan or the description and location of the property pledged. Within a few days, on April 5 and April 8, 1837 two additional mortgage loans were extended, one for $4,000 for six years and the other for $11,000 for five years. After twenty years of operation, the *Provident Institution for Savings* had a conservative and well rounded policy of diversifying its assets.

Early Increase in Savings Banks

The number of mutual savings banks grew slowly but steadily. By 1820 there were only ten savings banks with aggregate deposits of $1,138,576, or $131.86 per depositor. Only four were located outside of New England, one each at Philadelphia, Baltimore, New York City, and Albany. In the following ten years the number of savings banks increased to thirty-one with total deposits of $6,973,304 or $183.09 per depositor. By 1840 there were sixty-one mutual savings banks with deposits of $14,051,520 or $178.54 per depositor. The concentration continued in the New England States, as only fifteen out of these sixty-one institutions were located in other States.

Building and Loan Associations

Shortly after the rise of mutual savings banks, along came another type of savings institution to encourage regular habits of thrift in small amounts, the building and loan association. Here was the sixth credit institution to play a part in our economy. In this type of institution, shares were issued to members who were required to make regular weekly or monthly instalments, called dues, to pay for each share. These dues received a compound rate of dividend (interest), and the shares became fully paid, or matured at their face value, at a definite date. The funds accumulated in this way were loaned to members to purchase or erect homes. There existed an element of mutuality between savers and borrowers; many individuals saving and borrowing at the same time.

The first building and loan association was organized in 1831. By this time the development of the factory system had given rise to a class of wage-earners, many of whom had settled in the eastern urban cities. The receipt of regular wages, even though small, permitted them to save according to some systematic plan. At this period there were only thirty-six mutual savings banks in existence. Outside of these few savings banks in restricted territories, wage-earners had no place where they could place their savings for an emergency or for old age. Under these conditions, times were ripe for the appearance of some new type of institution which would accept small savings and at the same time assist the saver in acquiring a home in his community.

Oxford Provident Building Association

The *Oxford Provident Building Association,* the first building and loan association in the United States, was organized at Frankford, Pennsylvania, in 1831. At this date Frankford was an independent borough; since 1854 it has been part of the city of Philadelphia. There were two industrial pioneers in Frankford, Samuel Pilling who in 1820 opened a factory for printing calico, and Jeremiah Horrocks who in 1821 founded the Frankford Dyeing, Finishing, and Bleaching Works, the first dye house in Philadelphia County. These two men were both natives of England and realized the beneficial results to be achieved by encouraging workingmen to save systematically. With their business associates, they now advertised a meeting to be held on the night of January 3, 1831 to discuss this very practical subject.

At this meeting it was agreed to organize what would be known as the *Oxford Provident Building Association* to assist every member to acquire a home. Shares with a par value of $500 would be sold to each member, the members agreeing to make an initial or membership payment of $5, and then pay $3 a month on each share. Money received as dues would be offered as loans to the highest bidder among the stockholders who would be entitled to borrow $500 for every share held. It was also agreed that the association would continue in existence until every member had had an opportunity of building or purchasing a dwelling house, after which the balance in the treasury would be divided equally among the members according to their respective shares. No loans were to be made for building houses at a distance greater than five miles from Frankford.

The early records of loans of the association are somewhat confused. It appears, however, that the first loan made from the funds collected from instalment payments was for $375 and was made to Comly Rich. This record occurred in the minutes of the meeting of April 11, 1831, when Rich offered a premium of $10 for the privilege of borrowing this sum. With these funds, Rich purchased a piece of real estate improved with a small house on Orchard Street, and gave a mortgage as security for the loan. Rich apparently had difficulty in carrying this modest burden, as his stock in the association was transferred to one Duffield in July, 1836 and the same time, Duffield acquired title to the property.

The premium, such as that which Rich offered, was used as a means of determining priority in granting loans. Money was offered for sale to members, and the one who bid the highest premium at the auction was awarded the loan. All loans carried interest at six per cent per annum, the interest being payable in twelve equal monthly instalments. During the first year, loans were also made to James Wright and to Henry R. Shock. As funds were acquired in the treasury, loans were made to members, but only to erect or to purchase homes.

The *Oxford Provident Building Association* was, what became known in later years, a terminating association. At a predetermined date all shares would be paid in full, and every member would have had the opportunity to borrow a specified sum of money to acquire a home. The shares in this first association matured January 11, 1841 and the final meeting of the members was held on June 10, 1841. A second *Oxford Provident Building Association* was now organized, on January 30, 1841, and when its stock matured in 1852, a third *Oxford Provident Building Association* was organized.

Brooklyn Building and Mutual Fund Loan Association

Before the second *Oxford Provident Building Association* had been established, a similar association had been started in Brooklyn, New York. In 1836 a group of Brooklyn citizens had visited Frankford to investigate the operations of the first association. So impressed were these men that on their return, they organized the *Brooklyn Building and Mutual Fund Loan Association,* the second building and loan association in the United States. The monthly payments were $2.50 per share and the stock matured at $600 per share. As a terminating association, operations ceased when the shares matured.

Like most credit institutions, there was very little growth in building and loan associations for many years after they were first organized. Little literature was published regarding the development of this institution, and the idea was spread largely by the movement of individuals from communities where associations were operated to new communities. By 1841 they were still going through an experimental period.

ASHE, THOMAS, *Travels in America, Performed in 1806, for the Purpose of Exploring the Rivers Alleghany, Monongahela, Ohio, and Mississippi;* London, Reprinted in Newburyport, 1808.

ATHERTON, LEWIS E., *The Pioneer Merchant in Mid-America;* Columbia, Missouri, 1939.

BENNETT, FRANK P., *The Story of Mutual Savings Banks;* Boston, 1924.

BODFISH, H. MORTON, Editor-in-Chief, *History of the Building and Loan in the United States;* Chicago, 1931.

CAREY, H. C., *The Credit System in France, Great Britain, and the United States;* Philadelphia, 1838.

CAREY, MATTHEW, *Essays on Public Charities of Philadelphia;* Philadelphia, 1830.

Commerce of Rhode Island, 1775-1800, Volume II; Massachusetts Historical Society Collections, Seventh Series, Vol. X; Boston, 1915.

DOMETT, HENRY W., *A History of The Bank of New York, 1784-1884;* New York, 1884.

Executive Documents, 1st Session, 22nd Congress, *Documents Relative to the Manufactures in the United States, Collected and Transmitted to the House of Representatives, in Compliance with a Resolution of January 19, 1832, by the Secretary of the Treasury;* Two Volumes, Washington, 1833.

FEARON, HENRY BRADSHAW, *Sketches of America;* London, 1818.

First National Bank of Boston, 1784-1934; A brief history of its 150 years of continual existence with emphasis on the early days of its first forebear, the Massachusetts Bank—Organized in 1784. Privately printed; Boston, 1934.

FOSTER, B. F., *The Merchant's Manual, Comprising the Principles of Trade, Commerce and Banking;* Philadelphia, 1838.

GOUGE, WILLIAM M., *A Short History of Paper-Money and Banking in the United States;* New York, 1835.

GRAS, N. S. B., *The Massachusetts First National Bank of Boston 1784-1934;* Boston, 1937.

HARRIS, T. M., *The Journal of a Tour into the Territory Northwest of the Alleghany Mountains;* Boston, 1805.

HENDRICK, BURTON J., *Bulwark of the Republic;* Boston, 1937.

JONES, FRED MITCHELL, *Middlemen in the Domestic Trade of the United States, 1800-1860;* Urbana, Illinois, 1937.

Knox, John Jay, *A History of Banking in the United States;* 1900; Revised Edition 1903, New York.

Leach, Josiah Granville, *The History of the Girard National Bank of Philadelphia;* Philadelphia, 1902.

Levine, Samuel W., *The Business of Pawnbroking;* New York, 1913.

Michaux, F. A., *Travels to the West of the Alleghany Mountains in the States of Ohio, Kentucky, Tennessee, and Back to Charleston, by the Upper Carolinas;* London, 1805.

Millar, Bruce, *A Calendar of Walter Baker & Company, Inc. and its Times, 1765-1940;* New York, 1940.

Minutes of the Common Council, New York City, 1805-1830; New York.

Montgomery, Thomas H., *A History of the Insurance Company of North America of Philadelphia;* Philadelphia, 1885.

Nevins, Allan, *History of the Bank of New York and Trust Company, 1784 to 1934;* New York, 1934.

Records of New Amsterdam, 1653-1674; Minutes of the Court of Burgomasters and Schepens; Volume I, New York, 1897.

Wilcox, James M., *A History of The Philadelphia Saving Fund Society, 1816-1916;* Philadelphia, 1916.

Volumes Previously Cited

Bolles, Albert S., *The Financial History of the United States, 1774-1789;* New York, 1880.

Clark, Victor S., *History of Manufactures in the United States, 1607-1860;* 1929 Edition, New York.

Davis, Joseph Stancliffe, *Essays in the Earlier History of American Corporations,* Two Volumes; Boston, 1917.

Dewey, Davis Rich, *Financial History of the United States;* 1902; Second Edition 1903, New York.

East, Robert A., *Business Enterprise in the American Revolutionary Era;* New York, 1938.

Harrington, Virginia D., *The New York Merchant on the Eve of the Revolution;* New York, 1935.

Nettels, Curtis P., *The Roots of American Civilization;* New York, 1938.

Porter, Kenneth Wiggins, *The Jacksons and the Lees;* Two Volumes, Cambridge, 1937.

Weeden, William B., *Economic and Social History of New England, 1620-1789;* Two Volumes, Boston, 1890.

V · Evolution of Credit Institutions, 1841-1941

*I*N 1837, the fourth and most stunning depression in our history up to that time, materialized. A depression in 1784 had followed the excessive importation of English merchandise by the seacoast importer-wholesalers who expected a tremendous demand for English manufactured products and luxuries after the years of struggle for independence. In 1792, excessive speculation, especially in the stock of the early banking institutions including the first Bank of the United States, brought about a sharp financial crisis and a short panic. In 1819, a depression was precipitated when the second Bank of the United States presented an accumulation of notes to State banks for redemption, and these banks unable to meet their demand obligations, suspended specie payment and the brightly colored bubble of artificial bank note credit collapsed. A readjustment period of three to four years ensued.

The panic of 1837 far overshadowed these earlier commercial and financial escapades. Here was real, high pressure trouble. It was widespread and fundamental. The economic and financial difficulties leading up to the climax are of particular interest, as the succession of events had a salient influence, at least upon the mind of one well-known business man, Lewis Tappan, for the need of comprehensive credit information regarding business enterprises in a rapidly expanding commercial and industrial country. These events are unfolded in chapter VII.

From 1837 up to the days of the Civil War, credit outside of the mercantile field was extended entirely by pawnbrokers in the personal loan field; by commercial banks to industry and commerce; by fire, marine, and life insurance companies, mutual savings banks, and build-ing and loan associations primarily in the long-term mortgage loan field. There was little need for the wide variety of specialized credit granting organizations which compete so earnestly with each other for profitable, and sometimes unprofitable business in the world of 1941.

During and after the Civil War the industrial cities of the North attracted masses of wage-earners. With this rapid increase in concen-trated population, a substantial portion coming directly from Europe, there developed an extension of instalment merchandising to low-income classes and an expansion in the small loan business. In the latter part of the nineteenth century and the early part of the twentieth century, additional types of credit granting organizations were evolved, factors, title guarantee and mortgage companies, personal loan com-panies, credit unions, industrial banks, sales and discount finance com-panies, Stock Exchange commission houses, to serve both the business enterprise, the consumer, and the speculator. During the nineteenth century, the use of credit expanded as a means of developing commerce, industry, and speculation; in the twentieth century these new specialized types of credit institutions arose as a means of stimulating and support-ing commerce and industry, and in the flowering years leading up to the Great Depression, of intensifying speculation. Today some form of credit is available to everyone.

Mercantile Credit

The last chapter described the gradual change in typical mer-cantile credit terms from twelve months during the colonial era to six months in the first third of the nineteenth century, and with a tendency toward the use of specialized terms by different divisions of industry and commerce. Eight years before the outbreak of the Civil War, in 1852, Edwin T. Freedley wrote in a footnote in his volume, *A Practical Treatise on Business,* "everybody knows that goods can be bought in the eastern cities from ten to fifteen per cent lower for cash, than upon a credit of six months." This assertion referred to purchases by retailers from eastern wholesalers. The reference did not relate to discount terms but to the fact that it was customary, at this late date, as in the colonial days, to have different prices for the very same mer-chandise, depending upon the length of time which the buyer expected to take in liquidating his complete indebtedness.

A collection of eighty-five actual invoices covering merchandise sold in the years from 1843 to 1860,* showed eighteen invoices with no terms of sale printed on the billhead and sixty-seven with terms of sale. These invoices covered actual sales made by manufacturers, importers, jobbers, and wholesalers of almost as many kinds of merchandise as there were invoices; watches, clocks, music boxes, silverware, jewelry, drugs, gloves, thread, hosiery, scarfs, ribbon, umbrellas, parasols, canes, paints, looking glasses, brushes, feather dusters, pots, brass and iron fittings. The sellers were located in New York, Philadelphia, Boston, Providence, Buffalo, Troy, Trenton, Waterbury, New Haven, Lowell, Worcester, and Springfield.

Among the sixty-seven invoices which contained actual selling terms, there were a variety of terms, but by no means the variety which would be found today in the examination of a similar number of invoices of concerns in as many different lines of industrial and commercial activity. The most commonly used selling terms called for "5% off" which was quoted in twenty-three instances. On six invoices the terms of "4% off," and on three the terms of "6% off" were used. On other invoices, allowances were quoted on different types of merchandise up to "30% off" in the case of manufacturers and dealers in stoneware.

The vast majority of the invoices carried the simple terms of "5% off," "4% off," "6% off," or "30% off." Apparently on these particular purchases, a discount of the percentage specified on respective invoices was allowed for immediate cash payment, although one of the terms indicated that the discount would be allowed if taken within thirty days. Several of the terms also provided for payment by notes drawn for four months, several at six months, and a few at eight months, if the accounts were to be settled on net terms. In other words, the customary mercantile terms up to the Civil War called for payment by notes or trade acceptances running from four to eight months, but with a very respectable allowance, the word "discount" was only occasionally used, for immediate payment in cash.

Terms Before the Civil War

In a paper presented at a meeting of the Massachusetts Historical Society entitled *Reminiscences of Seventy-five Years,* William Endicott, a venerable Boston business man, outlined the mercantile terms of sales in customary use prior to the Civil War. He carefully explained:

* Warshaw Collection, Albany, N. Y.

Domestic goods were sold by the mill agents to jobbers upon eight months [credit], and cotton goods for export to China and the East upon twelve months' credit. The jobbers sold to retailers upon six months [credit] with a liberal discount for cash within thirty days. It will be observed that the eight months' credit accorded to jobbers enabled them to double up their indebtedness; that is, the large purchases for the beginning of one season would be made before the purchases of the previous season had been paid for, so that the domestic goods commission houses were practically supplying capital for the jobbers, who, in turn, were to a great extent carrying the retailers. When the jobbing houses had attained great importance, say by 1850, they found it quite convenient to buy domestic goods upon eight months [terms] and sell them without profit to retailers upon thirty or sixty days, thus procuring capital with which to import foreign goods.

This description was concerned particularly with the commission dry goods trade in and around Boston. The terms of sale varied with the trade sold. Sales of cotton goods for export to China and the Far East were made on twelve months' terms, to jobbers on eight months, and from jobbers to retailers had been reduced by 1850 from six months to thirty and sixty days. All obligations were settled by the usual promissory notes or trade acceptances.

That payment by notes, generally running for six or four months, was the most customary arrangement just prior to the outbreak of the Civil War would also seem to be emphasized by three trade announcements, which were distributed about this time. The first announcement dated January 1, 1855 was made by James M. Beebe & Co. of Boston, importers and wholesalers of woolen cloth, carpets, hosiery, gloves, dress goods, linen and linen goods, to the effect that ". . . . we shall, from this date, aim to offer sufficient inducements to our customers, to limit the term of credit to six months." The second announcement appeared in a form letter dated March 24, 1857 written by W. E. Coffin & Co., also of Boston, importers and wholesalers of pig iron, fire bricks, clay, wrought ship spikes, railroad spikes, and rolled iron. This letter read, "As usual at the close of the month we hand you Account, for amount of which, (if found correct), please forward us Note at six months from average time, say March 19th . . . ." The third announcement was signed by four dealers in "Iron, Steel, &c.," Cornett & Nightingale, G. Congdon & Co., Duty Evans, and Levi A. Packard, all of Providence, Rhode Island, on December 23, 1857, and stated that ". . . . believing the system of long credits to be unwise and injurious, ... have resolved to be governed by the following rules, to take effect on and after the first day of January, 1858, viz: 1st. All accounts in our favor, not settled sooner, will be made up to the first days of January and July in each year, and when they amount to less than One Hundred Dollars, they will be considered due in Cash, on presentation. 2d. The credit on all accounts amounting to One Hundred Dollars or more, shall in no case exceed an average of four months. 3d. No extension of time on accounts, or renewals of notes, in whole or in part, will be granted, unless additional and satisfactory security by endorsements or otherwise, is furnished."

The fact that mercantile credit terms were being shortened in some lines of trade but not in the dry goods trade was discussed in an article in the Providence *Journal* and partially reprinted in *Hunt's Merchant Magazine and Commercial Review* in 1858.* An analysis had been made for this article giving the exact selling terms used by a commission house at Providence in selling cotton bleached goods during the three months ending September 30, 1857 for a local mill, ". . . . fifty packages sold on eight months credit; forty on nine months; eleven on ten months; seventy-nine on average of eight-and-a-half months; and sixty-six on average of nine-and-a-half months, making 246 packages sold on the total average of very near nine months credit." This study then continued to explain that it was customary to sell fancy goods such as prints and other colored fabrics on even longer credits. "Prints were sold in the summer of 1857, in large lines, on eighteen months credit. An extensive manufacturer of heavy brown and colored goods, reports that he had nearly one thousand packages sold by one commission house in New York, for the quarter ending October 1, 1857, and the principal partner acknowledged to him that two-thirds of them were sold on ten months' credit. . . . . All other departments of trade are shortening their credits; groceries and provisions are sold mostly for cash, and never on a longer credit than four months; the hardware dealers have reduced their terms from six to four months; all the supplies for our [Providence] mills are either for cash or credit; cotton and wool are sold in all the markets at the South and New York for cash; why should we continue to sell the articles when manufactured on eight months' or ten months' credit. . . . ?"

The typical method by which New York wholesale dry goods distributors transacted business about this very time, has been described by a prominent nineteenth century New York merchant, Edward D. Page, one time Chairman of the Committee on Commercial Law of the Merchants' Association of New York. In this description, Page wrote that eight months' credit was the customary terms of sale used by the New York wholesalers, but he also mentioned "two liquidations

* Volume XXXVIII, March, 1858, pp. 394-395.

per annum" which would mean that six months' terms were likewise used here as in the other important distributing centers. The detailed picture which Page painted is very enlightening:

The records [1861] of my business show that in New York alone there were over three hundred wholesale dry goods merchants selling goods to western and southern retail houses, and financing the merchandise sold for a long enough term to provide for its complete turnover and cash liquidation from the proceeds of the crops. The customary term of that credit was eight months, and one, or at the most two, liquidations per annum were all that were commonly expected. The retail buyer had no general credit; he established relations with one or two wholesalers who made themselves familiar with his character, his ability, and the conditions under which he made his sales. The fabric of the trade was built up upon this intimate knowledge of personality, which often resulted in the complete assumption of a buyer's indebtedness by a single wholesaler in each of the merchandise lines which he handled, dry-goods, groceries, leather goods, hardware, etc. The goods themselves were mostly staple, accumulated by the wholesaler in anticipation of his busy season, and purchased in his warehouse by the personal selection of the buyer. The goods were then billed, the bill approved by the buyer, and settled immediately either by a note or draft for acceptance at eight months' sight. The transaction so far as the sale was concerned, was closed; the seller knew exactly the amount and terms of the credit extended, and the buyer often pledged himself to seek no further credit until the note was paid. ¶ At home he had no credit, for there was nobody to extend it; the country bank was almost unknown; its functions, so far as they were the needs of a rural or semi-rural community, were performed in large measure, by the retail merchant himself, who traded upon an elaborate system of accounts receivable and payable, which needed very little cash. My father, who graduated from one of these country stores, has often told me that they frequently went through a week's business without so much as five dollars in real money. At the harvest season the consumer settled by turning over his crop to the retail merchant; he, in turn, shipped it to a market, where it was sold and with the proceeds the note was paid. ¶ The farmer was so dependent upon the credit extended by the country merchant, and he upon that given by the wholesaler, that the seller practically charged whatever price he pleased for his merchandise, profits were several times what they now [1914] are under our cash system, and New Yorkers who had never done a business of over three or four hundred thousand dollars a year retired early with fortunes or competences. To obtain money with which to pay the manufacturer or importer for his stock in trade, the wholesaler discounted the notes of the country merchant, of course endorsing them and thus made the double name paper. . . . ¶ The system had other disadvantages than those of excessive profits due to credit control. It was easy to counterfeit the bill receivable with the endorsed accommodation note, and great losses ensued in various lines of trade from this practice. A crop failure or other disaster in any section not only bankrupted its local merchants, and dishonored their paper, but strained or broke the wholesalers operating in that region.*

---

* "Single-Name Commercial Paper under New Banking System—The Merchant's Viewpoint" by Edward D. Page in *Trust Companies*, March, 1914, Volume XVIII, Number 3, pp. 206-207.

This quotation gives a fascinating description of the typical retail merchant who came to New York twice a year and selected the exact merchandise he desired in the warehouse of the seller. Merchandise was sold on the premises after an examination, not by sample or by catalogue with the implication that when delivered it would be the same quality as the sample, or as described in the catalogue. The retailer purchased his requirements of dry-goods from one dry-goods distributor, groceries from one concern in the wholesale grocery trade, and leather goods from one concern in that line. Then came the Civil War and the every-day methods of transacting business changed.

Terms During the Civil War

From 1862 until 1879, when specie payment was resumed, the purchases of all raw materials by manufacturing plants, and finished merchandise by wholesalers and retailers, were made in a fluctuating unit of monetary value. In July and August, 1864, when military success was running against the Union forces, the average monthly value of paper money dropped to thirty-nine cents on the gold dollar. The constant daily fluctuations in the value of every-day currency in terms of gold naturally brought an increased hazard into the extension of credit by mercantile houses. Manufacturers and wholesalers that had been selling merchandise on terms of eight, six, or four months' credit, or for cash with "5% off" were naturally unwilling to continue to use the long net terms, even though established by custom, for fear that the greenback currency with which an invoice would be paid at maturity, would be worth less than at the time of sale. The very same situation had existed during the Revolutionary War. Uncertainty and apprehension have never been conducive to the use of long terms of sale. Moreover, a seller's market developed with demand for merchandise greater than the supply, so that the manufacturer was in an ideal position to select strong customers who could meet obligations on shorter terms. Mercantile credit became customary for thirty days and in some cases for only ten days. In addition, a premium in the form of a cash discount for early settlement became widely used.

Terms Since the Civil War

The seller's market which developed during the years of the Civil War was gradually succeeded by a buyer's market after the War as the production of articles for peaceful consumption began to outrun demand. This changed background, together with the resumption of specie payment in 1879, became the signal for selling on somewhat longer terms, such as sixty days instead of thirty days, but a discount for cash payment within a short period, continued to be allowed.

The shift to shorter net terms which developed out of the economic and financial conditions of the Civil War now became quite generally established at thirty and sixty days, and was facilitated by the rapid growth in the means of communication and transportation. Buyers could travel comfortably to their market several times each year, order by mail, or from samples carried by salesmen, instead of once or twice each year on the floor of the warehouse of the wholesaler. This trend to shorter selling terms became stabilized but with an almost infinite variety in the terms of sales as we entered that period of tremendous industrial and commercial expansion with increased specialization in every form of economic activity.

Since the resumption of specie payment in 1879, we have been in the modern era of commerce so far as the use of mercantile terms of credit have been concerned. Two broad influences, which have been just as constant and just as effective as air pressure and gravity upon an airplane in flight, have gradually modified terms of sale in most divisions of industry. These two forces have been classified as the nature of the product being sold, and the competitive conditions of the market. Each of these two influences on the constant evolution of terms of sale has several contributing factors. Terms of sale, for example, are constantly being affected under the intensive conditions of existing business activity by six factors which have to do with "the nature of the product":

1. Perishable articles are sold generally on shorter terms than articles which can be easily kept. Fresh fruits and vegetables, for example, are sold to retail grocers on ten and fifteen day net terms, while canned fruits and vegetables are sold on terms of two per cent discount in ten days, net thirty days.

2. Merchandise for immediate consumption is sold on terms which are materially shorter than products which are sold for seasonal use. Fresh meats, for instance, are sold by the packers on seven day terms, while automobile tires in the Winter are sold on Spring dating.

3. Raw products are sold on short terms and finished products generally on longer terms. This tendency is exemplified in the textile industry; cotton grey goods are sold uniformly on ten day net terms, while finished print goods are customarily sold on seventy day terms.

4. Standard articles which are well advertised have terms which are somewhat shorter than unadvertised brands. Plated silverware is sold on thirty to ninety

day net terms, while miscellaneous jewelry is sold to retail jewelry stores on terms of four to six months' promissory note.

5. Fixed assets, such as machinery and fixtures tend to be sold on short terms, as the buyer should have sufficient cash to pay for fixed investments. These terms, however, have become modified during recent years by the inter-position of the specialized finance company that pays cash to the seller, and then accepts instalment payments on an extended period of time from the buyer.

6. A small sale has a tendency to be made on short terms and a large sale on long terms. Candy and most immediately consumable products, for example, are sold for cash on short terms, whereas pianos and houses are sold on long terms.

No-one of these greatly varied factors is the determining feature in the evolution of terms of sale in a particular division of industry or commerce. Many forces working together result in certain terms which are then modified still further by competitive conditions in that line of business and between competing lines of business. Four influencing factors arise from these competitive conditions:

1. A weak seller tends to receive cash from a strong buyer. For instance, a farmer sells hogs to the meat packers for cash. Prior to the passage of the Robinson-Patman Act in 1936, however, large buyers tended to force concession from weak sellers, such as the practices which existed in chain store and mail order house buying. This pressure usually took the form of additional concessions.

2. A strong seller sometimes shortens terms. This practice is exemplified by the packers' selling terms which have gradually been reduced over a period of many years, to seven days. Sometimes, however, when a strong seller is anxious to increase sales, buyers are given longer terms to create the desired volume.

3. As competition becomes more intense among sellers, additional concessions are offered to buyers.

4. Manufacturers of well-advertised products make their own terms. This is typically shown by the selling terms used by the manufacturers of the well-known brands of cigarettes. Any terms which they should use would undoubtedly be freely accepted by their customers.

The modifications in mercantile selling terms which have taken place during this entire modern era have been very gradual and have had no disturbing effect upon the distribution of merchandise. Instead of twelve months' credit which was used so widely in our colonial period, or six months' terms used so widely one hundred years ago, different terms of credit have come to be used by the almost infinite number of different divisions of industry and commerce. Sugar is sold by refineries to wholesale grocers on terms of two per cent discount in ten days, while automobiles are most widely sold on terms of twenty-five per cent down payment and the balance in eighteen monthly instalments. Between these two extremes are such lines of business activity as manufacturers of automobile parts and accessories, canners of fruits and vegetables, and wholesalers of paper, which customarily extend credit on terms of two per cent discount in ten days, net thirty days; manufacturers of chemicals, and wholesalers of drugs and drug sundries, which sell on terms of one per cent discount in ten days, net thirty days; manufacturers of ladies' coats and suits, infants' clothing, and knitted outerwear, which distribute their merchandise on terms of eight per cent discount on the tenth of the following month; manufacturers of furniture, and wholesalers of men's and women's shoes, which sell on terms of two per cent discount in thirty days, net sixty days. Within particular divisions of industries, individual concerns are always departing from the generally accepted terms. These changes occur as a result of the interplay of the wide variety of national and local economic forces, and the more specialized influences which have been outlined. Changes are still taking place in terms of sale and will continue to take place just as long as competition and the democratic way of life predominates in American industry and commerce.

A survey covering the year, 1939, made by the Department of Commerce indicated that sales by all manufacturing enterprises in the country aggregated $56,828,000,000, and by all wholesalers aggregated $55,112,000,000. Of the manufacturing sales 90.4 per cent, and of the wholesale sales 92.2 per cent, it was estimated, were made on the infinite variety of mercantile terms of sale gradually evolved since 1879 to suit the peculiar needs of particular divisions of industry and commerce in our unfolding technological economy.

Pawnbrokers

As late as 1869 the regulation of pawnbrokers was left in the hands of "local governments of such towns and cities" as were "duly authorized for the purpose in their several charters." The result was a wide diversity in the regulations as well as in the rigor of their enforcement. This situation was carefully described at the time:

Thus while Albany .... lets the pawnbrokers pretty severely alone, Buffalo allows (or did a short time since) the collection of 3 per cent. per month, with a forfeiture at one year. Rochester restricts the interest to 20 per cent. per annum, but allows a forfeiture at the end of six months. Baltimore not very adroitly strives to dodge the woeful enormity of exacting usury by a funny device which fixes the interest at 6 per cent. per annum, but forces a renewal of the pawnticket every month, and the payment of a "ticket fee" of 6¼ cents for each ticket under $3; of 9 cents for

$5 and under, and so on up, in a gradually diminishing scale, as the sum climbs out of the reach of the really starving poor. By the system, a loan of a dollar pays 6¾ per cent. per month, with a forfeiture and sale at the end of six months, the surplus, "if any," to be held for the owner. Philadelphia somewhat resembles Baltimore in various respects, and allows 3 per cent. additional on sums of one dollar, with sale and forfeiture at the end of one year.*

Evolution in Operations

During the second half of the nineteenth century, pawnbrokers, to a limited degree served the purpose of commercial banks for those immigrants who seemed reluctant to keep their savings in banking institutions. Surplus cash, carefully and slowly saved would often be invested in diamond rings, sometimes for the wage-earner himself, and sometimes for his wife, wealth which seemed far more real and tangible to these individuals than records in a bank book. When ready to start a business, the jewelry would be taken to a neighboring pawnshop for a loan, and if the enterprise succeeded, the property redeemed.

Loans were made on almost any article of value with which the pawnbroker was reasonably familiar. One pawnbroker who was quite a fisherman became widely known for his loans on fishing tackle, one who was a musician, for his loans on valuable violins. In these fields they were expert judges of values. Others would loan against laces, clarinets, embroideries, shotguns, rifles; mariners would pledge their sextants, newspaper photographers their cameras, and railroad men their watches. Before the days of five and ten cent stores, many loans were made to carpenters against tools. A hammer which cost one dollar, or one dollar and one-half, was always good for a loan of 25c. to 50c. Today this business has disappeared with the price of tools near the low point for all time.

Some business was even handled by mail and by express. Jewelry would be sent in by actors and actresses on the road in need of funds. If the loan requested was too high from the viewpoint of the pawnbroker, a telegram would be sent stating the maximum loan which would be made. Even today a reasonable volume of business is handled by New York pawnbrokers for out-of-town borrowers.

Although the bulk of the loans at this time is made against diamonds, jewelry and silverware, there are pawnbrokers who will loan against almost every type of article including clothing. One of the strange modern corollaries of this ancient business is the extent to which

* *Harper's New Monthly Magazine*, Volume XXXIX, Number 1, June, 1869, p. 125.

policemen and firemen borrow $5 on Winter overcoats in the Spring of the year. This practice has grown up, not because of the need of funds but because the overcoats will be more safe from theft and moths in the care of the pawnbroker than at home. The payment of interest is really in the nature of a storage charge, a by-product of pawning.

Growth in Number

According to the census of 1850 there were seventy-two persons engaged as pawnbrokers in the United States. The twenty-fourth annual report of the *Boston Society for the Prevention of Pauperism* in 1859 mentioned that there were upwards of fifty pawnbrokers established in the city at that time, more than two-thirds as many as in the entire country nine years earlier. The yearly volume of business of pawnbrokers increased substantially after the Civil War.

In 1869 there were seventy-one licensed pawnbrokers in New York City. It was estimated that the profits of the licensed pawnbrokers were moderate and that at least two-thirds of the loans made on the pledge of personal property in New York City were made by unregulated lenders at higher rates. In 1860, 19.8 per cent of our population was urban, in 1880, 28.6 per cent, and in 1900, 40 per cent. With this rapid growth in urban population, wants were multiplied, literature flourished, and the number of active pawnbroking establishments increased steadily. The census of 1870 showed 384 pawnbroking establishments in the country, five being owned and operated by women.

On January 1, 1911 there were 1,976 pawnbrokers. Then the number decreased very materially, probably the result of increased competition from remedial loan societies, personal loan companies, credit unions, and more recently, from the personal loan operations of commercial banking institutions. The census of 1930 showed 1,509 pawnbrokers in existence, and the business census of 1935 a drop to 1,142.

Fire and Marine Insurance Companies

In 1841, there were one hundred and thirty-one domestic mutual and stock fire and marine insurance companies, and branches of five English companies, active in the United States. Thirty-eight of these particular domestic mutual and twenty-two of these particular domestic stock fire and marine insurance companies were in active operation in 1941, one hundred years later.

The great New York fire of 1835 closed what may be termed the pioneer period in American fire insurance underwriting. This fire was probably the most spectacular early tragedy to insurance companies; for three days it burned, completely laying waste to the business section, consuming six hundred and forty-eight houses and business premises. The destruction to property was fearful but no less terrible were the economic consequences. There had been forty active fire insurance companies in New York City operating under the laws of the State of New York and all but two became hopelessly in debt over-night as a result of this single catastrophe. These two enterprises had under-written very few risks on lower Manhattan property.

To resuscitate the other thirty-eight companies from utter ruin the State legislature passed an act on January 18, 1836, allowing them to pay their losses on a pro-rata basis to the extent of their assets, and then to continue operations on new capital to be raised from their stock-holders, but entirely released from the responsibilities of meeting the unpaid portion of their former claims. Ten companies availed them-selves of this legislation and obtained additional capital to continue in operation. The remaining twenty-eight never recovered.

Evolution in Operations

The public now demanded greater stability in fire insurance companies. Massachusetts led the way in 1837 by providing that a reserve fund be maintained to carry out their contracts. Here was the beginning of the unearned premium fund. In 1853 the New York legislature followed Massachusetts by enacting a similar law.

Special agents, better known as field men, became necessary as aggressive companies underwrote fire insurance at greater distances from their home offices. The strictly local company could supervise and care for its business through the employees of the home office. When distance became too great for direct home supervision, men had to be employed for this special type of work.

The incompleteness of the information furnished to the home or to the branch office regarding the physical characteristics of a distant risk and its environment presented a basic problem. Occasionally, special agents would make diagrams of the smaller towns they visited, indicating on these rough maps the risks of the company. On May 1, 1856, William H. Martin, a civil engineer, was employed by the *Aetna Insurance Company*, Hartford, Connecticut, to make maps of important points where risks had been assumed. At the outbreak of the Civil War, surveyors at work on these diagrams in the South for the *Aetna Insurance Company* were arrested as suspected spies, their notes were confiscated, and they themselves were turned over to vigilance committees and held until they proved the innocence of their activities. This highly specialized business was developed by one of Martin's assistants, D. A. Sanborn, into the very successful concern, now nationally known as the *Sanborn Map Company, Inc.*

Growth in Number and Assets

Records have been compiled since 1860 from the figures of fire and marine insurance companies licensed to operate in New York State. These compilations probably give the most reliable indication of the growth in this field of activity in the absence of comparative yearly data for all companies in the United States. In 1865 there were 174 fire and marine insurance companies operating in the Empire State. The number increased to 227 in 1875, and then decreased gradually but steadily to 144 in 1895. From this point an expansion took place to a peak of 403 companies in 1930, dropped off to 350 in 1934, and then fluctuated to rest finally at 395 fire and marine insurance companies as of December 31, 1939, the latest year for which this compilation is available.

The invested assets of the enterprises operating in New York State amounted to $97,630,000 in 1865. The figure has fluctuated somewhat since that time but with a general upward tendency to reach a peak of "admitted" assets for the 395 companies on December 31, 1939 of $2,698,290,000. These assets were invested in a far different manner than those of the early fire and marine insurance companies which placed such a large percentage of their funds in mortgage loans. Of the total "admitted" assets as of December 31, 1939, 39.9 per cent was invested in stocks mostly of corporations listed on stock exchanges but including a fairly noticeable proportion of bank stocks. The second largest division of investments consisted of United States Government securities, municipal, industrial, public utility, and railroad bonds representing 39 per cent of the total. Then followed cash representing 11.4 per cent, uncollected premiums 4.6 per cent, real estate both used in the business and repossessed 2.9 per cent; mortgage loans only $38,038,000 or 1.4 per cent, and collateral loans $730,000 or .03 per cent. Other assets made up the difference of .8 per cent. Readily marketable securities comprised the greater part of the assets of these companies.

Great New York Fire of 1835

Over the years, fire and marine insurance companies gradually invested more and more of their funds in liquid assets and a smaller portion in mortgage loans as mutual savings banks, building and loan associations, life insurance companies, and title guarantee and mortgage companies, played an increasingly stronger rôle in the mortgage loan field. As of December 31, 1940 there were approximately 682 fire and marine insurance companies of all types in existence in the United States with total "admitted" assets of about $3,076,000,000.

Mutual Life Insurance Companies

Although life insurance in the United States is primarily a development of the past one hundred years, it was occasionally, very occasionally, taken out in earlier years. In 1717, *The Fund for Pious Uses* was created by the Synod of Philadelphia, to be used primarily for the relief of needy ministers and their families, but also for other purposes. In 1759 this fund became *The Corporation for Relief of Poor and Distressed Presbyterian Ministers and of the Poor and Distressed Widows and Children of Presbyterian Ministers,* and a charter was secured from Thomas and Richard Penn to operate a life insurance company. Part of the funds were used for the redemption of ministers' families from Indians who held them in captivity. Only a small amount of life insurance business appears to have been transacted in the early years as in 1845 one policy was in force and that for only $1,000. In 1875, authority was obtained to transact a general life insurance business, and since that time the corporation has become an important enterprise, operating under the shortened title of the *Presbyterian Ministers' Fund.*

Several of the early fire and marine insurance companies also had authority to insure lives, the first being the *Insurance Company of North America.* No active effort was made to solicit this type of business as little scientific knowledge was available regarding life risks, but the board acted on applications which were submitted to it. On May 26, 1796, for example, policies of $24,000 on the life of John Holker to run from June 6 to September 19, and $5,000 on the life of Bon Albert Briois de Beaumez for eighteen months, were issued. It was not uncommon at this time to grant policies on the lives of ship owners or masters against capture by pirates, principally on the Barbary coast. Policies of this kind usually read that should the insured "be killed in any attempts made to defend the said ship against the said Algerians or Corsairs, or should he die before or after his captivity, the insurers should not be bound to pay any other sum or sums than would have been expended in attempting the ransom." Such policies were a supplementary mercantile side line to the marine insurance business.

In 1812 the *Pennsylvania Company for Insurance on Lives and Granting Annuities* was chartered. Six years later the *Massachusetts Hospital Life Insurance Company* was established, and in 1830 *The New York Life Insurance and Trust Company* was organized. All of these concerns were business corporations which were organized to earn a profit for stockholders. Like the early fire and marine insurance companies they operated in an experimental way in this little understood field of life insurance, but gradually the handling of corporate trusts and personal trusts, and the operation of commercial banking departments became their primary objects.

During these experimental years, life insurance policies were issued under very rigid restrictions and only for short periods. Absolute forfeiture resulted from the non-payment of any premium to all companies, except the *Presbyterian Ministers' Fund* which had modified this provision in 1792. Forfeiture also resulted from such varied causes as death by the insured's own hands, any untrue statement in the application, death upon the high seas, death in consequence of a duel, death by the hands of Justice, death in the known violation of any law of the United States, or of any State or Province wherein residence and travel were permitted, residence or travel south of the southern boundaries of Virginia and Kentucky between July 1st and November 1st, or at any time beyond the settled limits of the United States and the British Provinces of Canada, Nova Scotia and New Brunswick, or military or naval service, the militia not in actual service excepted.

Many of the insurance companies that had become financially involved by the New York City fire of 1835, had carried on incidental operations in the life insurance field but in the rather inadequate method of the day had kept no segregation of premiums, reserves, or assets to apply to the different types of insurance. As a result of the bankruptcy of thirty-eight out of the existing forty insurance companies operating in New York State, individuals who had been paying premiums for life insurance were suddenly bereft of any present or future benefits. They were wiped out just as completely as a speculator on a stock exchange who could put up no more margin in a falling market. The New York State legislature finally passed a very appropriate act in 1849 prohibiting a "company making insurance on the health and lives of individuals . . . . to take any other kind of risks."

The Mutual Life Insurance Company of New York

In 1842, Alfred Pell, an expert in marine insurance, Morris Robinson, who had been cashier of the New York branch of the second Bank of United States, Joseph Blunt, and John V. L. Pruyn, organized *The Mutual Life Insurance Company of New York* to introduce into the United States the mutual life insurance principle practiced by the famous *Old Equitable Company* of London. On February 1, 1843, this new enterprise, the first typically mutual life insurance company to become active in the United States, issued its first life insurance policy. This event marked the beginning of a new era in American life insurance development and just as important a development in the creation of tremendous funds which would seek constant outlet through the extension of various forms of credit into our economic world. By the end of its first year of active life, 470 policies amounting to $1,480,718 had been underwritten. By the end of 1845, 908 policies were in force for nearly $3,000,000 of insurance.

The cash premiums which were received for the payment of these policies built up reserves which needed to be invested much more rapidly than the capital and the reserves of the early fire and marine insurance companies. In its charter which had been passed by the State legislature on April 12, 1842, *The Mutual Life Insurance Company of New York* was conservatively restricted to investing its funds in bonds and mortgages on unencumbered real estate within the State of New York, the real property to secure such investments to be worth twice the amount of the mortgage. Not more than one-half of the premiums received could be placed "in public stocks [bonds] of the United States, or of this state or of any incorporated city in this state."

At a meeting of the finance committee on February 9, eight days after the first policy was sold, the president was "authorized to purchase Three thousand Dollars of the Six per cent Stock [Bonds] of the United States Loan of 1862, with Cash on hand, at a rate not to exceed 102% and . . . . a further purchase of $7000 of the Same Stock [Bonds] at the same rate, as the funds of the Company came in." At the next meeting of the committee, the president reported that the bonds could not be purchased at 102. The committee then authorized the acquisition of "$4,000 of the New York City 6% Water loan at par" and to extend the purchase as the funds accumulated to $10,000. By March 7, ninety-four policies had been issued and aggregate premiums of $7,627.97 had been received. Of this amount $7,000 was immediately placed in the New

York City Water loan, the very first investment of the company. By April 4, the limit of $10,000 had been reached.

The second investment was the typical mortgage loan. On June 2, 1843 it was agreed to lend "Gouveneur M. Wilkins Esq on three houses in Grand Street — Ten thousand dollars for One year at 6 per cent — $6000 to be paid as soon as the papers shall have been performed, and the balance at the convenience of the Company." A little over five months later, on November 28, it was agreed to lend Doctor Benjamin Beldon $7,000 at 6 per cent per annum, secured by a mortgage on "Two four Story Brick Houses & Lots N° 345 and 347 Rivington near Mangin Street — 22 by 75 feet. One vacant lot adjoining — 22 by 75 feet. One three Story Brick house and Lot N° 68 Mangin Street near Rivington — 20 feet 7 inches by 100 feet." The loan to Gouveneur M. Wilkins was discharged on June 1, 1852, while the loan to Doctor Beldon was repaid partly on March 1, 1851 and the balance on June 1, 1858.

When December 31, 1843 came around the company had taken in cash of $35,610.13 since the first policy had been issued. Of this sum $10,000 was invested in New York City Water loan bonds, $2,055 in New York State bonds bearing five and one-half per cent interest, and $17,000 in mortgage loans. This practice of investing a greater part of its accumulating reserves in mortgage loans became a basic policy. As of December 31, 1844, $50,250 was invested in mortgage loans and $21,997.50 in city and State bonds. On December 31, 1845, $146,650 was invested in mortgage loans, $31,920 in State and city bonds, $16,730.40 was on deposit with the Bank of New York, and $202.82 cash was on hand.*

New England Mutual Life Insurance Company

The *New England Mutual Life Insurance Company* located at Boston was chartered April 1, 1835 by the Commonwealth of Massachusetts but its first policy was not issued until February 1, 1844. The members of the State legislature seemed to have been a little wary of new ideas like life insurance and so stipulated that a guaranty fund of $100,000 would have to be raised by Judge Willard Phillips, the founder, and his associates, one-half to be paid in cash before the company could issue a policy. This fund was finally raised by 1844, many of the contributors having assisted under the impression that they were giving away money for benevolent purposes. By 1854 the business was on a

* *Minute Book of the Board of Trustees, March 7, 1843 to June 4, 1855,* pp. 4-80; and *Minute Book of Finance Committee, February 9, 1843 to January 27, 1858,* pp. 1-6, of The Mutual Life Insurance Company of New York.

firm foundation and the guaranty fund had actually been returned to the ninety-eight astonished subscribers.

For the first ten months of its operations, the *New England Mutual Life Insurance Company* invested its steadily increasing funds in bonds and stocks. The very first investment was made January 10, 1844 when the Finance Committee "voted That the Actuary be authorized to purchase $30,000 of Mass. State Stock [Bonds] at 4% advance Also —100 Shares of Eagle Bank Stock at not exceeding one per cent advance. Also 100 Shares of State Bank Stock at not exceeding $58. per share." On January 24 and February 8 it was voted to purchase United States five per cent bonds and on February 17 "Nashua Manf. Stock at ½% advance." In succeeding meetings, the Finance Committee decided to invest in a wide variety of securities; stock in the Providence Rail Road, more "Eagle Bank Stock," shares in the Boston & Maine Rail Road Co., and stock in the Appleton Manf. Company.

On October 12, 1844 the first mortgage loan was made. The Committee authorized "a loan of $5,000 to Asa Stearns on bond & Mortgage & 2000 when house mortgaged shall be finished. The House being located in Emory Street." The second mortgage loan was authorized on November 4, a loan of $4,000 to John Hunon on property located on Charleston Street, Boston, and the third loan was authorized on November 23, a loan of $7,500 to E. H. Derby secured by a bond and mortgage on property on Hanover and Brighton Streets, Boston.

When the annual report was prepared as of November 30, 1845, the aggregate investments amounted to the quite substantial sum of $107,844.55 of which the largest single item was "Notes and mortgages" of $58,600. In this phrase, "notes" did not refer to promissory notes. The word was used in the place of "bond" as many loans were made "on note secured by mortgage." Then followed investments in bank stocks of $20,971.50, "manufacturing stocks" of $11,000, United States and city bonds $9,000, railroad stocks $7,000, and premium notes of $1,273.05. Premium notes were instruments received along with part cash for the payment of yearly premiums. If such a note was not met at maturity it was a claim against the cash surrender value or the death claim. In succeeding years the amount of premium notes increased quite substantially.

The first loan against collateral was granted on July 11, 1848. The minutes of the Finance Committee read, ". . . . Six thousand five hundred & thirty one 19/100 dollars in notes endorsed by S. Lawrence Treaˢ Bay State Mills, including one of 2000$ secured by collateral security of C. P. Curtis & four hundred & fifty dollars in 5 shares Boston & Prov R R Co. also a loan of 1500 dollars to Ja^s Savage secured by collateral sec^y" Apparently the *New England Mutual Life Insurance Company* was diversifying its investments by discounting endorsed notes receivable for representative business enterprises. At the very next meeting of the Finance Committee held on September 12, 1848, an investment of this nature which had been made in the interim was approved, "2895 83/100 dollars in notes endorsed by S. Lawrence Treasurer of Bay State Mills." This transaction covered two notes, one drawn by J. W. Blodgett & Co. for $2,587.27 and the other drawn by Wilkinson Stetson & Co., for $308.56."*

On November 30, 1853, after almost ten years of successful operations, the investments aggregated $697,137.07 representing a wide diversification in credits. The largest single item continued to be mortgage loans which amounted to $235,873.75. Then came investments in banks and other stocks of $165,679.10, loans secured by collateral of $154,-360.97, premium notes which now had reached $59,273.25, city securities of $58,000, railroad bonds of $18,950, and real estate of $5,000.

Creation of Cash Surrender Value

In the early days of life insurance, a surrendered policy was considered by many companies to be a justifiable source of profit. Elizur Wright, the great actuary who made scientific valuation of policies imperative as the Insurance Commissioner of the State of Massachusetts, visited England in 1844. During this visit he was invited to witness an insurance auction at the Royal Exchange. "The first thing he saw was an old man standing on the life insurance auction block, his policy being offered by an indifferent auctioneer to the highest bidder. The old man was pathos incarnate. For forty-four years, Wright learned, he had been paying his regular annual premium and now he could carry the burden no longer. His entire investment, representing lifelong thrift, went under the hammer for whatever it would bring. Somebody who cared nothing for the insured bought the policy at a small fraction of its obvious worth and waited impatiently for the unfortunate old man to shuffle to his grave. Or perhaps he did not wait. Wright heard some very ugly rumors of policy buyers who thought nature too slow and hired the handiest villain to dispatch the insured. He investigated with the thoroughness and persistence that were characteristic of him and

* Minute Book No. 1 of the Finance Committee of the New England Mutual Life Insurance Co., January 10, 1844-January 21, 1880.

uncovered certain cases where the evidence fairly shouted 'Murder!' "

The year after Elizur Wright made this very enlightening visit to England, Ephraim Paulk of Bangor, Maine, holder of policy number 78 of the *New England Mutual Life Insurance Company,* surrendered his policy and was paid a fair sum in cash for it, apparently the first time a surrendered policy was given a cash value. In 1853, Elizur Wright completed his tables of "net valuation," establishing the first scientific basis for determining the cash value of a life insurance policy. In 1858, the State of Massachusetts enacted these tables into law.

Growth in Life Insurance Companies

The life insurance companies authorized to operate in New York State increased from fourteen in 1859 to seventy-one in 1870, dropped to twenty-nine in 1885, increased to forty-three in 1906, and then fluctuated up and down to arrive at thirty-seven companies which operated from 1919 to 1922. From that date the number increased steadily to fifty-seven life insurance companies in 1938, and to sixty in 1939, the latest year for which figures are available. In the meantime the "admitted" assets of these companies made the most spectacular growth ever recorded in the history of finance. In 1859, the fourteen companies operating in New York State had assets of $20,536,000. By 1875, the amount had increased to $403,142,000, by 1900 to $1,723,000,000, by 1925 to $10,016,000,000, and by 1939 "admitted" assets had jumped to the immense total of $25,615,000,000.

In 1906, at the time of the Armstrong insurance investigation in New York State, there were approximately 138 legal reserve life insurance companies in the country. A legal reserve life insurance company is one that agrees to pay a definite sum or benefit which cannot be scaled down, that charges a definite premium which cannot ordinarily be increased, and which is required by law to establish a basic reserve for each policy issued and in force. A study of life insurance companies of the country made by the Securities and Exchange Commission for the Temporary National Economic Committee indicated that there were approximately 365 legal reserve life insurance companies in existence in 1938 with total assets in excess of $28,000,000,000. The fifty-seven companies which were active in New York State in 1938 represented only 15.6 per cent of the total number, but their "admitted" assets represented 91.5 per cent of the aggregate "admitted" assets of all legal reserve life insurance companies in the United States.

Of these tremendous assets held on December 31, 1938, the study of the Securities and Exchange Commission pointed out that the largest item, representing 27.69 per cent, consisted of industrial, public utility and railroad bonds. The second largest item representing 26.28 per cent was bonds of the Federal Government, States, municipalities and other political divisions. Then came mortgage loans on urban and farm properties comprising 19.17 per cent, policy loans and premium notes of 11.62 per cent, real estate owned 7.3 per cent, stocks in business enterprises 2.17 per cent, and miscellaneous items of 5.77 per cent. Mortgage loans comprised a representative percentage of these tremendous assets.

Notwithstanding the fluctuation in the number of companies operating in New York State, the "admitted" assets had gone steadily upwards. The rapid growth in the amount of these assets has been one of the outstanding phenomena of our day and age. The *Metropolitan Life Insurance Company,* New York, on December 31, 1940 had "admitted" assets of $5,357,000,000 and was the largest financial institution in the country. Of this sum $1,063,435,000 was invested in securities of the Federal Government and $937,226,000 represented mortgage loans.

Specialty Insurance Companies

On February 12, 1850 the *Franklin Health Assurance Company* was given the privilege by the Massachusetts legislature to insure against loss of wages from accident or otherwise. On April 23, 1850 the *Haverhill Health Insurance Company* was empowered to write similar accident insurance. In succeeding years there followed the organization of companies to insure against an almost infinite variety of possible contingencies, casualty and surety companies, burglary, fly-wheel, plate-glass, automatic sprinkler leakage, steam boiler, title, tornado, automobile, and credit insurance.

As insurance companies engaged in one or several of these underwriting specialties, additional funds were brought together in the form of capital, surplus, and reserves which were invested to bring a monetary return. No comparative figures are available over the years giving the full number of insurance companies engaged in these various types of activity or the total amount of their "admitted" assets. There would seem little doubt that their assets have gone steadily upward.

The first figures issued by the Superintendent of Insurance of the State of New York on this group of companies was published in 1865 and disclosed assets of $998,000 for three concerns. In 1880 five specialty insurance companies were listed with assets of $2,312,000, by 1900 there were thirty-one with $47,326,000, and by 1920 eighty-eight with "admitted" assets of $529,088,000. This field of specialty insurance has shown its most rapid growth since 1920, the latest compilation for 1939 giving one hundred and thirty-four companies operating in New York State, with their "admitted" assets at a record high point of $1,744,000,000.

Of the total "admitted" assets of $1,744,000,000 fifty-two per cent represented investments in United States government, State, municipal, railroad, public utility, and industrial bonds. Then followed investments in stocks of all kinds but mostly listed securities of 20.1 per cent, cash 14.2 per cent, uncollected premiums 7.8 per cent, owned real estate 3 per cent, while mortgage loans only amounted to $22,122,000 or 1.3 per cent, and other miscellaneous assets 1.6 per cent.

Commercial Banks and Trust Companies

Second in importance only to mercantile credit in the development of the ever-increasing tempo of our commercial and industrial activity, has been the strategic part played by commercial banking institutions since the *Bank of North America* opened for business in Philadelphia in 1782. During the early years of the nineteenth century, both mercantile and banking credit continued to be granted by retail merchants in the less populated sections of the country, just as similar credit had been freely extended by importer-wholesalers located in the eastern seaport trading cities during the entire colonial era.

Typical operations of this nature were carried on as late as the 1840's. J. M. D. Burrows of Davenport, Iowa, for example, regularly received money on deposit from his customers. "At this time, and for a number of years afterward," he wrote, "we had no bank. Some of our farmers had money that they were afraid to keep at their homes. Especially was this the case at the Groves, and on the Wapsie, and even in Clinton County. The farmers, consequently, brought their money in and deposited it with me, the same as if I were a banker." This service ceased only when a bank was finally organized nearby. Customers withdrew their money as needed or took it out in merchandise.

Banking During the Independent Treasury System

In 1834, over a year before the expiration of the charter of the second *Bank of the United States,* Federal funds were gradually being withdrawn and placed on deposit with what economic historians have termed Jackson's "pet" banks. Federal funds were kept in this manner until August, 1846 when the independent treasury system under which the Federal Government was to keep its own funds, was established. Vaults and safes in new treasury buildings were now provided at Washington, and at the mints and customhouses; New York, Philadelphia, Charlestown, New Orleans, and St. Louis were the principal centers of deposit. This system was really a protest against the laxity in the operations of State banks as well as of a national bank.

Losses from poor banking practices in the western States were greater than in the East. In Indiana fifty-one institutions failed between 1852 and 1857, with serious losses to note-holders as well as to other creditors. In Michigan tricks were employed to deceive the official bank commissioners regarding the amount of specie on hand, the same boxes or bags of specie being quickly transferred from one institution to another to perform a continuous service of reserves.

Almost as important a defect in the banking practices of this period from a business viewpoint, was the lack of uniformity of security in bank-notes. In the colonial days, a merchant might receive several different kinds of paper currency with different current values, but now a large retail store might actually receive and pay out hundreds of different kinds of notes, some good, some doubtful, and some presumably worthless as every bank had its own individual notes in circulation. This ambiguous situation grew worse as the circle of business activity was enlarged by the construction of railroads.

A steady increase took place in the number of commercial banking institutions, from 691 in 1843, to 879 in 1851. No figures are available for 1852 but by the following year, the number of active banks had dropped to 750. Then a rapid expansion to 1,208 took place by 1853 and the upward tendency continued to 1,601 in 1861.

The measure of the credit extended by these banks was the volume of outstanding loans. Over the years from 1841 to 1862 there occurred a constant oscillation in the amount of loans and discounts but with a constant upward trend. The low point was reached in 1843 when the outstanding volume only amounted to $254,500,000. The high point materialized at the opening of the Civil War in 1861 when the loans and discounts aggregated $696,800,000. The figures of deposits and circulation, showed somewhat similar hills and valleys.

On January 1, 1862, the number of banks had dropped to 1,496 with aggregate capital of $420,000,000 and note circulation of

$184,000,000. These banks were established under the laws of twenty-nine different States and their circulation was based on a great variety of security, of different qualities and quantities. "In some States the bill-holder was secured by the daily redemption of notes in the principal city; in others by the pledge of State stocks [bonds]; and in others by coin reserves." In some States there were boards of bank commissioners who made frequent and thorough examinations of the condition of banks under their supervision, while in others no such boards existed or existed only in name; in a few States the public was informed as to the condition of the banks by the publication of periodical statements, but as a rule, publicity was not customary. These defects were forceful arguments in favor of the establishment of a national banking system.

National Banking Act

The election of November, 1860 gave a severe shock to public and private credit; southern banks withdrew large amounts of money on deposit in northern banks; loans were contracted; and by the middle of the month the "panic" was widespread. The government resorted to an issue of treasury notes under the Act of December 17, 1860, but so low was the public credit and so disturbed the public mind that to float the notes at par it was necessary to pay between ten and twelve per cent interest. The banking situation grew steadily worse and on December 30, 1861 under the lead of the New York City banks, specie payment was suspended throughout the country.

In November, 1862 only nine of the States required the circulation of notes to be secured by State bonds. The State securities pledged to support outstanding notes only amounted to $40,000,000, leaving over $120,000,000 provided for by other assets, sometimes by none. About 7,000 different kinds of bank notes were in circulation, to say nothing of successful counterfeits. Over 3,000 varieties of altered notes were afloat, 1,700 varieties of spurious notes, and approximately 800 varieties of imitations, making more than 5,500 varieties of fraudulent notes.

The act to provide a national currency secured by a pledge of the United States bonds was approved February 25, 1863. The system provided that a commercial banking institution, upon depositing bonds with the Treasurer of the United States, could receive circulating notes to the amount of ninety per cent of the current market value of the bonds deposited but not exceeding ninety per cent of the par value. After the passage of this act, the national banking system developed slowly.

The new banks were organized for the most part in the western States of Ohio, Indiana, and Illinois, due to the greater need of circulation in that part of the country. On October 1, 1863, 66 national banks had deposited less than $4,000,000 of United States bonds; a year later there were 584 with a circulation of $65,000,000. It was not until the Civil War was over, when the State bank issues felt the heavy hand of taxation, that the national system took more complete possession of the commercial banking field.

Rise of Trust Companies

The *New York Life Insurance and Trust Company*, which was organized in 1830, was the first concern to incorporate with the word "trust" in its title. Although the early stock life insurance companies immediately began to take on trust functions, it was not until well after the Civil War that the trust companies began to make real strides. The cumulative growth in private fortunes in the decades following the Civil War, both in number and size, provided increased personal trust business in the lifetime of wealthy individuals as well as after their decease. In 1869 the New York Stock Exchange required that the shares of all listed stocks be registered at some independent agency as a result of the questionable issue of securities by the Erie Railroad Co., in the historic squabble between Jay Gould, Jim Fisk, and Daniel Drew on one side and Commodore Vanderbilt on the other. In 1875 the Comptroller of the Currency reported only thirty-five active trust companies, all located in New York City; in 1900 he reported 290, widely distributed geographically.

In the development of their operations, trust companies prior to the Civil War began to accept "trust deposits" which were in the nature of savings accounts. It was a short step to accept demand deposits and to grant loans in direct competition to commercial banks. As this development took place, State commercial banks retaliated by organizing trust departments. Finally national banks were permitted to assume certain trust powers by section 11(k) which became a part of the Federal Reserve Act in December, 1913, when not in contravention of State or local laws. An amendment to the Federal Reserve Act passed by Congress on September 26, 1918 increased the list of trust powers which national banks could exercise, and finally the McFadden Act of 1927 granted perpetual charters to national banks which greatly facilitated their conduct of trust activities.

At the present time there is little or no practical difference between commercial banks which carry on extensive trust functions and trust companies. Increased competition has gradually brought each type of institution into the other's field. On June 29, 1940, 1,540 national banks in large cities were exercising extensive fiduciary powers.

Growth in Commercial Banking Institutions

By 1880, seventeen years after the National Banking Act had become the law of the land, there were only 2,726 national, State, and private commercial banks and trust companies. By 1900 the number had increased to 9,730. During the years of our great industrial and commercial expansion the number increased rapidly and steadily to a peak of 29,770 commercial banking institutions in 1922 with aggregate deposits of $35,347,000,000. In the following eight years the number of banks dropped to 23,473 but in the meantime deposits continued their upward climb to $50,631,000,000. The latest available figures covering operations for the year ending June 29, 1940 disclosed a continued drop in the number of commercial banking institutions to 14,466 but a still greater increase in aggregate deposits to the high point of all time, amounting to the tremendous sum of $60,522,000,000.

Federal Reserve Banks

Under authority of the Federal Reserve Act of 1913, twelve *Federal Reserve Banks* were organized in different parts of the country "to furnish an elastic currency, to afford means of rediscounting commercial paper, to establish a more effective supervision of banking in the United States, and for other purposes." National banks were obliged to become members and to subscribe to capital stock of the *Federal Reserve Bank* in their district, while State banking institutions, both commercial and savings, were given the privilege of becoming members.

The twelve *Federal Reserve Banks* hold the large part of the banking reserves of the nation and perform many of the basic banking functions of the country. From a credit viewpoint, however, they have been essentially bankers' banks, having the power and the resources to rediscount commercial paper as defined by law for member banks. Prior to the organization of these institutions one of the most serious defects in our banking system had been the absence of any strong centralized agency to which the banking institutions of the country could turn in time of need. This function has been adequately performed by the *Federal Reserve Banks* since their organization. On December 31, 1920 rediscounts of $2,719,100,000, the largest year-end volume on record, had been made for 6,941 member banks. Twenty years later, on December 31, 1940 rediscounts amounted to only $2,915,000.

By an Act of June 19, 1934, Congress enlarged upon the powers of these banks as reserve institutions by authorizing loans directly to established business enterprises to furnish working capital. An established concern that was unable to obtain a loan from its own depository bank or banks for any reason could now make application for a loan directly with two other institutions, the *Reconstruction Finance Corporation* and a *Federal Reserve Bank*. From June 19, 1934 to December 31, 1940 the twelve *Federal Reserve Banks* received 9,609 applications for loans directly from business enterprises amounting to $431,236,000. Of these applications 2,908 for aggregate loans of $212,-510,000 were approved. From June 19 to the end of 1934, 5,108 applications for loans of $190,798,000 had been received; in 1940 applications had fallen to 191 and the amount of loan requests to $26,011,000.

The largest amount of outstanding direct loans and commitments amounted to $61,142,000 and was recorded at the end of 1935. The amount then gradually decreased to $14,378,000 as of December 31, 1940 of which $9,152,000 were loans and $5,226,000 were commitments to purchase such loans. It is evident from these figures that the volume of loans made directly to established commercial and industrial business enterprises by *Federal Reserve Banks* has never been large.

Mutual Savings Banks

In 1834, seventeen years after the *Provident Institution for Savings* was organized at Boston, the State of Massachusetts passed the first general law pertaining to savings banks. This law made obligatory the issuance of an annual financial statement, limited deposits to $1,000 per individual, and limited investments to bank stocks, mortgages (to the extent of 75 per cent of the deposits), bonds of the United States, of the State, and of any county, city, or town in the State, and loans upon the credit of individual names. The last permission seemed to have been granted only in the event that the deposits could not "be conveniently invested in any or all of the other modes." In 1838 Virginia passed a general law governing the operations of savings banks, in 1843 Connecticut, in 1858 Rhode Island, and in 1875 New York State.

Insurance and Liquidity Funds

In 1900, 40.9 per cent of the resources of all mutual savings banks were invested in mortgage loans; in 1910, 50 per cent; in 1920, 47.6 per cent; and in 1931, 54.6 per cent. Over these years there had been a tendency to invest a larger and larger portion of the assets of the mutual savings institutions in obligations secured by real estate, even though the percentage remained well below the figures permitted by the laws of the various States. Mutual savings banks are not expected to be liquid institutions like commercial banks with their demand deposits. The collapse of the real estate market, both urban and farm in the early years of the depression did, nevertheless, present a potential problem to mutual savings banks which could turn to no reserve institution to raise liquid funds in an emergency.

The savings banks of Massachusetts solved this problem in 1932 by furnishing the capital to organize the *Mutual Savings Central Fund, Inc.,* to which they could turn for loans against collateral in time of real need. An amendment to the act in 1934 provided for the insurance of the full deposits and accumulated interest of mutual savings banks within the State by this Fund. In 1933, Connecticut chartered the *Mutual Savings Banks Central Fund, Inc.,* not to insure deposits but to provide liquidity in an emergency by granting loans to mutual savings banks within the State, with or without security at rates of interest determined by the board of directors. It may also buy the assets of any member mutual savings bank at any value which the corporation may determine, even in excess of market value. In 1933 the Savings Banks Association of New Hampshire created a "loan fund," which is unincorporated, and which stands ready to provide liquidity by extending credit to member mutual savings banks against collateral. This Association has the right to borrow from all member banks for the aid of any member bank. It does not insure deposits.

In 1933, New York State with greater potential problems, made more elaborate preparations by organizing three agencies as reserve institutions for the mutual savings banks within the State; the *Savings Banks Trust Company* to furnish liquidity by purchasing the securities of mutual savings banks or making loans to members against the pledge of assets; the *Mutual Savings Banks Fund,* which is not a corporation, to insure the deposits up to the full legal limit of $7,500; and the *Institutional Securities Corporation* to purchase mortgages from savings banks and so provide a central market for mortgages held by them.

Two credit agencies of the Federal Government provide additional reserve facilities for mutual savings banks as well as other financial institutions, but very few mutual savings banks have taken advantage of these facilities. These two agencies are the *Federal Deposit Insurance Corporation* to which fifty-three mutual savings banks were members on December 31, 1940, and the twelve district *Federal Home Loan Banks* to which eleven mutual savings banks were members. The functions and operations of these two Federally controlled credit agencies are described in the following chapter.

Growth in Number and Deposits

From the 61 mutual savings banks in existence in 1840, the number went up slowly but steadily to a peak of 652 in 1900. The years of greatest growth were encompassed by the decade between 1860 and 1870 when 239 mutual savings banks were opened. By 1930 the number had fallen off largely through mergers and consolidations to 606. At the same time the number of depositors and the aggregate deposits continued their upward trend without interruption. In 1900 there were 5,370,000 depositors with total deposits of $2,134,000,000 or $397 per depositor. In 1930 the 11,895,000 depositors had aggregate deposits of $9,191,000,000 or $772 per depositor.

Early in 1941 when the one hundred and twenty-fifth anniversary of mutual savings banking was celebrated, there were 540 mutual savings banks in existence in seventeen States holding deposits of approximately $11,000,000,000 or almost one-sixth of the total bank deposits of the nation. Massachusetts led all States with 192 mutual savings banks while Pennsylvania, the first State to have established one of these institutions, had only seven. New York State had 134 and these banks held more than one-half of the deposits in all mutual savings banks. As of January 1, 1941 there were 15,624,440 depositors in mutual savings banks with average deposits of $679.56.

There are no mutual savings banks south of the Potomac River, only three west of Minnesota, and none at all in the great expanse of territory that lies west of the Mississippi River except those in Minnesota, Washington, and California. Thus in the whole cotton belt, the corn belt, and the wheat belt, except Minnesota, there is not one mutual savings bank. Over the years the farmer has been disposed to use his savings to acquire more land, more livestock, more farming tools, or to erect more buildings. The individuals who need savings banks are those who are unable to put their savings back into their occupations. In other words, only where there is a numerous employee class has there seemed to exist the real need for mutual savings banks.

Building and Loan Associations

The oldest building and loan association in continuous operation in the United States is the *Decatur Building Association,* of Frankford, Pennsylvania. This concern had its inception at a meeting held in Decatur Hall on December 12, 1848. Ten days later a constitution was adopted and officers were elected for the first year. The books were opened for business on January 10, 1849, when the second *Oxford Provident Building Association* was eight years old.

At this meeting the first loan which amounted to $1,200 was made to Jos. H. Comly who paid a premium of $107.50 to borrow this sum of money. The second loan was made on April 11, 1849, a loan of $500 to Sarah Ann Woodington who paid a premium of $100. At the meeting of the directors held in the following month, on May 9, 1849, the third and fourth loans were granted, one for $400 to Mary Ann Campbell who paid a premium of $82, and one of $600 to Joseph Meelick who paid a premium of $120. Rather high premiums were paid for these early loans. The loan to Joseph Meelick for some reason did not go through as the minutes of the directors' meeting held on August 8, 1849 carried the following information without explanation, "On motion it was resolved that the Secretary shall be directed to charge Joseph Meelick with two months interest on loans bought by him and given up; and that said loans be sold to the highest bidder."*

The *Decatur Building Association* like the three *Oxford Provident Building Associations* was organized as a terminating association. The by-laws were amended in 1852 to authorize issuance of four series of shares each year and that system has been continued. The association was incorporated in 1855, reincorporated in 1866, and chartered perpetually in 1886.

Geographical Spread

No early accurate records are available regarding the number of active building and loan associations. By 1893, sixty-two years after the first association had been organized, and the first year for which

* *Minute Book No. 1, Decatur Building Association, pp. 1-7.*

accurate information is available, there were 5,598 in existence with 1,349,437 members and total assets of $473,137,000. Associations of this nature, which assisted wage-earners by the extension of credit to purchase or to erect homes, spread rapidly when the basic idea of their existence became widely known.

After the initial start in Pennsylvania and New York, the movement seems to have spread to the south where an association was opened in South Carolina in 1843. Maryland, New Jersey and Connecticut were credited with having associations by 1849. Then came Massachusetts in 1852; Maine, 1854; Virginia, 1859; District of Columbia, 1861; Georgia and California, 1865; and Texas, 1866. The last section of the country to have a building and loan association was what is now the State of Oklahoma. Here one was organized in 1890.

Types of Associations

Four major types of organizations have been used, the terminating plan, the serial plan, the permanent plan, and the permanent capital plan. The *Oxford Provident Building Association* was a typical example of the terminating type of organization. The distinguishing characteristic was the fact that the existence of the association ceased when the object for which the members became associated, had been accomplished. Its life was rather definitely fixed and when the shares of stock which were purchased in the process of repaying a loan had matured, the affairs of the association were officially wound up. In this process all stock would be issued as of the same date; new members could be taken in after organization only if they paid all back dues, plus a bonus, to place themselves on an identical footing with the original subscribers. As the association progressed toward the maturity of its shares, the number of potential borrowers decreased. Since the funds could be lent only to members, the names of those who had not borrowed, would be placed in a hat and drawn to determine who must take the money. If the member thus selected was not ready to utilize the loan, he had to find some other non-borrowing member who would be willing to assume his place; if he failed to find such an individual, he was obligated to take the loan.

In the 1850's, the serial plan arose. Under this plan, instead of issuing only one series of stock, several series would be issued at stated intervals. Dues would begin on each series when the stock was issued and the shares accordingly would mature at different dates. The members of each series would constitute practically a terminating association among themselves. Profits would be distributed to the shares of each series in proportion to the amount of dues paid and the length of time the money had been on deposit with the association. In many States the terminating plan was never used, for the advantages of the serial system had become so established by the time building and loan activity in those States began, that the serial form was immediately adopted. The serial form quite completely dominated the building and loan picture until the entrance, upon a wide scale, of the permanent plan about 1880. It is still in wide use throughout the country.

Under the permanent plan, the issuance of stock at stated regular intervals in series and the payment of a large sum upon the maturity of a series, were eliminated. The distinguishing features of the permanent plan are that shares may be issued at any time, that the accounts of individual members are kept separately, that is, individual shares may start and mature without reference to the status of other shares. This type of organization attracted more money to associations and the necessity for the premium payment on loans began to disappear.

The basis of the fourth plan, the permanent capital plan is the issuance of a non-withdrawable class of stock which has definite contractual liabilities to the other classes of members of the association. Following the panic of 1894-1895 the *Equitable Savings and Loan Association of Oregon,* like most savings and loan associations of the day, found itself in possession of considerable real estate acquired under foreclosure. As the disposal of this real estate might ultimately have involved a direct loss, the inequity of permitting members to withdraw or to receive payment of matured shares was fully recognized, as such accounts would not have borne their share of the potential loss. Accordingly, in 1899, this association issued $150,000 of non-withdrawable, reserve-fund stock. Each shareholder contributed his pro-rata portion toward the payment of this stock. From that date the shareholders suffered no loss of earnings from capital tied up in real estate, and they were permitted to withdraw freely as they secured no undue advantage over members who remained in the association.

Federal Savings and Loan Associations

Since 1933 it has been possible to organize building and loan associations under Federal charters. In accordance with the Home Owners' Loan Act of 1933, they are termed *Federal Savings and Loan*

Associations and are organized and supervised by the Federal Home Land Bank Board. On December 31, 1933 there were 59 of these institutions in existence. As of June 30, 1940 there were 1,429 in forty-five States.

Federal savings and loan associations operate similar to State building and loan associations. Loans are restricted to $20,000 and must be on properties located within fifty miles of the office, except that fifteen per cent of loans need not be restricted to $20,000 and may be outside this area (but secured by first liens), and State-converted associations may lend in areas where they formerly operated. Loans are restricted to seventy-five per cent of the appraised value of the home or combination property and to fifty per cent of the value of other improved real estate. Maturities range from five to twenty years. Loans are amortized monthly in amounts sufficient to retire the debt at maturity; instalments are equal in amount, with interest and principal varying.

During the year ending June 30, 1940 Federal associations made new mortgage loans of $457,816,000, an increase of thirty-seven per cent over the volume of the preceding fiscal year. At the end of the calendar year of 1939, the combined assets of Federal associations represented twenty-six per cent of the assets of all associations in the United States. These institutions, however, accounted for forty-two per cent of the volume of new mortgage loans during the fiscal year of 1940 and their mortgage holdings were equivalent to thirty-two per cent of the total mortgage portfolio of all savings, building, and loan associations.

The number of shareholders in Federal associations increased during 1940 to 1,562,079 from 1,299,915 or twenty per cent; their investments at the end of the fiscal year totaled $1,268,048,000 against $900,-872,000 the previous year, a growth of twenty-eight per cent. Shareholders in all Federal savings and loan associations are protected up to $5,000 by the *Federal Savings and Loan Insurance Corporation.* Federal associations are also required to be members of the Federal Home Loan Bank System from which they may borrow funds against collateral in time of need. State building and loan associations may obtain similar protection for their shareholders by joining the *Federal Savings and Loan Insurance Corporation,* and the Federal Home Loan Bank System, but they are not obligated to do so.

Growth in Number and Influence

From 1893 to 1908 no increase took place in the number of building and loan associations. The membership and the total assets, however, went steadily upward. From 1908 to 1927 the real progress was made; the number of associations more than doubled, increasing from 5,599 to 12,804. Then in the following twelve years the number, including Federal savings and loan associations, dropped to 8,328 which were active in 1939. Over these years the total membership expanded to a peak of 12,343,254 in 1930 and then gradually receded to 6,499,511 in 1939. Total assets reached a high point of $8,828,000,000 also in 1930 and then gradually liquidated to $5,674,000,000 in 1939. The drop in urban real estate values during the depression, the stagnant condition of the real estate market due to the heavy foreclosures by insurance companies, mutual savings banks, liquidating agents of title guarantee and mortgage companies, and investors, and the rather moderate amount of new home construction very materially affected the operations of savings, building, and loan associations in all parts of the country.

Evolution of Factors

The factor, as a specialized banking institution, is a comparative newcomer in the world of credits. Its evolution, however, goes back to the very early days of our colonial history.

When the Pilgrims made their partnership trading agreement with James Sherley, John Beauchamp, and Richard Andrews, these three men were termed "agents & factors." Throughout the colonial era, the term *factor* was used over and over again as descriptive of an intimate, personal agent who took care of the local financial interests of one or several distant business enterprises. He was really a merchant who performed supplementary specialized services. A British factor, for example, was the principal correspondent of one or several colonial business merchants. He sold on a commission basis the products of the new land, tobacco, furs and skins, fish, lumber and lumber products, which the colonial exporter shipped to him. He sold merchandise out of his own stock at the current prices which the colonial trader ordered from Britain. Merchandise which he did not carry and which the colonial importer ordered, from thread and needles to guns and gunpowder, he purchased from other British merchants on a commission basis. He arranged insurance on his customers' ships and cargoes, forwarded letters, made payments, and advanced funds when necessary, if the colonist's credit was good. Typical British factors of the colonial period were Neate, Pigou & Booth of London; Henry Cruger, Jr., and Peach & Pierce of Bristol; John Markland, and Touchet & Co., of Manchester; Clay, Midgely & Co., and Hyde & Hamilton of Liverpool, all well-known English houses.

Some British merchants, in turn, also kept factors in the colonies. In this use of the term, the factor generally was an employee sent from the home office of the British exporter. He kept a stock of consigned merchandise for his employer, developed sales, and acted as financial agent and confidential advisor. Many were natives of Scotland. They soon acquired the reputation of being shrewd, capable, business men.

Colonial merchants, at times, also had factors in trading centers which were of particular importance to them, such as on the islands of Jamaica and Antiqua in the West Indies, in Nova Scotia, Newfoundland, or located at the Spanish settlement of St. Augustine in Florida. These factors generally were energetic young men sent out by the colonial merchant for the purpose of developing profitable business. Occasionally he might be someone already established at a particular location, but well able and willing to take a personal interest in the affairs of some aggressive distant merchant. Often they were relatives of the merchants who sent them out.

Early Part of the Nineteenth Century

By the second quarter of the nineteenth century the business of the factor in the United States had developed into that of a distributor of merchandise largely for European manufacturers and exporters on a commission basis. The other services which he had earlier performed continued as supplementary but of minor importance. The terms *factor* and *commission merchant* had become quite synonymous, although the factor was probably more representative of the concern that handled imported merchandise. He customarily received a commission of five per cent on the value of foreign products which he sold, and two and one-half per cent on domestic products. Generally he had authority to sell on credit unless otherwise directed by his principal. Moreover, if the principal so desired, the factor would guarantee that the sales made on credit would be paid at maturity for another commission of two and one-half per cent. If collections were undertaken still another charge of two and one-half per cent was made. If it was necessary to engage in litigation, a commission of five per cent was added.

Facilities for the storage of merchandise in important centers were frequently provided. For purchasing, remitting, or collecting bills of exchange, the factor usually received one per cent, and for drawing, endorsing, accepting, or selling drafts or bills of exchange, two and one-half per cent. What was probably a more important financial function at this particular time was that of making advances of funds, usually two-thirds or three-fourths of the market value of merchandise to those for whom the factor sold merchandise.

In 1800 the population of the United States was 5,308,000, in 1820 it had increased to 9,638,000, and in 1840 to 17,069,000. As our population increased and spread westward an expanding market was created for European manufactured merchandise. The one product for which there existed the greatest demand was textiles of all kinds to be made into wearing apparel, bedding, and furnishings for the home. Over these years an increasing number of business enterprises were started in the United States as representatives of European textile mills, those of Lyons and Paris in France; Bremen, Cologne and Hamburg in Germany; Liverpool and Manchester in England; and Zurich in Switzerland; mills which produced woolen cloth for men's and women's suits, fine silk goods, cotton cloth, pile fabrics, felts, and mohairs.

These new enterprises were factors. They received merchandise on consignment for the particular European mills which they represented, they sold that merchandise on a commission basis, guaranteed the credits of their American customers, made advances generally once a month against these receivables, and made additional advances against the consigned merchandise. Most of these factors originally imported merchandise on their own accounts and only gradually did the bulk of their business consist of handling consigned merchandise. *Rusch & Co.,* for example, started in business in 1827 as importers on their own account. The handling of consigned merchandise became a more important part of their business as the firm made connections with French and Swiss mills which were anxious to increase their business with the United States. Frederick Vietor arrived in New York from Bremen in 1828; Thomas Achelis, a cousin in 1834, and after operating individually for several years formed the firm of *F. Vietor & Achelis* in 1843. Originally this firm purchased and imported European merchandise on its own account but its operations gradually changed so that factoring became the primary activity.

Most of the men who became factors at this time were Europeans. They were relatives or employees of families that controlled or operated textile mills in the manufacturing centers of Europe. The businesses which they started grew rapidly and profitably as the demand constantly increased for more and more woolen, cotton, and silk piece goods.

Factor Becomes Specialized Bank

Between 1889 and 1905 the factoring business underwent a radical change. The selling function was gradually discontinued and the factor became a specialized banking institution for the textile industry. On December 1, 1889, *Oelbermann, Dommerich & Co.,* was one of the larger factors representing many European mills and handling an annual volume of sales of around $15,000,000. Emil Oelbermann resided in Cologne and handled the European end of the business while Louis F. Dommerich managed the New York end. The work involved in supervising the sales in the United States for mills producing a great variety of products, keeping in touch with markets, styles, and prices, and constantly advising with the European manufacturers was so great that Louis F. Dommerich finally decided to discontinue selling merchandise on a commission basis. With the elimination of the selling function, the factor now became a specialized banker. He continued to perform all of the other services. Before an order for merchandise was filled, the order would be turned over to the factor who would decide if the buyer was or was not financially responsible. If responsible, the factor would guarantee the payment of that account to the mill making the sale, and at monthly intervals would buy these receivables outright from the mill without recourse. Advances of funds would also be made, as from time immemorial, against merchandise.

The McKinley tariff of 1890 completed this evolution which had been started by *Oelbermann, Dommerich & Co.* This tariff repealed the duty on raw sugar, and reduced the duty on steel rails, iron and steel plates. On the other hand, duties were increased on woolen cloth, and the finer grades of cotton, lawns, laces, embroideries, linens and plush goods. The general level of all duties was increased to an average of 49.5 per cent. In the case of textile products, these duties now became almost prohibitory.

Overnight the business of factors dropped off as the prices of European textile merchandise, with the added duty, became too high to sell broadly in the American market. The only solution was to concentrate on domestic business, so one and all, the factors began to make arrangements to provide the services to American cotton, woolen, and silk mills, and converters, which they had been providing to European mills. The selling end of the factoring business dried up as the American mills preferred to retain their own sales departments, and the business came to have three distinct attributes; passing upon the credits of customers from whom orders for merchandise had been received and in most cases cashing the sales, that is, buying these receivables outright without recourse; advancing credit to textile mills, selling agents, and converters against finished merchandise as security; and in some cases performing a group of special services such as providing space for the display and storage of merchandise, handling insurance, billing, packing, shipping, and making city deliveries.

The first of these attributes, that of passing upon credits and cashing sales involved the study, at a moment's notice, of the credit standing of concerns placing orders for merchandise so that the shipment of that merchandise could immediately be made. If the buyer became financially embarrassed or went into bankruptcy, any credit loss on that particular account would be assumed by the factor and not by the mill, selling agent, or converter, that shipped the merchandise. From a sales agent with supplementary functions, the factor had now become a banker, specializing in financing manufacturers and distributors of textile piece goods. By 1905 this evolution had been completed.

From the passage of the McKinley tariff by Congress in 1890 to around 1930, factors did business only with those mills, selling agents, and converters that sold their products primarily to the manufacturers of women's, men's and children's clothing, to chain stores, and to department stores. By confining their activities to these fields, the sales of many of the factored concerns overlapped, that is, several of the mills, selling agents, and converters would be selling some of the very same customers. The same credit information would be used by the factor in passing upon the worthiness of these buyers in behalf of different clients, and the receivables created by these sales would be collected by one billing. The distinctive feature of the business came to be this overlapping of the customers of the factored concerns.

Around 1930 several factors began to experiment with business in fields outside of the textile industry, in such lines as manufacturers and distributors of shoes, chinaware, furs and leather; fields where credit investigations and credit files would need to be created for a single customer. A variety of bases were used by factors in handling these accounts, in some cases receivables would be purchased outright without recourse as had been customary; more generally, loans would be secured by receivables on different margins depending upon the analysis of the receivables, a field which had been previously preempted by discount finance companies and those commercial banks that would lend on assigned acccounts receivable. This development has continued to the present time. Factors are going more and more into other lines of business under modified arrangements. There were seventeen factors in existence in 1940. These seventeen concerns handled an aggregate volume of business in that year of approximately $800,000,000.

Finance Companies Enter Factoring Business

Commercial Investment Trust Corporation entered the factoring field in 1928 by acquiring control of *Peierls Buhler & Co., Inc.,* one of the smaller but typically representative textile factors which had been established in 1893. In 1929 the business of *F. Vietor & Achelis,* one of the older and larger factors was acquired. These two concerns were merged on March 8, 1929 to form *Commercial Factors Corporation.* In January, 1930 *Commercial Factors Corporation* acquired the factoring business of *Schefer, Schramm & Vogel,* and in October of the same year, the business of *L. Erstein & Bro.*

In the latter part of 1931, *Commercial Investment Trust Corporation* acquired the business of *Morton H. Meinhard & Co., Inc.,* a successful textile factoring organization, and took over certain accounts of *Greeff & Co.* This concern now became known as *Meinhard, Greeff & Co., Inc.* In November, 1931, *Commercial Investment Trust Corporation* acquired the factoring division of *William Iselin & Co.,* one of the older prominent textile factors. This business was transferred to another newly organized subsidiary, namely, *William Iselin & Co., Inc.* Late in 1934 *Passavant & Co.,* was acquired and as of January 1, 1935 this business was transferred to *William Iselin & Co., Inc.*

In an agreement dated September 18, 1936 between *Commercial Investment Trust Corporation* and the stockholders of *Bachmann, Emmerich & Co.,* factors, *Commercial Investment Trust Corporation* acquired all of the capital stock of *Bachmann, Emmerich & Co.* The accounts of *Bachmann, Emmerich & Co.,* were transferred to *Commercial Factors Corporation.*

At the present time *Commercial Investment Trust Corporation* has three wholly owned subsidiaries engaged in the factoring business which represent the consolidation, merger, and purchase of the assets of nine textile factors. These subsidiaries are *Commercial Factors Corporation, William Iselin & Co., Inc.,* and *Meinhard, Greeff & Co., Inc.*

In September, 1933 the *Commercial Credit Company* purchased control of the *Textile Banking Co., Inc.,* the one textile factor operating under a banking charter obtained from the State of New York. At the present time *Commercial Credit Company* owns 99.25 per cent of its outstanding capital stock. On July 1, 1935 *Commercial Credit Company* acquired all of the capital stock of a second factor, *Ed. Wright Ginsberg Corporation*. These two concerns have continued in existence as separate organizations and subsidiaries of the *Commercial Credit Company*.

Title Guarantee and Mortgage Companies

The technique of extending credit in the form of guaranteed mortgages which were then sold to investors, was an outgrowth of the business of title insurance. This highly specialized technique which in the end proved so unsound and costly was confined largely in New York State. Probably less than twenty-five per cent of the volume of guaranteed mortgages sold, were originated in all of the other States.

The first general statute permitting the incorporation of companies to guarantee real estate titles was passed by the New York State legislature in 1885 under the title, "An Act to provide for the organization and regulation of corporations to examine and guarantee bonds and mortgages and titles to real estate." It has been said that the legislature probably contemplated that corporations formed under this act should have the power to do nothing more than insure titles and guarantee mortgages against title defects. In 1892 credit guaranty corporations were given the power to guarantee credits for merchants. In 1904 corporations were given the specific power to insure "the payment of" bonds and mortgages.

The original acts of 1885 and 1892 which apparently did not contemplate the guarantee of the payment of bonds and mortgages, made provision for a so-called "Guaranty Fund." This guaranty fund, the benefits of which proved so completely illusory, apparently originated as a fund to guarantee title insurance, the losses of which have always been negligible.

Expansion in Guaranteed Mortgages

Notwithstanding the apparent lack of power, four corporations appear to have engaged in the business of guaranteeing the payment of mortgages prior to the legislation of 1904; the *Title and Guarantee Company of Rochester*, organized February 14, 1887, the *Bond and Mortgage Guarantee Company*, New York City, organized April 19, 1892, the *Lawyers Mortgage Company*, New York City, organized

February 9, 1893, and the *Westchester and Bronx Title and Mortgage Guaranty Company,* New York City, organized December 4, 1902.

The guaranteed mortgage business was not very substantial until the World War, when the boom in building operations, accompanied by the decline in the yield of high grade bonds, caused an enormous expansion in this type of credit operation. By 1920 there were eleven corporations operating in the guaranteed mortgage field in New York State with an aggregate capital and surplus of about $60,000,000. These corporations had outstanding guarantees of approximately $529,000,000. From that time on the number of companies and the amount of guarantees outstanding, as well as the ratio of additional guarantees to capital and surplus, increased steadily and rapidly. The number in New York State reached a maximum of fifty in 1930 and in 1931. The increase of the business is shown by the following table:

Year	No. of Companies	Combined Capital and Surplus	Total Guarantees Outstanding
1921......	12	$64,000,000	$548,000,000
1922......	14	71,000,000	652,000,000
1923......	15	55,000,000	781,000,000
1924......	20	64,000,000	981,000,000
1925......	26	93,000,000	1,214,000,000
1926......	28	121,000,000	1,522,000,000
1927......	37	141,000,000	1,837,000,000
1928......	45	183,000,000	2,169,000,000
1929......	47	200,000,000	2,407,000,000
1930......	50	204,000,000	2,867,000,000
1931......	50	200,000,000	2,851,000,000
1932......	47	184,000,000	2,823,000,000

The tremendous growth of these companies was partly due to the excellent condition of business generally, but particularly to the activity of the real estate market which at this time reached unprecedented "boom" heights. Possible loss in the event of a depression was rarely, if ever, taken into consideration. The banker, the successful business man, the lawyer, the doctor, the small merchant, and even those with small salaries wished to take advantage of an investment which yielded five and one-half per cent interest and was unconditionally supported by a guarantee of the payment of the principal at maturity. Lawyers, trustees, and other fiduciaries bought blindly without examining the property which provided the security behind the investment.

Nature of the Business

The certified type of mortgage, for which title guarantee and mortgage companies became best known, came into existence but only on a small scale in 1906. It was not until 1918 that a certificated mortgage was a legal investment for trustees, executors, and guardians, in New York State. This type of mortgage was developed in order that the small investor could place his funds in real estate mortgages as an investment. Under this arrangement certificates of participation in denominations as low as $100 were sold to the public, the underlying security being a first mortgage on real estate. These "conservative" investment certificates were guaranteed as to principal and interest by the mortgage guarantee companies.

The greatest growth in the real estate mortgage field began in 1922 and carried through the tragic year of 1929. It was during this interval that the certificated mortgage came into prominence due to the construction of numerous large office buildings, hotels, and apartments. By 1932, it has been estimated "some 500,000 individuals" had invested in guaranteed mortgages and certificates secured by real estate in the one State of New York. There were 22,000 separate issues of guaranteed certificates based on mortgages on 150,000 separate properties in New York City alone.[*]

During this period of rapid growth very little attention was given to determining just how far the corporations could reasonably go in guaranteeing mortgages and still maintain a margin of safety and be in a position to weather a crisis. Some of the companies had by-laws which specifically stated that only mortgages equal to less than 66 2/3 per cent of the value of the property could be guaranteed as to principal and interest. While the intent of this rule was good, it was subject to considerable abuse. Values were sometimes inflated to a point where mortgages were actually double the true value of the property and this inflation was naturally one of the principal causes for the trouble that subsequently beset the mortgage companies.

The value of a guaranty depends, of course, on what is behind it. These companies were growing by leaps and bounds and issuing guarantees in continually increasing volume. The need of some safeguard in the law requiring a fixed relationship between capital and guarantees seems obvious. California limited the amount of guarantees that a company of this type could issue to twenty times its capital stock.

[*] "The Guaranteed Mortgage Situation from the Inside," by Gerhard Kuehne, *The Magazine of Wall Street*, Volume 53, Number 12, March 31, 1934.

Oregon had a similar restriction. New York, where the bulk of this business was done, placed no limit upon the amount of contingent obligations which such a company might assume.

While the issuance of new mortgages fell off sharply after 1929, the larger and more prominent mortgage companies did not begin to encounter financial troubles until 1931. Rents decreased sharply, so that building owners were unable to meet amortization and interest charges, affecting the income of the mortgage companies. It now became impossible to cover all interest payments on the guaranteed mortgage certificates. Defaults on interest brought about the maturity of the principal sums. It was not long before liabilities mounted beyond all proportions to the ability to pay. The authorities in New York State took over the companies in August, 1933 and began a rehabilitation program.

The *Reconstruction Finance Corporation* was created in January, 1932 and attempted to aid these companies with loans. It made one loan to the *State Title and Mortgage Company* as early as April, 1932, and encouraged large borrowings by other companies. Loans were also made to *New York Title and Mortgage Company, Lawyers Title & Guaranty Company, Long Island Title Guarantee Company, National Title Guaranty Company, First Mortgage Guaranty and Title Company,* and *Union Guarantee and Mortgage Company.*

Both the *Lawyers Title & Guaranty Company* and the *Bond and Mortgage Guarantee Company,* were taken over by the New York State Insurance Department in August, 1933 and were subsequently ordered liquidated. The *Bond and Mortgage Guarantee Company,* was reponsible for nearly one-third of all New York guaranteed mortgages. Its outstanding guarantees on November 1, 1932 totaled $917,966,000. Next in size came the *New York Title and Mortgage Company,* and third was the *Lawyers Mortgage Company.* These three companies accounted for approximately seventy-five per cent of the outstanding mortgage guarantees of the fourteen concerns taken over by the Superintendent of Insurance in the State of New York. In 1938 a law was passed by the legislature of the State of New York outlawing the practice of guaranteeing the payment of principal and interest on mortgage loans.

Sales and Discount Finance Companies

During the second quarter of the nineteenth century an evolution took place in the extension of credit to the consumer. Prior to that time there had been no distinct group of wage-earners except those employed in the shipyards, in shipping, and in rope-walks. Farmers who comprised most of the population obtained credit on the typical mercantile terms, and if they were unable to meet their obligations with money, they liquidated their debts by payment with part of their crops.

In the 1840's a class of urban wage-earners came into existence. City bakers, retail clothing stores, drug stores, dry-goods stores, grocers, and shoe stores began to grant open-book credit to these individuals. This practice appeared to have become increasingly common up to the days of the Civil War. As wage payments became more frequent in centers of manufacturing, the time for which consumer credit had been customarily granted, was shortened. As the terms shortened, the hazards of credit-granting were reduced and merchants became more and more willing to accord consumer credit.

Evolution in Instalment Sales

The selling of merchandise on the instalment basis which had earlier developed in the sale of horses, carriages, farm equipment, and furniture, now spread to newer products such as pianos, household organs, and stoves, these sales being made directly to the consumer through agents of the manufacturers. The *Singer Sewing Machine Company* is said to have gone into the instalment field by 1850, selling a machine which was priced from twenty-five to thirty-five dollars with a down payment of one dollar and weekly payments of fifty cents.

Instalment credit, however, was used very moderately prior to the Civil War. Such sales were confined almost entirely to products which had a satisfactory resale market; the down payment notwithstanding the practice of the *Singer Sewing Machine Company* generally being substantial, and the terms of repayment relatively short. Most merchants who sold furniture, pianos, organs, and stoves in industrial areas continued to sell only for cash, and presumably those who used instalment terms, handled the substantial portion of their sales for cash.

Shortly after the Civil War, the liberalization of instalment terms occurred in the growing industrial centers. By 1870, pianos and melodeons were being offered on terms calling for "$5.00 to $25 monthly until paid," which presumably meant several years. Encyclopedias and sets of books were offered on the instalment basis as early as 1871. Retail furniture stores specializing in instalment sales now offered all kinds of household equipment and furnishings from rugs to kitchenware. In the late 1870's clothing stores began to appear which sold suits, coats, and dresses on a down payment of one-fifth of the price with the balance in weekly payments over two months. In the 1880's watches and jewelry were being sold on instalment terms. During these years a remarkable increase in instalment selling in a growing number of lines took place, largely in the field of low-priced merchandise. Wants were multiplying and in that process, the demand for credit was expanding. It took the twentieth century, however, and the automobile, to put instalment selling on the map in a big way.

The increased sale of merchandise on the instalment basis meant increased receivables on the books of the seller. In the early sales of articles such as sewing machines and book sets, the increased receivables appeared on the ledgers of the manufacturers as the sales were made largely by the agents of the manufacturers. In the sales of furniture, household furnishings, and pianos, the increased receivables generally appeared on the ledgers of the retail stores which made the sales.

Larger receivables meant the increased use of credit; in the case of manufacturers in healthy financial shape that credit could be readily obtained from commercial banks; in the case of retail stores, occasionally a modest amount would be obtained from a depository bank or banks, but mostly from manufacturers that now granted larger and longer credit terms to the retail stores. It was no unusual situation for notes given in payment of such merchandise purchases to be renewed time and time again with moderate reductions at successive renewals.

Early Specialized Finance Companies

The first instalment finance company was organized in 1904. In that year the *Foster-Armstrong Company* of Rochester, New York, manufacturers of pianos, organized a subsidiary, the *Fidelity Contract Company* to purchase instalment contracts from the retail dealers that sold these particular pianos on a deferred payment plan. This concern is now known as the *Bankers Commercial Corporation,* its operation over the intervening years having been broadly expanded to include the purchase of instalment lien paper covering the sale of industrial machinery, durable consumer goods, and automobiles.

The earliest accounts-receivable finance company was organized in 1904 in Chicago. This concern purchased accounts receivables; that is, open book accounts in contrast to instalment accounts. After nine months of operation had proved that the venture was practical and profitable, it was incorporated as the *Mercantile Credit Company of*

Chicago. This business was later reorganized as the *Continental Credit Trust of Chicago.* In 1908 the *National Trust and Credit Company,* Chicago, and the *Commercial Credit Investment Trust,* of St. Louis, whose style was later changed to *Commercial Investment Trust Corporation* were organized to operate in this specialized field. Most of the accounts-receivable finance companies gradually entered the instalment field, first purchasing the instalment contracts covering the sale of pianos, later automobiles, and finally of the large number of durable consumer products such as radios, vacuum cleaners, washing machines, electric refrigerators, and oil burners which came to be sold extensively on this basis.

Automobiles Gave Impetus to Finance Companies

The big development of the finance company business came along with the expansion in the automobile business. The first automobile financing on an instalment basis was handled by *W. P. Smith and Company* of Seattle in 1910. The earliest passenger automobile instalment business was undertaken three years later by *L. F. Weaver,* a wagon and carriage dealer in San Francisco. A few months later, *C. Trevor Dunham* of Philadelphia began to finance the sale of passenger cars. By 1917 there were at least twenty-five concerns financing instalment sales of automobiles and several had spread their operations into many States. Gradually operations included the purchasing of instalment contracts covering sales of all kinds of durable consumer goods such as washing machines, vacuum cleaners, furniture, phonographs, and water pumps in addition to automobiles. During the 1920's electric refrigerators, radios, automatic oil furnaces were put on the market and found their way into the American home largely through the medium of instalment selling.

The increase in the number of finance companies and the volume of business they handled were dominated after the first World War by the expansion in the sales of automobiles. *General Motors Acceptance Corporation* was organized in January, 1919 to fill this need and its immediate success brought about the organization of a large number of small finance companies in all parts of the country. This growth in instalment finance companies solved the problem of retail financing and the automobile industry led the revival of general business activity in the latter part of 1921. The limits of the potential market for automobiles was progressively extended by constant improvements in the product at lower selling prices and by the expansion, liberalization, and improvement in the facilities for financing retail sales.

The profitable operation of a finance company required that a large volume of business be transacted in relation to the invested capital so credit three to five times as large as its tangible net worth was generally made available by commercial banks. The commercial banks thus became the ultimate source of a substantial part of the credit extended to automobile purchasers. The large organizations like *General Motors Acceptance Corporation, Commercial Investment Trust Corporation* and *Commercial Credit Company* were later able to float issues of collateral trust notes secured by the pledge of underlying sales contracts in the investment market, and still later issues of debentures. In this way the finance company bridged the gap between the buyer and the commercial bank, the finance company investigating the credit standing of the buyer, making collections, repossessing goods in case of defaults, and in this process, practically guaranteeing banks against loss. The finance company invariably secured additional protection in its operations by obtaining a repurchase agreement from the dealer who would agree to substitute new paper for, or repurchase those contracts where the buyer did not make his instalment payments reasonably on time. Experimentally during 1934 and more aggressively since 1936 commercial banking institutions have entered the sales finance field directly and have operated along with credit unions and industrial banks in competition to finance companies. In 1939, 10,381 of the 13,493 commercial banks insured by the *Federal Deposit Insurance Corporation* reported that they were handling retail instalment paper.

Growth in Number

Very few finance companies, either sales or accounts-receivable finance companies were organized until the years from 1912 to 1915. By 1922, according to Robert G. Merrick, who published a brief volume about finance companies during that year, there were approximately 125 doing business in most of the industrial States. The growth in this field of activity, up to that time was very slow and very cautious.

The years of 1919 and 1920 were years of wide economic depression, but by 1921 the automobile industry had shown the way to remarkable recuperation. Specialized finance companies now began to attract the careful, thoughtful attention of the aggressive leaders in the automobile industry as a means of increasing sales. In the two years from

1922 to 1924 the number of finance companies increased to about 1,400. Naturally a large number of the newcomers were small enterprises with very limited financial resources. By June, 1926 the number had dwindled to around 850. In 1929 an authoritative estimate placed the number at 918.

Ten years later, the business census of 1939 found 1,086 sales finance companies engaged exclusively or mainly in purchasing and holding retail instalment paper arising from sales to consumers of motor vehicles and consumer goods of all kinds. Their aggregate volume of business for the year was placed at $1,990,000,000 and their holdings at the end of the year at $1,348,000,000. There were a limited number of finance companies which specialized in purchasing or making advances against accounts receivable that were not included in this total. The volume of business and the holdings at the end of the year were not total figures for sales finance companies, as many of the important concerns also handled instalment notes arising out of the sale of industrial machinery to manufacturers, the sale of furnishings and equipment to retail stores, made loans on assigned accounts, and purchased receivables arising from factoring operations, none of which fell under the survey classification of "instalment paper arising from sales to consumers." Finance companies have made tremendous progress in the past twenty years. They have become a recognized integral part of our ramified credit structure.

Personal Loan Companies

The first effort to make an impression upon the usurious activity of unregulated small loan lenders and upon the operations of licensed pawnbrokers was attempted by what has become known as remedial loan societies. The first of these enterprises was the *Collateral Loan Company of Boston,* organized in 1857 to lend against pledges. In the same city, the *Workingmen's Loan Association* was organized in 1888 by public-spirited individuals to make loans at the lowest possible rate consistent with a moderate profit. Then followed the *St. Bartholomew's Loan Association* of New York to grant chattel loans, and the *Provident Loan Society of New York* to extend credit on pledged articles, both organized in 1894. Similar societies were organized in Worcester, Massachusetts, in 1896, and in Providence, Rhode Island, in 1898. By 1909 there were fifteen such enterprises in active operation.

The capital for most of these organizations was contributed by wealthy individuals but with the understanding that the return would be fixed at a definite rate, generally six per cent per annum. Accordingly, more reasonable rates for loans could be charged than by the unregulated lenders or by licensed pawnbrokers. From these experiments it was found that capital could be attracted to the small loan business if rates, somewhat higher than the legal interest rates of commercial banks, but only a fraction of the excessive rates of the unregulated lender, were charged.

Development of Uniform Small Loan Act

Studies undertaken by the Russell Sage Foundation in 1907 and 1908 disclosed the anti-social characteristics of the existing small loan business and widespread efforts were then made to remedy the situation by encouraging the organization of additional limited dividend companies to make chattel mortgage and pledge loans, and by sponsoring the passage of State laws which would regulate all loans of $300 or less. In 1916, the Russell Sage Foundation drafted a model regulatory act, known as the Uniform Small Loan Act which has since served as a basis for legislation in the thirty-nine States and the District of Columbia which have such laws on their statute books. Enterprises operating under this law have come to be known as personal loan companies.

Loan companies licensed to operate under the small loan law of respective States originally used household furniture and wage assignments as their principal security, although an increasing volume of loans was made on unsecured endorsed and co-maker notes. Such loans were made payable generally in instalments over periods ranging from five to twenty months, and the charges on outstanding balances were limited by State laws from two per cent to three and one-half per cent a month, computed on the unpaid balance of the loan.

Personal finance companies, unlike sales and discount finance companies, deal directly with the borrower, extend only cash loans, state the aggregate charges usually as a per cent per month of the unpaid loan balance, and for security have come to rely chiefly upon the character of the borrower or his co-makers. Loans, although often used for the purchase of a commodity such as a refrigerator, a radio, or a washing machine, are also sought for an infinite number of other purposes, such as the desire to liquidate a large number of small debts or to pay a doctor's bill. Borrowers are drawn almost entirely from urban residents whose annual incomes are between $500 and $3,500 a range which contains over three-quarters of the non-farm income groups of the country, and a range that bears the brunt of unemployment and of curtailed purchasing power due to cyclical and seasonal fluctuations in industrial and commercial activity.

Growth in Legal Personal Loan Agencies

No early records are available indicating the number of remedial loan societies in existence or the growth in their yearly volume of outstanding credits. In 1910 sixteen were in active operation. Then the number gradually expanded to a peak of forty organizations in 1915. As personal finance companies increased in number to fill the need and operated under the Uniform Small Loan Act, a gradual but steady decrease took place in number of remedial societies. By 1920 there were thirty-two, 1930 twenty-six, and 1940 only nineteen. Among these nineteen was the *Provident Loan Society of New York* which is the largest organization in this field with its twenty branches in New York City through which 734,881 loans were made in 1940 for $35,357,000.

A portion of the early unregulated lenders immediately changed operations to conform with the requirements of the Uniform Small Loan Act as it was passed by successive State legislatures. Among these were the two largest organizations, the *Beneficial Industrial Loan Corporation* and the *Household Finance Corporation*. By 1910 there were two chains of personal loan companies with more than 100 offices and many with more than 30 offices; there were also hundreds of independent local small loan offices.

No adequate records are available regarding the number of personal loan companies in existence over the years. Although the banking departments in most States were supposed by law to keep records of the number of licensed offices of small loan companies, no complete records were kept prior to 1929. Compilations for the five following years show a steady drop, not in the number of companies, but in the number of licensed offices from 3,766 in 1929 to 3,347 in 1934. Then the number increased slowly but steadily to 3,619 in 1938 with a 11.5 per cent jump to 4,036 in 1939. Rolf Nugent of the Russell Sage Foundation has estimated that the outstanding loans of all personal loan companies expanded year by year from $195,000 in 1912 to $288,816,000 in 1931, then dropped to $232,004,000 in 1933, and from that time, increased steadily to $495,000,000 in 1940.

At the end of 1940 the two largest chains, the *Beneficial Industrial Loan Corporation* with 394 offices and the *Household Finance Corporation* with 288 offices held approximately thirty per cent of the reported outstanding loans of all personal finance companies in the country. This thirty per cent is not of all so-called personal loans but only those of licensed personal finance companies operating under the Uniform Small Loan Act, as an increasing volume of loans of this type have been made by commercial banking institutions since the *Hudson County National Bank* of Jersey City opened up this field in 1924.

Credit Unions

At the same time that personal loan companies were being organized in increasing numbers to operate under the Uniform Small Loan Act, a type of cooperative credit organization was in process of development known as the "Credit Union." This particular type of loan organization was modeled after what is now known as the Raiffeisen credit societies originated in Germany about 1850, and which spread to Canada in 1900 under the leadership of Alphonse Desjardins, a Canadian journalist, and then from Canada into New England.

The first credit union in the United States, *La Caisse Populaire Ste. Marie* was organized in 1909 within a French-Canadian parish in Manchester, New Hampshire by this same Alphonse Desjardins. During the same year a bill authorizing the operation of credit unions was enacted by the Massachusetts legislature, in 1913 by New York, and in 1915 by North Carolina.

Nature of Operations

Credit unions are generally organized within groups of people who have some specific mutual interest, such as employment by the same organization, membership in the same church, a labor union, a fraternal order, a club, or residence in the same neighborhood. A credit union is the most convenient bank for its members. It brings the bank to the saver rather than waiting for him to come to the bank. It generally operates where he works or lives and its hours are set to suit the convenience of its members.

These institutions supply members with cooperative credit by furnishing the machinery which enables members to accumulate savings in a common pool. This machinery consists of a thrift plan whereby a member instead of making a deposit as in a mutual savings bank, buys a "share" on an instalment basis, somewhat like the technique of building and loan associations. In actual practice, such a purchase on an instalment has been found to inculcate a habit of saving, of thrift. A share which is generally five dollars would be paid at the rate of twenty-five cents each week.

If a member would like to save fifty cents each week, he would agree to purchase two shares. By having the unit of weekly payments small, the plan adapts itself to members who can save the least. While this unit is called a "share" it is not a share in the investment sense of the word. The member may withdraw whatever amount he has put into shares at any time; it is more in the nature of a deposit but the share technique was developed to foster the routine of systematic savings which is so essential to the wage-earner. Actual deposits in irregular amounts from members are also permitted by many credit union laws.

Loans are made by a credit union to its members for provident and constructive purposes; to pay a doctor, a nurse, the hospital in time of need; to enable a member to improve his position economically, to shingle his house, pay his taxes, build a garage, pay for an education; to break up the instalment purchasing system by furnishing funds to members to purchase for cash at lower prices. Applications for loans are studied and approved by a credit committee which is composed of members themselves so that they know each other's problems, reputation, earnestness, and reliability.

Credit unions have developed rapidly because they are of aid to the wage-earner who is often in need of a small loan and who previously, and in many communities today, is an easy victim for the loan shark. The typical charge is one per cent a month on the unpaid balance, which is materially below the charges allowed by the statutes in all States to personal loan companies operating under the Uniform Small Loan Act and even more below the typical charge of the unregulated lender.

These savings are managed through officers of their own choosing and from their own number. The money is invested exclusively in loans to the members of its own group and only for provident or productive purposes. All of the net earnings, after the full expenses of operation and twenty per cent of the net earnings has been set aside as an indivisible surplus, are divided among the members of the society as dividends on their savings in the common pool, except that credit unions operating under Federal laws are not allowed to pay annual dividends in excess of six per cent. "There is no exterior capital and no-one outside of the specific group may have anything to do with the credit union in question directly or indirectly." In all matters each member has a single vote.

Loans generally range from $25 to $100 although the extension of credit is allowed in most States up to $2,000, usually on the security of endorsed notes to be repaid in instalments over a period of one year. Many State laws and the Federal law limit the amount of an unsecured loan which may be made to a member to $50. As a cooperative organization, profits belong to the members. Credit unions accept endorsements of those who have no more responsibility than the borrower, which often means moral responsibility and little or no financial responsibility.

Federally Chartered Credit Unions

Impetus was given to the credit union movement by the passage of the Federal Credit Union Act by Congress in 1934. Under this law interested groups located in a State which had no credit union act may obtain a charter from the Governor of the Farm Credit Administration at Washington, D. C. By the end of 1934 there were 42 Federal credit unions, by 1936 there were 1,675, and by 1940 there were 3,782. Federal charters were granted to 666 credit unions in 1940, and 529 in 1939. It is estimated that the Federal credit unions had 1,125,000 members at the end of 1940, that these unions had accumulated "total assets of more than $71,000,000" and that members were borrowing $58,000,000. The average loan was approximately $110.

Growth in Number of Credit Unions

Like most innovations in the financial world the early growth of the credit union movement was very slow. From the one credit union in 1909, the number gradually increased to 142 in six States with 39,800 members and outstanding loans of $3,100,000 in 1920. By 1930 there were 1,017 active unions with 292,800 members and outstanding loans of $19,000,000. The rapid growth now took place between 1930 and 1940 when literature became more widely read on the movement and Congress enacted helpful legislation in 1934. By 1940 there were 8,700 credit unions, both State and Federal with 2,514,000 members, outstanding loans of $200,000,000 and aggregate assets of $214,000,000.

Here is more than an eight-fold increase in the number of credit unions and members during the past decade, and more than a ten-fold increase in outstanding loans.

Industrial Banking Companies

The first of a type of lending organizations which has since become known as industrial banking companies was created in 1910 when Arthur J. Morris, an attorney, organized the *Fidelity Savings and Trust Company,* at Norfolk, Virginia. In his experience as counsel for commercial banks, Morris had learned that banking institutions invariably refused loans on salaries and wages to many worthy applicants who could not offer adequate security. He attempted to solve this problem by the origination of a new type of commercial bank with a special lending technique, just about the time that credit unions were getting an initial hold in New Hampshire and Massachusetts. These banks have little or nothing to do with industry. The descriptive word "industrial" came to be used as the institutions were set up primarily to serve industrial workers.

Field of Operation

This special technique consisted of an elaborate arrangement to increase the amount of interest return on a loan without conflicting with State usury laws. Under this arrangement, instalment payments on a loan were credited to non-interest-bearing certificates instead of being used to reduce the loan. In this way "the actual interest rate on a loan discounted at $8.00 per hundred and payable in fifty-two equal weekly instalments, amounted to 17.7 per cent if the contract was met promptly, and a higher rate if the borrower was delinquent in his payments." This newcomer into the field of small loans, provided a respectable source of funds for borrowers who could not obtain credit elsewhere except at far greater rates.

These institutions thus differed originally from existing commercial banks in two respects, they extended consumer loans which were repayable on an instalment basis, and they operated as savings or thrift institutions by obtaining part of their loanable funds from deposits, or more commonly, as they were prevented in many States from accepting deposits, by selling investment certificates. In their early years, they dealt almost exclusively in co-maker loans.

Industrial banking companies as a general rule, grant loans from $25 to $1,000, although in many States they are authorized to grant loans up to $5,000, usually on the security of endorsed notes, payable in instalments over one year. Endorsements by persons who are in the same economic status as the borrower are acceptable as with credit unions and so loans are extended to those who often would be unable to obtain endorsements strong enough for the typical commercial bank. Operations originally were carried on under existing banking laws with interest charges at the maximum State discount rate, an investigation fee amounting usually to two per cent of the note, plus a charge for delinquency, but the legality of these operations under usury laws was questionable and special enabling statutes were subsequently enacted by many States to authorize special features of operation.

As a result of the increased competition among and between the various types of banking and credit institutions, the types of loans originally made by industrial banks have been greatly broadened since 1935. Co-maker loans continue to be the most important part of their activities, but in addition, loans are now made on single name paper, on single name commercial paper, and to finance the retail instalment purchase of such products as automobiles, refrigerators, oil burners, radios, and similar articles, operating either through dealers or by direct contact with the individual purchaser. In an increasing number of States they have also been given the privilege of accepting deposits and of granting loans for commercial purposes. This diversification has brought them into competition as lenders or as recipients of savings with almost all types of credit institutions, commercial banks and trust companies, mutual savings banks, personal loan companies, credit unions, sales finance companies, and to some extent pawnbrokers, and remedial loan societies.

Rates used by industrial banks vary according to competition and locality. Discount rates range from three and one-third per cent to eight per cent plus a credit investigation charge generally of 50 cents per $100, or from 6.87 per cent per annum to 16.06 per cent per annum, plus charges.

Growth in Industrial Banks

Industrial banking corporations unlike credit unions are private profit-making enterprises. They are generally organized with capital funds obtained by the sale of stock to local business men. The promo-

We the Subscribers, Brokers for the Purchase and Sale of Public Stock, do hereby solemnly promise and pledge ourselves to each other, that we will not buy or sell from this day for any person whatsoever, any kind of Public Stock, at a less rate than one quarter per Cent Commission on the Specie value of and that we will give a preference to each other in our Negotiations. In Testimony whereof we have set our hands this 17th day of May at New York. 1792.

Leond. Bleecker   Sutton & Hardy
Hugh Smith   Benjn. Seixas
Armstrong & Barnewall
Saml. March   John Henry
                         John A Hardenbrook
Bernd. Hart
Alexr. Zuntz   Amrus. Rutin
                         Benjn. Winthrop
Andrew D. Barclay   Jn. Ferrers

"Buttonwood Agreement," May 17, 1792
Founding New York Stock Exchange

tion, enfranchisement, and supervision of "Morris Plan Banks" were and are carried out by the *Morris Plan Corporation of America* and its predecessors. Somewhat similar groups were developed to transact the same type of lending activity, the *Trusteed System* in the South and the Middle West, the *Hood System* in North Carolina, the *Morgan Plan* and the *White System* in the South, the *Peoples Finance and Thrift* companies mainly in California, the *Consumer Discount* companies in Pennsylvania, the *Citizens System* companies in the Middle West, and *Wimsett Systems* with affiliated companies across the continent. Some of the companies have been merged with other units, and most of those now in existence operate as independent industrial banks.

The second industrial bank was organized in Atlanta in 1911 and was followed by similar institutions in Baltimore, Washington, D. C., and Richmond in 1912. Nine were established during 1913 and 1914, twelve in 1915, twenty-eight in 1916 and in 1917, and eight in 1918. By 1923 there were about 190 such companies in existence and by 1929 there were approximately 620. Ten years later, in 1939 the Consumer Credit Institute of America, Inc., made a compilation showing 678 industrial banks in forty-five States and the District of Columbia. There were three States without such institutions, North Dakota, South Dakota, and Vermont.

Yearly estimates of the outstanding loans of all industrial banking companies have been made by the Russell Sage Foundation. These estimates begin with $80,000 for 1910 when the *Fidelity Savings and Trust Company* of Norfolk, Virginia, was the sole industrial banking company in existence. The outstanding loans expanded to $219,037,000 in 1929, gradually decreased during the early years of the depression to $120,664,000 in 1933, and then increased steadily to a new high point of $288,000,000 in 1940.

Stock Exchange Commission Firms

The final important credit institution is the stock exchange commission firm. These houses, of which there were 373 that owned seats on the New York Stock Exchange on May 31, 1941 are engaged in buying and selling securities on exchanges for the cash and the margin accounts of customers.

Purchases of registered securities on a national stock exchange made through these houses on margin have been subject to regulation by the Board of Governors of the Federal Reserve System since 1937.

When securities are purchased on a margin the difference between the cost price and the amount advanced by the buyer is furnished by the commission house for its customer.

The New York Stock Exchange was formally organized in 1792. John T. Flynn has written that as late as 1817 "it was a simple trading market to which men went to buy and sell for cash." No exact or general information is extant regarding the rise of margin trading on funds provided by stock exchange brokers, but this development undoubtedly took place simultaneously with the early growth in the New York City call money market prior to 1860.

Unfortunately there is no record of the dollar volume of loans made by commission firm members of the New York Stock Exchange to their customers during the great peak of the last speculative period. In December, 1935 loans of this nature amounted to $1,258,000,000. Since that date the Federal Reserve Board has compiled these fascinating figures at monthly intervals. Such loans expanded to a peak of $1,489,-000,000 in June, 1937, and then gradually decreased with some moderate fluctuation to $677,000,000 in December, 1940.

Funds which are lent to customers by stock exchange commission firms are largely borrowed from depository banks and on the call money market. Records of the volume of loans incurred by members of the New York Stock Exchange have been kept for a longer period than the record of loans made by commission firms to margin investors and speculators. The peak of such borrowings, both on demand and on time, amounted to the very substantial figure of $8,549,000,000 in September, 1929. Of this amount $6,498,000,000 was lent by the banking institutions of New York City or through them for outside lenders. It is probable that by far the greater portion of these funds were re-lent by commission firms to their margin customers. This enormous flood of funds into the stock market was one of the fundamental causes of the rise in speculation, and the inflation in the prices of securities to such unprecedented heights in the years leading up to the crash of 1929.

In 1940, the average sales per trading day on the New York Stock Exchange amounted to 751,000 shares, compared with 4,165,000 in 1929. The drop has been a steady one for several years. As a result, the borrowings of margin customers from commission firms have been low, and the demand and time borrowings of members of the New York Stock Exchange dropped to $322,492,000 in August, 1940, the lowest amount in the last eight years. These borrowings then expanded very moderately to $413,467,000 which was outstanding on December 31, 1940.

Bibliographical References to Chapter Five

ALGER, GEORGE W., *Report to His Excellency Herbert H. Lehman, Governor of the State of New York, covering the examination and the investigation of the management and affairs of the Insurance Department with reference to the operation, conduct and management of title and mortgage guarantee corporations under its supervision;* 1934.

ATHERTON, LEWIS E., *The Pioneer Merchant' in Mid-America;* Columbia, Missouri, 1939.

BERGENGREN, ROY F., *Cuna Emerges;* 1935, Fourth Edition 1939, Madison, Wisconsin.

BURPEE, CHARLES W., *A Century in Hartford;* Hartford, Connecticut, 1931.

BURROWS, JOHN McD., *Fifty Years in Iowa; being the personal experiences of J. M. D. Burrows, concerning the men and events, social life, industrial interests, physical development and commercial progress of Davenport and Scott County, during the period from 1838 to 1888;* Davenport, Iowa, 1888.

CHAPMAN, JOHN M. and ASSOCIATES, *Commercial Banks and Consumer Instalment Credit;* New York, 1940.

CLARK, SYDNEY A., *The First Hundred Years of the New England Mutual Life Insurance Company;* Boston, 1935.

DUNHAM, HOWARD P., EDITOR, *The business of Insurance;* Three Volumes, New York, 1912.

FLYNN, JOHN T., *Security Speculation;* New York, 1934.

FOULKE, ROY A., *Behind the Scenes of Business;* New York, 1937.

FREEDLEY, EDWIN T., *A Practical Treatise on Business, or how to Get, Save, Spend, Give, Lend, and Bequeath Money;* 1852, Edition of 1866, Philadelphia.

GALL, HENRY R., and JORDAN, WILLIAM GEORGE, *One Hundred Years of Fire Insurance;* Hartford, 1919.

GROBBEN, MARGARET, *Industrial Banking;* New York, 1940.

HOFFMAN, FREDERICK L., *Fifty Years of American Life Insurance Progress;* Published by American Statistical Association, 1911.

JOSEPHSON, MATTHEW, *The Robber Barons;* New York, 1934.

Life Insurance Operating Results and Investments; Hearings before the Temporary National Economic Committee, Seventy-sixth Congress, Third Session, Pursuant to Public Resolution No. 113; 1940.

MASSACHUSETTS HISTORICAL SOCIETY, *Proceedings October, 1912-June, 1913,* Volume XLVI; Boston, 1913.

NEIFELD, M. R., *Personal Finance Comes of Age;* New York, 1939.

New York Insurance Reports, 1939-1940.

NUGENT, ROLF, *Consumer Credit and Economic Stability;* New York, 1939.

ROBINSON, LOUIS N., and NUGENT, ROLF, *Regulations of the Small Loan Business;* New York, 1935.

SAULNIER, RAYMOND J., *Industrial Banking Companies and Their Credit Practices;* New York, 1940.

SELIGMAN, EDWIN R. A., *The Economics of Instalment Selling;* Two Volumes, New York, 1927.

SHERMAN, FRANKLIN J., *Modern Story of Mutual Savings Banks;* New York, 1934.

SMITH, JAMES G., *The Development of Trust Companies in the United States;* New York, 1928.

STEINER, W. H., *The Mechanism of Commercial Credit;* New York, 1922.

Study of Legal Reserve Life Insurance Companies; Monograph No. 28 of the Investigation of Concentration of Economic Power for the Temporary National Economic Committee; 1940.

TUCKER, DONALD S., *The Evolution of People's Banks;* New York, 1922.

WELFLING, WELDON, *Savings Banking in New York State;* Durham, North Carolina, 1939.

YOUNG, RALPH A. and ASSOCIATES, *Personal Finance Companies and Their Credit Practices;* New York, 1940.

ZARTMAN, LESTER W. and PRICE, WILLIAM H., *Property Insurance, Marine and Fire;* New Haven, 1926.

Volumes Previously Cited

BENNETT, FRANK P., JR., *The Story of Mutual Savings Banks;* Boston, 1924.

BODFISH, H. MORTON, EDITOR-IN-CHIEF, *History of the Building and Loan in the United States;* Chicago, 1931.

CLARK, VICTOR S., *History of Manufactures in the United States, 1607-1860;* 1929 Edition, New York.

DEWEY, DAVIS RICH, *Financial History of the United States;* 1902, Second Edition 1903, New York.

HARRINGTON, VIRGINIA D., *The New York Merchant on the Eve of the Revolution;* New York, 1935.

KNOX, JOHN JAY, *A History of Banking in the United States;* 1900; Revised Edition 1903, New York.

LEVINE, SAMUEL W., *The Business of Pawnbroking;* New York, 1913.

SCHLESINGER, ARTHUR MEIER, *The Colonial Merchants and the American Revolution;* 1918, New Edition 1939, New York.

VI * Governmental Lending Agencies

*T*HE early policy of the colonies and of local settlements in extending credit for the actual organization and development of business activities, was immediately carried over into our national existence. Subscriptions of individual States became important sources of funds in the creation of early public utility enterprises such as canals, toll bridges, and toll roads. Virginia, for example, subscribed $60,000 between 1785 and 1790 to the *James River Company* which constructed a seven-mile canal around the Great Falls beginning at Westham; $190,000 between 1791 and 1837 to the *Great Dismal Swamp Company* which constructed a canal to open communication between Elizabeth River and the North River; and with Maryland from 1785 to 1799, Virginia granted larger sums to the *Potomac Company* to improve navigation up the Potomac River. George Washington was president of this enterprise and assiduously devoted himself to its affairs until he became President of the United States in 1789.

The State of New York adopted the same policy, and between 1792 and 1804, subscribed and paid $92,000, and then donated an additional $12,500 to the *Western Canal Company* which opened a connecting link between the Mohawk River and Lake Ontario. New Jersey subscribed and paid $10,000 in 1791 to the historic *Society for establishing useful Manufactures* of Paterson, New Jersey. This corporation has not engaged in direct manufacturing since 1796, but it has continued in existence as an inactive enterprise, holding water rights on the Passaic River which were leased to others until 1934, when it completed a hydroelectric power plant at Great Falls, and now produces and distributes electric power. The Federal Government assisted in the organization and retained substantial stock interests in both the first and second Banks of the United States.

Even small towns and villages occasionally assumed a modest stake in developing a toll bridge company or a canal company. The amount and extent of these early monetary aids may easily be exaggerated, but the fact remains, that funds were invested and loans were actually made by national, State, and local governmental units to assist in the organization of business enterprises which often took on the nature of public improvements. That was a long time ago, years before the days of excess bank reserves, of specialization in credit knowledge, investigation, and interpretation. In the meantime, canals and toll roads, if not toll bridges, have gone largely out of style as transportation methods have become streamlined, and as fashions in investment and speculative securities have gradually changed.

Then, the era of railroad empire building overwhelmed politics. The policy of making gifts and of extending loans was resurrected, improved, and extended. The *South Carolina Canal and Railroad Company* completed its road of one hundred and thirty-six miles in 1833 only after the city of Charleston had purchased $20,000 of its stock and the State had extended a loan of $100,000. Ohio, in 1837, authorized loans to railroad companies, amounting to one-third of their capital, provided the other two-thirds had been otherwise subscribed. Indiana went one step farther, but a step with seven-league boots, and permitted railroad corporations to issue paper money to pay for labor and materials!

When the question reached Congress, the Federal Government positively refused to grant direct aid to assist in the construction of railroads. Politicians have always found the way around the mulberry bush and they did here. Lavish grants of land were now made to the States, and the States, in turn, proceeded to pass these grants over promptly to the railroads. This simple procedure solved a complex problem. The first of these land grants consisted of alternate sections, six miles on each side of the proposed route for the *Illinois Central Railroad* from Chicago to Mobile, and was made to the States of Illinois, Mississippi, and Alabama. Similar gifts were subsequently made to Michigan, Wisconsin, Iowa, Missouri, Arkansas, Louisiana, and Florida. By 1861 there had been granted for internal improvements, mostly to railroads, no less than 31,600,852 acres of government-owned land. With this awesome spectacle before the country, it was no wonder that Henry

George popularized the theory of the single tax in 1879 in his remarkable volume of *Progress and Poverty*.

Foreign Credits During First World War

The greatest experiment and experience in extending credit ever undertaken by the Federal Government was made, however, not at home but abroad. Not only did we advance billions and billions of dollars on credit to our allies to purchase war supplies during the first World War but additional advances were made after the War, supplies in Europe were sold on credit, and occupational expenses were incurred. In payment, the various European governments gave their demand notes but made no effort to pay them until the suggestion was gently and diplomatically advanced in 1922 that it would be desirable to the United States if these immense obligations were funded. Funding agreements were then made with fifteen European nations, the total principal of the debts under these agreements being fixed at $11,522,000,000 to be repaid over a period of sixty-two years. Here was the extension of credit on a high-powered wholesale scale. In addition, unfunded obligations totaling over one billion dollars were due from Germany, Russia, Armenia, and Nicaragua.

Payments under these funding obligations were made each year according to schedule until 1931. In June of that disastrous year a breakdown in European finance appeared imminent, and President Hoover helpfully suggested a moratorium of one year on all war debts including the German indemnity arranged under the Young Plan in June, 1929. When the so-called Hoover moratorium expired in June, 1932, France advanced the specious claim that the inter-ally debts had been ended by President Hoover's action and so refused to pay. Great Britain, paid her instalment in full. One year later, in June, 1933 only Finland paid in full. As of June 30, 1940, the unpaid principal of these funded debts, no interest included, aggregated $11,231,000,000, and of the unfunded debt $204,000,000. In addition, unpaid principal due from Germany as of the same date under the debt funding agreement of June 23, 1930 covering the costs of the American Army of Occupation and the awards of the Mixed Claims Commission, amounted to $1,225,000,000. Here was a grand total due from foreign countries of $12,660,000,000.

As a result of the inability or the lack of desire of these nations with the exception of Finland to meet their obligations, the Johnson Act was passed by Congress in April, 1934, closing the capital market in the

United States to all defaulting nations. No loans were made by the Federal Government from that time until July, 1937 when the Treasury Department announced that it was setting aside $50,000,000 from the Gold Stabilization Fund to promote stability between the American dollar and the Chinese yen. In March, 1941, the Lend-Lease bill was passed by Congress providing for billions of dollars of credit in kind, in merchandise, food, airplanes, guns, tanks, and ammunition to the democracies of the world attacked by warring powers. We are now in the midst of this second great experience in the extension of credit to foreign governments.

Federal Credit Agencies

After a lapse of many decades, the extension of credit to individuals and to business enterprises by the Federal Government under the New Deal, zoomed upward as never before in our history. This more recent extension of credit, however, is so vast when measured either by the types of loans, the number, or the amount of loans, and is available under such an unlimited variety of circumstances, that previous excursions of governmental units into the domestic credit field, by comparison, seem almost infinitesimal. Perhaps this is the third revolution in our history, not as fundamental as that which gave us our freedom, but perhaps quite as fundamental as the second revolution in which control of our national policies changed from the agricultural south to the industrial and commercial north and culminated in the Civil War. Here is government in business again, and this time in a gigantic way; certainly a modest, if not a generally recognized trend toward State capitalism.

On December 31, 1940 there were twenty-nine active credit agencies of the Federal Government. These agencies fell into six general categories, those which engaged in: (1) the general extension of credit and insurance such as the *Reconstruction Finance Corporation* and the *Federal Deposit Insurance Corporation;* (2) home financing and insurance such as the *Federal Home Loan Banks* and the *Federal Savings and Loan Insurance Corporation;* (3) agricultural finance such as the *Banks for Cooperatives* and the *Commodity Credit Corporation;* (4) construction financing such as the *Public Works Administration;* (5) transportation finance such as the *Inland Waterways Corporation* and *United States Maritime Commission;* and (6) other lending agencies such as the *Tennessee Valley Authority* and the *Puerto Rico Reconstruction Administration.* The complete schedule of all governmental credit agencies as of December 31, 1940 classified under these six major divisions with their year of organization, and brief descriptions of their major functions and purposes, is as follows:

Federal Credit Agency	*Organized*	*Principal Functions*

I. GENERAL FINANCE AND INSURANCE:

RECONSTRUCTION FINANCE CORPORATION.	1932	To aid in financing agriculture, commerce, and industry; to purchase preferred stock, capital notes, or debentures of banks, trust companies, and insurance companies; and to make loans to local public bodies.
ELECTRIC HOME AND FARM AUTHORITY.	1934	To finance the instalment sale of electrical and gas apparatus, equipment, and appliances.
EXPORT-IMPORT BANK OF WASHINGTON.	1934	To assist in financing exports and imports.
RFC MORTGAGE COMPANY.	1935	To make mortgage loans to apartments, hotels, business and office buildings, either for construction or refinancing.
FEDERAL NATIONAL MORTGAGE ASSOCIATION.	1938	To establish a market for National Housing Act mortgages, and to facilitate the financing of low-cost housing projects.
DISASTER LOAN CORPORATION.	1937	To provide loans made necessary by catastrophes since 1936.
FEDERAL DEPOSIT INSURANCE CORPORATION.	1933	To insure accounts of depositors in national banks and in insured State banks; to extend credit to facilitate bank mergers in case of threatened loss, and to receivers of closed insured banks.

II. HOME FINANCE AND INSURANCE:

FEDERAL HOME LOAN BANKS.	1932	To provide reserve credit for thrift and home financing institutions.
HOME OWNERS' LOAN CORPORATION.	1933	To extend emergency long-term mortgage loans to distressed urban home owners.
FEDERAL SAVINGS AND LOAN INSURANCE CORPORATION.	1934	To insure savings in thrift and home financing institutions.
FEDERAL HOUSING ADMINISTRATION.	1934	To insure advances for alterations, repairs, and improvements on real property, to insure home mortgages, to organize and supervise national mortgage associations.

Federal Credit Agency	*Organized*	*Principal Functions*
III. AGRICULTURAL FINANCE:		
FEDERAL LAND BANKS.	1917	To make long-term first mortgage loans on farm lands.
FEDERAL INTERMEDIATE CREDIT BANKS.	1923	To make loans to, and discount farm credit paper for Government and private agencies engaged in financing farmers and farm production activities.
AGRICULTURAL MARKETING ACT REVOLVING FUND.	1929	To make loans to farmers for the production and orderly marketing of certain farm products.
REGIONAL AGRICULTURAL CREDIT CORPORATIONS.	1932	To make loans to farmers and stockmen for agricultural purposes.
PRODUCTION CREDIT CORPORATIONS.	1933	To organize Production Credit Associations and to assist in financing them. These associations make short-term loans to farmers.
EMERGENCY CROP AND FEED LOAN OFFICES.	1933	To make loans to farmers for any purpose in connection with producing and marketing crops.
BANKS FOR COOPERATIVES.	1933	To finance farm cooperatives and business concerns that serve agricultural needs.
COMMODITY CREDIT CORPORATION.	1933	To make available to producers or associations of producers, loans on those agricultural commodities for which the Department of Agriculture has a general plan or program for production or market adjustment.
FEDERAL FARM MORTGAGE CORPORATION.	1934	To assist in financing the operations of Federal Land Banks, to make loans to farmers on notes and first or second mortgages up to seventy-five per cent of the appraised, normal value of farm land.
TENNESSEE VALLEY ASSOCIATED COOPERATIVES, INC.	1934	To promote and finance cooperatives especially in the Tennessee Valley drainage basin.
FARM SECURITY ADMINISTRATION.	1935	To extend loans to qualified farm tenants to purchase farms; to make rehabilitation loans to low-income farm families for land, crop, or farm and home maintenance; to administer direct relief in stricken rural areas.

Federal Credit Agency	Organized	Principal Functions
III. Agricultural Finance, Continued:		
RURAL ELECTRIFICATION ADMINISTRATION.	1935	To make loans to persons, corporations, public bodies, and cooperative associations for financing the construction and operation of generating plants and distribution lines, and for financing wiring and plumbing installations and electrical equipment for persons in rural areas who are not receiving central-station service.
IV. Construction Finance:		
PUBLIC WORKS ADMINISTRATION.	1933	To make loans and grants to public bodies for construction purposes, and to finance and construct Federal projects.
UNITED STATES HOUSING AUTHORITY.	1937	To assist public bodies through loans in the improvement of housing conditions.
V. Transportation Finance:		
INLAND WATERWAYS CORPORATION.	1924	To promote and develop water-transportation services and facilities in connection with the commerce of the United States.
UNITED STATES MARITIME COMMISSION.	1936	To develop a merchant marine for commercial and national defense purposes and to encourage private industry in marine transportation.
VI. Other Lending Agencies:		
TENNESSEE VALLEY AUTHORITY.	1933	To maintain and operate the properties at Muscle Shoals, Alabama, in the interest of national defense, for agricultural and industrial development, and so far as may be consistent with flood-control and navigation programs, to generate and sell electrical power.
PUERTO RICO RECONSTRUCTION ADMINISTRATION.	1935	To provide relief and work relief, to finance cooperative associations, to promote rural rehabilitation, and to improve housing and living conditions on the island of Puerto Rico to the end that it will become self-sustaining.

Corporations as Government Instrumentalities

The twenty-nine credit agencies of the Federal Government which actually have outstanding billions of dollars of credit under the six primary classifications given in the above schedule, are of three structural types. The first is the typical corporation such as the *Reconstruction Finance Corporation* and the *Federal Farm Mortgage Corporation* that obtain their entire capital from the Federal Government and also sell notes, bonds, or other debt obligations guaranteed by the Federal Government to the public, or to the United States Treasury to obtain adequate working funds. The second is the cooperative form of organization such as the *Federal Land Banks* and the *Banks for Cooperatives* that obtain their initial capital directly or indirectly from the Federal Government. A borrower is required to purchase stock in the cooperative lending organization in proportion to the amount of his loan. Theoretically, cooperative agencies of this type should ultimately pass wholly under the ownership of their borrower-stockholders at which time government capital would be retired or repaid. The third is an organization without a corporate charter such as the *Federal Housing Administration* and the *Farm Security Administration* that operate directly or indirectly as arms of the Federal Government.

Our entry into the first World War brought an end to the long period during which governmental corporations had been little used. To assist in carrying on the tremendous coordinated work of the war period, the Federal Government incorporated or authorized the incorporation of the United States Emergency Fleet Corporation, the War Finance Corporation, the United States Housing Corporation, the Sugar Equalization Board, the Spruce Production Corporation, and the Russian Bureau, Inc. These organizations were created as emergency rather than as permanent agencies, and all of them ceased active operations after the close of hostilities. The United States Emergency Fleet Corporation, however, was succeeded many years later by the existing *United States Maritime Commission*.

During the fourteen years which followed the close of that war, very few additions were made to the ranks of governmental corporations. The twelve *Federal Land Banks* were organized in 1917, the twelve *Federal Intermediate Credit Banks* were set up to supplement the Federal Farm Loan System in 1923, and Congress chartered the *Inland Waterways Corporation* to develop inland water transportation and to coordinate it with railroad transportation in 1924.

As the depression which began in 1929 eased into the great national emergency, the Federal Government again turned to the corporate form of organization as a basic means for discharging new and emergency functions. The record since 1929, however, would seem to indicate that although most of these units have come into existence chiefly during a period of national emergency, they have in many instances being utilized to discharge permanent as well as temporary administrative functions of the government. The opinion has received wide currency over the intervening years that the corporate form of organization provides freedom of operation, greater efficiency as measured by business standards, and flexibility for purposes of experimentation. The report of the President's Committee on Administrative Management discussed this viewpoint in a particularly enlightened manner:

Freedom from the necessity of appropriations carries with it freedom from various governmental controls and restrictions, such as budget procedures; personnel regulations governing appointment, discharge, and compensation; and various governmental rules regarding purchase, travel, space, and property. Ordinarily corporations devise their own systems of accounts, and within the limits of their enabling statutes, may incur obligations and settle claims. These exemptions from ordinary governmental routines and procedures give corporations the power to act with a speed and economy, necessary for those enterprises set up in national emergencies, such as war and panic, and for others that are rendering continuing economic services that compete with, and will inevitably be compared with, private enterprise.

Extent of Government Credit

The aggregate "loans" of all "governmental corporations and credit agencies" compiled by the Treasury Department have been reported as follows as of June 30 each year from 1933 to 1940:

June 30	Aggregate Loans
1933	$3,603,000,000
1934	5,764,000,000
1935	8,019,000,000
1936	8,312,000,000
1937	7,785,000,000
1938	7,645,000,000
1939	7,600,000,000
1940	7,687,000,000

The amount of outstanding "loans" in the above table expanded at a very rapid rate during the difficult years from 1933 to 1935. Then the total "loans" increased moderately from $8,019,000,000 in 1935 to a peak of $8,312,000,000 in 1936. At the end of the 1937 fiscal year, the "loans" had decreased to $7,785,000,000 and from that time to the end of the calendar year of 1940, the fluctuation has been very moderate. Included in these figures are loans of almost every kind ranging from short-term loans of three months made by the *Federal Intermediate Credit Banks* to sixty years by the *United States Housing Authority*.

A combined statement of assets and liabilities of governmental "corporations and credit agencies" is published in the report of the daily statement of the United States Treasury for the last day of each month. This combined statement as of December 31, 1940 reflected a moderate expansion in aggregate outstanding "loans" during the last six months of 1940 from $7,687,000,000 to $7,945,000,000.

The full extent of the outstanding credits of all governmental "corporations and lending agencies" is not represented by these totals as these figures only represent "loans." On December 31, 1940 there were additional outstanding credits extended by the twenty-nine lending agencies amounting to $275,785,000 in accounts receivable, exclusive of accrued interest; $127,889,000 in investments in securities guaranteed by the Federal Government; and $1,553,788,000 in investments in other securities. The accounts receivable included $139,368,000 due to the twelve *Federal Land Banks* and $28,523,000 due to the *Federal Farm Mortgage Corporation*. The investments in securities guaranteed by the Federal Government represented credit extended to other lending agencies which borrow on the guarantee of the Government, principally $102,589,000 bonds of the *Home Owners' Loan Corporation* owned by the *Federal Savings and Loan Insurance Corporation*. The investments in other securities included in its existence list $761,130,000 consolidated farm loan bonds of the *Federal Land Banks* owned by the *Federal Farm Mortgage Corporation*, $452,279,000 in preferred capital stock or notes of banking institutions owned by the *Reconstruction Finance Corporation*, and $154,682,000 in the shares of *Federal Savings and Loan Associations* owned by the *Home Owners' Loan Corporation*. The aggregate of these various "forms of credit" granted just by the twenty-nine governmental credit agencies reached the formidable total on December 31, 1940 of $9,867,000,000.

Even this figure is not the grand total of all outstanding credits. It does not include three loans made by non-lending agencies; namely, $2,647,000 lent to Indians by the Interior Department, $30,080,000 lent to railways and still outstanding under the Transportation Act of 1920, and $2,123,000 in securities received by the Treasury Department from the *Reconstruction Finance Corporation* under the Act of February 24, 1938. Neither does it include securities of $60,000 held by the United States Railroad Administration of the first World War, or $295,000 of securities held by the *Panama Railroad Company,* both governmental corporations but not strictly credit agencies. Likewise it does not include receivables, exclusive of accrued interest, of $9,000 due to the *Federal Crop Insurance Corporation,* another governmental non-credit agency, $5,773,000 to the first World War Emergency Corporation and agencies in liquidation, $766,000 to Federal Prison Industries, Inc., and $432,000 to the *Panama Railroad Company.* The inclusion of the scattered miscellaneous "credits" with those of the twenty-nine strictly credit agencies gives a final grand total of $9,910,000,000 on December 31, 1940 for "all governmental corporations and credit agencies."

Now let us break the six broad groups of strictly governmental credit agencies into their component parts, ascertain the types of every-day credit in which each specializes and to whom, for how long, and on what basis each lending agency grants credit. The vast organization of credit-granting business enterprises evolved by private capital and described in the preceding chapter represents no simple arrangement. Each type of enterprise operates in a specialized field but each type also overlaps portions of other fields so that there is a maze of interference with each other in our highly competitive capitalistic system. The operations of government credit-granting organizations, as one may readily realize from the preceding paragraphs, is no whit simpler. Competition with each other and with the thousands of private credit-granting enterprises is constant and immense.

General Finance and Insurance

There are seven credit agencies of the Federal Government that operate in the general finance and insurance field, the *Reconstruction Finance Corporation,* the *Electric Home and Farm Authority,* the *Export-Import Bank of Washington,* the *RFC Mortgage Company,* the *Federal National Mortgage Association,* the *Disaster Loan Corporation,* and the *Federal Deposit Insurance Corporation.* The first six of these credit agencies come under the supervision of the governmental unit known as the Federal Loan Agency. The four credit agencies which operate in the home finance and insurance field, as outlined on page 239, also come under the general supervision of this Agency. The *Federal Deposit Insurance Corporation* has no supervisory authority.

Reconstruction Finance Corporation

The greatest house of financial power ever created in the United States, an agency of the Federal Government which has made loans to an almost infinite number of types of enterprises and whose funds have flowed freely into every State in the Union is the ubiquitous *Reconstruction Finance Corporation*. This organization was created by Congressional legislation on January 22, 1932 at the suggestion of President Hoover as an emergency agency, with limited lending powers, to function for one year. It was created to supplement the credit facilities of banks and other financial institutions that appeared unable to cope with the tightening credit conditions resulting from the expanding depression. The idea of the organization was born of conservative economic thinking but its constant expansion into fertile new fields of credit has been the result of typical New Deal thinking. It is the resurrection of the second Bank of the United States which Andrew Jackson fought and killed, only with infinite more power, influence, and prestige.

Loans have been made by this organization to commercial banking institutions to forestall runs, to closed banks to bail out depositors; to finance drainage, levee and irrigation districts and to build aqueducts; to railroads, insurance companies, building and loan associations, public school authorities, and mining companies; loans where funds have gone to meet payrolls, to pay past due invoices for the purchase of merchandise, to assist in refunding operations, and to construct so-called income producing properties. In 1934, Congress authorized the extension of loans directly to commercial and industrial business enterprises to supplement the credit facilities of the licensed and operating commercial banks and trust companies. Moreover, the *Reconstruction Finance Corporation* has furnished the permanent capital to many of the other governmental credit agencies such as the *Federal National Mortgage Association, Regional Agricultural Credit Corporations,* and the *Disaster Credit Corporation;* it has furnished working capital to others, such as the *Rural Electrification Administration,* and the *Federal Land Banks;* and it stands ready to consider loan applications which other governmental agencies have turned down. It is the "granddaddy" of the governmental credit agencies. These extensive operations are carried on through the headquarters office located at Washington, D. C., and what are known as loan agencies in twenty-seven other cities.

The management of the corporation is vested in a board of directors of five persons appointed by the President of the United States by and with the consent of the Senate. Of the five members of the board not more than three may be members of one political party, and not more than one may be appointed from any one Federal district. The outstanding capital stock amounts to $500,000,000, all subscribed and paid for by the Secretary of the Treasury on behalf of the Federal Government. It has been said that the *Reconstruction Finance Corporation,* under the direction of Jesse Jones, has grown into a fourth arm of the government not provided for in the Constitution:

All other Federal agencies undergo a double checking, by both the President and Congress, before getting any money to spend. Jones, who handles more of Uncle Sam's coin than any other one person, submits no accounting to the President, nor has he ever appeared before an appropriation's committee. The ceiling on Jesse's lending power is so high as to be meaningless. Jones, not Congress, decides how much of the billions, entrusted to him is or is not to be loaned. Again, the purposes for which the RFC can lend money are so all inclusive that, in practice, Jones, not Congress, decides what kind of loans the RFC will or will not make. ¶ Countless matters of policy come up in making loans. It is Jesse who decides what is or is not in the national interest, Jesse can decree whether textile mills or coal mines are to be abandoned, whether sick one-industry towns are to be saved. He can start new industries, like the Lufkin, Texas mill for the manufacture of newsprint from Southern pine, or can balk them. It happens that Jones is inclined to feel that the manufacture of synthetic substitutes for some raw materials not obtainable in this country is "uneconomic." He can stimulate competition in any field—with $15,000,000 of RFC financing, Reynolds Metals is about to produce aluminum—or can cut down competition. . . . The RFC constantly is making the same sort of decisions as Congress. Unlike Congress, though, the RFC affords no representation for our many diverse economic groups. No hearings are held; there is no opportunity for debate on the merits of its decisions. If Jones wants to hammer down railroad interest rates, the public gets no chance to hear what the likely effects will be on the whole field of private employment and investment.[*]

The original Reconstruction Finance Corporation Act, authorized loans to commercial banks, savings banks, trust companies, building and loan associations, insurance companies, mortgage loan companies, credit unions, Federal Land banks, Joint-Stock Land Banks, Federal Intermediate Credit Banks, Agricultural Credit Corporations, livestock credit corporations, and loans secured by the assets of banks, mutual savings banks, and building and loan associations, which were closed or in process of liquidation. It was under this authority that the loan of $90,000,000 was made in June, 1932, to the bank in which General Charles G. Dawes was chairman of the board of directors, the Central Republic Bank & Trust of Chicago. Up to March 18, 1941, the sum of $48,482,-

[*] "New Deal's J. P. Morgan," a Story of Jesse Jones, Federal Administrator, by Samuel Lubell in *Saturday Evening Post*, November 30, 1940, p. 90.

191.10 had been repaid on the principal of this loan and $20,431,731.43 in interest. Here was unlimited reserve power to support our entire banking structure and to keep banking institutions of all kinds open during the heightening difficulties of 1932 and the early part of 1933, but it failed to work; more fundamental support was needed.

That additional support came from Congressional legislation immediately provided by the Roosevelt administration. To meet the unprecedented banking crisis confronting the country, the President proclaimed a "holiday" for banking institutions. All banking transactions were suspended except those authorized under regulations issued by the Secretary of the Treasury. It now became necessary not merely to reopen the banks, but also to strengthen the entire financial system of the nation. In this situation the *Reconstruction Finance Corporation* was empowered to purchase preferred stock, or if that expedient was unlawful in a particular State, to extend credit against preferred stock, or to purchase capital notes or debentures of any commercial bank or trust company. Very substantial loans were made in accordance with this Act and outstandings are still heavy.

Congress subsequently in 1933 authorized the *Reconstruction Finance Corporation* to support insurance companies, national mortgage associations, mortgage loan companies, or similar financial institutions in the same manner by subscribing to their non-assessable preferred stock. Such support has been made to only ten insurance companies and has never been large. Where such financial institutions were not permitted to issue non-assessable stock, their legally issued capital notes or debentures could be purchased.

With the approval of the Interstate Commerce Commission aid in the financing, reorganization, maintenance, or construction of railroads may be extended by purchasing the obligations of railroads engaged in interstate commerce, or by guaranteeing the payment of such obligations when funds were not available on reasonable terms through investment or credit channels. Of all of the funded securities issued by railroads since 1932, the *Reconstruction Finance Corporation* has acquired almost thirty per cent. The Baltimore and Ohio Railroad Company has had the greatest support with aggregate loans of $95,343,000. On the other extreme, railroad loans have been made as small as $13,915 which was extended to the Greene County Railroad Co., which operates a twenty-mile line in the State of Georgia.

Loans were authorized to States, territories, and municipalities for relief purposes, for financing the repair or replacement of State and municipal property damaged by floods or other catastrophes, and to aid in financing projects authorized under Federal, State, or municipal law. Loans were authorized to or for the benefit of tax-supported public-school districts or similar public-school authorities, to or for the benefit of drainage districts, levee districts, irrigation districts, and similar organizations devoted chiefly to the improvement of lands for agricultural purposes. Such loans may not run for more than forty years. Because of their long term nature, repayments have been very moderate.

During 1932 and 1933 legislation was passed by Congress enlarging the powers to make loans to processors or distributors of agricultural commodities for the purpose of paying Federal processing taxes, and for the purpose of financing sales or surpluses of agricultural products. These functions became dormant as loans for agricultural purposes were gradually taken over by agencies of the Farm Credit Administration, and by other credit agencies not under the supervision of the Farm Credit Administration, such as the *Commodity Credit Corporation* and the *Export-Import Bank of Washington*. Outstanding loans of the *Reconstruction Finance Corporation* for crop, livestock, and commodity loans on December 31, 1940 had been reduced to a nominal amount.

Self-liquidating loans were made to finance the $200,000,000 aqueduct to carry water from the Colorado River in Arizona two hundred and forty-two miles to Los Angeles and to eighteen other cities in Southern California; the $75,000,000 Oakland Bay Bridge at San Francisco; the Niagara Frontier Bridge at Buffalo; and the bridge across the Mississippi River at New Orleans. On the cross-bay bridge from San Francisco to Oakland, one of the very early loans, a profit of $4,000,000 was recorded when the securities of $73,000,000 received for the loan were re-sold to investment bankers. On the one hundred and sixty-mile Harrisburg-Pittsburgh toll super-highway $40,800,000 was lent, with a bond profit exceeding $2,000,000 when these securities were sold. The functions of the *Reconstruction Finance Corporation* to make loans of this type were subsequently taken over by the *Public Works Administration* but this agency has been financed since its inception by selling the marketable securities received for its loans to the *Reconstruction Finance Corporation*.

Loans may also be made to business enterprises when capital or credit, at prevailing rates for the character of the loan applied for, are not otherwise available. In addition to the direct loans to business enterprises a modified insurance scheme was worked out by which the *Reconstruction Finance Corporation* may guarantee banks participating with it in loans against a percentage of their losses. Specific authority was given to extend loans to develop quartz ledge, or veins which surveys indicated contained gold, silver, or tin. "Development" has been said to be a Congressional euphemism for grub-staking. Congress might have decided that the Federal Government should hardly be expected to grub-stake any proposition as speculative as prospective mining and so the problem was turned over to the *Reconstruction Finance Corporation* with the one restriction that no loans in excess of $40,000 would be made to any mining enterprise for development purpose. No limit exists on the size of loans which may be made to established mining enterprises.

The most important amendment of June 12, 1940 provided for increased assistance to aid in national defense. Loans may be made to or capital stock purchased in any corporation for the purpose of producing, acquiring, and carrying strategic raw materials as defined by the President, for plant construction, expansion and equipment, and for working capital to be used in the manufacture of equipment and supplies necessary to national defense. Corporations may be specifically organized to carry on these activities, to purchase and produce equipment, supplies, and machinery, for the manufacture of arms, ammunition, and implements of war, to lease such plants to private corporations to engage in the manufacture, and if necessary for a government agency to engage in such production, to engage in and to carry on manufacturing processes. Under this amendment, capital has been furnished for expanding aircraft plants, for manufacturing motors, machine tools, parts, and uniforms. Authority actually exists to go into any line of business considered essential for national defense.

Under this defense amendment the *Reconstruction Finance Corporation* had organized four corporations prior to January 1, 1941 and had made commitments which aggregated no less than $1,099,298,000. The Reserve Rubber Company was organized June 28, 1940 to accumulate a reserve stock of 430,000 tons of crude rubber in 1940 and 1941 at a cost of approximately $190,000,000. The *Commodity Credit Corporation* had previously acquired 95,000 tons of crude rubber in 1939 in exchange for cotton in a barter agreement with Great Britain. The Metals Reserve Company was also organized June 28, 1940 to accumulate reserve stocks of antimony, chrome ore, copper, graphite, managanese ore, tungsten, trioxide, tin, wolframite, and toluol, an essential of T.N.T. By December 31, 1940 outstanding orders for these commodities totaled $376,724,-200. The Defense Plant Corporation was organized August 22, 1940 to construct plants, docks, and to acquire machinery and equipment to manufacture airplanes and parts, tanks, tank engines, ordnance and other products essential for national defense. These plants are leased to the manufacturers. Outstanding commitments on December 31, 1940 totaled $349,780,000 and actual defense loans to business enterprises $51,809,000. The Defense Supplies Corporation was created August 29, 1940 to acquire and to carry a reserve supply of critical and strategic materials and supplies such as high-test aviation gasoline, nitrate of soda from Chile, and Australian wool.

The outstanding credits extended by the *Reconstruction Finance Corporation* as of December 31, 1940 under these many and varied authorizations amounted to the very substantial sum of $1,531,599,000. The variety and extent of the credits made by this great financial institution are clearly evident from the following table:

Loans to:

Agricultural Credit Corporation	44,000
Banking Institutions	$148,800,000
Building and Loan Associations	4,268,000
Business Enterprises, for National Defense	51,809,000
Business Enterprises, not for National Defense	121,268,000
Credit Unions	11,000
Crop, Livestock, and Commodity Loans	490,000
Insurance Companies	24,513,000
Joint-Stock Land Banks	3,265,000
Mortgage Loan Companies	43,628,000
Railroads	486,172,000
States and Territories	103,409,000
Other Loans	79,113,000
Total Loans	$1,066,790,000
Accounts and Other Receivables	4,229,000
Bonds in Tennessee Valley Authority	8,300,000
Stocks and Debentures in Banking Institutions	452,280,000
Stocks and Debentures in Insurance Companies	100,000
Total Outstanding Credits	$1,531,699,000

Electric Home and Farm Authority

This enterprise was first organized under Delaware laws on January 17, 1934, as the Electric Home and Farm Authority, Inc. A new corporation was formed August 1, 1935, under the laws of the District of Columbia. The assets of the Delaware corporation were then transferred to the new corporation which was given the existing title of *Electric Home and Farm Authority.*

In the development of the power program by the Tennessee Valley Authority, it was found that the existing sales finance companies confined their operations principally to the larger cities and the surrounding territories, and that as a result, consumers living in small towns and in rural areas had difficulty in purchasing electrical and gas appliances, apparatus, and equipment on the typical instalment basis. Moreover, the cost of such services as were available in restricted territories was so high that purchases of equipment and the use of electrical energy were materially restricted. The *Electric Home and Farm Authority* was created with a paid-in capital of $850,000 to provide these financing facilities at a rate, and on terms, which would encourage the instalment purchase of domestic and farm electrical and gas appliances in rural areas in all parts of the country.

Unlike most of the governmental lending agencies, the outstanding capital stock was not issued to the Federal Government, a cabinet office, or some other lending agency, but to its seven trustees. The stock is held by them in trust for the Federal Government. The members of the board of trustees are all officers or employees of the *Reconstruction Finance Corporation.* The principal office is located in Washington, D. C., and district offices in five important widely-spread centers, Chattanooga, Tennessee; Chicago, Illinois; Los Angeles, California; Minneapolis, Minnesota; and Portland, Oregon.

The *Electric Home and Farm Authority* is a sales finance company. Conditional sale contracts, chattel mortgages, and instalment notes are purchased with recourse from retail distributors who sell refrigerators, water heaters, water pumps, coal stokers, gas furnaces, cream separators, electric motors, milking machines, feed grinders, radios, and similar durable goods products. Credit instruments average $150 which covers the sale price, less the down payment, plus the finance charge. Minimum down payments range from five per cent in the purchase of such products as refrigerators, water heaters, and coal stokers, to ten per cent for radios and milking machines. The actual down payment, however, averages sixteen per cent. In this way credit is made available indirectly to the individual buyer. The face amount of the instrument includes the time payment charge computed on the basis of five per cent per annum on the principal amount being financed. Thus the charge amounts to $5 on an unpaid balance of $100 when repaid in twelve equal monthly instalments, $9.92 when covered in twenty-four equal monthly payments, and $14.84 when repaid in thirty-six equal monthly instalments.

When a purchaser fails to meet an instalment the dealer is requested to repurchase the contract in full. If collection is not accomplished in this manner, steps are then taken to foreclose and obtain possession of the collateral. Renewals or extensions are often granted in delinquent cases. Copies of all contracts purchased are filed with the utility which serves the purchaser under an agreement for billing and collecting the monthly instalments. Under this agreement the utility receives a fee of twelve and one-half cents per month for each contract serviced and one dollar for each contract at the time it is purchased and filed for collection.

Facilities are also provided for financing the installation of electrical wiring in existing dwellings and farm buildings. Indebtedness of this character is retired in twenty-four equal monthly instalments or less. Agreements with utility companies for billing, collecting, and remitting the monthly payments on these installations provide that no fees will be paid on these particular contracts. After inspection of the completed work, a monthly instalment note, endorsed without recourse, is purchased from the contractor.

All financial requirements, above that obtained from its paid-in capital stock of $850,000 have been provided from accumulated surplus, collections, and from borrowings on its unsecured notes from commercial banks. On December 31, 1940 the earned surplus amounted to $280,000. All notes outstanding on that date had been discounted by depository banks at one per cent per annum. This low rate had been obtained as the *Reconstruction Finance Corporation* had agreed to repurchase any notes not met at maturity.

For the year ending December 31, 1940 purchases of contracts and notes amounted to $12,479,000 compared with $9,962,000 for 1939, an increase of twenty-five per cent. This volume represented a national spread as operations were carried on in thirty-six States. Losses have been small since the inception of the business, amounting to approximately one-sixth of one per cent. About two-thirds of the purchasers in the fiscal year of 1940 reported monthly incomes of $150 or less.

Outstanding loans on December 31, 1940 amounted to $14,305,000 and accounts receivable due principally from dealers to $22,000, or total credit of $14,327,000. While this volume of business is relatively small compared with the activities of the well-known sales and discount finance companies, these operations of the *Electric Home and Farm*

Authority are significant because business is carried on principally in areas where instalment facilities have been unavailable, and because its finance charge is below that made by typical finance companies in larger cities throughout the country.

Export-Import Bank of Washington

As a gesture in connection with the recognition by the United States of the Union of Soviet Socialist Republics, the *Export-Import Bank of Washington* was incorporated under the laws of the District of Columbia on February 12, 1934, to assist in financing trade between the two countries. The board of trustees of the bank decided that this trade should not be financed in the absence of the complete settlement of the long-standing debts and claims between the United States and the Soviet Union.

In order to extend certain credits to the Republic of Cuba, the second Export-Import Bank of Washington, D. C., was created in March, 1934. This bank now developed its activities to place American manufacturers and exporters more on a par with foreign subsidized competitors by financing trade on longer terms with other countries, except with the Soviet Union. When the breakdown in the negotiations to settle the Soviet debts occurred early in 1935, the trustees authorized the second Export-Import Bank of Washington, D. C., to transfer its commitments and loans to the *Export-Import Bank of Washington*. The second bank was finally liquidated and went out of existence on June 30, 1936. Thereafter, the facilities of the *Export-Import Bank of Washington* were available to assist in financing trade between the United States and any foreign country. The Departments of State, Treasury, Agriculture, and Commerce are represented on its board of trustees.

The capital stock of the bank was increased from $75,000,000 to $175,000,000 in January, 1941, divided into $1,000,000 of common stock and $174,000,000 of preferred stock. All common stock, except eleven shares in the names of the trustees, stand in the names of the Secretary of State and the Secretary of Commerce, jointly, for the benefit of the United States. The preferred stock is all owned by the *Reconstruction Finance Corporation*.

The bank operates in four major export fields. Until the outbreak of the second World War, the most important field was the extension of short-term credits to finance the exportation of agricultural products, especially cotton and tobacco, where necessary facilities were not readily available through existing financial institutions. The bank assisted in the sale of raw cotton to foreign spinners and to foreign dealers by establishing, through American commercial banks, lines of credit available to American cotton shippers and guaranteed by prominent banks in the countries of the purchasers. Prior to the present war such lines of credit had been established for spinners and dealers in Italy, Yugoslavia, Czechoslovakia, Latvia, and Poland, upon terms of six months, with the privilege of renewing obligations for an additional three months. Early in 1939, lines of credit had also been established for Spanish spinners, upon the obligation of Spanish banks, to mature over a much longer period of twenty-seven months. It had been customary for commercial banks to limit similar cotton credits to three or four months. The longer credits, however, had been made necessary as a result of the lack of dollar exchange in many of the countries constituting the foreign market for our agricultural products. In 1940, a number of such loans were authorized to foreign governments and to the agencies of foreign governments to assist in financing the exportation of other agricultural products such as wheat and lard along with certain manufactured products, but in only a few instances have these credits been more than partly used.

The second important field is the extension of credit directly to American firms engaged in exporting industrial products, particularly heavy machinery, electrical, and railway equipment. These credits cover particular transactions; they are not revolving. The practice of the bank, until the opening of the present war, had been to offer credit terms approximating those made available by foreign manufacturers, the average having been in the neighborhood of five years. In some cases, the bank agreed to assume a portion of the risk without recourse to the American manufacturer or exporter. These transactions have usually been accomplished by discounting the obligations of the foreign purchaser, endorsed or otherwise unconditionally guaranteed by a foreign bank, or in a few cases, by a foreign government. This type of financing has increased moderately during the past year but principally with Latin-American countries. Brazil has been the principal recipient with eleven such loans outstanding on December 31, 1940 and with ten other substantial loans authorized but not yet utilized. These loans covered the exportation of railway cars and equipment, locomotives, ships, steel rails, electrical equipment, and road building equipment. Other substantial commitments and loans were outstanding to Argentine, Chile, Colombia, Ecuador, Paraguay, Peru, Venezuela, Uruguay, Costa Rica, Cuba, Dominican Republic, Haiti, Mexico, Nicaragua, and Panama. The only countries outside of Latin America to which such credits have been extended are China and Portugal.

The third field represents the extension of credit up to $20,000 to smaller American exporting and importing houses that have been hampered by lack of capital in obtaining accommodation from commercial banks. It has been the practice to designate a commercial bank to handle such an account as agent for the *Export-Import Bank of Washington*. These credits are revolving and are made available by the agent bank to the exporter or importer upon presentation for discount of ninety day drafts on approved foreign purchasers. Twelve such loans were outstanding on December 31, 1940.

The fourth field represents an increasing number of special transactions such as making dollar exchange available solely for the purpose of meeting obligations promptly to American exporters. Credits of this nature have been granted to leading banks in Argentine, Brazil, Colombia, Ecuador, Nicaragua, Paraguay, Peru, and Uruguay. This field has become the most important part of the activity of the *Export-Import Bank of Washington* during the past year. In the case of Brazil the credits were designed to alleviate a temporary adverse exchange situation and to restore trade with the United States as far as possible to a free exchange basis. In the other cases they were intended to eliminate unusual fluctuations in the supply of exchange, including those resulting from the seasonal exportation of major crops. Credit has also been extended to the Republic of Cuba at five different times to finance the purchase of silver bullion and the minting by a United States mint into standard Cuban pesos. Payments in these cases have been made against the delivery of pesos in Havana.

Interest rates and charges depend upon maturities and risk. Rates have ranged from three and one-half to six per cent per annum, and commissions from one-half of one per cent to five per cent flat on the amount of participation. On December 31, 1940, the *Export-Import Bank of Washington* was operating on a paid-in capital of $75,000,000, and an earned surplus of $6,030,000. On that date outstanding credits were represented entirely by unpaid loans of $82,836,000.

R F C Mortgage Company

On January 31, 1935, Congress passed legislation allowing the *Reconstruction Finance Corporation* to subscribe for stock in various kinds of corporations, including mortgage loan companies. One and one-half months later, on March 14, 1935, the *RFC Mortgage Company* was incorporated under the laws of the State of Maryland and the entire capital stock was taken by the *Reconstruction Finance Corporation.*

At the time there were in existence the twelve *Federal Home Loan Banks,* the *Home Owners' Loan Corporation,* and provision had been made for the establishment of *Federal Savings and Loan Associations.* The National Housing Act had been enacted to make mortgage money available to home owners on reasonable rates and terms. Credit facilities had also been made widely available to farmers through the various institutions supervised by the Farm Credit Administration. Mortgages on income-producing business properties, such as apartment houses having more than four apartments, hotels, business structures, and office buildings, could be refinanced by no existing governmental instrumentality. Likewise there were no credit facilities for those interested in the construction of properties of this type. The *RFC Mortgage Company* was organized to fill these needs.

The lending activities of the *RFC Mortgage Company* have been of three types, refinancing loans, new construction loans, and certificate loans. Refinancing loans, secured by first mortgages, are made on income-producing business properties where financing cannot otherwise be obtained upon reasonable terms, and where the income in sufficient to pay operating expenses, taxes, insurance, interest on indebtedness, and reasonable amortization. New construction loans, secured by first mortgages, are made to assist in the erection of new income-producing buildings. Certificate loans are made to distressed holders of first mortgage bonds and first mortgage certificates upon their promissory notes secured by bonds and certificates, provided sufficient information is available to determine that the income value of the property or properties securing the bonds or certificates is sufficient to warrant the loan. Very few loans of this type have been granted as the borrower in each instance must establish extreme distress to be eligible for the loan. With few exceptions all loans are amortized monthly.

Operations are carried on through a principal office located in Washington and agents located in thirty-one cities. Financing operations and general cash requirements are met through the repayment of loans, the sale of mortgages, the collection of interest, and through borrowings from the *Reconstruction Finance Corporation,* secured by the pledge of underlying collateral. On December 31, 1940 operations were carried on with a paid-in capital of $25,000,000, and surplus and reserves of $639,000. Outstanding loans amounted to $67,299,000, securities guaranteed by the Federal Government were carried at $385,-000, and accounts receivable representing principally purchase money mortgages on repossessed properties which had been sold amounted to $413,000; providing total outstanding credit of $68,097,000.

Federal National Mortgage Association

The National Housing Act of 1934 made provision for the establishment of a new type of mortgage lending institution that would operate under Federal charter and supervision. These institutions would supplement local mortgage lending companies, and would furnish a market for long-term amortized mortgages through the authority to purchase mortgages from local institutions. Each such concern was given authority to issue and to have outstanding bonds or debentures ten times the aggregate par value of its outstanding capital stock. It was felt that this authority would enable a national mortgage association to sell notes or debentures in those sections of the country where an excess of mortgage money was available, and that the funds thus obtained could be used in financing residential construction in other sections where a scarcity of mortgage funds existed. The system was planned to work like the open market for short-term commercial paper.

In May, 1935 and in February, 1938 liberalizing amendments were enacted by Congress. No national mortgage associations, however, had been organized with private capital and so the President, on February 7, 1938, directed the *Reconstruction Finance Corporation* to organize such an association and to provide it with management.

On February 9, 1938, the *Federal National Mortgage Association* was organized with a paid-in capital of $10,000,000, and a paid-in surplus of $1,000,000. The entire capital stock was purchased by the *Reconstruction Finance Corporation*. Operations are carried on through the principal office located in Washington, D. C., and through agents located in twenty-nine cities throughout the United States.

The *Federal National Mortgage Association* is prohibited from making real estate mortgage loans. It will, however, purchase mortgages insured by the *Federal Housing Administration* for the principal unpaid balance plus accrued interest to the date of purchase. Such mortgages are serviced by the institutions from which the mortgages are purchased, or by other approved mortgagee institutions operating in the territory in which the properties are located.

On December 31, 1940 operations were conducted on a paid-in capital of $10,000,000, a paid-in surplus of $1,000,000, and earned surplus and reserves of $6,190,000. On that date outstanding mortgage loans amounted to $181,100,000, securities guaranteed by the Federal Government were carried at $584,000, and accounts receivable at $13,000, or total outstanding credit of $181,697,000. The funds to carry these obligations were obtained largely by the sale of its own notes, with maturities up to five years. On December 31, 1940 $80,304,000 of these notes were owned by the *Reconstruction Finance Corporation* and $85,240,000 were in the hands of private investors.

Disaster Loan Corporation

Immediately after the floods occurred in New England and Pennsylvania in 1936, Congress authorized the *Reconstruction Finance Corporation* to grant loans for financing the repair, the reconstruction, and the rehabilitation of property damaged or destroyed by floods or other catastrophes in 1935 or 1936. The amount of these loans was limited by this initial legislation to $50,000,000.

When the Ohio-Mississippi Valley was devastated by a flood in January, 1937, no part of these funds were available. Senator Alben W. Barkley of Kentucky desired the *Reconstruction Finance Corporation* to make additional loans to the extensive number of individuals and business enterprises that had suffered from this particular disaster, but as such loans would not be "adequately secured," it was decided to set up a separate corporation for this particular purpose. Congress accordingly passed legislation on February 11, 1937 creating the *Disaster Loan Corporation* with an authorized capital of $40,000,000, of which $24,000,000 was subscribed by the *Reconstruction Finance Corporation* and was outstanding on December 31, 1940. This stock was subsequently assigned to the Secretary of the Treasury and is held by him in behalf of the Federal Government.

In order to be eligible for a loan from the *Disaster Loan Corporation,* an applicant must have suffered property loss or damage from a flood, a hurricane, or some other catastrophe in the years from 1936 to 1940 inclusive. A loan as small as $15 and many for $25 have been made to southern sharecroppers. The largest loan which amounted to $13,906,605 was made to the Federal Surplus Commodities Corporation, controlled by the Department of Agriculture, in 1939. This corporation, in turn, organized the Northeast Timber Salvage Corporation, an operating company to measure, value, and cut the timber destroyed by the extensive sleet storm which had caused widespread damage to New England forests in the Spring of the year. These funds were used to advance cash equal to ninety per cent of the value of this timber to the owners of the land, the loans to be repaid as the timber was sold.

The typical loan of the *Disaster Loan Corporation* is in the neighborhood of $2,000. Repayment provisions and other terms are determined by the exigencies of each borrower but maturities generally run from four to five years. These particular loans differ from somewhat similar extensions of credit authorized by the *Reconstruction Finance Corporation,* principally by the fact that little or no security is required. Operations are carried on from the principal office located in Washington, D. C., and eighteen regional offices located in all parts of the country from Boston to Los Angeles.

Loans are serviced by the field facilities of the *Reconstruction Finance Corporation.* The proceeds of collections and income are used to make new loans and to carry on the general operations of the corporation. No appropriations have ever been received from Congress, its entire operations having been carried on with the capital of $24,-000,000 contributed by the *Reconstruction Finance Corporation.* Outstanding credits of the *Disaster Loan Corporation* on December 31, 1940 consisted of 15,552 loans aggregating $20,905,000, and accounts receivable principally representing purchase money mortgages taken in the sale of properties of $137,000, a total of $21,042,000.

Federal Deposit Insurance Corporation

The *Federal Deposit Insurance Corporation* was chartered by Congress on June 16, 1933. It is the outgrowth of conditions which existed prior to and at the time of the declaration of the memorable banking holiday in March, 1933. After that dramatic episode in our economic history, only the banking institutions that were certified as solvent by their supervising authorities were licensed and reopened.

The primary functions prescribed by law for the *Federal Deposit Insurance Corporation* are to insure national and State banks admitted to membership in the Federal Reserve System, to examine and admit to insurance State banks not under the Federal Reserve System which apply for insurance, to pay off depositors in closed insured banks, to terminate the insurance of insured banks continuing unsafe and unsound practices, to liquidate closed insured banks when appointed receiver, and to make loans to banks in order to facilitate mergers where threatened losses might be averted or diminished. The principal office is located in Washington, D. C. In addition there are twelve district examination offices and numerous but a constantly fluctuating number of field liquidation offices.

The deposit balance of each depositor in each insured bank is insured up to $5,000. An annual premium of one-twelfth of one per cent of total deposits is paid by each bank for its insurance. This premium is just one-third of what previous experience would indicate, would be necessary. Whether or not this rate will be sufficient over a period of years to take care of future bank losses is a matter which only time will tell. As of December 31, 1940, the membership of insured banks consisted of 5,144 national banks, 1,342 State banks that were members of the Federal Reserve System, 6,956 State banks that were not members of the Federal Reserve System, and 53 mutual savings banks.

The very nature of the banking structure in the country has made bank supervision an extremely difficult task. There are national banks chartered by the Comptroller of the Currency that are members of the Federal Reserve System subject to supervision and regulations issued by both the Comptroller of the Currency, the Board of Governors of the Federal Reserve System, and the Federal Reserve Banks. There are State banks chartered under the laws of the forty-eight States, subject to the supervision of the State banking departments in the respective States, and in cases where the State banks are members of the Federal Reserve System, the banks are also subject to both regulation and supervision by the Board of Governors of the Federal Reserve System and by the Federal Reserve Banks. Heretofore, no single agency has been concerned with the entire banking system. With the establishment of the *Federal Deposit Insurance Corporation* and with approximately ninety-four per cent of the operating banks in the country insured with this agency, with the uninsured banks for the most part being small banks in isolated communities, there has finally been established a common meeting ground for most of the banks in the country.

The *Federal Deposit Insurance Corporation* is authorized to make loans only to banks and only under two sets of circumstances: to facilitate a merger with another bank, if by so doing a threatened loss may be averted or diminished; and to the receiver of a closed bank to permit a distribution of funds to creditors of the bank, provided that, in case of a loan to a receiver, if the closed bank is not a national bank or a State bank that is a member of the Federal Reserve System, it must have been an insured State bank. Up to December 31, 1940 loans had been made to 129 insured banks to facilitate mergers and of these loans 115 were wholly or partly outstanding. Loans had also been made to the receivers of 226 insured banks to pay off depositors. The New Jersey Title Guarantee & Trust Company of Jersey City with deposits of $23,000,000 became financially involved in February, 1939. This was the largest banking institution to have received assistance from the *Federal Deposit Insurance Corporation.*

In view of the fact that loans may only be made to a bank to avert or to diminish a threatened loss, there is no legal provision as to the adequacy of security which must be pledged. In all cases the security includes so-called unacceptable assets in the bank to which the loan is made, and which is being merged. The typical loan and merger trans-action provides that the purchasing bank assumes all liabilities of the selling bank (the bank to which the loan is made), takes over the so-called acceptable assets which are considered to be of sound value and suitable for a bank, and then receives the cash proceeds of the loan made by the *Federal Deposit Insurance Corporation* to the selling bank. In this process the *Federal Deposit Insurance Corporation* acquires all remaining, or so-called unacceptable assets as collateral to its loan. This collateral has generally consisted of real estate mortgages, unsecured notes, real estate, and stocks and bonds, including a great many items that may have previously been charged off by the bank. In almost all cases it is evident that a loss will be sustained. It must be determined, however, that such a loss will be less than the loss which would have been sustained had the bank been allowed to close, depositors been paid off, and the bank placed in receivership. The loan agreement provides that any collateral remaining after the payment of all liquidation expenses, repayment of the principal in full, and payment of the interest at four per cent per annum, shall be returned for distribution to the stockholders of the bank to which the loan was made.

The *Federal Deposit Insurance Corporation* is authorized to issue and to have outstanding its notes, debentures, bonds, or other such obligations, aggregating three times the amount of its capital stock plus the assessments upon insured banks for the year 1936. These notes, debentures, bonds, and other obligations may be secured by assets in such manner as may be authorized by its board of directors. The law authorizes the Secretary of the Treasury to purchase any of these obligations. Up to December 31, 1940 no notes, debentures, bonds, or other such obligations had been issued.

On December 31, 1940 operations were being conducted on outstanding no par, non-voting, non-dividend stock carried at $289,299,000. Of this paid-in capital stock, $150,000,000 was purchased and is held by the Secretary of the Treasury on behalf of the United States and $139,-299,000 by the twelve *Federal Reserve Banks* equivalent to fifty per cent of their respective surpluses on January 1, 1933. There was no credit or debit surplus but there had been accumulated substantial reserves of $238,689,000. Outstanding loans amounted to $58,981,000, in addition to which there were accounts receivable of $36,730,000 representing claims on the assets of closed banks as a result of payments made to insured depositors, or aggregate credit accommodation of $95,711,000.

Home Finance and Insurance

The four credit organizations that operate in the home finance and insurance field also come under the supervision of the Federal Loan Agency. These four organizations were created to effect reforms in the home mortgage field, the *Federal Home Loan Banks,* the *Home Owners' Loan Corporation,* the *Federal Savings and Loan Insurance Corporation,* and the *Federal Housing Administration.* The first three of these organizations are supervised by an intermediate agency known as the Federal Home Loan Bank Board.

Great developments have been made in the encouragement of thrift and home ownership by thousands of financial institutions over the years since *The Philadelphia Saving Fund Society* was organized in Philadelphia in 1816, and the *Oxford Provident Building Association* in Frankford, Pennsylvania, in 1831. Each new institution, however, had been an isolated unit with no reserve of credit upon which it could draw in an emergency. The Federal Home Loan Bank System was developed to remedy this situation by providing a reservoir of credit in the home financing field somewhat analogous to that already established in the commercial banking field by the Federal Reserve System and in the farm-mortgage field by the Federal Land Bank System.

Federal Home Loan Banks

Twelve district *Federal Home Loan Banks* were organized in October, 1932. They are located in strategic centers from Boston to Los Angeles to serve all sections of the country. Federal savings and loan associations, which are federally chartered, are required to be members of the system, and State-chartered home-financing institutions such as mutual savings banks, building and loan associations, cooperative banks, and insurance companies which are engaged in home financing, are eligible for membership. On December 31, 1940 membership consisted of 3,864 institutions of which 1,437 were Federal savings and loan associations, 2,387 were State building and loan associations, 11 were mutual savings banks, and 29 were insurance companies.

The sum of $125,000,000 was made available by Congress and $124,741,000 was actually used by the Secretary of the Treasury to purchase stock and provide the initial paid-in capital for these twelve *Federal Home Loan Banks*. The paid-in capital on December 31, 1940 ranged from $7,284,000 for the bank in Portland, Oregon to $23,887,000 for the bank in New York City. Member institutions must subscribe to stock in their district bank to the extent of one per cent of the aggregate unpaid principal of their home-mortgage loans, but not less than $500. Borrowing members must at all times hold stock in their district *Federal Home Loan Bank,* amounting to not less than one-twelfth of their outstanding advances from the bank. On December 30, 1940 the member institutions had an invested interest of $55,741,000 in the twelve banks. Paid-in capital amounted to $169,282,000, while total capital, surplus, and reserves from all sources amounted to $180,482,000.

Each bank has the authority to issue debentures, bonds, or other obligations. The Federal Home Loan Bank Board may also issue consolidated Federal Home Loan Bank debentures which become the joint and several obligations of the twelve banks. Obligations of these banks, whether issued by the board or a bank, are not guaranteed by the United States, either as to principal or interest. All securities which had been issued through 1940 have been the unsecured consolidated Federal Home Loan Bank debentures of which $90,500,000 were outstanding on December 31, 1940, all held by investors.

As reserve banks, the twelve *Federal Home Loan Banks* are empowered to make both long and short term advances to member institutions. Short term advances, not to exceed one year, may under certain circumstances be unsecured. Long term advances, up to ten years, must be secured by home mortgages or obligations of, or guaranteed by, the United States. If an advance runs for more than one year, repayment must be amortized on a monthly or quarterly basis. On all advances, whether secured or unsecured, a statutory lien is held on the borrowing member's stock in its district *Federal Home Loan Bank*. On December 31, 1940 the outstanding loans of the twelve *Federal*

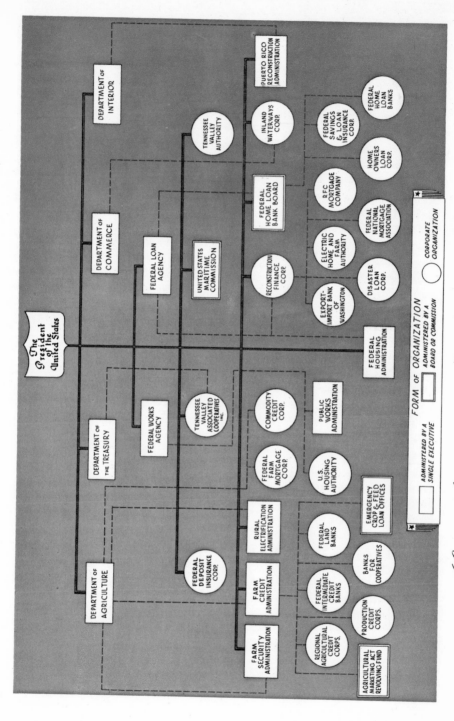

Credit Agencies of the Federal Government, 1941

Home Loan Banks amounted to $201,491,000. Of this sum $284,000 was due from member insurance companies and $201,207,000 from member savings, building, and loan associations. In addition, the twelve banks had accounts receivable of $8,000, providing total outstanding credit of $201,499,000.

Home Owners' Loan Corporation

The estimated volume of non-farm mortgage foreclosures increased from 68,100 in 1926, to 248,700 in 1932, and 252,400 in 1933. Approximately twenty to twenty-five per cent of outstanding urban mortgages, were foreclosed in the two years of 1932 and 1933. Foreclosures, moreover, only represented a modest part of the loans which were in default. Some immediate action was essential to alleviate the distress that existed among the home-owning public, and to stabilize the real estate market which had become glutted with an unprecedented volume of foreclosed properties. At the same time, it was necessary to support the mortgage credit structure during this crisis.

In this situation, the *Home Owners' Loan Corporation* was chartered in June, 1933 by the Federal Home Loan Bank Board to refinance home mortgages. It was given a capital of $200,000,000 paid in by the Secretary of the Treasury. Headquarters are located at Washington, D. C. and ten regional offices carry on operations in all parts of the country.

Initially the *Home Owners' Loan Corporation* was authorized, for a period of three years, to exchange its bonds and advance cash for first mortgages on urban homes in actual danger of foreclosure, or to recover a home lost within two years. Loans were limited to $14,000 or to eighty per cent of the appraised value of the property, whichever was smaller. These refinancing operations ceased on June 12, 1936, and since that time its activities have been confined to collecting and servicing outstanding loans, and managing and selling properties which had been acquired.

Loans were limited to non-farm real estate upon which there was located a dwelling or dwellings for not more than four families, and which were used, in whole or in part, by the owner as his home, and which had a value of not more than $20,000. During the three years in which loans were made, a total of 1,886,491 applications aggregating $6,173,355,000 were filed. Loans were actually made to 1,017,827 borrowers for a total of $3,093,450,000. These loans were extended on the direct reduction plan providing for the payment of interest, and the gradual and orderly retirement of the principal indebtedness through regular monthly payments, generally over a period of fifteen years.

Every effort has been made to hold foreclosures to the minimum. Where a default is willful or where the property has been abandoned, action is promptly taken. Likewise, where a default is not willful but its continuance is clearly unavoidable, action is taken. Properties owned and in process of acquisition as of December 31, 1940 numbered 65,084 compared with a peak of 121,107 on May 31, 1938.

In addition to the power to refinance moderate size urban home-owned mortgaged property, the *Home Owners' Loan Corporation* was empowered to purchase shares, make deposits, purchase certificates of deposits and investment certificates in State-chartered building and loan associations, when insured; and in Federal savings and loan associations, all of which must be insured. This provision was for the purpose of assisting in the organization and the financing of building associations in communities where local home financing needed encouragement on reasonable terms and conditions. This support has enabled established institutions that were in a frozen or inactive condition, and located in communities handicapped by a shortage of home-mortgage funds, to resume normal mortgage loan operations.

On December 31, 1940, the *Home Owners' Loan Corporation* had outstanding loans of $1,956,267,000. At the same time, investments in shares, deposits, and certificates of deposits in State building and loan associations amounted to $39,580,000, and in Federal savings and loan associations to $154,683,000, while accounts receivable amounted to $62,000. Outstanding credits totaled the very substantial sum of $2,150,592,000. To carry on these extensive operations the corporation had a paid-in capital of $200,000,000. Operations to December 31, 1940 had entailed a deficit in this sum to the extent of $85,489,334. Most of the funds which had been used to grant loans had been obtained by the issuance of bonds guaranteed by the Federal Government. These bonds aggregated the very substantial sum of $2,614,919,000 on December 31, 1940 and were largely owned by investors.

Federal Savings and Loan Insurance Corporation

The *Federal Savings and Loan Insurance Corporation* gives a protection to shareholders in savings, building, and loan associations somewhat similar to that provided by the *Federal Deposit Insurance*

Corporation for depositors in commercial banking institutions and mutual savings banks. It was created by Congress in June, 1934 to provide ultimate insurance to shareholders in insured savings, building, and loan associations up to $5,000. On December 31, 1940, 2,276 institutions were covered by this insurance protection; all of the 1,437 Federal savings and loan associations which by law were obligated to join the system, and 839 of the State-chartered building and loan associations.

The funds of the *Federal Savings and Loan Insurance Corporation* are being created by two methods: through the initial capital of the corporation, and by the payment of an annual premium by insured associations equal to one-eighth of one per cent of share and creditor liabilities until a reserve of five per cent is accumulated. The initial paid-in capital amounting to $100,000,000 was provided by the *Home Owners' Loan Corporation* in exchange for the entire capital stock, and was made not in the form of cash but by three per cent bonds of *Home Owners' Loan Corporation* due May 1, from 1944 to 1952. The $3,000,-000 interest which is received on these bonds each year is transferred from earnings to a reserve for contingencies which on December 31, 1940 amounted to $16,500,000. The premiums paid by insured associations approximate $2,300,000 annually. No funds have been obtained directly or indirectly from the Federal Treasury. On December 31, 1940 capital, surplus and reserves amounted to $126,449,000.

The fundamental purpose of this organization is to prevent default or to restore an insured institution in default to normal operations by means of a loan, the purchase of assets, or a contribution. No contribution, however, may be made to any institution in an amount in excess of that which would be reasonably necessary to save the expense of liquidating the association. In case of default and liquidation of an insured association, the *Federal Savings and Loan Insurance Corporation* does not make cash immediately available like the *Federal Deposit Insurance Corporation*. It makes available to each of the insured investors a new account of the same amount in an insured institution, not in default, or if the investor prefers, he may obtain ten per cent of his insured investment in cash immediately, forty-five per cent in negotiable non-interest-bearing debentures of the *Federal Savings and Loan Insurance Corporation* due within one year from the date of the default, and forty-five per cent in similar debentures due within three years. Up to the present time, no such debentures have been issued. No loans had been made to impaired insured associations up to December 31, 1940, all settlements of such situations having been effected by making contributions to restore their assets and thereby to prevent default.

From the time of its establishment up to December 31, 1940, the *Federal Savings and Loan Insurance Corporation* has handled the cases of twenty-one distressed associations. Contributions aggregating $1,165,000 were made to twelve institutions, with additional contingent commitments of $394,000. Three of the twenty-one associations were merged with other insured institutions in their communities; six continued to operate as separate units; and three subsequently went into voluntary liquidation, paying all insured investors. Three associations were placed in liquidation by the supervisory authorities and the optional methods of settlement were made available to the insured investors; the outlay in these cases amounted to $503,000, a substantial portion of which, it is expected, will be returned as the assets are liquidated. Four cases were pending solution at the close of 1940, and the remaining two were in need of no immediate assistance.

On December 31, 1940 accounts receivable, exclusive of accrued interest, were outstanding to the extent of $1,415,000 represented principally by claims against the assets of insured associations which had been taken over by other savings, building, and loan associations.

Federal Housing Administration

The *Federal Housing Administration* is one of the agencies of the Federal Government that is not a corporation. This agency was created in June, 1934 for three purposes: to insure lending institutions such as commercial banks, mutual savings banks, and insurance companies against losses on loans extended on personal notes, the proceeds of which were to be used in financing alterations, repairs, or improvements of existing structures; to insure lenders on home-mortgages, including small-home properties and large-scale rental or group-housing projects, against loss of principal from default of the borrower and subsequent foreclosure on the mortgage; and to charter and supervise the operations of national mortgage associations that would operate as purchasers of insured mortgages.

The success of the property-improvement plan in tapping idle funds is indicated by the fact that through December 31, 1940 financial institutions scattered in every State in the Union had reported 3,009,224 notes for insurance in the total amount of $1,242,959,000. Up to December 31, 1940, claims for insurance had been paid on 122,098 notes with an aggregate value of $30,511,000. Prior to June 30, 1939 no charge was made for this insurance. After that date a premium of three-fourths of one per cent per annum was collected.

Insured mortgages may represent from eighty to ninety per cent of the appraised value, and may run from twenty to twenty-five years, depending upon the value of the property. An annual premium of one-half of one per cent on the outstanding reducing balance of the mortgage is charged. On December 31, 1940 there were 7,785 separate financial institutions holding *Federal Housing Administration* premium-paying mortgages on small homes. At the same date only 3,547 of the 634,023 premium-paying small-home mortgages had been foreclosed by the lending institutions, and in only 2,311 of these cases had the mortgagees turned over title to the *Federal Housing Administration*. In these cases the *Federal Housing Administration* issued to the lending institutions its debentures guaranteed by the United States Treasury in exchange for title to the foreclosed property. In this way lending institutions obtained a liquid, income producing asset guaranteed by the Federal Government in exchange for a fixed asset of doubtful value. On December 31, 1940 there were $12,945,000 of these guaranteed debentures outstanding. Debentures have a maturity date which is three years subsequent to the maturity date of the original mortgage, and bear interest of two and three-quarters per cent per annum.

Operations are carried on from headquarters in Washington, D. C., and from eighty-eight field offices. On December 31, 1940 the *Federal Housing Administration* had assets in excess of actual liabilities of $54,837,000 which represented its net worth as a business enterprise, and a modest amount of only $12,945,000 of outstanding debentures, guaranteed by the Federal Government, given in exchange for mortgaged property. From the date of its organization through December 31, 1940, notes and mortgages which totaled $4,345,000,000 had been insured. On that date investments were carried at $14,000, and accounts receivable, largely purchase money obligations received from the sale of repossessed properties, were carried at $23,211,000.

Agricultural Finance

Twelve governmental credit agencies operate in the agricultural field. The entire twelve agencies come under the supervision of the Department of Agriculture. Interposed between the the first seven of these agencies listed in the table on page 216 and the Department of Agriculture is an administration and supervisory organization known as the Farm Credit Administration. The remaining five credit agencies come under the direct supervision of the Department of Agriculture.

The Farm Credit Administration was organized in 1933, during the depth of the depression, to provide a complete and coordinated credit system for agriculture by making facilities available to farmers for long-term and short-term credit. This powerful, far-reaching agency now has under its supervision most of the credit agencies making loans to farmers and operating under Federal supervision; these institutions comprise a nation-wide system of permanent agricultural credit-granting organizations and a group of emergency agricultural credit organizations.

The entire country is divided into twelve farm districts. In each of these twelve districts there is in active operation one *Federal Land Bank,* one *Production Credit Corporation,* one *Federal Intermediate Credit Bank,* and one *Bank for Cooperatives.* The offices of these four institutions operating in each district, are located in the same city and in the same building. In nine out of the twelve districts, the offices of a fifth credit agency, the *Emergency Crop and Feed Loan Section,* are also located in the same buildings.

The extensive activities of the Farm Credit Administration are directed and supervised by a governor who is assisted by two deputies and four commissioners, all appointed by the President of the United States with the consent of the Senate. Each of the four commissioners is in charge of one of the four divisions of national activity which have permanent offices together in the twelve districts; one known as the Land Bank Commissioner supervises the twelve *Federal Land Banks,* one known as the Production Credit Commissioner supervises the twelve *Production Credit Corporations,* one known as the Intermediate Credit Commissioner supervises the twelve *Intermediate Credit Banks,* and one known as the *Cooperative Bank Commissioner* supervises the *Central Bank for Cooperatives* at Washington which operates across State lines and the twelve *Banks for Cooperatives.* One board of directors of seven members serves simultaneously as the board for each of these four agencies in the same district so that the activities of the four organizations are fully integrated and correlated.

Federal Land Banks

The twelve *Federal Land Banks* were established in March, 1917 as permanent institutions to provide long-term credit for agriculture on first mortgages. In 1935, these banks were also given the power to make loans under certain conditions to corporations engaged in raising livestock. Prior to that time individuals engaged in raising livestock were eligible to become borrowers but not corporations.

Slightly over ninety-six per cent of the operations of the *Federal Land Banks* are carried on through underlying National Farm Loan Associations. These associations are cooperative credit organizations created by groups of farmers who have united for the purpose of obtaining long-term mortgage credit. In a typical case, the farmer obtains a first mortgage loan from his local association, and simultaneously purchases shares of capital stock in his local association to the extent of five per cent of his loan. These shares of stock are pledged with the association along with the first mortgage as collateral security for the loan. The association then endorses the loan and turns it over to its district *Federal Land Bank*. These loans are limited to fifty per cent of the agricultural value of the land plus twenty per cent of the insured improvements.

The association, in turn, purchases capital stock in its district *Federal Land Bank* equal to five per cent of its aggregate loans. The land bank stock is now pledged with the bank as additional collateral to secure the association's endorsement. In other words, the farmer obtains long-term, first mortgage credit from his local National Farm Loan Association, which then pledges that mortgage to the district *Federal Land Bank* as the principal security for a loan of similar size. The shares of capital stock purchased by the farmer in his local association, and by the association in the district land bank, are the bases of cooperative interest of the borrower in the workings of this system. This procedure is somewhat complicated because it is indirect, but the technique is the practical way in which cooperative farm organizations function. On December 31, 1940 there were 3,635 National Farm Loan Associations in existence, a steady decrease from the peak of 5,034 associations on December 31, 1935.

Federal Land Banks are authorized to make loans directly to farmers only in localities not served by National Farm Loan Associations. The interest rate on such loans is one-half of one per cent higher than on loans made through local farm loan associations. During 1940, the *Federal Land Banks* made eighty-five loans direct to farmers, amounting to $247,800.

The consolidated balance sheets of the twelve *Federal Land Banks* on December 31, 1940 disclosed paid-in capital stock of $177,-

940,000, paid-in surplus of $145,225,000, earned surplus, undivided profits and reserves of $105,332,000, an aggregate of invested funds of $428,497,000. Of the total invested funds, 48.6 per cent was owned by the Treasurer of the United States, and the remaining 51.4 per cent by National Farm Loan Associations and by farmers who had borrowed directly from these banks.

The greater portion of the funds required to carry on operations from day to day, are obtained by the issuance of consolidated farm loan bonds for which the twelve *Federal Land Banks* are jointly and severally liable for the payment of both principal and interest. On December 31, 1940 there were $1,755,810,000 of these obligations outstanding. These bonds unlike those of the *Home Owners' Loan Corporation* are not guaranteed in any way by the Federal Government. They are secured by the pledge of underlying mortgages as collateral.

On December 31, 1940 there were first mortgage loans of the *Federal Land Banks* outstanding for a total of $1,851,218,000. Loans were at their high point in 1935 when $2,071,924,000 was outstanding. Since that time, there has been a gradual and moderate reduction each year. In addition, the twelve banks had outside investments of $756,000 consisting almost entirely of securities of the *Federal Intermediate Credit Banks*, and accounts receivable consisting principally of purchase money mortgages taken in the sale of repossessed farms of $139,368,000, providing total outstanding credit of $1,991,342,000.

Federal Intermediate Credit Banks

The twelve *Federal Intermediate Credit Banks* were organized in March, 1923 to grant credit of certain types to farmers' cooperative associations, and to serve as reservoirs for financing institutions which, in turn, made loans direct to farmers and to stockmen. These banks were not empowered to extend credit directly to individuals. Considerable use was made of the discount facilities of the *Intermediate Credit Banks* during the first ten years of their operation, but farmers and stockmen benefited only indirectly. With the establishment of the nation-wide system of local Production Credit Associations in 1933 with capital funds obtained largely from these twelve banks, the modified system has become much more widely and generally used.

The principal activity of the *Federal Intermediate Credit Banks* at the present time is to discount and to purchase the promissory notes given by farmers and stockmen to Production Credit Associations and which have been endorsed by one of the twelve *Production Credit Corporations;* they also discount and purchase similar credit obligations given by farmers and stockmen to national and State commercial banking institutions, privately capitalized agricultural credit corporations, incorporated livestock loan companies, and similar agricultural lending organizations. To be eligible, discounted notes must bear the endorsement of the original lending institution. The *Federal Intermediate Credit Banks* may also make loans directly to such financial institutions on the security of paper eligible for discount.

Maturities acceptable to the *Federal Intermediate Credit Banks* usually coincide with normal marketing or liquidating seasons in order that obligations will come due when funds are available for their repayment. Ordinarily, the maturities range from three months to one year. Under the law they may not exceed three years.

These banks may also make loans direct to farmers' cooperative marketing, purchasing, and business service associations, and may rediscount loans made to such cooperatives when endorsed and offered for discount by any one of the *Banks for Cooperatives.* However, the *Federal Intermediate Credit Banks* have withdrawn almost entirely from the field of direct lending to cooperative associations. Most of the loans direct to cooperative associations are now made by the twelve *Banks for Cooperatives.* Only the larger of such loans are offered by these institutions to the *Federal Intermediate Credit Bank* of its district for rediscount.

Of the total volume of business in 1940, loans to and discounts for financing institutions amounted to $475,868,000, or 92.9 per cent; loans aggregating $31,797,000, or 6.2 per cent were rediscounted for *Banks for Cooperatives,* and loans to cooperative associations totaled $4,593,000, or 0.9 per cent. Of the total volume of credit extended to financing institutions in 1940, 81.4 per cent, represented loans to and discounts for Production Credit Associations, and 18.6 per cent for privately capitalized institutions such as commercial banks, agricultural credit corporations, and livestock loan companies.

Most of the funds used in the lending operations of the twelve *Federal Intermediate Credit Banks* are derived from the sale of debentures to the investing public. To this end the banks issue and sell consolidated collateral trust debentures having a maturity of not more than five years. Ordinarily they are issued for three to twelve months, with interest payable at maturity. The Federal Government assumes no liability, direct or indirect, for these debentures. The twelve institutions are jointly and severally liable for both the principal and the interest of consolidated debentures.

On December 31, 1940 operations of the twelve *Federal Intermediate Credit Banks* were conducted on aggregate paid-in capital of $60,000,000, surplus and reserves of $23,579,000, and debentures, practically all in the hands of the investing public, of $200,635,000. The entire outstanding capital is owned by the Federal Government. Outstanding loans amounted to $206,764,000 and accounts receivable to $518,000, making total credit of $207,282,000.

Agricultural Marketing Act Revolving Fund

The *Agricultural Marketing Act Revolving Fund* is neither a corporation nor a separate governmental organization. As the title implies it is solely a fund. The Agricultural Marketing Act, approved June 15, 1929, created a Federal Farm Board and authorized an appropriation of $500,000,000 to be used as a revolving fund in promoting the effective merchandising of agricultural commodities. The Federal Farm Board administered this fund until May 27, 1933, when the Farm Credit Administration became its successor and was given the administration of the remaining balance of the fund and of the outstanding loans due from farmers' cooperative associations and stabilization corporations. Active lending operations have been curtailed and a program of orderly liquidation of outstanding loans has been under way since the establishment of the *Central Bank for Cooperatives* and the twelve district *Banks for Cooperatives* in 1933. A number of properties consisting largely of grain elevators, grain warehouses, and related machinery and equipment which were acquired by assignment or foreclosure, have and are being sold.

The Farm Credit Act of 1933 under which the *Central Bank for Cooperatives* and the twelve district *Banks for Cooperatives* were established, provided for the payment from the revolving fund for the capital stock of these institutions. Net disbursements from the fund for this purpose aggregated $149,000,000, of which $50,000,000 represented the purchase of stock in the *Central Bank for Cooperatives* and $99,000,000 the purchase of stock in the twelve district *Banks for Cooperatives*.

On December 31, 1940, outstanding loans from the revolving fund amounted to $16,462,000 compared with $466,243,000 on May 27, 1933, when the Farm Credit Administration succeeded the Federal Farm Board, and outstanding accounts receivable to $94,000. Outstanding loans were all to cooperative associations, $12,168,000 in merchandising loans and $4,294,000 in facility loans.

Regional Agricultural Credit Corporations

The Emergency Relief and Construction Act of 1932, authorized the *Reconstruction Finance Corporation* to create in any of the twelve farm credit districts a *Regional Agricultural Credit Corporation* with a paid-in capital of not less than $3,000,000. Twelve corporations were subsequently created, one in each district, to meet the existing needs in agricultural communities for short-term credit. On May 1, 1934, these twelve *Regional Agricultural Credit Corporations* were placed in orderly liquidation, inasmuch as the Production Credit Associations, a permanent source of short-term credit, had been organized to provide farmers and stockmen with appropriate short-term credit facilities.

On December 31, 1940 the aggregate paid-in capital of the twelve corporations had been reduced to $5,000,000, all assigned to the Secretary of the Treasury. The paid-in surplus amounted to $16,512,000 and a deficit in earned surplus to $832,000. On the same date 6,021 outstanding agricultural loans had been reduced to $5,855,000, and accounts receivable to $92,000, total outstanding credit of $5,947,000.

Production Credit Corporations

The twelve *Production Credit Corporations* were established from August to December, 1933 to provide cooperative credit facilities adaptable to the short-term and intermediate-term credit needs of agriculture. *Production Credit Corporations,* however, do not extend credit. Their funds are invested primarily in class A capital stock of underlying Production Credit Associations to the extent of approximately twenty per cent of the actual or expected volume of loans to be made by respective local associations. Surplus funds of the *Production Credit Corporations* are invested in three other classes of securities, in bonds of the Federal Government, in government-guaranteed bonds of the *Federal Farm Mortgage Corporation,* and in consolidated farm loan bonds of the *Federal Land Banks*.

The capital stock of each local Production Credit Association is divided into two classes, "A" and "B." Class A capital stock is non-voting. It is preferred as to assets in case of liquidation, and is held principally by the district *Production Credit Corporation*. The class

B capital stock may be purchased only by member-borrowers and those eligible to become members. Each member of an association subscribes to class B stock in an amount equal in fair book value (not to exceed par) to the extent of $5 for every $100, or fraction of $100, borrowed. Class B stock, if not sold to another member of the association, must be converted into class A stock within two years after a stockholder ceases to be indebted to the association. This provision makes certain that control of all associations will rest in the hands of their active member-borrowers, one of the basic cooperative principles.

The proceeds resulting from the sale of class A capital stock to *Production Credit Corporations,* are not lent but are invested by each association in approved securities. Associations do not extend credit. They serve as intermediaries by endorsing and rediscounting the notes of their member-borrowers with the *Federal Intermediate Credit Banks* as already explained. This process is even more indirect than the manner in which a farmer obtains credit from a *Federal Land Bank*. Notwithstanding the circuitous route, the method works out in practice. They act more like London bill brokers who endorse the notes they sell, or somewhat like the acceptance activities of commercial banks.

More than one-half of the loans made by local Production Credit Associations during 1940 were for amounts less than $450. In four districts, slightly more than one-half of the loans were for less than $250. Loans generally are made to mature within one year, the maturity date being fixed at the time the livestock or crops which are being financed, are expected to be marketed.

Within prescribed limits, a local association may extend credit upon approval of the loan by its loan committee without forwarding the member's note for discount to the district *Federal Intermediate Credit Bank*. This practice enables associations to make loans to its members within a few days' time. Notes offered to a *Federal Intermediate Credit Bank* which are not rediscounted, and which cover loans already made; are carried by the local association until placed in discountable condition or until they are collected.

The underlying organizations, the Production Credit Associations are local cooperative groups of farmers and stockmen that operate under Federal charters granted by the Governor of the Farm Credit Administration. On December 31, 1940 there were 529 active associations, a drop from the peak of 599 on December 31, 1934.

The twelve *Production Credit Corporations* on December 31, 1940 were operating on aggregate paid-in capital of $105,000,000 and earned surplus of $3,922,000. The entire outstanding capital stock is owned by the Treasurer of the United States. The amount of the paid-in capital ranged from $8,500,000 for the *Production Credit Corporation* of New Orleans, Louisiana, to $13,500,000 for the *Production Credit Corporation* of Columbia, South Carolina.

The rediscounts of the Production Credit Associations with *Federal Intermediate Credit Banks* on December 31, 1940, amounted to $143,799,000, represented 83.4 per cent of the total loans made by the associations. The remaining 16.6 per cent of the loans were being carried by the local associations. During 1940, farmers and stockmen obtained 230,906 loans, including renewals, for a total of $349,693,000 compared with 234,266 loans for $320,961,000 during 1939.

The par value of the capital stocks of the 529 active Production Credit Associations on December 31, 1940, was $78,340,000, of which $16,895,000 represented class B stock owned by 254,159 farmers and stockmen. The investments of the twelve *Production Credit Corporations* in class A stock on December 31, 1940 was the quite respectable amount of $61,445,000. In addition, the *Production Credit Corporations* had $10,425,000 invested in bonds of the *Federal Land Banks,* and outstanding accounts receivable of $11,000, making aggregate outstanding credit accommodation of $71,881,000.

Emergency Crop and Feed Loan Offices

The *Emergency Crop and Feed Loan Offices* are not corporations. They represent governmental credit agencies created in 1933 to lend funds obtained directly from the United States Treasury pursuant to appropriation acts of Congress. They function as a division of the Farm Credit Administration in making small loans direct to farmers who have been unable to obtain loans from any other source.

Credit is extended for the purpose of financing the fallowing of land, the production and harvesting of crops, and the purchase and production of feed for livestock. All loans are made on a secured basis. Loans for the production of cash crops are secured by a first lien on all crops financed, and loans for the purchase or production of feed for livestock are secured by a first lien on the livestock. Credit of this nature is limited to $400 except that the Governor of the Farm Credit Administration may make loans in excess of this amount in any area certified by him to the President as a distressed emergency area. Of the total loans made since 1931, only one-tenth of one per cent have been secured by liens on livestock. Since practically all of the loans are secured by liens on the crops financed by the loan, repayments have been materially affected by crop yields and market prices.

Liens given to secure crop production loans are limited to the crops grown during the current crop season. The government, with only an occasional exception, holds no security for unpaid crop loans made in prior years, although such loans are still evidenced as existing valid obligations by promissory notes. Despite the unsecured character of these prior unpaid loans, substantial repayments continue to be made each year in areas where crop conditions are satisfactory. As an interesting illustration, $4,845,000 was repaid in 1940 on loans made in 1939 and prior years, and of this sum $322,000 represented collections on loans made as far back as 1933.

For the purpose of administering the loan program, headquarters are located in Washington, D. C., and eleven regional offices are maintained throughout the country, nine of which are located in cities where other units of the Farm Credit Administration are located.

The First Deficiency Appropriation Act, approved February 9, 1937, earmarked the sum of $50,000,000 and provided that these funds should be available until June 30, 1938. In each following year, Congress has provided that the unexpended balance of this $50,000,000 appropriation, together with all collections made on 1937 and subsequent loans, should be available for making future emergency crop and feed loans. As a result of this policy, it has not been necessary for Congress to appropriate any funds for making emergency crop and feed loans during the fiscal years of 1938 or 1939. At the beginning of the fiscal year of 1940, Congress supplemented the funds already authorized by an additional appropriation of $15,000,000.

The *Emergency Crop and Feed Loan Offices* in 1940 made 160,989 loans to farmers amounting to $19,471,000, an increase of 15.4 per cent in the number of loans and 29.1 per cent in dollar volume compared with 1939. Of the 1940 emergency crop and feed loans, 63.3 per cent had been repaid at the close of the year, compared with 68.3 per cent repaid on the 1939 loans at the end of 1939. Outstanding loans as of December 31, 1940 amounted to $167,385,000.

Banks for Cooperatives

The *Central Bank for Cooperatives* at Washington, D. C., and the twelve district *Banks for Cooperatives,* were incorporated from

August to December, 1933, to extend credit to farmers' cooperative organizations. They were designed to meet the credit needs of farmers' cooperative associations that market farm products, purchase farm supplies for their members, or furnish farm business services. For the most part, the credit needs of farmers' cooperative associations are met by the twelve district *Banks for Cooperatives*. When the operations of an association are on a national or a broad regional basis, thus extending over several farm credit districts, financing is generally obtained from the *Central Bank for Cooperatives* at Washington, D. C.

The law provides that each cooperative association that obtains an operating capital or facility loan from its district *Bank for Cooperatives,* must, at the time the loan is made, own $100 of capital stock in the lending bank for every $2,000, or fraction of $2,000 it borrows. Cooperative associations, however, need to own only $100 of stock for every $10,000, or fraction of $10,000 when borrowed on the security of approved commodities. Where the purchase of stock by cooperative associations is contrary to a State law, the required amount may be paid into the guaranty fund of the bank. Upon full repayment of a loan, the borrower's capital interest may be retired at par, unless the stock of the bank has become impaired, in which case the stock is retired at par, less its pro rata share of the impairment.

Three distinct types of loans, commodity loans, operating capital loans, and facility loans, are made available to eligible cooperative associations. Commodity loans, which are made on the security of staple farm products and supplies, are short-term loans, usually for the duration of the borrower's marketing or purchasing season. Loans on unhedged commodities may be made up to seventy-five per cent of the current market value of the commodity pledged as security, while loans on hedged commodities may be made up to ninety per cent of the commodity's value. By agreement the *Banks for Cooperatives* submit all commodity loans of $100,000 or more to the *Federal Intermediate Credit Banks* for rediscount. Operating capital loans are also made for short terms, primarily to supplement the borrower's working capital during seasons of peak activity. There are no statutory provisions regarding the type of security required as collateral for loans in this category. In general, liens on real estate, on equipment, or on inventories are acceptable. Facility loans are made to enable borrowers to finance or refinance the acquisition of land, buildings, or other facilities. Security generally consists of a first lien on the property itself, although additional collateral is sometimes taken. Facility loans are limited by law to sixty per cent of the fair appraised value of the security offered and may not be made for a term in excess of twenty years. In actual practice most of the loans are scheduled for repayment within ten years.

The *Central Bank for Cooperatives* was originally capitalized at $50,000,000, while the initial capital of each of the district banks was $5,000,000. From time to time, additional subscriptions to the capital of each of the district banks have been made, and on December 31, 1940 the aggregate capital of the thirteen banks amounted to $112,620,000, and the earned surplus and reserves to $19,091,000. Of the total invested funds, $4,174,000 represented the interests of cooperative associations and the balance represented the interest of the Federal Government.

Outstanding loans on December 31, 1940 amounted to $74,740,-000, investments in securities of the *Federal Farm Mortgage Corporation* guaranteed by the Federal Government amounted to $10,030,000, other investments $27,233,000, and accounts receivable $530,000, or total outstanding credit of $112,533,000.

Commodity Credit Corporation

In the Fall of 1933 President Roosevelt was anxious to have the *Reconstruction Finance Corporation* grant loans of ten cents a pound on cotton, then selling at nine cents a pound. The law, since liberalized, required the *Reconstruction Finance Corporation* to lend only on "full and adequate security." There was no law, however, to prevent the *Reconstruction Finance Corporation* from lending to another Governmental corporation, which, in turn, would make the loan on cotton. By executive order, the *Commodity Credit Corporation* was incorporated under Delaware laws on October 17, 1933 to serve this purpose.

The *Commodity Credit Corporation* makes loans principally to producers to finance the carrying and orderly marketing of agricultural commodities. All such loans have been made upon the recommendation of the Secretary of Agriculture, and each loan program has been specifically approved by the President. Loans made to individual producers upon basic commodities—cotton, corn, wheat, wool—are made under an arrangement whereby the producer may either secure the loan directly from the *Commodity Credit Corporation,* or from banks and other local credit institutions under an arrangement whereby such loans will be repurchased at face value plus accrued interest.

Loans are made either to individual producers or associations of producers. All loans made to individual producers have been without liability to the producer for any deficiency arising from the sale of the collateral unless fraudulent statements or misrepresentations are established. With the exception of loans on corn, and approximately thirty per cent of the loans on wheat, all loans are made upon the security of negotiable warehouse receipts issued by approved public warehouses. All loans on corn, and approximately thirty per cent of the loans on wheat, are made upon the security of the commodity stored on the farm and sealed by the county agricultural conservation associations.

On December 31, 1940 operations were conducted on a paid-in capital of $100,000,000, paid-in surplus of $170,129,000, and a deficit in earned surplus of $169,541,000 indicating that some substantial losses had been taken. Of the capital stock $3,000,000 was initially subscribed by the Secretary of Agriculture and the Governor of the Farm Credit Administration; subsequently $97,000,000 was subscribed by the *Reconstruction Finance Corporation*. In 1938 the entire capital stock was turned over to the Federal Government. Additional funds, when needed, have been obtained by selling debentures guaranteed by the United States in the investment market. On December 31, 1940 $696,-252,000 of these guaranteed obligations were in the hands of investors. Outstanding loans on that date amounted to $280,218,000, and accounts receivable to $1,165,000, making aggregate credit of $281,383,000.

Federal Farm Mortgage Corporation

The Emergency Farm Mortgage Act of 1933 made available to the Land Bank Commissioner a fund of $20,000,000 to meet any demand for more liberal farm mortgage credit than could be provided by the existing permanent units of the Farm Credit Administration. The Federal Mortgage Corporation Act, approved January 31, 1934, extended and broadened these emergency facilities and established the *Federal Farm Mortgage Corporation* with the entire capital stock owned by the Federal Government. Headquarters are located in Washington, D. C., and branches in the twelve land bank cities.

The *Federal Farm Mortgage Corporation* thus makes loans for the same general purposes, but on a more liberal basis than the *Federal Land Banks*. These loans may be granted upon the security of first or second mortgages on farm property, either real or personal, not exceeding, together with all prior encumbrances, seventy-five per cent of the appraised normal value or "prudent investment value" of the property mortgaged. The maximum loan which may be made to any one farmer is $7,500.

These loans are payable on an amortization plan with annual or semi-annual instalments maturing within forty years. Most of the loans, however, are payable over ten years, with no principal payments during the first three years. Loans generally represent first mortgage accommodation on security not eligible for Federal Land Bank loans, or second mortgage accommodation to supplement existing or new Federal Land Bank loans. The availability of these supplemental lending facilities, where the amount loanable by the *Federal Land Banks* within their limit of fifty per cent of the value of the land and twenty per cent of the value of the buildings is insufficient to meet the applicant's requirements, has enabled many thousands of farmers to obtain additional funds, as well as assisted thousands of young farmers and tenants in the purchase of farms.

Funds to grant these loans are obtained from the paid-in capital of $200,000,000 and by the issuance of bonds which are fully and unconditionally guaranteed both as to principal and interest by the United States Government. On December 31, 1940 outstanding guaranteed bonds amounted to the substantial sum of $1,269,620,000.

The proceeds of approximately one-half of the bonds issued by the *Federal Farm Mortgage Corporation* have been used to furnish the *Federal Land Banks* with funds for making land bank loans. Here was a perfectly legal but subtle financial arrangement. At the time the *Federal Farm Mortgage Corporation* was created, the demand for Land Bank loans was greater than the banks could readily finance through the issuance and sale of consolidated farm loan bonds in the investment market. During the calendar years of 1934 and 1935, the *Federal Farm Mortgage Corporation* accordingly assisted the *Federal Land Banks* in financing their large volume of loans by accepting their consolidated bonds in exchange for an equivalent amount of its own bonds. The fact that the bonds of the *Federal Farm Mortgage Corporation* were fully guaranteed by the United States Government gave them a wider market at lower rates of interest. In this way the *Federal Land Banks* were enabled to finance and to make a large volume of Land Bank loans at interest rates considerably lower than they could otherwise have done. Since the early part of 1936 the *Federal Land Banks* have sold their own bonds directly in the investment markets to obtain funds to make new loans as well as for refunding purposes.

On December 31, 1940, 433,226 loans were outstanding to farmers with an unpaid principal balance of $648,296,000, compared to 439,076 loans with an unpaid balance of $690,880,000 on December 31, 1939. In addition the *Federal Farm Mortgage Corporation* owned $761,130,000 consolidated farm loan bonds of the *Federal Land Banks*, $760,000 securities of the *Federal Intermediate Credit Banks,* and had accounts receivable, largely purchase money obligations, of $28,523,000 outstanding, or total outstanding credit of $1,438,709,000.

Tennessee Valley Associated Cooperatives, Inc.

This corporation was chartered under the laws of the State of Tennessee in January, 1934, to assist in organizing and fostering a chain of cooperative enterprises to improve the economic welfare of the lower-income families in the Tennessee Valley drainage basin. The entire outstanding capital stock is owned by the Federal Government.

Potential borrowers must be organized under the cooperative laws of the State in which they are located; their officers and members must be producers; and there must be a need to relieve distress among the small farmers and idle workers in the area of activity of the borrowing association. Under these conditions, the *Tennessee Valley Associated Cooperatives, Inc.,* will make loans evidenced by demand notes, will invest in the preferred stock of the cooperative, and in certain cases will make outright grants of funds to them.

The amount of a loan is governed by the volume of business which the borrowing cooperative expects to handle. This amount is determined by the presentation of a budget showing their need in advance of the operating season. As the program is more or less a relief program, limitations of loans have been governed more by the needs of the borrowers than by the appraisals of its actual security. The *Tennessee Valley Associated Cooperatives, Inc.,* takes a lien on the fixed property of the borrowing association and on the inventory of finished goods created through the use of the loan. Repayment is made when the products of the borrowing association are sold. The proceeds of repayments are returned to the *Tennessee Valley Associated Cooperatives, Inc.,* and used for making further loans. In other words, the proceeds are used as a revolving fund.

The *Tennessee Valley Associated Cooperatives, Inc.,* was given a grant of $300,000 by the Federal Emergency Relief Administration through the Tennessee Emergency Relief Administration. As this money has been used as a revolving fund, no other appropriations have been made by the United States Treasury. On December 31, 1940 operations were being conducted on a paid-in capital of $1,000 and a paid-in surplus of $294,000. Outstanding loans amounted to $258,000, investments in preferred stocks of cooperatives to $34,000, and other investments $2,000, making total outstanding credit of $294,000.

Farm Security Administration

The *Farm Security Administration* is not a corporation; it is a Bureau in the Department of Agriculture. It is a change in name, made in September, 1937, of the Resettlement Administration which had been set up two years earlier principally to resettle destitute or low-income families and to make loans to needy farm families. Activities are carried out by twelve regional offices spread from Raleigh, North Carolina, to Portland, Oregon.

The work of the *Farm Security Administration* has assumed three major phases, rehabilitation loans to farm families and to cooperative associations of farmers, direct relief to farmers, and loans to farm tenant families to assist in acquiring farms. All contacts with families who are assisted by loans or by direct relief are ordinarily made through the county office which serves as the rehabilitation center in all rural areas. Each of the nearly two thousand county offices is run by a rural rehabilitation supervisor. Through this office, applications for loans are made, farm and home management plans upon which the loans are based are drawn up, and the actual work of supervision, debt adjustments, and loan collection is carried on.

Farm owners, farm tenants, sharecroppers, farm laborers, or persons who, when last employed, obtained the major portion of their livelihood from farming operations are eligible for rehabilitation loans. At the time of application for a loan, an applicant must be unable to obtain adequate funds from any other source. He must give some evidence of previous managerial ability, and must show that the land available to him is capable of providing a satisfactory return if intelligently worked. The applicant must also agree to accept and to follow farm and home management plans developed with the assistance of the local county office staff which call for the raising and the canning of sufficient vegetables and fruits to provide an adequate diet for the family, the growing of sufficient livestock for farming operations and food purposes, the diversion of adequate acreage in feed crops for the livestock, and the raising of a specified acreage in cash crops.

The advance of credit is then made to enable the farmer to obtain the bare essentials for his farming operations, such as a mule or a plow, and to help him secure necessary services such as medical care which will improve the health and the efficiency of himself and his family. The purpose of the loan is to put the farmer on his feet, while guidance is being offered to help him operate his farm with the greatest possible efficiency. Loans range from an average of about $250 in areas where the type of farming requires a smaller physical outlay, to somewhat over $800 in areas where normal operations make a larger investment in stock and equipment necessary. These loans are ordinarily made for periods from one to five years, although in certain special instances loans are granted for ten years; they are evidenced by one or more promissory notes secured by a first lien on crops growing or to be grown by the borrower, and a first lien on any livestock or equipment purchased with the proceeds of the loan.

Loans may also be made to establish cooperative services, or to existing cooperative business enterprises to finance or extend facilities or services where clients of the *Farm Security Administration* are materially benefited. These loans have been made to acquire property, to construct buildings, to purchase equipment, to provide operating capital, and to refinance or reestablish existing cooperative activities. They are secured by mortgages, chattel mortgages, or liens on the property or crop so acquired or produced, with different types of security being required in different areas. The period for which a loan of this type is made varies considerably according to the purpose, the financial resources of the individuals concerned, the estimated life of the property where it exists, and depreciation on that property. The maximum period is forty years.

Direct relief in the form of outright grants of money is provided for emergency conditions in stricken agricultural areas. Farm owners, farm tenants, sharecroppers, farm laborers, and other persons who now live on farms and who, when last employed, received the major portion of their income from farm operations are eligible. An applicant's need is established when it is determined through personal investigation that his material and credit resources are inadequate to meet accepted subsistence requirements, to maintain health, or to prevent human suffering. Grants of money are made to meet emergency needs for food, fuel, clothing, shelter, indispensable medical services, and other essential subsistence goods or services. A total of 1,079,800 grants averaging approximately $20 each was made during the year ending June 30, 1940.

Loans are also made to farm tenants, farm laborers, sharecroppers, and others who are engaging or have recently engaged in farming operations for the major portion of their income, to assist them in purchasing farms. To be eligible, the head of the family must be a citizen, have a good reputation among his neighbors, have demonstrated resourcefulness and farming ability, and be unable to obtain financial aid elsewhere. A variable payment plan is available under which the borrower makes payments on his loan according to the amount of his yearly net cash income, paying more in good years and less in poor years. No final payment is required in less than five years.

The *Farm Security Administration* has no legal authority to borrow for any purpose. It has no authority to establish special revolving funds to finance future activities with the proceeds of recoveries of past expenditures. Therefore, its proposed program is subject each year to scrutiny by the Bureau of the Budget and pertinent Congressional committees before funds can be made available.

It was obvious from the beginning that expenditures for such activities as direct relief and voluntary farm-debt adjustment would produce no revenue. The benefits would be in the form of alleviating and preventing distress and suffering from hunger, cold, and disease, and in enabling debt-burdened farmers to get a new start. In a lesser degree all other activities were expected to involve some cost to the Federal Government. On December 31, 1940 outstanding loans amounted to $375,353,000 and accounts receivable to $10,804,000, or total outstanding credit of $386,157,000.

Rural Electrification Administration

The *Rural Electrification Administration* was established in May, 1935. It is a direct arm of the Department of Agriculture and not a corporation. All sums authorized for loans and for administrative expenses are made available by annual appropriations and at the direction of Congress.

Loans many be made to "persons, corporations, States, Territories, and subdivisions and agencies thereof, municipalities, people's utility districts, and cooperative, non-profit or limited-dividend associations." More than ninety-eight per cent of all loans made in dollar amounts have been "for the purpose of financing the construction and operation of generating plants, electric transmission and distribution lines or systems for the furnishing of electric energy to persons in rural areas who are not receiving central station service." The remaining two per cent of loans have been "for the purpose of financing the wiring of the premises of persons in rural areas and the acquisition and installation of electrical and plumbing appliances and equipment." Cooperative associations have taken 91.5 per cent of all loans, public bodies 6.8 per cent, and utilities companies for profit 1.7 per cent.

As of June 30, 1940, this agency had made loans or entered into obligations to make construction loans with 692 borrowers totaling $269,518,000, or an average of $389,000 per borrower. Of the aggregate contracts $135,949,000 were executed in the 1939 fiscal year, the peak volume. In the 1940 fiscal year $47,625,000 contracts were signed. Wiring and appliance loans must be repaid within five years and all other loans within twenty-five years.

Although most loans are secured by first mortgages upon the properties financed, certain loans are protected by collateral or other security. In some States, public bodies borrowing funds for rural electrification cannot lawfully mortgage the properties, and in these instances revenue bonds have been accepted. Certain loans to utility companies have been secured by the deposit of general mortgage bonds of the borrowing corporation or an affiliate corporation by way of collateral security. Under the provisions of the Rural Electrification Act of 1936, the *Reconstruction Finance Corporation* was authorized and directed to make loans to the *Rural Electrification Administration* upon the approval by the President. On December 31, 1940 outstanding credits of the *Rural Electrification Administration* were represented by loans which aggregated $249,229,000.

Construction Finance

During the first half of the year 1933, virtually no new construction work was undertaken by private capital. Although the Federal Government had increased its program of public building, the total volume of contracts for new construction awarded in the first six months of 1933 was only fourteen per cent of that awarded in the corresponding period of 1929. In this emergency, two Governmental lending organizations were created to operate in the construction field to combat the problems of steadily shrinking construction, the *Public Works Administration* and the *United States Housing Authority*. Both of these extensive oranizations are supervised by an administrative body known as the Federal Works Agency.

Public Works Administration

The *Public Works Administration* is an agency of the Federal Government. It is not a corporation. The title to all of its assets is acquired in the name of the United States. From its inception in June, 1933 to June 30, 1940 the *Public Works Administration* financed the construction of 34,512 projects with an estimated aggregate cost of $6,140,000,000. Public works of every type and description—from small rural school houses to giant bridges and dams—have been undertaken in all but three of the 3,071 counties in the United States.

Outright grants of money could be made only to States, municipalities, and public agencies. Any non-Federal applicant was also eligible to receive a loan, provided it was a duly organized public body such as a State, county, city, town, village, school district, or other political subdivision. These loans were used to assist in the construction of schools, waterworks, sewer and power systems, hospitals, city halls, auditoriums, jails, streets, highways, bridges, tunnels, flood control, water power, and reclamation. Where outright grants of money were made, in contrast to loans, on non-Federal projects they were limited until 1935 to thirty per cent of the cost of labor and material, and after that date to forty-five per cent.

Private corporations were eligible to receive loans to finance the construction of such projects as bridges, tunnels, docks, viaducts, waterworks, canals, and reservoirs. Specific authority was also given to make loans to hospitals partly supported by public funds, to railroads to aid in financing maintenance work and equipment; and to limited dividend housing corporations.

Loans have ordinarily been effected by purchasing bond issues with fixed serial maturities from borrowers commencing not later than the third year after the date of the bonds. The ultimate maturity date has in very few cases exceeded thirty years from the date of issuance except for a few large nationally-known projects of a permanent nature, such as massive dams. There are no statutory provisions restricting the length of loans. These securities, in turn, have been repurchased by the *Reconstruction Finance Corporation,* and many of them resold to the investing public at a profit.

On December 31, 1940 the outstanding credits of the *Public Works Administration* were represented solely by loans of $89,738,000 representing bonds which had not been purchased up to that date by the *Reconstruction Finance Corporation.*

United States Housing Administration

The *United States Housing Authority* was created by the United States Housing Act of October, 1937 to take over that part of the activity of the *Public Works Administration* which had to do with a more or less permanent Federal program for eradicating slums and erecting low-rent housing projects. It was chartered by an Act of Congress with capital stock of $1,000,000 all held by the Treasurer of the United States. Loans are extended to local authorities to finance the erection of low-rent housing projects up to ninety per cent of the total development cost, including land, to be amortized over sixty years. A "local authority" is any State, county, municipality, or other governmental entity or public body authorized to engage in the development or administration of low-rent housing or slum clearance.

After a project is completed and ready for tenants, the *United States Housing Authority* pays annual rent subsidies to help bridge the gap between total annual charges against the project, including debt retirement, maintenance, and operation, and the rents which slum or blighted-area dwellers can afford to pay. These annual contributions cannot exceed the "going Federal rate of interest" plus one per cent upon the total development cost. The term "going Federal rate of interest" is defined as "the annual rate of interest specified in the then most recently issued bonds of the Federal Government having a maturity of ten years or more." At present, authority exists to contract for $28,000,000 annual contribution of this character, but several years will elapse before this figure will be reached. The *United States Housing Authority,* itself, cannot construct a single project; it may only finance them.

Funds to be lent to local housing authorities had been obtained as of December 31, 1940 from its paid-in capital of $1,000,000, paid-in surplus of $140,922,000 (there was a deficit in the earned surplus of $4,640,000), and by the sale of its own notes and bonds to the Federal Government. The Treasury Department has sold these obligations in the open market with the unconditional guarantee of both principal and interest by the Federal Government. On December 31, 1940, $226,956,000 of such obligations were outstanding. Funds to be contributed to local authorities during the period when a project is becoming rented to a point to carry itself, are obtained from yearly appropriations payable from the general funds of the United States. For the fiscal year 1940, $5,000,000 had been appropriated for this purpose.

On December 31, 1940, the *United States Housing Authority* had outstanding loans of $185,520,000, and accounts receivable of $675,000, or total credit of $186,195,000. These loans are repayable over a period not exceeding sixty years.

Transportation Finance

There are only two Federal organizations in the transportation field which extend credit, the *Inland Waterways Corporation* and the *United States Maritime Commission*. The activities of the *Inland Waterways Corporation* are supervised directly by the Department of Commerce. The *United States Maritime Commission* is a direct agency of the Federal Government.

Inland Waterways Corporation

The *Inland Waterways Corporation* was incorporated by Congress in June, 1924 to reorganize the inland, canal, and coastwise water services which were being operated at that time by the Secretary of War. At the time of organization, operations extended from New Orleans to St. Louis on the Mississippi River; from New Orleans through the Industrial Canal and Mississippi Sound to Mobile, Alabama; then up the Warrior River system to Port Birmingham, Alabama. Subsequently the service was extended on the upper Mississippi River to Minneapolis; on the Illinois Waterway system to Chicago; and on the Missouri River to Kansas City, Missouri.

In 1926 the rail line switching facility extending from Port Birmingham, Alabama, to Ensley, Alabama, was purchased at a cost of $500,000. This was a part of the Ensley Southern Railway which the Southern Railway had operated at a loss for several years and finally had petitioned the Interstate Commerce Commission for abandonment. Under a court order the property was sold to a corporation organized under the laws of the State of Alabama, and ownership acquired by *Inland Waterways Corporation* through the purchase of the capital stock. The line has been completely rehabilitated and modern rolling equipment provided at a cost of about $1,200,000. The acquisition of this concern, now a subsidiary of the *Inland Waterways Corporation,* known as the Warrior River Terminal Co., has turned the Warrior River system into a profitable operation.

The *Inland Waterways Corporation* is a credit agency of the

Federal Government to a very moderate extent; it is empowered to make loans to any State, municipality, or transportation company for the construction of terminal facilities. Generally the terminal facilities so constructed have been leased for operation by the *Inland Waterways Corporation*. The use of these facilities has materially aided successful operations, and has permitted the exchange of traffic between water and rail carriers, thereby extending the benefits accruing from water transportation to inhabitants in the interior who enjoy the same savings as those located on the rivers.

On November 30, 1940 the figures showed a healthy condition with capital and surplus of $24,416,000, no funded debt, and moderate liabilities of $980,000. The entire outstanding capital stock is owned by the Secretary of the Treasury. On the same date, outstanding loans amounted to the very moderate sum of $435,000, and accounts receivable to $333,000, a total of $768,000.

United States Maritime Commission

With the exception of a few limited services, there were practically no American-owned and operated steamship lines maintaining regular sailings from the United States to foreign ports at the outbreak of the first World War. Ninety per cent of our water-borne exports and imports were being transported by foreign vessels. After the outbreak of the War, the foreign vessels upon which we had depended for the carriage of American goods were gradually withdrawn from our trade. Seaboard warehouses and terminals became congested with export commodities and ocean freight rates increased, in many instances to a prohibitive degree.

The first legislative action designed to fulfill this need was the shipping Act of 1916 creating the United States Shipping Board for the purpose of encouraging, developing, and creating an adequate American merchant marine. This Board functioned throughout the first World War. In 1920 Congress created a revolving loan fund of $125,000,000 and authorized the Shipping Board to make loans to assist American shipowners in financing the construction of vessels in domestic yards. In 1928 supplementary legislation increased this fund to $250,000,000. The Postmaster General was also authorized to award contracts to American steamship companies serving our foreign trade routes.

By 1935, construction loans and liberal mail compensation had failed to accomplish the establishment of a permanent American merchant marine. In his message to Congress on March 4, 1935, the President advocated the termination of the construction loan and mail-contract systems and the substitution of annual appropriations for the payment of direct, rather than disguised, subsidies sufficient to cover the differential between American and foreign costs in three respects: the difference between the cost of building American and foreign flag ships, the difference between the cost of operating such ships, and the difference between the subsidies that foreign governments provided for their shipping. Out of this recommendation there emerged the Merchant Marine Act of 1936 creating the *United States Maritime Commission*. The Commission is an independent establishment of the executive branch of the Federal Government. It is not a corporation.

It is evident from this description that the *United States Maritime Commission* makes grants of funds outright, it does not normally make loans. The Commission did, however, take over from its predecessor outstanding loans of $85,511,000 as of October 26, 1936 representing construction loans. It has continuously serviced these loans which by December 31, 1940 had been reduced to $36,214,000. The total construction loans which had been made by the earlier agency amounted to $147,943,000, and, in most instances, had been made for a twenty-year period. These loans are secured by first preferred and blanket preferred mortgages on the vessels. Repayments on principal are made in annual or semi-annual instalments.

Since its organization the *United States Maritime Commission* has made only one direct loan. This loan, amounting to $2,000,000 was made in October, 1938, to an operating company to effect repairs on eleven vessels. The loan was made in conjunction with a credit of $2,500,000 granted by the *Reconstruction Finance Corporation*. The principal is due in quarterly instalments of $60,000 running from October 1, 1939 to October 1, 1943 when the unpaid balance falls due.

In addition to the outstanding loans of $36,214,000 on December 31, 1940, the *United States Maritime Commission* held notes of $34,-991,000 for the sale of ships, other investments of $635,000, and had accounts receivable of $18,619,000, making total outstanding credit accommodation of $90,459,000.

Other Lending Agencies

Finally there are two credit agencies which cannot be classified with any of the above specialized five groups. These are the *Tennessee*

Valley Authority, an independent Federal agency, and the *Puerto Rico Reconstruction Administration* which is supervised by the Department of the Interior.

Tennessee Valley Authority

The *Tennessee Valley Authority* is a corporation created by Congress in May, 1933. Its major and far-reaching purposes are to maintain and to operate properties owned by the United States in the vicinity of Muscle Shoals, Alabama, in the interest of national defense, agricultural and industrial development; to improve navigation on the Tennessee River; and to control the destructive floodwaters in the Tennessee River and the Mississippi River Basins.

In carrying out these extensive objectives, dams have been constructed across the Tennessee River. Electric power generated at these dams is sold wholesale to municipalities and cooperatives, preferably, and to industrial consumers and others when a surplus exists. In this process loans have been made to certain of its municipal and cooperative power customers to enable them to acquire, rehabilitate, and operate existing electric distribution properties and interconnecting transmission lines. Electric properties constructed or otherwise acquired by the *Tennessee Valley Authority* have also been sold on a deferred-payment basis to municipal and cooperative power customers. These loans and deferred-payment sales run from twenty to twenty-five years and are reduced by serial maturities.

On December 31, 1940 operations were conducted on a paid-in capital of $293,478,000 all owned by the Federal Government. There was no surplus. The only outstanding credits were accounts receivable which amounted to $6,268,000.

Puerto Rico Reconstruction Administration

The economic depression which began in the United States in 1929, had an immediate effect upon business and employment in Puerto Rico. The island was just beginning to recover from the effects of a severe hurricane which had caused great damage in September, 1928. In 1932 another disastrous hurricane struck, causing great losses principally in the northern and western sections of the island. Early in 1933 the insular government attempted to alleviate the situation by means of a public works program to be financed through loans from the *Reconstruction Finance Corporation.* The financial condition of the island government, however, had been so affected by the events responsible for the general economic distress that its borrowing capacity was insufficient to permit any widespread reconstruction.

In the meantime a commission from Puerto Rico had been invited to Washington for the purpose of drawing up a plan to expedite the permanent economic rehabilitation of the island. This analysis, known as the Chardow report, stressed the urgent necessity of projects for the resettlement of agricultural workers on subsistence farms, slum-clearance programs, the establishment of agricultural and industrial cooperatives, the establishment of new industries on the island, the reconstruction of the sugar, coffee, tobacco, and citrus fruit industries, the extension of the insular hydroelectric system, and the development of insular and Federal forestry programs.

On the basis of these findings and recommendations, the *Puerto Rico Reconstruction Administration* was established by the President in May, 1935, as a separate Federal agency within the Department of the Interior. A wide range of activities was immediately undertaken including rural rehabilitation, rural electrification, forestation, slum clearance, low-cost housing construction of buildings and improvements at the University of Puerto Rico, construction of a cement plant, and the eradication of the cattle tick and the coconut bud-rot.

In addition to carrying out an extensive program of improvements of these types, loans were granted to farmers, farm tenants, croppers, farm laborers, stockmen, cooperatives, and partnerships. Loans to needy farmers range from a minimum of $50 to a maximum of $3,000 with the provision that individual loans in excess of $3,000 may be made in special cases. These credits are granted for the time required to grow, harvest, and market the crops, or to raise and market poultry or livestock, but in no case for a period in excess of three years. Loans to cooperatives are generally made on a long term basis varying from ten to thirty years. Some loans, such as the one to the Associacion Azucarera Cooperativa Lafayette for the purchase of a sugar mill, are payable in twenty-seven equal annual installments over a period of thirty years with no amortization during the first three years.

On December 31, 1940 the outstanding loans of the *Puerto Rico Reconstruction Administration* amounted to the moderate sum of $4,216,000, stock interest in local enterprises to $1,220,000, and accounts receivable to $2,502,000, or total outstanding credit of $7,938,000.

Bibliographical References to Chapter Six

Commodity Credit Corporation, Annual Report, 1940.

COPPOCK, JOSEPH D., *Government Agencies of Consumer Instalment Credit;* New York, 1940.

CRAGG, ALLISTON, *Do You Need Some Money?;* New York, 1941.

Electric Home and Farm Authority, Annual Reports, 1935-1940.

Export-Import Bank of Washington, Annual Reports, 1936-1940.

Farm Credit Administration, Annual Reports, 1934-1940.

Farm Security Administration, Annual Report, 1940.

Federal Deposit Insurance Corporation, Annual Reports, 1934-1939.

Federal Home Loan Bank Board, Annual Reports, 1933-1940.

Federal Housing Administration, Annual Reports, 1934-1939.

Federal Works Agency, Annual Report, 1940.

Financial Statements of Certain Government Agencies; Letter from the Secretary of the Treasury Transmitting in further Response to Senate Resolution No. 150, certain Information Relative to Financial Statements concerning certain Government Agencies; Senate Document No. 172, in Two Parts; 76th Congress, 3d Session; 1940.

Government Lending Agencies; Published by the American Bankers Association, 1937.

Inland Waterways Corporation, Annual Reports, 1938-1939.

Reconstruction Finance Corporation, Annual and Quarterly Reports, 1933-1940.

Rural Electrification Administration, Annual Reports, 1936-1940.

SECRETARY OF THE TREASURY; *Annual Report on the State of the Finances for the Fiscal Year Ended June 30, 1940.*

United States Maritime Commission, Annual Reports, 1936-1940.

Volumes Previously Cited

BOGART, ERNEST LUDLOW, *Economic History of the American People;* 1930, Edition of 1935; New York.

CLARK, VICTOR S., *History of Manufactures in the United States, 1607-1860;* 1929 Edition, New York.

DAVIS, JOSEPH STANCLIFFE, *Essays on the Earlier History of American Corporations,* Two Volumes; Boston, 1917.

KIRKLAND, EDWARD C., *A History of American Economic Life;* 1932, Edition of 1939, New York.

NETTELS, CURTIS P., *The Roots of American Civilization;* New York, 1938.

PART FOUR

☆   ☆   ☆   ☆

Evolution of The Mercantile Agency

ONE hundred years ago, in 1841, Lewis Tappan, a merchant of New York City established the first national organization to act as an impartial center for gathering and disseminating credit information regarding merchants engaged "in the country trade." That organization was The Mercantile Agency which now has a record of one hundred years of intimate service to American industry and commerce.

Lewis Tappan started his enterprise in New York City but branches were rapidly opened in all of the important wholesaling centers. The democratic air of America with its lack of class distinction, its widening horizon, and its innate willingness to put confidence in character, enabled this original contribution to our expanding economic system to take root quickly.

The following five chapters give a picture of the economic conditions in the United States out of which The Mercantile Agency arose, a description of its present-day activities, and an interpretation of the basic work of the credit reporter and of the credit correspondent. These chapters also explain the function of the credit report and the part it has played and is playing in the healthy development of American trade by easing the tremendous flow of daily credit in every city, town, country village, and seaside hamlet in the United States.

VII ⁑ *Rise and Growth*
of The Mercantile Agency

A LITTLE over one hundred years ago, on May 10, 1837 the banks of New York City suspended specie payment. The currency in circulation at that time consisted almost entirely of paper money issued by the 788 existing State banks, with very little in the way of gold or silver reserves behind the notes. During the early years of the nineteenth century, our bank note circulation was a rather provincial, unsuccessful, profit-seeking attempt at a managed currency.

There were no Federal Reserve notes, there were no National bank notes against which United States Government securities had been pledged as collateral. There were no gold certificates similar to those called in from general circulation by Sections 3 and 4 of the Gold Reserve Act of 1934. There were no silver certificates or United States notes colloquially known as greenbacks. That there was substantial bank credit in existence is evidenced by the circulation of $149,185,890 of the notes of the State chartered banks, many of which had earned the term "wild cat" by the inefficiency of their managements, the ease with which they could be organized, the lack of supervision, and the facility with which they could become financially embarrassed.

Certain of these local bank notes used in day-to-day business were so poorly regarded as credit instruments that they were not even acceptable as currency by merchants and bankers in neighboring States. Counterfeits were numerous and *Counterfeit Bank Note Detectors* were in almost universal use among merchants and others taking in paper money. "No one was safe without them—nor especially with

275

them," remarked a merchant of that period. Bicknall's *Counterfeit Detector and Bank-Note List* of January 1, 1839 contained the names of fifty-four banks that had failed at different times; of twenty fictitious banks, the pretended notes of which were in circulation; of forty-three other banks for whose notes there were no sale; of two hundred and fifty-four banks, the notes of which had been counterfeited or altered; and enumerated thirteen hundred and ninety-five descriptions of counterfeited or altered notes then supposed to be in circulation, with denominations from one dollar to five hundred dollars.

Many years later, Matthew Josephson pointed out in his widely read book, *The Robber Barons,* that shortly after this enterprising period in our economic history, Jay Cooke, then in the employ of the well-known banking house of Clark & Dodge "boasted of knowing the counterfeits at sight, all the broken banks in America, an education which in those days of hazardous currencies, he candidly reckoned was 'worth a mint to him.' "

When the banks in New York City suspended specie payment, those in other commercially important cities immediately followed, ushering in the panic of 1837.

Origin of the Panic of 1837

On the day in 1837, following that on which the New York banks had suspended specie payment, the banks in Philadelphia, Baltimore, Albany, Hartford, New Haven, and Providence suspended payment; on the twelfth of May, the banks in Mobile and New Orleans; on the fifteenth, those in the District of Columbia; on the seventeenth, the banks in Charleston and Cincinnati; and on the nineteenth, the banks in Louisville and Augusta closed their doors.

At this period in our history a few railroads with wooden rails were experimenting with steam as a means of propulsion, and a few isolated miles of experimental telegraph lines were carrying halting messages. We had no telephones, no automobiles, no airplanes; news traveled relatively slowly, and as a result, the banks in the different important trading centers were closed on successive days as the news of the financial difficulties in New York City spread and affected banks located farther and farther away. In 1933, all banks failed to open their doors on the same day; the accelerated pace of business brought about by the introduction of telephones, teletype machines, radios, and high speed rotary newspaper presses had knit our commercial and industrial centers closer and closer together.

In 1837, there were no bank credit departments, mercantile credit departments, credit investigators, and no detailed credit reports, but one thing we had in common—business depressions. Hard times came just as easily and were considered just as difficult to eradicate as today; students of political economy knew just as little about how to control the business cycle as do an army of authoritative economists in the twentieth century. In Europe, at that very time, Karl Heinrich Marx was studying law, history, and philosophy at the University of Bonn, laying a foundation for those theories which today are striking at the very roots of the popular conception of ownership rights on widely scattered portions of our civilized world.

Business Failures in 1837

In two months in 1837, it is said that over two hundred and fifty commercial enterprises failed in New York City. The number of failures among mercantile houses for the entire year was not recorded but it was probably the greatest in proportion to the number of business enterprises in existence in our entire history, including 1932.

In the memorable year of 1932, there occurred 31,822 business failures in the United States, the greatest number in any one year. This number represented 1.53 per cent of the active commercial and industrial business enterprises of the country. Only in 1878 when the number of failures was 10,478 was this percentage exceeded, and even then by only 2/100th of one per cent, reaching 1.55 per cent of the active manufacturing and trading business enterprises.

Proponents of the economic interpretation of American history have outlined several fundamental reasons for this early panic of 1837. Probably the outstanding reason was also characteristic of our last sad depression. Speculation! The desire to get rich quickly and easily without a great deal of mental or physical effort was just as widespread immediately prior to 1837 as in 1929, when the common stock of the Radio Corporation of America sold on the New York Stock Exchange at $114¾ per share, the common stock of The Baldwin Locomotive Works at $66⅝, and the cumulative participating preference stock [par $35] of the International Match Corporation under the masterful touch of Ivar Kreugar at $102½ per share. Speculation was rampant in city real estate, in uncultivated country land, in securities, in commodities.

Speculation Fostered by Local Banks

This early nineteenth century speculative fever was fostered among other things, by the political and economic agitation not to renew the charter of the second Bank of the United States. As the bank prepared to close its doors and to cease operations in 1836, government funds were gradually withdrawn and placed in selected local banks in different parts of the country. In fact, several hundred new banks had been organized with the hope of obtaining government deposits, and of making substantial profits by expanding their circulation of notes to fill the need which would surely be felt by the withdrawal of the notes of the Bank of the United States. They were quite successful in expanding their circulation of notes!

Local merchants were invited by the organizers and the inexperienced officers of these new banking institutions, as well as by the experienced officers of the rather limited number of established State chartered banks, to borrow funds for enlarging their business operations. The merchants were no more hesitant to accept these offers than men of limited resources from 1927 to 1929, who in their mad haste to take advantage of the last sophisticated opportunity to become wealthy, bought country land, city office buildings, merchandise of all kinds to handle an increasing volume of business, securities on moderate margins, and experienced no great difficulty in obtaining credit to carry on these "profitable" undertakings. While Andrew Jackson was carrying on his "war" against the wide economic influence and power of the second Bank of the United States, over-trading, speculation, and the confident investment for a profit had become the very temporary and enlightened dominant note of American life.

Widespread Speculation in Land

The greatest speculation at this time was centered in unimproved public land, wild lands, and swamp lands, although town and city lots came in for their share of reasonable attention. The Federal Government in 1820 had reduced the size of the minimum tract of unimproved public land which would be sold to one individual from one hundred and sixty to eighty acres, and the price from $2.00 to $1.25 per acre. Here the price remained during the years immediately preceding 1837, even though the general level of wholesale prices was headed decidedly upward. The market price of more desirable subdivisions frequently and quite naturally rose above this initial level just as prices now do on the New York Stock Exchange during a period of improving business, and then suddenly jump up like a jack-in-the-box during a period dominated by a widespread boom psychology.

Credit was readily granted by the existing State banks on the security of the land, and the borrowers then often used these funds to carry on the process again simultaneously. That's called pyramiding when applied to modern speculation. Only the experienced speculator should attempt it and even he, very, very often comes to the same unsuccessful ending as did so many of the early trans-Atlantic flyers. From an average of less than $2,000,000 a year before 1830, the receipts to the Federal Government from the sale of public lands rose to $25,000,000 in 1836. So unprecedented were these sales that the expression, "doing a land office business" became synonymous with great commercial activity and has remained one of our typically American colloquial expressions.

In his annual report to Congress for the year 1836, Levi Woodbury, Secretary of the Treasury, pointed out that these unexpectedly large receipts were of comparatively recent origin. "The unusual receipts during the last two years," he wrote "have chiefly accrued from the unprecedented sales of public lands. It is remarkable that those sales assumed their extraordinary character chiefly between July, 1835 and October, 1836—a period of little more than fourteen months." The finances of the Federal Government had never been in such flourishing condition, and we now know only too well, that our national finances have never been in the same unique condition since.

Inflation in Bank and Mercantile Credit

This vast speculation in public lands could only have been financed with a corresponding inflation in credit, in an expansion in the loans, and in the circulation of notes of the existing banks. Between 1830 and 1837 the number of banks increased from 329 to 788, their aggregate capital from $110,186,608 to $290,722,091 and their loans over threefold, from $159,800,000 to $525,115,702. These figures are small when compared with the 22,759 commercial banks and trust companies in active operation in 1930, and 14,466 in 1940, but nevertheless, the expansion from 329 to 788 active banking institutions within such a relatively few years was a very noticeable and substantial increase of 136 per cent. The commercial banking business was on the up and up.

The concurrent overtrading in commodities became manifest in the tremendous growth in the floating debt which American merchants owed to European—principally British—manufacturers for merchandise, to be re-sold to the American retail merchants on credit terms which were now customarily six months. Between 1830 and 1836, the volume of Anglo-American trade actually doubled, and in the year ending September 30, 1836, the imports from Great Britain exceeded our exports to that country by more than twenty million dollars. Everyone was as happy as a kitten in a fish bowl and spending money. With emphasis on the upward swing of business activities, importers, both wholesalers and large retailers for their own account, were purchasing greater varieties and more merchandise in Europe to fill the anticipated demands of customers, than at any previous time in our history.

The seeds of all depressions are sown when people are happy, naïvely acquisitive, and irresponsible. It was so in Florence, in the days before Girolamo Savonarola began to thunder forth predictions of heavenly wrath; it was so in the flagrant disregard of the quiet conscientious New England virtues so characteristic of the years immediately preceding 1929, and it was so in the years prior to 1837, notwithstanding the early flowering of New England. The unprecedented sale of public land actually created a Federal surplus. The Treasury Department, believe it or not, was actually receiving more funds than it could spend. The concurrent widespread speculation in public land on credit, and in commodities by business men and business enterprises, were having full effect.

"Specie Circular" Brings a Halt

On July 11, 1836 to curb the speculative activities in connection with the sale of western public lands, what has since become known in the economic history of our country as the "Specie Circular" was issued by the Treasury Department, providing that only gold or silver would be acceptable in the future for the payment of land. Eloquent notices were even displayed in post offices reading, "No Bank Notes taken—nothing received or known here as money but the hard coin itself."* No longer would the bank notes of "wild cat banks" be acceptable to the government. A check was thereby placed upon land speculation, the market value of public land immediately dropped, and

* *The American Review*, Volume III, Number V; May, 1846, p. 467.

loans extended by eastern as well as by western banks became impaired, just as loans on securities became impaired in 1930 and 1931.

In the meantime, the entire public debt of the United States had been liquidated, and an act to place surplus Federal funds of $37,468,859.97 on deposit with State banks became a law on June 23, 1836. Preparatory to this distribution of the surplus revenue, funds were to be withdrawn in four quarterly instalments in 1837 and placed in the State banking institutions. The first three instalments aggregating $27,063,430 were so deposited, but the fourth was postponed, year after year, and never made. Years later, in 1883, the State of Virginia made a claim upon the Secretary of the Treasury for the fourth instalment, and even appealed, but unsuccessfully, to the Supreme Court for a mandamus to compel the payment of its share amounting to $732,809. The Treasury Department actually carried the sum, representing the first three instalments, on its books as a part of its cash balance until the 61st Congress by an Act of June 25, 1910 provided that the entire amount be written off.

The effect of the "Specie Circular" was to force the buyers of land to ask their banks for gold or silver in the redemption of local bank notes to obtain the specie with which to pay the Federal Government, and the banking institutions which had over-issued the most, were the first to suspend specie payment.

The transference of the public funds naturally caused the banks from which funds were being withdrawn, to call upon their customers to repay or reduce their loans. This process implied the slowing up of industrial and commercial expansion as well as speculative activity, just about the time when foreign creditors of American importers were pressing for their payments. In the two months of February and March, 1837, the price of raw cotton fell 25 per cent, putting many merchants in the southern States in a weakened financial condition and unable to meet their maturing obligations to northern creditors at the very time when the speculative bubble was near its peak. Without more ado the panic of 1837 was well on the way.

Need for Mercantile Credit Agencies

Among the failures which received the widest publicity in 1837 was that of the well-known, established business of Arthur Tappan & Co., wholesale and retail dealers in dry goods, largely imported from France and India, located at 122 Pearl Street in New York City, then in the very heart of the fashionable shopping district bordering Wall Street. Walter Barrett in one of his volumes entitled, *The Old Merchants of New York City* succinctly described this concern as "doing the largest silk business in the city . . . in 1826. It was a better class store than any of its neighbors, being built of granite."

Arthur Tappan & Co. had one of the largest wholesale and retail silk and cotton goods businesses in the country with annual sales materially in excess of one million dollars. Liabilities at the time of the failure amounted to what was then, and in fact still is, the very impressive sum of $1,100,000. The obligations comprising this aggregate debt were renewed by notes falling due in six, twelve, and eighteen months, and were promptly met and paid as they fell due.

Influence of Arthur Tappan

Arthur Tappan was one of the well-known characters in New York City, a foremost merchant, an ardent abolitionist in the front of every movement for freeing the slaves, a believer in equal rights and the education of negroes, a prohibitionist, an anti-tobacconist (he considered its use wasteful and injurious alike to body, intellect, and soul). With his brother Lewis, he started the *New York Journal of Commerce.* He was also one of the founders of Oberlin College, a "munificent patron." When William Lloyd Garrison was convicted in Baltimore of libel for publishing an article in the *Genius of Universal Emancipation,* to the effect that a vessel owned by Francis Todd, of Newburyport, Massachusetts, had taken slaves "as freight" to New Orleans, it was Arthur Tappan who paid Garrison's fine to release him from jail.

When this wide awake, energetic Yankee merchant opened his business in New York City, he had, contrary to all established business practices, decided to sell merchandise only for cash and at one price. The institution of either of these policies would have been radical; the institution of both together was revolutionary. As his business expanded, he continued to sell only at one price, but at the solicitation of his customers and incidentally to increase the profits so close to the heart of a typical Yankee, he began to depart, little by little, from the policy of selling only for cash, until over a lapse of years his principal sales were being made on credit terms. In his later years, Arthur Tappan was convinced, that as a broad business policy, sales should only be made for cash, or on short terms paid by promissory notes which should fall due at a bank, and to this change in his early policy he ascribed his financial difficulties during the panic of 1837.

Customary Credit Terms

Travel and transportation were too difficult and the market too scattered for the wholesaler to seek out retail customers. Consequently, the retailers to obtain supplies, came to the wholesale markets. Ordinarily they arrived twice each year, in the Autumn before transportation became too difficult, and again in the Spring when the Winter stocks had been sold and transportation had opened up.

The retailer gave his note in settlement of his purchases, as explained in chapter V, at the time of each visit and simultaneously took up the note for his last previous purchases. Invariably he procured his requirements of one type of merchandise, food, hardware, or leather goods from one wholesaler, selecting the merchandise he wanted at the dealer's own warehouse. By this practice, the city wholesaler became a banker as well as a distributor of merchandise. Like his colonial ancestors, he carried the receivables of his customers for many months. He also sold his merchandise at prices which varied with the length of the terms of sale and his margin of profit was generally high.

The country retail merchant, after he had obtained his merchandise from city wholesale distributors, also in turn, often served as a banker, extending credit to farmers for miles and miles around, being paid with the farmers' crops at the harvest season. This was a continuation of the practice which had been followed in colonial days by the country general store. These crops were shipped to market, and out of the proceeds the local retail merchant retained the amount due to him, and then turned the balance over to the grower.

Credit the Basis of Mercantile Agencies

Out of the financial embarrassment of Arthur Tappan & Co., came Lewis Tappan, a brother of Arthur, who proceeded in 1841 to organize *The Mercantile Agency*, now widely known by the corporate style of DUN & BRADSTREET, INC. Here is one of the strange contradictions of human nature, that an individual convinced in his own mind of the fundamental soundness of the economic theory which Edward Fitzgerald interpreted about this time in England in one of the quatrains of the *Rubaiyat of Omar Khayyam*, "Ah, take the Cash, and let the Credit go," nevertheless went ahead at the very same time to develop a procedure unique among existing business services by capitalizing upon a practice which was the exact opposite to that theory. Like a dictator who would dictate democracy, like a pacifist who would fight for peace, so Lewis Tappan believing with his brother Arthur, in the fundamental soundness of selling for cash or on short terms, organized an enterprise whose progress and very existence has depended during the intervening decades upon the extension of credit.

In the succeeding one hundred years of its existence, the expansion of the services of *The Mercantile Agency* into every county and parish in the United States, into every province and county in Canada, and into foreign lands, has been built upon the sale of merchandise on credit terms, and the lending of funds unsecured and secured by commercial banks, trust companies, and private bankers, locally, nationally and internationally. Along with intensification in the industrial way of life has come an ever wider and wider use of credit, and the ever increasing specialization in the forms and extentions of credit.

Economic Conditions of the 1840's

This period—the quarter of a century before the internecine strife burst out between the industrially expanding North and the agricultural South—was one of constant compromise in the field of politics, but one of the most fascinating, progressive, and alive periods in our economic life. Forward looking businessmen, bankers, speculators, and investors were beginning to wonder about the profitable possibilities of organizing and operating railroads commercially. At the same time, the expansion in the use of the corporate form of business organization was beginning to place larger and larger funds in the hands of aggressive operating managements. The broad background of economic conditions which created these urges was the same background which created the fundamental need for the unique services of mercantile credit agencies.

The cities mentioned on page 276, whose banks suspended specie payment following the action of the New York banks on May 10, 1837, were the important trading centers in the rather limited area which then comprised the United States. In 1840, with a population of 17,059,000, of which 2,873,000 were colored—mostly slaves—we were hardly an embryonic world power. There were only three States, Missouri, Arkansas, and Louisiana west of the Mississippi River, trade

Lewis Tappan
Founder of The Mercantile Agency

was carried on largely in boats along the coast, up the rivers, and through the network of canals which were still being financed as experiments in speculation and investment. The important trading centers were located largely along the Atlantic seacoast where a substantial portion of the imported luxuries and manufactured products from Europe and Asia were landed.

Machinery, iron products, and textiles, for use and consumption west of the Allegheny Mountains were being manufactured in the Atlantic States; grain and food supplies were being produced on the western farms. The East, with increasing population in the urban industrial centers following a flood of foreign immigrants, had become dependent upon the West, that is, the States across the Allegheny Mountains, for food supplies; the southern States were experiencing a rapid expansion in the growing of cotton; and raw cotton comprised the greater part of our total export business.

Transportation Handicaps

The broad picture of commercial life at this stage of our economic expansion was that of a growing number of economically detached communities, increasing rapidly in population, industrial and commercial importance, and each possessing the foundation for profitable commercial interchanges, provided transportation costs could be brought to a reasonable level, and provided that bad debt losses could be kept to a moderate figure by the judicious weeding out of undesirable distant customers and prospective customers.

Until after the War of 1812 up-country freighting, that is, from the seaport cities and towns inland, was by pack-horses and wagons; down-country freighting, that is, from inland settlements to the coast, was mostly by "arks," sloops, barges, and keel-boats. "Arks" were large flat-bottomed boats, made with planks fastened upon ribs with wooden bolts, which were carried down the rivers, principally the Ohio and Mississippi Rivers to New Orleans. These particular vehicles of travel were from twelve to eighteen feet wide, and from forty to sixty feet long. They commonly carried sixty to eighty tons of corn, ham, dried pork, flour, whiskey, peach brandy, cider, bacon, iron and cabinet works, products of the interior country, and would float with the current down a river. Oars were used only to direct and propel them to the shore, as occasion required. After discharging its cargoes, an ark would be taken apart and sold for lumber with very little loss. They were picturesque, practical, and peculiarly adaptable to long trips of fifteen hundred to two thousand miles down the broad Mississippi River in the early years of the nineteenth century. When the merchandise was finally disposed of at New Orleans, the traders would generally go by sea to Philadelphia or Baltimore and then overland to Pittsburgh and the environs where most of them resided. Here it was certainly true that the longest way round was the shortest way home.

Shortly after 1815, steamboats and canals transformed inland transportation in three ways: they cheapened the cost and shortened the time for carrying bulky freight to the interior; they connected formerly isolated transportation systems; and they opened to settlement country previously unavailable because it was not accessible to natural waterways. Arks and canal boats carried bulk loads at low costs. Waterways were comparatively smooth avenues for commerce, while transportation over primitive roads offered daily adventures in which human ingenuity was tested by a constant variety of problems in getting the load over boggy roads and fords.

So long as pack-horses or wagons remained the only means of transporting merchandise inland, overland freight cost from 20 to 40 and even 60 cents a ton-mile, according to the condition of the roads and the distance covered. The saving effected by railways is sufficiently indicated by the single fact that transportation charges soon fell to three cents a ton-mile, or to about one-tenth the cost of wagon-carriage. This radical revolution in transportation was accomplished within a single generation, affecting the market range of commerce and industry.

The great obstacle to expanding trade between the different sections of our country, in addition to this slow and costly transportation, had been the lack of credit information regarding prospective distant customers, the records of the principals, their financial responsibilities, and their local reputations for honesty of purpose and ability. Routes of trade in colonial days had been confined almost exclusively to natural waterways. By 1841, however, some sections not served by such channels of commerce had obtained supplementary connecting facilities such as improved turnpikes, canals, steamboats, and rather primitive early narrow-gage railroads, but even these services were sharply restricted by geographic and climatic conditions.

Today it is possible for a New York or a Chicago banker to obtain comprehensive credit data within a few hours regarding any business enterprise in the country. Before the establishment of the first national mercantile agency in the United States in 1841, there were no well-established routines, no reliable channels for collecting credit information, and then making that information readily available to a New York or Chicago banker, a New England textile mill, a Philadelphia hardware manufacturer, or a Baltimore wholesaler of harness and leather goods. The need was awaiting systematic cultivation, our westward expansion, our steady increase in population, our developing wealth, a start toward the utilization of our immense store of natural resources, and the growth in the number of active commercial and industrial business enterprises in the freest democracy in the world.

History of R. G. Dun & Co.

In determining the amount of credit to be extended to a customer by the firm of Arthur Tappan & Co. it is said that Lewis and Arthur Tappan "were equally exacting," but the degree of exactness apparently was little better than that exercised by many banks, industrial, and commercial houses that have become financially embarrassed over the intervening years by the unwise, wholesale extension of credit.

There is no doubt that the two brothers had a more sincere interest in understanding the responsibilities of their customers than most competitors of their day. That interest, however, was not quite sufficient to guide the fundamental policies of a concern that undoubtedly was overtrading, and so owing a substantial sum of money to domestic and foreign creditors during what was the most critical economic period in our history, while at peace, up to that time.

Tappans Were Early Credit Authorities

"Each applicant was questioned individually, usually by Lewis, and no detail reported was ever forgotten," a careful student of the operations of Arthur Tappan & Co., heroically wrote many years later, "both brothers being noted for their very retentive memories. In this manner the firm gradually accumulated a large amount of information regarding buyers in all parts of the country. As an instance of the high esteem with which their fellow merchants regarded the Tappans as credit authorities, A. T. Stewart, in the early stages of his career—when doubts were expressed as to whether he was going beyond his resources—named Lewis Tappan 'as a fit and proper person, both from integrity and business shrewdness, to look into his accounts and make an impartial report of his pecuniary condition, so as to set all doubts at rest.' During the early thirties, as the extent and reliability of the information they had accumulated for their own use became generally known, Arthur Tappan & Co., were frequently consulted by fellow merchants on the subject of credits, and gave their advice freely whenever requested to do so."

After the temporary embarrassment of the house that the unwise extension of credit built, the business was reorganized. On July 20, 1841, Lewis Tappan retired as an active partner and was free to engage in some other occupation. His personal interest in the subject of credit investigation, his reputation in appraising the credit responsibilities of distant country traders when the West was a steadily receding frontier, suggested the idea of organizing a central, impartial credit reporting bureau devoted to collecting and disseminating such information for the benefit of the entire business community.

The great lesson of the panic of 1837 as he saw it—after studying closely its causes and effects—was not to devise some method to reduce the extent of the widespread speculation in unimproved public land, town and city lots, securities, and merchandise, or to develop a sounder currency, but it was to improve "the system of mercantile credits that had prevailed until then," a system which "was essentially unsound because it failed to take sufficiently into account the standing of the applicant for credit, based upon information obtained from intelligent and reliable sources." This theory was even more fundamental in the following years with the rapid expansion in our industrial and commercial activity, as our developing capitalism, in turn, was based upon the easy natural flow of credit as commerce wended its way across western mountains, rivers, wildernesses, and prairies.

Origin of "The Mercantile Agency"

On June 1, 1841 Lewis Tappan had sent an announcement to the leading merchants of New York City, and particularly to those engaged in the wholesale trade selling largely to retailers in other parts of the country—"in the country trade," it was termed in those days—regarding the establishment of an enterprise that he was calling *The Mercantile Agency*. In this announcement, the date of August 1 was set for beginning active operations, and on that day, this new institution, now the oldest of its kind in the entire world, opened its doors at No. 7 Dorr's Building, at the corner of Hanover and Exchange Streets in the City of

New York. Here was the earliest important attempt to centralize the national collection of impartial credit information.

The first step, which Lewis Tappan took to anticipate the needs of wholesale merchants for credit information on distant country customers, was to send a circular to lawyers and others at distant points inviting them to become his correspondents. In this way, he hoped to secure in advance, sufficient data regarding the standing of traders in other cities, towns, country hamlets, and trading posts to enable New York City wholesalers to determine what amount of credit, if any, could safely be accorded. Tappan's own experience had taught him that after a buyer had arrived, and according to the custom established in the colonial days, presented letters of introduction and recommendation, the seller was in possession of only a part of the information he required to arrive at a safe decision regarding the initial extension of credit. "Obviously, no man would refer him to those who knew any ill of him, while letters of introduction might be furnished by those who gave them merely to avoid the unpleasant necessity of explaining to the credit applicant in person why they refused to do so." That was natural in the colonial days. It was natural in 1841.

Seven years after *The Mercantile Agency* was organized, William P. M. Ross published a volume entitled, *The Accountants' Own Book and Business Man's Manual*. In that volume he included a short chapter of five pages which shed light upon Lewis Tappan's new business enterprise. Ross delicately intimated that commercial fraud was not uncommon at the time:

The wholesale merchants of the eastern cities were more or less at the mercy of their country debtors, or, at best, had to depend for their knowledge of the country trader's business character and condition, on such references or letters of recommendation as he was able to furnish them, or, on what was still more uncertain—the testimony of clerks or travelling agents, whom each house was in the habit of sending annually on collecting tours throughout the country—testimony too often obtained from any but reliable sources. The letters of recommendation, also, were frequently given from interested motives, and the writers too often shared, with the persons in whose favour they were written, the fruits of their conspiracy. At the best, this system was limited in its operations, as the information obtained by each house was necessarily confined to a small section of the country. Sometimes, several city houses would unite in sending some trust-worthy man, whose sole business it was to ascertain and report the condition of the country traders. Much valuable information was obtained in this way, but the system was still imperfect, as the agent might oftentimes have scarcely left a particular locality, before some trader reported good by him would fail, of which fact the agent would be unaware until his next visit to that section of the country. But few competent agents were ever sent out, and this plan has now [1848] fallen into disrepute. As the population of the country and the number of traders increased, it became a matter of the greatest importance to the merchants in the importing and jobbing cities to acquire, in some way, information respecting the conditions of the country traders, which should be complete, reliable, and constantly *fresh*.

The response to the preliminary circular sent out by Lewis Tappan proved quite satisfactory, and *The Mercantile Agency* rapidly accumulated a valuable mass of reports on frontier traders, southern retailers, and enterprising, if comparatively small manufacturers throughout the United States. These reports were all written in long hand—the invention of the typewriter was still many years in the future—in huge ledgers bound in sheepskin. It would be difficult to surpass the beauty of the handwriting in the brown ink of the day with which many of these early reports were recorded. Today millions of credit reports are sent to subscribers each month; in those early years the subscribers called at the office, and the reports in which they were currently interested, were read to them from these huge ledgers.

Branch Offices are Opened

It became increasingly apparent that the services of the new organization would be greatly improved if branch offices were opened in the principal cities. In February, 1843 the first branch was opened in Boston just about the time when Boston's princely merchants were being forced to relinquish their maritime China and India trade that had created so much of the wealth of New England to support the leisure of the young poets, the teachers, the historians, and the essayists, who for many decades would dominate the cultural life of our country. Hard-headed New England businessmen were turning to manufacturing. The second branch was opened in July, 1845 in Philadelphia, and the third, in 1846 at Baltimore. The West was then of relatively little importance commercially, Chicago having a population of but 4,470, while St. Louis was a modest bustling frontier river post and fur trade center with 16,469 inhabitants.

In June, 1847 Lewis Tappan took as a partner young Benjamin Douglass, who had been actively associated with him about a year. Benjamin Douglass was the eldest son of a successful West India merchant who was operating out of Baltimore and New York. After being associated with his father for several years, he had moved to Charleston, South Carolina, and then to New Orleans where he had extended his mercantile business up the Mississippi Valley. It had been his habit to investigate the credit standing of his customers, in person, just as Lewis Tappan had done. In this process, Douglass had been accustomed to make extensive trips throughout the South, the Southwest, and even as far North as Ohio. Although only thirty years of age, he was very familiar with the business methods of the "country trade" and with the loose system of granting credits to country buyers which was so common at the time. His own experience enabled him to appreciate the economic importance of a service business of this new type.

Lewis Tappan retired in 1849, and his place was taken by Arthur Tappan, who remained an equal partner with Douglass for five years, when he, in turn, sold his interest to Douglass. Young Douglass had political views at variance with those of Arthur Tappan; this difference in opinion, however, did not interfere with a very successful business relationship. Arthur Tappan thought of *The Mercantile Agency* in terms of service to large merchants in the coastal cities; Douglass turned his eyes inland toward the growing West and decided that the business should be brought closer to the distributing centers along rivers, new highways, and railway junctions.

In 1849, a branch was opened at Cincinnati, which was then the great metropolis of western trade, with a population of 115,435. In 1850, an office was opened at St. Louis. Within a very few years what had been a simple trading station had grown, along with the western settlement and expansion, into a "roaring hive of frontier industry and commerce. Long lines of steamers clung to the levee along the river front and the merchandise received and distributed bore the names of traders throughout the vast region drained by the Mississippi and its subsidiaries." In 1851 a branch was opened at New Orleans.

In June, 1851 the business had completed its first decade of existence. Thirty men were employed in the New York City office condensing, copying, giving out reports, and carrying on extensive correspondence, all by long hand. The credit reports collected during this ten-year period were contained in more than one hundred of the largest ledgers then available, each with six to seven hundred pages.

Recognition of Legal Status

A centralized system of impartial credit reporting had now become a recognized economic essential to the expanding commerce of sprawling America. A more competent, responsible, and systematic method, than that which had been used in the colonies and in the early years of the United States, had become necessary. Because of the almost total lack of legal precedents, however, the creation of original enterprises to render this new type of specialized credit service brought legal problems in their train. The most fundamental of these questions was whether credit reports issued to interested subscribers in response to their inquiries should be afforded protection as qualifiedly privileged communications.

During the first fifty years of their existence, mercantile agencies in the eyes of the courts, remained in a probationary stage. Inherent hesitancy on the part of the courts to accept this innovation in business activity before they had sufficiently demonstrated their economic justification was the natural course of judicial conservatism. Gradually, however, by the determination of questions brought before them, the courts handed down decisions which have served as benchmarks in surveying the pattern to which the operations of mercantile agencies should conform.

In one of the early cases, Benjamin Douglass was called as a witness to testify in an action for libel brought by John B. and Horace Beardsley of Norwalk, Ohio. The suit was tried in 1851 before Judge Betts of the United States District Court in New York City. Douglass declined to answer certain questions which he felt would require him to violate a confidence, principally to give the name of any agent or correspondent in Norwalk, Ohio who had furnished confidential information. His steadfast refusal to compromise with what he regarded as a sacred business principle, even when ordered by the court to answer, resulted in his commitment for twenty days in the Eldridge Street jail for contempt of court. Douglass had a profound respect for the dignity of the court and the administration of justice. When, however, the mechanics of the administration of justice came in conflict with the dictates of his conscience, he found it difficult to reconcile the two apparently contrasting principles. The stand of Douglass in going to prison rather than violate his moral obligation was highly commended by the business men of his day, clearly evidenced by a resolution of approval adopted by a committee of the New York Chamber of Commerce.

In one of the final hearings on the Beardsley case, Charles O'Conor, the venerable New York City attorney whose untiring labors assisted in the exposure of the Tweed ring and "whose Parian bust adorns the Appellate Division of the First Judicial Department," made one of the most lucid explanations of the essential need of centralized credit reporting organizations as a stimulant to trade. In this explanation O'Conor posed the fundamental question of utility and then answered it at length with simple commercial illustrations of his time:

What is the operation of these agencies? The country dealer who comes to any of the cities needs some evidence that he is worthy of trust and confidence. The ancient practice was for the country dealer to bring with him a certificate of his minister of the Gospel, or a letter from some country lawyer, or, perhaps, from some fellow-merchant; and then he would spend a week perhaps in New York, trying to satisfy the persons with whom he dealt that he was worthy of credit—in establishing for himself, as well as he could, a good character. What has been the result of establishing these agencies? Why, a merchant from this little town of Norwalk, Ohio, walks into the store of a wholesale merchant in New York, or Boston, or Philadelphia, and says: "I should like to purchase from you such and such goods." The city merchant replies: "Well, sir, look at our goods and whatever you desire to purchase shall be laid aside for you." After spending perhaps half an hour in making his examination and selection of goods, he goes back to the desk or counting room to talk about terms of payment and credit, etc. He asks, "How long a credit do you allow?" The answer is "Well, we give four or six months." "Do you require an endorser?" "No, sir." This answer, if the country dealer knew nothing about what is going on in the business world might very much surprise him for perhaps he never was in the store before, and so far as he can tell, he is wholly unknown there. He gets his goods and goes home. He is independent of lawyer and minister and everybody else, so far as this world's mere temporal interests are concerned. Upon the strength of his good character, if he has one, he gets credit. A person of doubtful reputation receives a different answer. ¶ This whole thing is done with a promptitude which is amazing and to all honest people in the country very delightful. They find indeed that "a good name is better than precious ointment," and "rather to be chosen than great riches;" that it accompanies them everywhere. And all this is through the action of these mercantile agencies. While the country merchant is looking at the goods, the mercantile agency reports that he is a man perfectly worthy of confidence, and upon the strength of this report the New York merchant is willing to trust him; and he does so with a pleasantly confiding manner, which is as gratifying to the pride of the country dealer as it is conformable to propriety.

After several intermediate steps, the courts finally recognized that the doctrine of qualifiedly privileged communication should be applied in instances of the issuance of credit reports to subscribers in response to their inquiries.* The taking of judicial notice by the courts of the function and the operations of mercantile agencies was accompanied by the full acknowledgment of the beneficial effects of their existence in the business community.†

The advocates before the courts in the early days of mercantile agencies stressed, and the logic of their argument was compelling, that

---

* Ormsby *v*. Douglass (1868) 37 N. Y. 477.
† Eaton, Cole & Burnham Co. *v*. Avery (1880) 83 N. Y. 31; Erber *v*. Dun (1882) 12 Fed. Rep. 526.

the unscrupulous individual in business, seeking to suppress his own defections, would be loud in his wails of alleged injury because of insignificant trivialities, and would attempt to conceal the truth by harassing litigation. Astute administrators of the law were quick to discern the distinction between hollow claims of this type from those made in good faith. Since the prosperity of mercantile agencies depends upon their good faith and accurate reporting, there has seldom been serious differences of opinion when the desires of all concerned have been to disclose a full, truthful, and fair statement of relevant credit facts.

Foreign Branches Established

Robert Graham Dun of Chillicothe, Ohio, was employed by *The Mercantile Agency* in 1851. His grandfather was the Rev. James Dun, for twenty years a minister of the Free Church of Scotland at Glasgow. In 1815 his father, Robert Dun, who had also been educated for the ministry, emigrated to the United States and settled at Chillicothe, at this time, the capital of the young State of Ohio. The trips made by young Benjamin Douglass to Ohio while he was a merchant at New Orleans may have been the indirect cause of Dun entering the service of the agency, for at that time he met Miss Elizabeth Dun, a sister of Robert G. Dun, whom he subsequently married. By a remarkable coincidence Benjamin Douglass also had a sister named Elizabeth, who married Robert Graham Dun.

On June 1, 1854 Douglass became the sole owner of *The Mercantile Agency*. He immediately made Robert Graham Dun a partner, the firm style changing to B. Douglass & Co. Under the aggressive leadership of these partners, the firm not only proceeded vigorously to extend its chain of offices into the West and into the South, but in the year 1857, set up branch offices in London and in Montreal.

As the population moved westward, opening up territories with trading stations, prairie posts, and mining centers, representatives of *The Mercantile Agency* immediately entered these communities to gather essential credit information regarding the business habits, records, and responsibilities of the buyers of merchandise. As these towns grew into cities, offices were established. Between 1871 and 1890, ninety offices were opened in the United States, four in Canada, three in Europe and one in Australia. Today there are one hundred and fifty-two cities in the United States in which offices are located and sixteen in the Dominion of Canada.

At the end of its first fifty years of existence, one hundred and twenty-six offices were in existence of which only five were outside of the United States and Canada; four of the five were in Europe, and one in Australia. During the next twenty-five years, from 1891 to 1916, the history of *The Mercantile Agency* was one of rapid expansion into a world-wide organization. Of one hundred and fifteen new offices which were opened during this period, eighty-three were located outside of the United States at such points as Mexico City, Cape Town in South Africa, Hamburg, Bremen, Amsterdam, and important points in Latin America and the West Indies. Immediately prior to the beginning of the present World War, offices of DUN & BRADSTREET, INC. and offices of foreign mercantile agencies in which DUN & BRADSTREET, INC. had an interest, were operated in one hundred and twenty-five cities in twenty-seven countries outside of the United States and the Dominion of Canada.

Steady Expansion in Activity

On May 1, 1859 at the age of thirty-two, Robert G. Dun became the sole proprietor of *The Mercantile Agency,* changing the name shortly thereafter to R. G. Dun & Co. The keynote of operations of this business from the very beginning, had been one of expansion, constant expansion southward and westward as these territories became settled, as merchants and traders in these 'sections sought increased credit from eastern manufacturers and wholesalers. In fact, a detailed history of *The Mercantile Agency* from 1841 to 1900 would be an epitome of the expanding commercial and industrial importance of different parts of the United States, but always flowing westward. For forty-one years Robert Graham Dun remained the sole proprietor. He died in 1900. The business was then operated as a common law trust until 1931.

On January 1, 1931 the R. G. Dun Corporation was organized as a holding company to hold the entire interest in R. G. Dun & Co., a common law trust, and the National Credit Office, Inc. Arthur D. Whiteside, who had been the President and owner of the National Credit Office, Inc., became the President of the R. G. Dun Corporation, and since that time has been the active head, first of that enterprise, and then of its successor since 1940, DUN & BRADSTREET, INC. During these past ten years, the developments have been concerned with steady improvements in service, in the thorough education of credit reporters, in the production of improved specialized types of credit reports, in the expansion of continuous service, and in the rapid distribution of year-end statements, to produce a service which would more effectively and rapidly serve the essential needs of credit authorities in all circles of modern, American business life.

History of The Bradstreet Company

The economic conditions of a rapidly, geographically expanding country, when the flow of population and commerce was steadily westward, when transportation and communication facilities were being revolutionized, when merchandise was being purchased only once or twice during the calendar year by country retail dealers on credit terms of six or eight months, and when tremendous credit losses were being assumed during the depression swings because of these long terms, were likewise fundamental reasons for the organization of the second general mercantile agency, *The Bradstreet Company*. While the initial circumstances were quite different, the underlying economic causes for the need which resulted in its organization and its steady development, were the same as those which brought about the earlier organization of *The Mercantile Agency*.

Origin of "The Bradstreet Company"

The founder, John M. Bradstreet, had been a dry goods merchant in Cincinnati for almost twenty years,* first as a member of the firm of Yeatman & Bradstreet, and then from 1840 to 1850, under his own name as a proprietorship. Bradstreet had an illustrious colonial heritage. He was a descendant of Governor Simon Bradstreet, colonial Governor of Massachusetts from 1679 to 1686, and of Anne Dudley Bradstreet, America's first poet.

Edward Payson Bradstreet, a distant relative, has left a picture of the conscientious manner in which the founder of this second mercantile agency worked upon his plans for developing a system of credit ratings, while operating his own little retail dry goods store: "In this connection he was in need of constant legal advice. John Bradstreet was doing most of the actual work himself, saying he could not afford to hire much help. I was frequently sent on legal errands to his little

* From an advertisement of J. M. Bradstreet & Son which appeared in the *New York Daily Tribune*, Saturday, December 13, 1862.

office and would find him at noon holding his home-prepared lunch in one hand while writing with the other—so anxious was he to start his new enterprise. He was in fact transcribing in large books information which, through his system of indexes, enabled him to find in a moment the rating and general character of any party desired."[*]

John M. Bradstreet finally relinquished his retail business and began the practice of law. In 1848 he was made assignee of a large insolvent estate. While handling the affairs of this estate he acquired considerable, additional pertinent credit information concerning the moral and financial responsibilities of both debtors and creditors of the estate. Out of this setting he was able to make arrangements in 1849 to sell the available credit information as well as that which he had been collecting and meticulously ordering in the large volumes which his distant relative had so carefully noticed, to New York City wholesale distributors.

At this particular time, Cincinnati was the outstanding metropolis west of the Atlantic seaboard, and through it flowed a substantial portion of the western settlers and the western commerce, so it was quite natural that the opportunities for reviewing the credit responsibilities of a large number of commercial concerns should have become available at this point. These operations were so successful that in 1855 when the business had expanded sufficiently, an office was opened in New York City under the name, *Bradstreet's Improved Commercial Agency*. Shortly afterward, a son was admitted and the firm name became J. M. Bradstreet & Son, although the earlier more fluent style was also continued. From this time onward, *Bradstreet's* like *The Mercantile Agency* established offices at commercial and industrial centers as they took on importance, as the West became settled, and as railroads opened new territory for settlement, farming, cattle raising, mining, and trade.

"Bradstreet's" Printed the First Rating Book

An interesting advertisement which appeared in the *New York Daily Tribune* in 1862 briefly explained the operations of this business: "In 1857 we printed our first volume of 'Commercial Reports.' This volume contained reports of the business men of the Cities of New York, Philadelphia, Boston, Baltimore, Pittsburgh, Cincinnati, Louis-

[*] Quoted in an article, "The Evolution of the Commercial Agency, The Story of Bradstreet's," by C. W. Steffer in *Commerce and Finance*, February 22, 1928, Volume XVII, Number 8, p. 426.

ville, St. Louis, and Chicago, and we have issued a volume every six months since, adding reports of other cities and towns in each succeeding volume, until Volume XI issued in July, 1862 contains reports of nearly 200,000 business men in six thousand and four hundred of the cities and towns of the North. . . . We own and set the type for our books and sheets—the paper used in making the books is manufactured expressly for us. . . . We are at the present time revising all the Northern, Eastern and Western portions of the United States in order to correct and increase our Reports for our next volume (12), which will be the largest, most complete and correct Volume of 'Commercial Reports' ever issued in any country." Lewis Tappan, in the early years of his business, concentrated upon obtaining credit information on "country traders." John M. Bradstreet concentrated on the "city trade."

In 1863, the founder died and was succeeded by his son, Milton Bradstreet. In 1876, the business was incorporated. Upon the death of the son in 1876, the presidency devolved upon Charles Finney Clark, who had established the Detroit office in 1860. In 1869 and 1870 he managed the Philadelphia office and from 1870 to 1876 the Boston office. He remained President of the enterprise until his death in September, 1904. Clark was succeeded by Henry·E. Dunn who held the reins until May, 1927 when he, in turn, was succeeded by Charles M. Clark, the son of the former President.

John M. Bradstreet popularized the use of credit ratings. His early experiments on this unique problem, of having keyed information regarding business enterprises available for ready reference in a volume where a name could be "looked up" like a word in a dictionary, were brought to fruition in 1857 when the first book of commercial ratings was printed. This first volume of *Bradstreet's Improved Commercial Agency Reports* contained one hundred and ten pages, 17,100 names in nine locations, the intention at the time being to print ratings only on business concerns in the larger cities.

Two years later *The Mercantile Agency* followed with its reference book. This volume was bound in dark sheepskin and was closed with a bulky lock so that the subscriber might retain the key and thus keep its confidential contents from the prying eyes of subordinates and visitors. This volume contained five hundred and nineteen pages with 20,268 names located in what was then the United States and Canada.

Both agencies developed their reference books gradually to the point of printing four editions yearly, and finally in 1932, six editions yearly, to keep the entire business community informed of changes due to bankruptcies, liquidations, correct styles of all new concerns, and the modifications in credit responsibilities, as soon as possible. How important this is, may be realized by the fact that in the first six months of 1941, an average of 4,282 changes were made in the *Reference Book* of DUN & BRADSTREET, INC. for each business day.

History of Dun & Bradstreet, Inc.

On March 1, 1933 *R. G. Dun & Co.,* acquired the business of *The Bradstreet Company,* and subsequently changed the corporate style of the enlarged enterprise to DUN & BRADSTREET, INC. Both organizations had operated competitively since the formation of *Bradstreet's* in 1849, often opening offices in the same cities about the same time, employing credit reporters who called upon the very same business enterprises, printing reference books with corresponding information, and editing somewhat similar credit reports upon the same concerns. The facilities and activities of one organization duplicated those of the other. The combined facilities since the merger have made it possible to give a steadily improving standard of credit service to the banking, industrial, commercial, and insurance interests of the entire country.

During all of these years, many other mercantile agencies have entered the field. Specialized mercantile agencies operating in a limited locality or in specialized divisions of industry or commerce, have been developed from time to time, and many are in active existence today.

Foreign Affiliations of Dun & Bradstreet, Inc.

In addition to the one hundred and fifty-two offices maintained in the United States, DUN & BRADSTREET, INC., through its foreign affiliates, has direct connections, facilities, offices, or representatives almost everywhere on the face of the globe except in Soviet Russia and certain parts of Asia. With the exception of these points, the world is covered by an integrated system of closely affiliated or correspondent relationship. The names of the affiliated companies and the countries in which each operates, are given in the table on the following page. These concerns under normal conditions of world peace, operate similar to the way, but hardly as thorough as that in which DUN & BRADSTREET, INC. operates under the more liberally developed business and legal customs, habits, routines, and mores of the United States.

Affiliated Units	*Countries in which Active*
A. G. Auskunftei R. G. Dun	SWITZERLAND
Bradstreet's British Limited	GREAT BRITAIN, IRELAND
Dun & Bradstreet of Canada, Ltd. . .	CANADA, NEWFOUNDLAND
R. G. Dun & Bradstreet (Belge) S. A.	BELGIUM
R. G. Dun & Bradstreet Company . .	ARGENTINE, BRAZIL, CHILE, CUBA, URUGUAY
R. G. Dun & Bradstreet (France) S. A.	FRANCE
R. G. Dun & Co.	AUSTRALIA, NEW ZEALAND, PORTUGAL, PUERTO RICO, SPAIN, SOUTH AFRICA
R. G. Dun & Co., N. V.	HOLLAND
La Agencia Mercantil, R. G. Dun & Bradstreet de Mexico, S. A.	MEXICO

The nine mercantile agencies listed in the above schedule, operate in the most important commercial and industrial countries of the world with the exception of the Central European powers. These mercantile agencies have been established for many years in Great Britain and Ireland, Canada, France, Holland, Belgium, Switzerland, Argentine, Brazil, Chile, Uruguay, Australia, New Zealand, Mexico, South Africa, Cuba, and Puerto Rico. As a result of the present war with its concurrent military censorship, the status of most of the continental European offices of these affiliated units is unknown.

The direct offices which R. G. Dun & Co., formerly operated in Germany were taken over by an official Bureau of the German government when the United States entered the first World War. During that war, in 1918, these offices were acquired by the German mercantile agency, Deutsche Auskunftei, G.m.b.H. Since that time Dun & Bradstreet, Inc. has had no interest in any mercantile agency operating in Central Europe.

In the somewhat less important commercial and industrial centers of the world such as the countries located in Scandinavia, the northern part of South America, Central America, Africa outside of South Africa, Japan, China, India, the smaller Asiatic countries, and the East Indies, correspondent relationships are maintained with local sources of credit information such as agencies, individuals, or banking institutions that perform somewhat similar activities. By these established connections and arrangements, credit information is available through the facilities of Dun & Bradstreet, Inc. from all parts of the world.

Bibliographical References to Chapter Seven

ALBION, ROBERT GREENHALGH, *The Rise of New York Port, 1815-1860;* New York, 1939.

BARRETT, WALTER, *The Old Merchants of New York City;* Volume 1, New York, 1885.

JENKS, LELAND HAMILTON, *The Migration of British Capital to 1875;* New York, 1927.

LIGHTNER, OTTO C., *History of Business Depressions;* New York, 1922.

LYNCH, DENIS TILDEN, *"Boss" Tweed;* New York, 1927.

MCGRANE, R. G., *The Panic of 1837;* Chicago, 1924.

ROSS, WM. P. M., *The Accountants' Own Book and Business Man's Manual;* Philadelphia, 1848.

SAKOLSKI, A. M., *The Great American Land Bubble;* New York, 1932.

Treasury-Annual Reports 1829-36; Published by the Federal Government, 1837.

Treasury-Annual Reports 1837-44; Published by the Federal Government, 1851.

VOSE, E. N., *Seventy-Five Years of The Mercantile Agency;* New York, 1916.

Volumes Previously Cited

ASHE, THOMAS, *Travels in America, Performed in 1806, for the Purpose of Exploring the Rivers Alleghany, Monongahela, Ohio, and Mississippi;* London, Reprinted in Newburyport, 1808.

BOGART, ERNEST LUDLOW, *Economic History of the American People;* 1930, Edition of 1935, New York.

CLARK, VICTOR S., *History of Manufactures in the United States, 1607-1860;* 1929 Edition, New York.

DEWEY, DAVIS RICH, *Financial History of the United States;* 1902, Second Edition 1903, New York.

JONES, FRED MITCHELL, *Middlemen in the Domestic Trade of the United States, 1800-1860;* Urbana, Illinois, 1937.

JOSEPHSON, MATTHEW, *The Robber Barons;* New York, 1934.

KIRKLAND, EDWARD C., *A History of American Economic Life;* 1932, Edition of 1939, New York.

KNOX, JOHN JAY, *A History of Banking in the United States;* 1900, Revised Edition 1903, New York.

TAPPAN, LEWIS, *The Life of Arthur Tappan;* New York, 1870.

VIII ✧ Operations of
The Mercantile Agency

THE activities of *The Mercantile Agency* fall into nine divisions. The objective of each division is the collection, the analyzation, the editing, and the dissemination of information concerning some particular phase of commercial and industrial life. In this way, *The Mercantile Agency* assists in the more orderly flow of mercantile and banking credit according to American business practices and customs, terms of sale, and settlement, which have been evolved over the years since the early colonists first traded with the Indians "for corne." These nine divisions are:

1. The Credit Report Department which investigates, analyzes, and edits narrative credit reports on practically every business enterprise in the United States.
2. The Insurance Division of the Credit Report Department which prepares specialized reports for fire insurance underwriting corporations and general agencies.
3. The Reference Book Department which publishes a credit rating book on commercial and industrial business enterprises six times yearly.
4. The Advisory Service Department which gives a rapid service by telephone and telegraph to the manufacturers of women's, men's, and children's garments regarding the advisability of shipping specific orders received from retail stores.
5. The Foreign Department which collects information and edits credit reports on business enterprises throughout the world outside of the United States, Alaska, Hawaiian Islands, and the Dominion of Canada.
6. The Municipal Service Department which prepares comprehensive specialized reports on States, counties, municipalities, and similar borrowing units for investors.
7. The Mercantile Claims Department which collects past due accounts in behalf of concerns selling to business enterprises.
8. The Magazine Department which publishes *Dun's Review,* a business monthly.

9. The Research and Statistical Department which makes studies of current interest on problems of industry, commerce, banking, accountancy, and Congressional legislation affecting business.

Each department is uniquely important, each department serves a definite economic function and fills a definite niche in the American scheme of democratic business life. Of the entire nine departments, however, the one which is of outstanding importance and significance is the department which embraces all of the activities of collecting and analyzing credit information, and which prepares "credit reports," the function for which *The Mercantile Agency* was established by Lewis Tappan in 1841, and *The Bradstreet Co.,* by John M. Bradstreet in 1849. There is no touch of the synthetic in this activity. It is intensely and peculiarly practical. Both of these early mercantile agencies, during all of the years up to 1933, and the merged enterprise since that date, developed collateral services, but the collection and the analyzation of credit information on active business concerns, and the transformation of that information into credit reports to assist in the guidance of commerce, has always been the primary function.

This field covers practically every active business enterprise in every nook and cranny from Aroostook County in Maine to San Diego County in California, in every country town and hamlet, every sea-side fishing village, mining center, and Summer resort, whether the net investment is hundreds of millions of dollars in steel mills or two hundred dollars in trinkets in a country store catering to Summer visitors. Between 16 per cent and 20 per cent of all the active business concerns go out of existence each year and approximately the same percentage of new enterprises are organized. This ease in fading out of the business picture, and also with a little money and initiative, of setting up an independent business, is, along with the freedom of speech, freedom of the press, and freedom of worship, an outstanding expression of a democratic nation in an economic world currently torn between the totalitarianisms of Fascism and Communism.

These services of *The Mercantile Agency,* carefully developed over one hundred years, now provide credit reports on every active business concern with almost mechanical assuredness. These reports are available in answer to any request for credit information from any banking institution, manufacturing establishment, wholesale distributor, insurance underwriter, or subscriber in any other field of activity. By this service the barriers of distance have been completely broken down. Strength and elasticity have been added to every-day commerce.

Ebb and Flow of Business Enterprises

In 1929, an all-time peak was reached in the number of active commercial and industrial business enterprises in the United States. The number then coasted uncomfortably down hill each year until 1933, but since that time, the number has appreciably and steadily increased. In July, 1940 there were 2,156,000 concerns engaged in manufacturing, converting, assembling, importing, exporting, wholesaling, and retailing merchandise listed in the *Reference Book* for the United States. In general, financial institutions including commercial banks, trust companies, savings banks, and investment bankers; railroads; professional individuals, such as lawyers and doctors; farmers, and others not ordinarily users of commercial credit in the generally accepted sense, are not rated in the *Reference Book*. In July, 1940, however, there were 92,000 branches of established businesses acting as separate buying units which were included, resulting in a net figure of 2,064,000 active commercial and industrial business enterprises in the forty-eight States at that time.

During the calendar year of 1939, there were 376,000 new business concerns in the United States. Control of 45,000 of these enterprises had been retained by the principals of the predecessor concerns, while 113,000 were successions in which the old ownerships had been completely eliminated. The 376,000 new enterprises represented eighteen per cent of all active commercial and industrial concerns.

In 1939, there were 349,000 business enterprises that discontinued operations of which 158,000 are accounted for in the preceding paragraph. The remaining 191,000 concerns completely disappeared from the business arena. The 349,000 discontinuances represented sixteen and one-half per cent of the active commercial and industrial business enterprises. In other words, during every business day of 1939, an average of 1,338 new commercial and industrial concerns opened their doors in the United States and of this number, 563 succeeded previously existing enterprises, such as a corporation succeeding a partnership or a proprietorship, while 775 were entirely new ventures.

The figures in the preceding two paragraphs present a vital, moving picture of the continual daily change which takes place within our highly competitive, democratic, economic system. These figures are also indicative of the tremendous volume of work, and the size of the task involved in constantly gathering, sifting, and interpreting credit data on all units in our commercial and industrial life. A very large proportion of these business births are small scale enterprises with net invested funds well below $3,000. The large corporation seldom disappears, although its control may shift as its securities are bought and sold, as operating managements come and go, and as mergers, consolidations, and reorganizations take place. When the Supreme Court decided in 1886 that a corporation was a person in the meaning of the "due process" clause of the Federal Constitution, an element of unprecedented security was given to the existence of the large corporation which was becoming a dynamic power in our social and economic life.

The yearly number of business deaths is an indication that high hopes have not, and are not sufficient qualifications to survive in this highly competitive struggle for business existence. A moderate proportion are cases where men wish to retire so that the termination of ownership involves no particular stress or strain. The bulk of the cases, from year to year, however, represent situations where the limited amount of invested funds become exhausted, where sales drop off, and where there appears to be no solution except withdrawal from the daily business struggle. The lack of profits and natural economic laws provide the unquestioned authorities for this continual change.

Credit Report Department

In developing an organization of trained men to interview, investigate, analyze, and prepare commercial, narrative credit reports on each of these 2,064,000 commercial and industrial concerns which were in existence in July, 1940, DUN & BRADSTREET, INC., has divided the United States into forty-five districts, each district representing a geographical territory ranging from an entire State such as Colorado or Utah, where the population is widely scattered, down to a few counties in densely populated regions such as New York City, Chicago, and Philadelphia. These forty-five districts have under them "sub-offices" and "reporting stations" so that, all in all, the existing organization consists of one hundred and fifty-two offices of various sizes in the United States, and sixteen under the name of a wholly-owned subsidiary, DUN & BRADSTREET OF CANADA, LIMITED, in the Dominion of Canada. These offices are further supported by an extensive staff of correspondents and local representatives who reside in every city and important town in the United States, a most efficient development over the years since Lewis Tappan sent out his initial circular in

1841, inviting lawyers and others at distant points, to become his experimental correspondents "in the country trade."

Each of these one hundred and fifty-two offices in the United States, and the sixteen in the Dominion of Canada, have staffs of men who investigate, gather pertinent credit information, analyze the data, and prepare the final commercial, narrative credit reports on all business concerns domiciled in their respective territories. These staffs consist of four classes of reporters who are constantly gathering information for the current editing of credit reports; city reporters at points where offices are located, resident reporters living in important nearby cities, traveling reporters, and local correspondents living in other cities and towns. These various classes of credit reporters have been created over the years as the means of obtaining essential credit information with the maximum degree of efficient, rapid service from every part of the country throughout the year, no matter how densely or sparsely settled a section may be.

The City Reporter

In most offices, the credit investigations on business concerns located within the city limits, are handled by three to twenty trained, city credit reporters. A city generally is divided into geographical divisions, and all investigations on business enterprises located within a particular district are made by the same reporter. In this way, the reporter becomes intimately acquainted with all unusual sources of credit information, and the managements of all businesses located in his particular district. In larger cities, such as New York, Chicago, Philadelphia, Detroit, and Los Angeles, the division of work is broken down with greater refinements, business concerns being divided into four groups, depending upon their size, the complicated nature of their organization with subsidiary or affiliated enterprises, their methods of operation, and their financial condition. The credit investigations of concerns in these four groups are handled by different categories of specialized city reporters.

The first call which the city reporter makes in his investigation, is upon the concern itself, verifying its existence if the enterprise is newly organized, and ascertaining the previous business connections of the principals. These earlier business connections are subsequently verified directly from the tremendous storehouse of records of *The Mercantile Agency,* by direct calls if previous employers or associates are located nearby, or by correspondence with other offices whose reporters make the verification from their records or by direct calls. There are an infinite number of essential points of credit information varying with the size, the nature of the business, the method of operation, the financial condition of the business, and the method of financing, which the experienced credit reporter is then trained to follow up carefully and diligently in his investigation.

Besides gathering all essential credit information on local business enterprises, city reporters also analyze that information, and prepare the credit reports on these concerns. There are eight hundred and forty-eight city reporters in the entire system in the United States.

The Resident Reporter

Each office, in addition to its staff of city credit reporters, also has a smaller number of what are known as resident reporters. In the New York City office, for example, the resident reporting staff consists of seven reporters who gather the pertinent credit information on concerns located in the respective cities where they reside, and in nearby outlying territories; Middletown, Newburgh, White Plains, and Riverhead in New York State, Asbury Park and Hackensack in New Jersey, and Stamford in Connecticut.

Inquiries calling for investigations on concerns in their territories are mailed to resident reporters daily by their supervising office. These business establishments are investigated by resident reporters in the very same manner as city names are investigated by city reporters; the one resident reporter, however, handling all lines of business, factories, newsstands, delicatessen stores, corner drug stores, automobile distributors, and lumber dealers, large and small, in his territory. The credit information obtained in these investigations is then mailed daily to the home office, where members of another staff known as "report writers" analyze the information received from the resident reporters, from the bank and the trade investigations which are being made simultaneously, and prepare the finished commercial, narrative credit report.

Resident reporters provide speed in gathering credit information and in bringing credit reports up to date on concerns located in the more densely populated territories, but some distance away from any one of the one hundred and fifty-two offices, which could be obtained rapidly and efficiently in no other way. They are on the ground, they become widely and intimately acquainted in their respective territories, they know every source of available credit information, all local short-cuts, and they hear the day-to-day gossip regarding profitable and unprofitable ventures of local business men and business enterprises. There are sixty-five resident reporters from the Atlantic to the Pacific, and five hundred and twenty report writers.

The Traveling Reporter

In addition to the counties which comprise New York City proper, the New York City office has supervision over all investigations in the nine New York State counties nearest to the city, over all concerns located in Bergen and Monmouth Counties in New Jersey, and approximately one-half of Fairfield County in Connecticut. In these eleven and one-half counties there are 767 cities, towns, and villages in which there are located approximately 46,500 active commercial and industrial business enterprises. Each one of these concerns is visited each year automatically, irrespective of the fact that many of them are also investigated in the course of the year by resident reporters and by correspondents.

For this extensive field work, the New York City office employs ten traveling reporters. Each reporter is equipped with an automobile and a schedule of the cities, towns, and villages which he must cover during the succeeding eleven and one-half months. As he goes on this circuit, he calls upon and investigates locally every business enterprise at each location. This procedure is known as "automatic revision." The traveling reporter, unlike the city reporter, the resident reporter, and the correspondent, handles only occasional inquiries calling for immediate investigation. His main task is to revise and to bring up to date the credit information on every "name" in every city, town, and village on his schedule. At the end of each week he mails the results of his investigations and all financial statements he has obtained to his home office. Frequently he picks up information of vital current interest which he mails to his home office the very same day so that it may be distributed immediately to all interested subscribers.

Every county in the forty-eight States, the territory of Alaska, the nine Provinces and the two territories in the Dominion of Canada, and Newfoundland, are covered in this manner by travelers from the various offices. From Edmonton and Winnipeg in Canada, the traveling reporter eventually reaches the trading posts in the Arctic Circle over twelve hundred miles away, and in the same systematic way,

These sho have Pressing new Sub. papers sent

1. Nath. Wood &c.

2. A. Tappan &c.

3. Maltbie Wood

4. Rob. L. Smith & Henderson

5. Calvin W. How

6. Benj. D. Godfrey

Petit, Dunning & Co
11 Jan 1843 Petit, Bon

Jn. N. Leavitt

J. Cook, Anthony & Co

John W. Holberton

60 maiden Lane

Bowen & McNamee

Charles Stanton & Co

First Subscribers to The Mercantile Agency, 1841

traveling reporters from St. Paul, Minnesota, call upon every business establishment in every country town in Divide County in North Dakota, about seven hundred miles away. By this process every business enterprise is directly called upon and investigated locally at least once every year. The traveling reporter is the backbone of *The Mercantile Agency* in outlying country territories, just as the city reporter is the backbone at the locations where the one hundred and fifty-two offices are maintained in the United States.

The Local Correspondent

The New York City office also has approximately four hundred local correspondents. There is at least one such correspondent in every reasonable sized community; a banker, an insurance broker, an established merchant, an attorney at law, a real estate broker, someone who is willing and anxious to give a reasonable portion of his time and interest to outside work of this nature.

Correspondents are called upon for credit investigations on local businesses under two sets of circumstances. At certain peak seasons of the year when more inquiries flow through for investigation than can normally be handled by the resident reporter, the excess is sent to the local correspondent for immediate investigation. With this routine, speed and promptness which is so essential in all phases of credit activity, is always assured. In a smaller town and village, where no full time resident reporter is employed, all inquiries calling for immediate investigation between the visits of the traveling reporter, are forwarded directly to the local correspondent.

One or more correspondents are maintained in practically every city, town, and village in the country outside of those cities where offices are located. By 1846, when *The Mercantile Agency* was five years old, there had been built up a chain of 679 correspondents, 352 to the New York office, 115 to Boston, and 212 to Philadelphia. Today there are approximately 50,000 local correspondents of this character in the United States and about 8,000 in the Dominion of Canada.

Trade Investigations

While the city reporters are calling upon local business concerns, banking depositories, and larger merchandise creditors; while resident reporters, traveling reporters, and correspondents are following out their similar prescribed activities; each home office is sending out thousands of trade inquiries to merchandise creditors in all parts of the country to ascertain the manner in which each of these concerns is paying its current merchandise bills. Information is obtained simultaneously regarding the amount of recent high credit, the terms of sale, amount owing, amount past due, amount on order, whether payments are being made by notes or trade acceptances, whether the account has recently been collected by an attorney, and whether unjust claims are ever made.

A Detroit department store might purchase women's dresses in New York City, men's suits in Baltimore, Maryland, canned fruits and vegetables in California, furniture in Grand Rapids, Michigan, jewelry in Providence, Rhode Island, and men's hats in Danbury, Connecticut. Every important source of supply must be consulted. During 1940, over 21,000,000 trade slips, or approximately 70,000 daily, were mailed or personally delivered to creditors to ascertain from them the exact paying experiences of their business customers. A ceaseless round of activity must be carried on to obtain every piece of pertinent credit information at the earliest possible moment.

Supplementary Credit Information

Three supplementary practices exist in the collection and dissemination of pertinent credit information. First, in January of each year a financial statement form is mailed to every commercial and industrial business enterprise in the United States. As these financial statements are returned, they are incorporated into credit reports and promptly distributed to all interested subscribers. Secondly, a representative is maintained in most county seats whose responsibility it is to report all record items such as deeds, mortgages, suits, judgments, and similar instruments to his home office promptly. Thirdly, newspapers, financial journals, and trade periodicals are examined and clipped daily so that no published pertinent information affecting the credit risk of any concern, favorably or unfavorably, will be overlooked.

Continuous Service

An inquiry regarding a business enterprise is immediately answered by delivering or mailing a current credit report on that concern. This procedure is just the beginning of present-day, streamlined credit service. A copy of every additional credit report edited during the ensuing twelve months, including the results of regular revisions, automatic revisions, interim and fiscal financial statements, trade investigations, and special notices, is automatically furnished to the inquirer. In other words, every request for information is immediately answered by a credit report, but the inquirer, in addition, receives every item of supplementary credit information obtained and distributed on that enterprise for a continuous period of one entire year. This program of continuous service was instituted in 1931 and has been of infinite value to the credit community.

When the year of credit service expires on an account, a continuous service renewal slip is delivered to the inquirer. This slip merely states that service has been rendered for one year on a particular concern, and that if the ticket is returned, the service will be continued for another year. By this automatic vigil, the subscriber is informed when service on an interested account would cease, and if he has no further credit interest in the case, he retains the ticket; on the other hand, if he continues to sell the account and is anxious to receive all available information for another year, this simple routine provides the means.

Color Signal System

Commercial narrative credit reports are printed on sheets of paper which have a colored right hand border, either green, amber, or red, to assist users of the service in recognizing types of information as it flows into their credit files. A green border on the right margin of the report paper indicates that the rating carried by the current report is the same as the rating assigned at the time the previous report was edited. An amber border on the right margin indicates that the rating has just been changed. The change may be either upward or downward in either the capital or credit symbol. A red border on pink paper signifies that the report is a Special Notice covering some special current development. Information regarding suits, judgments, liens, petitions in bankruptcy, composition settlements, voluntary or involuntary liquidations, changes in ownership, fires, deaths, the placing of chattel mortgages, and similar information of immediate interest, is distributed on red bordered paper.

A blue bordered rider, blue on the upper margin, and attached to any report—regardless of the color of the right border—indicates that the report answers a specific inquiry. All other credit reports, that is, reports without this blue bordered rider are furnished as supplemental or additional reports under continuous service automatic routine. This color signal system provides a simple, effective means for the selective review of reports according to the probable relative degree of immediate interest.

Insurance Report Division

For many decades, fire insurance companies have made extensive use of the commercial, narrative credit reports of *The Mercantile Agency*. Until more recent years, it had been the almost uniform policy of the underwriting departments of fire insurance companies to underwrite any fire risk where there was no apparent question regarding the honesty, the integrity, the principles of the owner or owners of a business if a proprietorship or a partnership, and of the officers, if a corporation, provided the physical exposure of the location was satisfactory. In line with this policy, credit reports were used primarily to ascertain the record, the exact antecedents of the principals in a business, to learn if any individual or any business enterprise with which a principal may have been associated, had had questionable fires or questionable failures.

Relativity of the Moral Hazard

During recent years, however, this policy has been questioned by progressive fire insurance companies and general agencies. After all, is not such a policy somewhat general and ambiguous? Because an individual has had a clear record, is no indication that his moral backbone is strong enough to withstand the tragic strain when heading for the yawning chasm of bankruptcy. There is always the possibility that his reflex might end in "accidental" incendiarism. Morality is not a fixed reality. It changes with changing conditions, environments, financial stress and strain, professions, and associations.

When a business enterprise is operating unprofitably, when the outlook for improvement is clouded, when competition is strong and unfilled orders are rapidly shrinking, and when the management is unqualified, indifferent, or dominated by inertia, essential guiding policies are at times relaxed. Under such conditions, a management weighted by discouragement often exhibits a carelessness in its attitude toward policies which are essential to proper fire control; oil soaked cotton waste might be allowed to remain in the corners of a room; corrugated paper and excelsior might accumulate; matches and burning cigarettes might be casually discarded; any one of which would increase the fire hazard of a lumber yard, a mill, a loft building, or a retail store.

Furthermore, it is not the most unusual occurrence in the world for an owner's ethical resistance to break down under some such aggravated set of unusual circumstances. With inventories and liabilities high, with increasing difficulty in paying his bills, with bankruptcy staring him in the face, the one way out might seem to be a homemade fire. An individual, whose antecedents have been as clear as the rays of the rising sun, succumbs; his values of right and wrong are suddenly warped and the result is incendiarism, a fraudulent fire which no one may be able to prove was fraudulent.

Specialized Insurance Reports

To fill this particular need, special insurance reports of two types have been developed, one on a specialized question and answer blank, and the other on a tabulated form. These reports furnish fire insurance examiners, underwriters, general agents, and inspectors, concisely and completely, with pertinent and detailed antecedent data, show the current financial trend in the applicant's business, discuss the physical aspects of the location of the enterprise and its neighborhood from a fire insurance viewpoint, reveal the record of any previous fires, and such supplementary facts which are of particular interest when an application for fire insurance from a business concern is being examined. These reports are prepared under the direct supervision of reporters especially trained in understanding the requirements of fire insurance underwriters and general agents.

Reference Book Department

The *Reference Book* is a volume which contains the names of all active commercial and industrial business enterprises in every city, town, village, and hamlet in the United States, together with two symbols, one before, and one after each name. The symbol which appears before each name indicates the line of business activity, and the one which follows indicates the estimated financial investment in the business and its general credit worthiness. This volume also contains supplementary information for the banker and the mercantile credit man, such as a list of banks with important correspondents, State maps, and the population of every village, town, or city.

The most valuable feature of the *Reference Book*, and the one for which it is universally known and used, is the credit rating on each active commercial and industrial concern. With a *Reference Book* available, a banker or a credit man may, at any moment, look up the name of any active commercial or industrial business enterprise in the United States or in Canada, just as he would look up a word in a dictionary, or a name in a telephone directory, and obtain an approximate idea of its size and credit worthiness. The symbol at the left of each name refers to one of 293 trade classifications, an index to which appears in the front of the volume.

The Rating Key

The symbol at the right of most of the names consists of a letter and a numeral, the letter representing the "estimated pecuniary strength," and the numeral, the "general credit" standing. Sometimes it is difficult, notwithstanding the most painstaking investigation, to obtain sufficient facts on which to base both a capital and a credit rating, and in these cases, either one or both symbols may be omitted.

There are seventeen classifications for "estimated pecuniary strength" ranging from "Aa," which represents financial responsibility in excess of $1,000,000, to "M," which represents less than $500. There are only four classifications of credit worthiness: high, good, fair, and limited. Under these four classifications there are, in the aggregate, forty-eight symbols indicating the "general credit" standing. This key is a gradual development over a period of forty-one years, from 1859 when the first rating key was published by *The Mercantile Agency*, to 1900, when the present more elaborate key was adopted.

When a credit rating only appears as in "—1," the numeral takes on a different significance. A rating "—1," for example, indicates that a business concern has a pecuniary strength in excess of $125,000, but sufficiently exact financial information is not available for publication in the credit report to classify the tangible net worth under a particular letter symbol; all credit information, however, is of a general favorable nature. The "—2" rating carries a similar implication within the capital range of $20,000 to $125,000, "—3" from $2,000 to $20,000 and "—4" for less than $2,000.

Number of Listed Names

The number of names in the forty-eight States contained in the *Reference Book* increased with minor fluctuations from 20,268 in 1859, the date of the first volume published by *The Mercantile Agency*, to 2,212,000 in 1929. During the four years ending 1933, the number dropped to 1,960,700. In the following seven years ending June 30, 1940 the number gradually increased to 2,156,000, of which 92,000 represented branches that acted as separate buying units, as previously mentioned. These figures indicate the extensive nature of the national task involved in compiling the essential credit facts on every active commercial and industrial concern in the country, condensing that information into ratings, and then compiling those names with trade and rating symbols within the covers of a single volume.

Reference Books were revised yearly with the exception of 1862 and 1863 during the Civil War when none were printed. In 1866, a second edition was published during the year, and the announcement was made that thereafter the volume would be issued semi-annually. In 1873, the volume was published four times yearly and beginning in 1932, six times yearly. As manufacturers and traders gradually extended their operations across the continent and from the borders of Canada to the borders of Mexico, as the number of active concerns exceeded 500,000, then 1,000,000 and finally 2,000,000, it became necessary to publish the *Reference Book* more and more frequently so that changes, including the names of all new concerns; the elimination of those which went into bankruptcy; those which voluntarily liquidated, merged, or consolidated; and more important, the changes in capital and credit ratings, would be available to commerce and industry within the least possible lapse in time. The immensity of this task will be seen by the following tabulation of changes made in these volumes during the first six months of 1941, an average of 4,282 changes for each business day:

Number of Changes in Reference Book January-July, 1941

New Names Inserted	179,367
Names Obliterated	191,710
Changes Made in Ratings	205,261
Changes Made in Styles	31,696
Alterations in Bank List	38,624
Total Changes January-July, 1941	646,658
Average Changes for each Business Day	4,282

The complete *Reference Book,* including the names of all active commercial and industrial concerns in the United States and in the Dominion of Canada, is a volume 11½ by 16½ inches in size, and four inches thick. The July, 1941 edition contained 3,759 pages. Individual State *Reference Books* are also published in pocket editions, 6¾ by 4¾ inches in size, for the use of executives and of traveling salesmen.

Advisory Service Department

Probably the most efficiently organized credit departments around the turn of the century were those of the New York City factors which, as we have seen, operated exclusively in the textile field. As a result of maintaining up-to-date credit files and efficient personnel, their credit departments were able to pass upon almost any individual request for credit within a very few moments. They set the early pace for the developments of keen specialization, in the understanding and interpretation of extensive credit information, in the ability to translate comparative financial statements, and in the demand for being kept informed of comprehensive up-to-the-minute credit facts.

Need for Rapid Credit Decisions

Mercantile houses that failed to have such experienced credit personnel around the turn of the century had other problems. After an order for merchandise was obtained, it would go to the credit department for approval. The individual in the small concern who was responsible for, but not experienced or fundamentally trained to handle credit problems, would request a credit report from one of the mercantile agencies to obtain the information to assist him in making his decision. Unless the subscriber sent a special messenger for this report, it would invariably be delivered early the following morning.

In the textile industry, a new theory began to find expression to eliminate the over-night delay. If the enterprise receiving the order could telephone to a central bureau and receive qualified advice over the telephone that the concern placing the order was a legitimate business enterprise, that it was or was not financially responsible for reasonable credit, a decision could immediately be made. This theory was based upon the assumption that such a bureau would employ experts and would have a continual flow of pertinent information into its credit files.

Application to Retail Apparel Trade

This theory was developed, first, by textile mills and selling agents in passing upon the orders received from concerns in the cutting-up trades, that is, from the manufacturers of coats and suits, waists and dresses, men's and children's clothing, shirts, and underwear. This initial development of serving textile mills and selling agents, in turn, gradually gave way to the much larger field of serving the manufacturers of clothing selling direct to retail stores in all parts of the country, which handled apparel goods, women's, men's, and children's clothing, and accessories. This evolution came to be known in credit circles as an "advisory credit service."

In 1928, *The Mercantile Agency* organized an Advisory Service Department to give a credit service of this very nature to concerns everywhere in the United States selling to retail stores handling clothing and accessories. The headquarters of this department were located in the New York City office, and branches were gradually opened in ten other important centers, Boston, Chicago, Cleveland, Dallas, Kansas City, Los Angeles, Minneapolis, St. Louis, San Francisco, and Seattle offices. A staff of specialized credit analysts who are fully acquainted with the purchasing habits, trade customs, and buying seasons of retailers handling these lines of merchandise, assist manufacturers in this hazardous style field to make prompt shipments to desirable customers everywhere in the United States. There are approximately 130,000 retail concerns in the country, handling clothing and accessories, with the concentration in and around the important cities where branches of this specialized department are maintained.

Foreign Department

Three years before the outbreak of the Civil War, *The Mercantile Agency* started its extensive chain of foreign offices by establishing two branches, one in London, England, and the other in Montreal, Canada. The London office was opened as a service to British export houses that had become subscribers to the New York City office to obtain credit reports upon active American importers.

The London branch at the outset confined its relations to export and import houses trading between the two countries, but it was not long before the business community in Great Britain began to request reports upon British as well as upon American traders. In 1872, branches were established in Glasgow, Scotland, and in Paris, France; in 1876 in Berlin, Germany; and in 1887 in Melbourne, Australia. Resident agents were appointed in immediately succeeding years in other business centers in Australia and in New Zealand, and additional branches were subsequently installed on the European continent, in South Africa, South America, Mexico, and in the West Indies. Prior to the present World War, offices or branches of subsidiaries or affiliates of DUN & BRADSTREET, INC., were maintained at one hundred and forty-one locations in twenty-seven foreign countries. After one and one-half years of hostilities, the status of many of the European offices such as those in Belgium, Holland, Italy, and part of France, remain uncertain as military censorship has prevented all but the barest rumors from passing the borders of those countries. In the meantime, relations with Latin-American countries have steadily expanded.

All offices of subsidiaries and affiliates are engaged in the same type of credit investigation, analysis, and reporting which has become the customary business procedure in the United States, although in all countries with somewhat fewer refinements and somewhat less adequate results. Abroad, the practice of making comprehensive credit information available in its various ramifications has not become quite the recognized, normal, every-day, business procedure that it has in the United States. In certain Old World countries such as Great Britain and France, the information is quite fragmentary, more general, more in the nature of opinions and general reputation, while in the more recently settled and developing countries such as Argentine and Brazil, the practice and the expectancy of obtaining exact, reliable, financial data from those seeking mercantile or bank credit, more closely approximate our own technique, expectancy, and routine.

These credit facilities are available in accordance to the customs of each particular country to American bankers, manufacturers, and exporters who happen to be seeking essential facts regarding the moral and financial responsibilities of commercial and industrial concerns located in every business community on the face of the earth. These reports contain credit information based upon investigations at the home office of the business, supplemented by investigations in the American market, and in any foreign markets in which the debtor might be purchasing merchandise or obtaining bank credit. These credit facilities of the world are funnelled into the Foreign Department of *The Mercantile Agency* in New York City.

Operations of the Foreign Department

When the typical American exporter of cotton goods, automobile tires, or machinery, receives orders from foreign buyers who are located anywhere on the face of the globe, he immediately requests credit reports upon them. If these houses have been in existence one year or more, and had previously placed orders in the American market, the Foreign Department would have current credit reports on them. If the orders were the first to be placed in this market, current data would be rapidly obtained by writing or cabling the nearest foreign office of the subsidiary or affiliate operating at or near that point, or established correspondent in that country, for all available credit information. As soon as the reply arrived in the United States, the information would be translated into English and incorporated into a credit report. That report would also contain an up-to-the-minute supplementary trade investigation which would have been made simultaneously in the United States export market to determine whether other orders for merchandise had been placed here, and if so, what information, if any, those exporters had obtained regarding the credit worthiness of the foreign buyer and their experience with the account.

The credit files of the Foreign Department are constantly being kept current by reports which are sent in automatically as well as upon specific request. This practice, in particular, is followed by the seventeen offices located in Latin America. In countries which are less active in the American market such as China and India, connections are maintained with established correspondents who furnish information only upon specific request. Overlapping inquiries make it possible to keep up-to-date credit information available on practically all foreign buyers in the American market.

Credit reports are edited in the New York City office on all foreign concerns. A staff of credit specialists, who keep in touch with the respective markets throughout the world and their conditions, and who translate correspondence and credit reports received from almost every country, handle this rather intricate work. Credit reports on foreign establishments are modeled after the domestic reports. In addition, however, there is also included the current market rate, in dollars, of the foreign currency quoted in the report. Thus, at a glance, the credit man sees the approximate equivalent, in United States currency, of his client's capital even though the financial statement be in Argentine pesos, Brazilian contos, Venezuela bolivars, or Japanese yen.

Airmail has expedited foreign service materially, cutting down mail time, especially between the United States and South America. Occasionally, letters are received from Havana and from Mexico the day after they were mailed, instead of four or five days later. The "Clipper" airships are in current use to and from Portugal, the Philippine Islands, New Zealand, and Australia. Frequent cable advice is obtained from London, from Tokyo, from Buenos Aires, and in many instances, the replies are received the very same day. In the United States such rapid service is taken for granted, but in foreign trade, the marked difference in time must be kept in mind, as well as the fact that in certain foreign countries, telegrams are delivered by mail and not by messenger.

Latin America Sales Index

In 1938, a list of manufacturers, wholesalers, retailers, and professional men in the twenty-nine markets of South America, Central America, and the West Indies, was compiled by the Foreign Department in a volume measuring 11 by 14 inches and containing 1,060 pages, known as the *Latin America Trade Index*. Approximately 90,000 concerns are arranged in this volume, alphabetically by country, town, and business style. Many of these enterprises are turning to the United States for their merchandise and equipment requirements in the present disturbed state of world commerce. In addition to the name and the address, a capital code key gives an approximation of the invested capital, the nature of each business, and the principal products handled by each enterprise.

Moreover, a trade code key used in combination with a special type of gage, known as the trade selector, makes it possible to pick out accounts in any specific trade or capital group. The American manufacturing exporter is thus enabled to make an analysis of his potential market in any area, by number and by size of prospective buyers. For the first time, he may study the concentration of potential accounts in any Latin American territory. He has a ready guide to the selection of agents in any location, trade, or capital group.

The nearest banking connections, the nearest port, the population and the economic classification of cities and towns are also given. A statistical section containing a review of the various types of credit terms used in shipments by American exporters to Latin America, a chart of seasons which is helpful in planning sales promotional campaigns of seasonal merchandise, and tables showing the primary native products exported by each of the twenty-nine markets in Latin America, are included. To keep both the old and new listings up to date, over 120,000 foreign credit reports are examined yearly. These reports are checked against master records and all changes in name, street address, trade, or capital code are reported in a monthly supplement. In July, a special supplement which lists all changes reported in the preceding six months, as well as all new names, is published. This volume is completely revised once each year.

Municipal Service Department

In 1932, the Municipal Service Department was established to prepare specialized investment reports on States, counties, cities, and other governmental borrowing units in behalf of commercial banks and trust companies, savings banks, investment bankers, private estates, fraternal organizations, insurance companies, and individuals having substantial holdings of government and municipal securities. At that time, investors owned approximately $19,000,000,000 of State and municipal bonds without having in a readily available usable form, a great deal of exact information regarding the financial and economic strength behind particular issues of securities. With defaults in over three thousand governmental units, it became evident that thorough, unbiased credit analyses of these units had become most essential.

Government Finance Records Complex

The processes of government and of government finance are somewhat mysterious, even when expounded on the front pages of the press, and that mystery often deepens as one goes further into their records. States and local governments borrow, levy and collect taxes, make appropriations and spend money in accordance with laws which are laid down in constitutions, statutes, charters, local ordinances, and resolutions. No two States have the same legal system; no State has a uniform system for all classes of its municipalities; State and local law makers are constantly changing the systems; and the courts are perennially adding their sometimes disconcerting interpretations.

Government financial transactions are a matter of public record. Actually, however, this advantage is not so great as might appear. In the first place, States and local governments follow no standard system of accounts. A few States have prescribed standard accounting systems for some or all of their municipalities, but no two States have followed this procedure in quite the same way, nor with quite the same degree of success. The majority of cities, counties, school and other districts, have their own locally adopted systems, some admirably scientific and complete, but many antiquated and fragmentary. In the second place, a surprisingly large number of local governments either publish no periodic reports of their financial transactions, or issue reports which virtually defy intelligent interpretation. As a result, the unscrambling and simplifying of these records is a major undertaking.

The Municipal Service Department proceeds along three general lines in compiling its reports. First, the department collects in its library thousands of State and municipal official reports, audits, and financial statements, economic surveys and reports, and all available technical and professional literature bearing in any way upon municipal credit. Secondly, its staff maintains contact, personally and by correspondence, with hundreds of individuals throughout the country engaged in public administration and research, in order to exchange views and keep abreast with all developments. Thirdly, specialization is provided by the experienced analysts in the department.

This specialization centers in assigning to each analyst a territory consisting of a contiguous group of States. It then becomes his responsibility to familiarize himself with the governmental systems, finances, and economic characteristics of all important borrowing units in his territory. All pertinent new material for the library goes to his desk before it is placed on the shelves or in the files. About one-fourth of his time is spent in traveling, making regular and special investigations, obtaining first-hand pictures of the larger cities and counties, meeting public officials, and securing interpretations of obscure points in their financial statements. In general, he is responsible down to the final editing, for reports covering units in his territory.

Units on which Surveys are Made

Surveys are prepared on every governmental unit in the United States which publicly sells a general obligation issue of bonds of $250,000 or over, maturing in more than one year. Surveys are also prepared during the calendar year on each of one hundred and seventy-six cities with more than 50,000 population; seventy-four counties with more than 150,000 population; forty States, and ten special districts whose bonds are widely held. In the two States of New Jersey and Pennsylvania, surveys are prepared on all borrowing units with more than 10,000 population in whose bonds there is general investor interest.

Mercantile Claims Department

In 1857, the Mercantile Claims Department was organized to assist in the collection of past due accounts arising out of mercantile transactions. Operations were designed to render a practical collection service at minimum cost. No attempt is made to participate in activities connected with adjustments, assignments, receiverships, or bankruptcies. At the present time this department functions through thirty-two offices in the United States and six in the Dominion of Canada. If an account is not settled by the efforts of this department, it is referred at the direction of the creditor to an attorney for collection. That has been and is the last resort of creditors from colonial days down to the very present.

In the eighty-four years which this department has been in existence accounts have been referred for collection, in behalf of creditors, to many nationally known attorneys. Among them have been Chester A. Arthur, the twenty-first President of the United States, while practising law in New York City; Calvin A. Coolidge, the thirtieth President of the United States, while a resident of Northampton, Massachusetts; Garrett A. Hobart, Vice-President of the United States under William McKinley, while practising law in Paterson, New Jersey; and John G. Sargent, Attorney-General under Coolidge, while a practising attorney in Ludlow, Vermont, an individual of phenomenal memory for men and their activities.

Magazine Department

In 1893, *Dun's Review* was established as a weekly journal of finance and trade, continuing in its pages two series of current business reports which *The Mercantile Agency* had published in circular form for many years, a summary of business conditions based upon information gathered throughout the nation by the managers of the widely spread reporting offices, and tables recording the number of commercial and industrial business failures with the amount of their aggregate liabilities. As the magazine developed, other features helpful in measuring and in interpreting business activity were added: periodic data on prices, the volume of bank clearings, the amount of building permits, special articles, and economic surveys.

Historical Development of Dun's Review

In some degree the present *Dun's Review* is the inheritor of the experience of three business magazines no longer published, in addition to its own record of forty-eight years: *Dun's International Review* (1903-1931) and *The World's Markets* (1917-1924), both of which had been published by R. G. Dun & Co., and *Bradstreet's Weekly* (1879-1933), which had been published by *The Bradstreet Company.*

Dun's International Review first appeared in 1903 at a time when the foreign services of R. G. Dun & Co., were rapidly expanding. In the three years following the turn of the century, twenty-seven foreign offices had been opened. First printed in English only, *Dun's International Review* was soon published regularly in four languages, English, Spanish, French, and Portuguese. *The World's Markets,* also a magazine of international trade, first appeared in 1917, one month before the United States entered the first World War. In its initial issue the magazine was dedicated not only to publishing information regarding the rapidly shifting currents of wartime commerce, shifting predominantly toward the United States, but also to record the chaotic aftermath which in 1917 the editorial board clearly foresaw.

Originally a news letter, *Bradstreet's Weekly,* began publication in magazine form in 1879 with much the same purpose as the early *Dun's Review.* This magazine undertook pioneer work in the measurement of the level of prices, initiating in 1895 a Monthly Wholesale Commodity Price Index. When discontinued in 1937, this Bradstreet series was the oldest wholesale price index which had been published in this country without interruption. As has happened with other statistical activities of *The Mercantile Agency,* this index was discontinued after it had been followed by other reliable indexes and after its original contribution to the business world had been fulfilled.

When in 1933 the activities of *The Bradstreet Company* were absorbed by R. G. Dun & Co. to form Dun & Bradstreet, Inc., *Dun's Review* became, until December, 1936, the *Dun & Bradstreet Monthly Review. Dun's Review* as a monthly magazine with new editorial direction, new format, and new policies and objectives, began publication in February, 1937. This is the *Dun's Review* of 1941.

Editorial Contents and Features

The emphasis of *Dun's Review,* in the hundredth year of *The Mercantile Agency* is on current material of basic importance to an understanding of broad credit, economic, social, and legislative trends. To this end it reports authentic information developed in economic studies, partly developed within the organization of DUN & BRADSTREET, INC., and partly without. Subjects which have been recently and extensively explored in its pages include government regulation of business, marketing problems, municipal finance, standards of financial management developed from financial statement analysis, and the more recent economic aspects of the national rearmament program begun in 1940. The frank expression of opinion on controversial subjects is reserved for a series of articles contributed by leaders of industry, banking, labor, government, and education.

To supplement the business conditions data of longer standing, there was begun in 1937, Regional Trade Barometers, monthly indexes of consumer purchases for the United States and for twenty-nine broadly homogeneous regions having the same components and the same base year so that all indexes would be comparable. In *Dun's Statistical Review,* a supplement, tables only, no text, are published each month giving detailed statistics compiled by DUN & BRADSTREET, INC. These data, summarized and interpreted, are also reported to business—directly and through newspapers—in weekly and monthly releases on general business conditions, the number and liabilities of failures, volume of bank clearings, wholesale commodity prices, amount of building permits, and the up-to-the-minute condition of selected industries and trades.

Research & Statistical Department

The pioneer effort of *The Mercantile Agency* in business research was its early record of commercial and industrial failures and liabilities, originated in 1857. Next came figures covering the volume of bank clearings, and somewhat later, periodic analyses of current business activity by geographical areas and by divisions of industrial activity. The Research & Statistical Department was organized in 1935 to forward these existing research activities, and to explore and to develop new and commercially usable types of basic economic information, either as a by-product of the credit reporting service, or by virtue of the close touch which DUN & BRADSTREET, INC., maintains with the business community through its nationwide network of branch offices.

Research for the Business Public

The changing relationships have been followed between government and business, as revealed in the surveys and studies constantly published in *Dun's Review,* studies regarding such laws as the Robinson-Patman Act, the "fair trade" laws, and the defense program with all of its accessory legislation and intricate ramifications. Significant evidence on business problems of broad and acute public interest, such as the surtax on undistributed profits, and the extent and character of concentration in American industry, have been studied. The seasonal characteristics of sales, inventories, receivables, and liabilities in widely varied lines of industry have been analyzed in a series of "natural business year" bulletins. Surveys have also touched upon such subjects as the burden of taxes paid by business, the trend of yearly national sales, the amount of year-end and mid-year inventories, aggregate national capital expenditures for plant improvement and expansion, and retailers' operating cost figures in important divisions of retail trade.

The time-honored records of commercial and industrial failures with their liabilities not only have been maintained, but have also been re-analyzed with changes in the bankruptcy and receivership laws to permit comparison with earlier years. An Insolvency Index relates the number of failures to the number of active commercial and industrial concerns, and indicates the current level of business mortality.

Research for Trade Associations

Prior to the organization of the Research & Statistical Department, *The Mercantile Agency* had from time to time been requested by trade associations to act as a confidential and impartial agent in the collection and publication of industry statistics. This type of service has developed into an important, supplementary field of economic research activity. Such services have included surveys of wages and hours for particular industries, of annual operating costs and net profits in specific divisions of industry, the collection and pooling of association dues where members furnished confidential sales figures for proration of dues, the compilation of current monthly indexes of sales volume or shipments, and the reporting of contract commitments for building materials.

IX ☆ Work of the Credit Reporter

*T*HE early credit reporters were "commercial travelers" with a gift of acquiring and interpreting pertinent bits of information regarding an individual's moral and financial responsibility, his method of doing business, gossip, and rumors. Their judgments were based on long memories of faces and incidents, on their ability to incite local gossip in the trade, on the local reputation of a trader for integrity as well as his reputation in some distant buying market, on information obtained by word of mouth from an ever widening circle of acquaintances, and on a broad knowledge of trade practices. These early credit reporters, by the extensive nature of their activity, developed into individuals of wide and authoritative discretion. A study of their reports indicates that rarely, if ever, did they pull their shots.

The pioneer credit reporters in the United States were Thomas Wren Ward and Sheldon P. Church, both adventurous travelers and keen students of business operations, at a time when traveling was no bed of roses. Inland travel was entirely by stage, horseback, walking, canoe, and boat. Travel on the rivers and the canals was very much slower than by stagecoach. During the early years of the nineteenth century, boats rarely reached the mouth of the Ohio River from Pittsburgh in less than fifteen days. Twenty days was a good Spring passage. In the Summer, when the water was lower, six, eight, and even ten weeks were often required to make the same trip.

The scheduled time to go from New York to Boston, traveling on stagecoaches every minute of the day and night, was reduced by

1832 to forty-one hours, and the fare to $11 per person. It was a nerve-wracking trip with every bounce communicated to the weary joints of the passengers. There were no balloon tires, shock absorbers, or cushioned upholstery to ease the journey. The only comparatively recent improvement in carriages had been the development of elliptical springs in the year 1804. With the exception of the turnpikes constructed by the Federal Government, and the toll roads constructed by local groups of investors, it was not unusual for the eastern highways, especially in the Spring and in the Autumn, to be ankle to knee deep in mud. Roads in the States west of the Alleghany Mountains often dwindled into narrow, winding paths.

The forerunners of the present-day credit reporters took these early handicaps in their every-day strides. Moreover, they had large personal responsibilities in the presentation and interpretation of the credit information which they collected. There were no checks or balances against their individual judgments. Ward passed on enormous credits in his time; his reports were written on merchants, ship captains, super-cargoes, bankers, pioneer railroads, and States that were issuing long-term bonds. Church reported primarily on merchants, commission men, wholesalers, and retailers.

As will be seen by the examples of the reports of these two men, quoted in chapter XI, both were fearless and frank in their use of unmistakable English. Their reports, however, had restricted circulation and were of quite a confidential nature. Ward's reports were used solely by his British correspondent, Baring Brothers & Company, and those of Church by a restricted group of New York City wholesale merchants who finally organized as *The Merchants Vigilance Association* to protect themselves against the fraudulent buyer and the unsound credit risk "in the country trade."

Pioneer Credit Reporters

In 1798, Alexander Baring, the second son of Francis Baring, made a visit to the United States from England. Francis Baring was the founder of Baring Brothers & Company, the most powerful merchant-banking firm in England at this time and until the rise of the Rothschilds several decades later. Vincent Nolte in his memoirs mentioned two incidents regarding Alexander Baring's visit to the United States, "At his departure, his father confined his advice to two

especial recommendations, one of which was to purchase no uncultivated land, and the other not to marry a wife there: 'Because,' said he,
'uncultivated lands can be more readily bought than sold again and a
wife is best united to the home in which she was raised, and cannot be
formed or trained a second time.' "

In other ways, Alexander may have been a devoted and obedient
son, but when he returned from his extensive travels, he was the proprietor of vast territories in uninhabited parts of Maine and Pennsylvania, and in the very year of his visit, when just twenty-four years of
age, he married Anna Bingham, the eldest daughter of the wealthy,
successful merchant, William Bingham of Philadelphia. Alexander
Baring inherited $900,000 in 1804 upon the death of his father-in-law!
In 1810, the mantle of Francis Baring descended upon Alexander who
became the principal partner in the great firm. The earlier personal
interests of Alexander in American affairs now broadened, and Baring
Brothers & Company became the most important English firm trading
with business men across the North Atlantic Ocean.

After 1826, the group of London merchant-bankers financing
North American trade came to be dominated by about eight houses—
Wiggin & Company, Wildes & Company, Wilson & Company, Lizardi
& Company, W. & J. Brown & Company, Morrison, Cryder & Company,
N. M. Rothschild & Sons (after 1834), and Baring Brothers & Company
—and the competition became correspondingly more intensive.

Baring Brothers & Company had interests extending from Canada
to the Gulf of Mexico. They acted as agents for the United States
Government, for the second Bank of the United States until its liquidation in 1837, and for well-known private banking and mercantile firms
such as Prime, Ward & King of New York. They served as brokers in
the sale of Federal, State, and municipal bonds in England and on the
continent. They extended credit, largely in the form of acceptance
credits, to business enterprises in all of the important American cities,
and upon the financial soundness of these extensive clients in America,
did their own success and security fundamentally depend.

Agent for Baring Brothers & Company

In 1828, while on a vacation trip to England, Thomas Wren Ward,
visited his intimate friend and a former Bostonian, Joshua Bates, who
had recently become a partner in Baring Brothers & Company. As a
result of these conversations, Thomas Baring, a nephew of Alexander

who was now the senior partner, made an extended journey during the following year to survey American business firms and their operations, and in October, 1829, signed a contract with Thomas Wren Ward to act as the firm's special resident agent in the United States. Ward's responsibilities among other matters would be to obtain credit information, and to "rate" American business houses. Ward was a retired, well-to-do, experienced merchant of Boston, a former partner in the importing and exporting house of Ropes & Ward, and an individual who happened to have a wide acquaintanceship among American business men.

As resident agent in the United States, Ward held a position of very considerable importance. From 1828 to 1861, the greater portion of the business of Baring Brothers & Company consisted in the granting of credits to finance American commerce. Moreover, almost all of this business until 1853 passed through Ward's hands, a volume which amounted to several million pounds sterling annually; during his first three years as agent, he is said to have granted commercial credits to American merchants, which aggregated $50,000,000. He selected correspondents for Baring Brothers & Company, granted credits, arranged for the transfer of shipping documents, collected debts, negotiated loans, and reported upon the prevailing economic conditions, the financial market, and the national political outlook.

In these extensive activities, Ward exercised a wide range of discretion for the English firm. He might well have been characterized as a financial ambassador plenipotentiary. It was upon his initiative that Daniel Webster was retained as American counsel for Baring Brothers & Company. Daniel Webster and Alexander Baring were thus well acquainted in 1842, when Baring, now Lord Ashburton visited the United States as the representative of the British ministry, and negotiated the famous Webster-Ashburton Treaty which settled the long standing boundary dispute between Maine and Canada.

To Ward was given a large share of the credit that Baring Brothers & Company was the only one of the seven leading English firms of merchant-bankers doing an extensive business in the United States (N. M. Rothschild & Sons was just becoming established in American trade at this time), to emerge from the panic of 1837 and the ensuing six years of depression with unimpaired prestige, power, and credit. His ability and accuracy in judging men and conditions was most extraordinarily disclosed in the extensive reports which he constantly made to London. For many years, Ward played one of the very important but unobtrusive parts in the developing commercial life of the United States.

Reporting Activities of Thomas W. Ward

It was almost as difficult to obtain detailed, exact, credit information regarding a business enterprise at this time in our national history, as in our colonial days. Merchants were reluctant to put in letters what they really thought about their neighbors and their competitors. Moreover, in a day when writing continued to mean actual long-hand correspondence, the process was, to say the least, lengthy and laborious. Newspapers were still in the primitive state where they carried very little commercial and financial news regarding specific business enterprises, as public participation in ownership existed in very few concerns. Business was almost entirely privately controlled. It was much easier to pass credit information on by word of mouth, by friendly conversation. That meant almost continuous traveling.

Ward traveled extensively from Portland, Maine, to New Orleans, Louisiana, obtaining credit information from private conversations with the partners of former correspondents of his original firm of Ropes & Ward, by interviews with acquaintances of prospective clients, by conferences with prospective clients, and by his uncanny personal judgment of individuals. Here was the man who among his wide interests and extensive responsibilities, was the pioneer credit reporter, an individual with great business experience, many friends, financial acumen, and an exceptionally keen mind in appraising the character, the integrity, and the business ability of others.

By 1831, Ward had sent credit reports on several thousand commercial houses in the United States to London, sometimes several in a special letter, sometimes only one in a general letter in which he would cover other subjects. "These evaluations were quickly organized and systemized. An estimate included the location of the firm, its capital, its particular preoccupation (dry goods importing, iron importing, import and export commission business, cotton exporting, and so on), its character—whether trustworthy and honorable or unreliable, the amount of credit that it was safe to give to it, the special items that might have a bearing upon the business activities of the house. The Barings assigned a number to each new firm on their list and entered Ward's information in a Private Remarks Book. Until 1837 both agent and managing partners customarily used only the numbers in referring to correspondents, presumably to discourage such prying eyes as those of some of the more inquisitive sea captains carrying the mail."* In

---

* "Credit Rating Before Dun & Bradstreet" by R. W. Hidy; *Bulletin of Business Historical Society, Inc.*, Volume XIII, Number 6, December, 1939, pp. 81-88.

1835, Ward systematically went over his opinions of all houses in his list, made duplicate "Private Remark Books," and sent one to London. Not all revisions were made so thoroughly; very brief comments being considered sufficient in most cases in such years as 1833 and 1836.

For twenty-four years, Thomas Wren Ward continued to be the active special resident agent for Baring Brothers & Company in the United States. During these years he constantly investigated the moral and financial responsibilities of American business houses for London. He retired in 1853, when sixty-seven years of age, and the representation of Baring Brothers & Company was taken over by his two sons, John G. Ward and Samuel G. Ward. In 1856, John G. Ward died and the entire responsibility fell to Samuel G. Ward.

Reporting Activities of Sheldon P. Church

During the first half of the nineteenth century, wholesale distributors in New York, Philadelphia, Boston, and Baltimore handled a steadily increasing volume of business, and extended larger and larger credits to retailers located farther away to the south, the southwest, and the west. With the increase in distance, the problem of the wholesaler in obtaining reliable credit information regarding these buyers, became more and more difficult, particularly as many of the newcomers had little or no financial resources and were of questionable moral responsibility. No improvement, however, was made by wholesalers over the cumbersome method which had grown up in the colonial era, of obtaining credit information, until the days of Sheldon P. Church.

Occasionally, larger wholesale distributors with substantial outstanding receivables would send a member of the firm, or a trusted employee, on an extended collecting tour. Lambert Brothers of New York City, for example, sent a letter to John Thomas, Esq., of Augusta, Georgia, in November, 1823 to prepare him for the arrival of one of their partners, "We wrote you on the 22^{d} Oct last enclosing your acct on which will be due us $420⎯. Our S. F. Lambert expects to be in Augusta in about 3 or 4 weeks probably by the first day of Dec^{r} & as he will only stay a day or two he will be glad to find the money ready for the balance you owe us."* On these trips, bits of credit information were, at times, recorded by those travelers who realized the fundamental importance of securing and retaining accurate information.

* *Letter Book of Lambert Brothers, 1822-1829*, p. 167. (Baker Library, Harvard Graduate School of Business Administration)

In 1827,* Church began to investigate the credit standing and to render credit reports to a few of the larger wholesale dry goods merchants in New York City. This early activity was probably of a local and a part time nature as he was listed as a "saddler" under the style of Sheldon P. Church & Co., in successive *New York City Directories* from 1831 to 1838. About 1841, the New York merchants whom he had been representing, banded together and formed what then became known as *The Merchants Vigilance Association.* This association operated as a distinct organization about three years. Sheldon P. Church now increased the area of his operations as a traveling credit reporter in behalf of this group; the expenses of his services being pro-rated among the members. In 1842, he made his first extensive trip to the South, traveling from one city to another to investigate the local credit standing of those merchants who purchased, or might purchase, dry goods in the New York City market. Here, for the first time, greater emphasis was placed upon acquiring credit information, and only nominal emphasis upon the collection of outstanding accounts. This technique of extensive traveling worked so well that Church gradually included concerns outside of the dry goods trade among his clients.

Before leaving New York on his second extensive trip in November, 1844, Church described his route as follows: "After a few days in Petersburgh and Norfolk, I return to Baltimore, and from thence cross the mountains to Wheeling, Va.; then I go through parts of Kentucky, including various towns not visited heretofore; then to St. Louis, thence through Tennessee, North and South Alabama, and Eastern Mississippi, aiming to accomplish thus much in time for spring trade; then through the river counties of Mississippi, then to Florida, and to return through Georgia, the Carolinas and Virginia." Apparently he was unable to estimate how much time he would need to spend in each city and town on this trip, as he left word with his clients that they could ascertain from Messrs. Wolfe & Gillespie where a letter would reach him, in case clients desired him to make special investigations while en route.

In the following year, 1845-1846, he prepared his schedule more carefully beforehand, showing at what date mail could reach him at important cities as he went on his circuit, November 30 at Norfolk, Va., January 15 at Columbus, Ga., March 1 at New Orleans, La., April 1 at Little Rock, Ark., May 20 at St. Louis, Mo., July 15 at Chicago, Ill., and home in New York City on August 15, a trip of almost nine months. It was on this trip that Church came to the little village of Atlanta,

* *The Commercial Agency Annual for 1857,* p. 5, published by Tappan & McKillop.

Georgia, and wrote, "This place, being now established as the junction of a branch rail road, it is thought, will become hereafter of some importance as a place of business, say within two or three years."

Church forwarded weekly reports, containing information and his opinion in unmistakable terms of all houses that he investigated on these journeys, to New York. These reports, at first, were copied and distributed among the members of *The Merchants Vigilance Association,* later printed, and finally bound for his growing list of clients. Little is known regarding the latter years of Church's life, but apparently he continued active as a widely known credit reporter and traveler, as in 1857, he was in the employ of Tappan (no relation of Lewis Tappan who founded *The Mercantile Agency*) & McKillop, a general mercantile agency, operating in New York City.

Early Reporters of The Mercantile Agency

It was the policy of Benjamin Douglass, after he had become the sole proprietor of *The Mercantile Agency* in 1854, to follow closely on the heels of retail merchandise traders in the westward expansion of the country, and to open branch offices as frontier settlements became important wholesale distributing centers. This program was continued and developed after 1859 by Robert G. Dun. It brought a greater importance, co-ordination, and discipline into the expanding credit reporting system. Tappan's earlier operations had been predicated upon a dependable list of resident observers of local trade, they came to be known as correspondents, but Douglass improved on that original system by acquiring a constantly increasing number of full time employees who became experienced, skilled, credit reporters, and interpreters of credit information. A new profession was arising.

The ability to keep credit reports somewhat up to date under the earlier system of correspondents instituted by Lewis Tappan, represented a genuine improvement over the sporadic but sincere efforts of the commercial travelers such as Sheldon P. Church. Even this fundamental improvement, however, lacked the uniformity which could be expected only from a properly disciplined organization of trained, traveling, credit reporters who were full time employees, and who would cover the same territory at periodic intervals. The correspondent served a basic function, but his best service now became an auxiliary to the organized efforts of the full-time, skilled, credit reporter.

Reporters in the Post Civil War Days

The typical credit reporter in the years immediately following the Civil War was often recognized by a peculiar interest and aptitude for his job. Many of them were English, Scotch, or Irish by birth; men of education who enjoyed the excitement, the hardships, the ever-changing environment, and the more than occasional perils of travel in a frontier land. One credit reporter who rode the prairies related that he "didn't see his superior for a year." He would ride or trudge from town to town, chatting with the traders, bankers, sheriffs, and tavern keepers; he would spend long evenings correcting the names in the listings for the *Reference Book,* and mail his full reports every Sunday to his home office.

George Osmond, a retired manager of the St. Louis office and a credit reporter of the 1870's explained how he generally covered ground, "One method was to go on the railroad as far as possible, then visit the towns on horseback. I traveled many miles on the hot plains of Texas by saddle, buckboard, or mail hack. I called on the storekeepers, and usually paid a visit to the county seat to gossip with officials and to examine the assessment rolls for property descriptions."

Credit reports on business concerns in these small and remote communities were necessarily brief. Financial statements were rarely obtained and trade information was negligible. Credit decisions were made largely on the reporter's experienced analysis of the individual, the amount and condition of the merchandise in his store, his local reputation for honesty, shrewdness, capacity to earn a profit, and then to hold on to it. The reports upon arrival at the home office of *The Mercantile Agency* were recopied by clerks in huge volumes. The early ledgers reveal the Spencerian skill of these copyists, who looked upon the introduction of the typewriter in later years as an offense against the age-old chirographic art.

Early credit reporters were canny and resourceful; they learned from experience how to "size up" the honorable merchant or the fraud by the formula of the practical psychologist. They came to recognize from sheer experience the little badges of candor and deceit in the men they interviewed. As the itinerant printer and newspaper reporter developed into a "type," so the wandering credit reporter evolved out of the mold created by his nomadic life in a developing country. The work of making credit investigations coincided with an incurable wanderlust. Their powers of observation became sharply focused, and not limited by any means to mercantile evidence. A pilferer or footpad might suddenly run afoul of the law, never aware that a chance remark, or an overt act had been detected by a credit reporter in his routine of everyday calls and investigations.

Credit Reporters on the Frontier

In 1885, George Osmond was transferred to the office at Salt Lake City which at the time had jurisdiction over a tremendous district comprising Utah, part of Wyoming, Idaho, and Montana. Here he used "railroads when it was possible to do so, but as a rule" he traveled "through the bottoms and over mountains upon the mail hack. These hacks visited most of the towns and would usually carry two or three passengers. If it was impossible to finish the investigations in a small town during the period which the mail hack remained in it, a horse could always be hired," or he "could take another hack which would come along within a day or two." In this manner Osmond traveled through counties two hundred miles from railroads.

Eloquent testimony of the difficulties involved in credit reporting during the latter frontier days is offered in a memorandum written by an early reporter of the Denver office of *The Mercantile Agency:*

Denver was a rough and tough mining and cattle center. During the period from 1880 to 1890 the town experienced a terrific boom and the work of the credit reporter became one of great difficulty and responsibility. Merchants, traders, and shifty adventurers came from all parts of the country, started in business, and immediately sought credit. Prosperous towns like Leadville and Cripple Creek sprang up almost over night, huge ore bodies were discovered, and immense wealth was located within a few months—bringing with it all of its attending parasites. ¶Men would walk down the main street of the city of Leadville swinging their revolvers by a chain attached to their wrists, ready for use on the slightest provocation. Shooting scrapes in a gambling 'joint' next to our office were regular occurrences. During the entire period, we always had traveling reporters to cover the territory. The arduousness of their work may well be imagined. Railroads and trains were few and far between; most of the traveling had to be done on horseback or by stage through the ranches, hills, and mining towns in sparsely settled districts infested by desperadoes, half-breeds, cowpunchers, and tough characters of all kinds. Stage robberies were frequent and the rights of property were often decided either by the fitful laws of chance or by the quickness on the trigger.

Retailers in the nineteenth century issued very few balance sheets or income accounts as yardsticks of sound management. Storekeepers were mostly men of character and good intention. When financial difficulty arose, it was often the result of a too liberal credit policy by merchandise suppliers, as well as the lack of initiative, or the unwitting desire of the storekeeper to over-extend his own credit. Credit judgment in the post Civil War period was usually based on property assets, on the ability of the merchant, and on his recognized opportunities.

While a modest but a gradually increasing number of neatly arranged financial statements were obtained in the larger eastern communities in the 1870's and the 1880's, the traveler in the western and southern States had to search out and estimate the assets and the liabilities of wholesalers and retailers through adroit questioning. The typical frontier trader kept few or no records, and his progress or lack of progress was usually determined by the immediate goods on the shelves, the cash on hand, and the liabilities due to one or two principal suppliers. Some traders, insolvent but unwilling to quit, continued to be favored outlets for their jobbing suppliers. In judging such risks, the credit reporter could only pass upon the integrity of the proprietor, and the likelihood of the enterprise to remain in existence.

Credit Reporter of Today

Today, a credit reporter in an automobile will cover as much territory in one day as his prototype was able to encompass in a fortnight using the horse, the stagecoach, or the canoe, but the basic function of his mission has remained unchanged. Though credit reporting has developed into an intricate nerve system of business in which every active commercial and industrial business concern is part of the sensitized web of credit information, the face-to-face interview of the credit reporter with the storekeeper, the wholesaler, or the manufacturer, continues to provide basic information for the report. With this information is coupled the wide range of supplementary facts obtained in interviewing banking depositories, merchandise suppliers, and others who might have had business relations with, or who know the particular enterprise and its management staff.

Credit Reporter in Alaska

There continue to exist romantic and dramatic opportunities in the daily life of the credit reporter in some districts and in some divisions of modern industry. Reporters assigned to Alaska and to the Canadian Provinces still have their obstacles in distance and nature, but conquering inventions have provided ever faster, and more comfortable, modern transportation. A reporter who revised the credit reports on all business enterprises in Alaska in 1938, mostly by direct personal interviews, covered over three thousand miles in three months by steamer, railroad, caboose, and airplane.

Interior storekeepers in Alaska are extended the same mercantile credit terms today which were so prevalent throughout our entire colonial period, namely, twelve months. These terms of sale invariably call for settlement upon the opening of transportation in the Spring of the year, generally payable with the proceeds from the sale of furs. Wholesale houses, most of which have been located in Seattle and in Tacoma, have carried the brunt of these unusually long credit terms peculiar to Alaskan trade since its very inception.

From Anchorage to Fairbanks, the reporter used a gas-powered mail car and jounced for three hundred miles over the rocky roadbed on the Alaskan Railroad which rose and dipped with all of the thrills of a toboggan ride. A motor car served him in his daily excursions to the little towns in the shadow of the Arctic Circle: Gilmore, Fox, Chatanika, Central, and finally the town of Circle, itself, on the Yukon River. Tenderfoot visitors to these towns are few and far between, but everywhere the credit reporter on his investigating trip was cordially received. The hospitality of the people more than compensated for the lack of modern hotel comforts.

Credit Reporters in Canada

While correspondents are relied upon for much current credit information regarding traders in the remote sections of Canadian Provinces, the reporters working out of Winnipeg must make regular revisions which take them as far north as The Pas, a flourishing town of approximately 3,500 inhabitants. In days gone by, reports on concerns located in this part of Manitoba have been repeatedly revised with dog teams as the means of transportation, but the revisions are now accomplished by rail, a roundabout trip from Winnipeg of twelve hundred miles. Canadian offices report within a few degrees of the magnetic North Pole and occasionally receive inquiries far beyond that point.

The opening of new mines as a result of the increased value of gold in the world market, has created many boom towns, every one of which must be visited. In 1940, a reporter arrived at Yellow Knife, Alberta, a new and prosperous mining area, by airplane, and revised the credit reports on every business enterprise in that thriving community. Three years ago there was nothing here but a few Indian shacks and trappers' cabins. When the reporter had completed his revision he had information on twenty-three concerns that were seeking credit from distant merchandise suppliers. All freight in this section is taken in by scows in the Summer and by airplanes in the Winter.

Northwestern Canada is extremely difficult country to cover as most roads are new. There is, moreover, a continuous flow of inquiries regarding small merchants starting miles away in the "bush." This area, is becoming a rapidly developed region, and in the last few years there has been an increase of nearly twenty-five per cent in the number of active business concerns, many of them little wilderness general stores carrying extensive varieties of merchandise, first cousins of our own colonial, country general stores. Temperature in the northerly part of Edmonton's district has been known to reach 72 degrees below zero.

In Montreal and Quebec, the reporters are bi-lingual, requiring the ability and knowledge to use both French and English fluently. In the outlying districts, the vast distances of Canada provide additional challenges. The Quebec office has supervision over the territory along the south shore of the St. Lawrence River, a distance of over one thousand miles around the Gaspé Peninsula with its many French villages. It is also responsible for the bleak Labrador Atlantic coast line, a continuation of the north shore of the St. Lawrence River, where settlements are fewer and more distant from each other.

The Montreal office has supervision over northern Quebec Province, comprised largely of new mining areas such as Noranada, Malartic and Rouyn. To reach this territory, the reporter must travel five hundred miles by land. The distance is shorter by air, and sometimes airplanes are used. When making arrangements to revise these reports, the reporter may locate himself in a town fifteen miles long, with or without roads, probably with no registry office, and generally with no police. There are no lot or building numbers, and it is frequently a difficult task to locate the party upon whom an inquiry has been received.

One traveling reporter left his home in Montreal in January and returned home last November. In the Winter the temperature will average 20 to 25 degrees below zero. From time to time, the Montreal office receives inquiries on traders far within the Arctic circle, in fact, on the southern edge of the Arctic Ocean. The only way in which these inquiries can be handled is by means of the supply steamer of the Hudson's Bay Company which makes a round trip once each year.

Credit Reporters at Catastrophes

Reporters are first on the ground when catastrophes affect the mercantile life of a community. They visit and report rapidly on the losses caused by floods, fires, or earthquakes, obtaining estimates regarding the shrinkage in the financial resources of all affected concerns. These revised reports provide the up-to-the-minute credit information, so very essential to the prospective shipper in deciding whether goods on order for a particular business enterprise in the affected zone should, or should not be shipped.

After the twelve streams in the Northeast retreated in the Spring of 1936, leaving three hundred and eighty-seven communities suffering from flood damages to a greater or lesser degree, credit reporters were on the ground to make a rapid survey and to report to their nearest office. Reporters first determined the actual street areas affected by the flood waters so that stores on dry ground would not suffer any delay in the shipment of urgently needed merchandise and supplies. Each day, they sloshed through the wet and silty streets of the Golden Triangle of Pittsburgh, examining premises and interviewing merchants. They returned to cold, oil-lighted offices where the credit reports were typed, duplicated by the thousands, and immediately sent off to suppliers who had made previous inquiries on these accounts. It is estimated that more than one hundred thousand copies of these "Continuous Service" special notices were distributed within a few days by the Pittsburgh office alone, notifying suppliers all over the country whether or not the individual merchant was still an acceptable credit risk.

In squads of four, the reporters patrolled the three populous valleys in the western Pennsylvania district using automobiles wherever the highway conditions permitted. Along the river banks they found steel mills, potteries, and manufacturers of machinery and durable consumer goods under water. While hundreds of concerns suffered machinery damages and losses due to interrupted production schedules, in few instances was the loss sufficiently great to disturb the credit relations with merchandise creditors. Some large department stores in Pittsburgh had severe merchandise and property losses but they recovered rapidly and began necessary major alterations without any loss in time. It was the smaller merchants who were affected the most, many requiring additional credit for new fixtures and property repairs. The final check-up of commercial losses showed that 3,044 concerns in Pittsburgh, Johnstown, and Wheeling had suffered damage, 431 seri-

The Mercantile Agency, New York, 1875

ously enough to affect their purchasing power, and 192 were actually forced to discontinue operations.

When the wall of water from the Connecticut River reached Hartford, the crest of the river thirty-seven feet above normal, flooded the business and residential district for one-half mile on either side. Sufficient warning, however, had enabled the merchants to salvage large portions of their stocks. Credit reporters, after a complete check-up of the flooded shops and factories, revealed that about ten per cent of all of the concerns had suffered some damage.

The City of Providence, on the other hand, was caught entirely unawares by the hurricane of 1938 as it suddenly veered along the New Jersey coast, cut across Long Island, and left a corridor of pillage and wreckage in its train. The loss of life and property at Providence was immense. Providence stands on Narragansett Bay forty miles inland from the Atlantic Ocean. A wind, blowing into the perfect funnel of the bay at more than one hundred miles an hour, drove the unusually high tide into the very heart of the city around five o'clock on September 21, just as thousands of men and women were pouring from their offices into the streets. In less than one hour, salt water was ten feet deep throughout the entire downtown business district. Banks, department stores, hotels, restaurants, and offices were submerged to the top of the first floor. Thousands of automobiles were covered. On the following day the credit reporters went to work. Within one week, every business enterprise within the flood district had been visited, and estimates had been obtained regarding the amount of damage in every case.

Credit Reporter as a Specialist

As the various steps in the distribution of merchandise have become more and more specialized, the problems of credit investigation have called for an increasing amount of technical knowledge. The reporter calling at the sources of raw material supply must be familiar with subsequent steps of processing. He must know peculiarities of the trade and industry, of markets and seasons, of maximum and minimum activity. He must know that the independent oil driller is a creature of chance and that his ability to meet obligations often depends upon his success in finding a paying well. He must be aware of the method of sending the crude oil to the refinery. Will it go by pipe line or by tanker? What is the quality of the crude and what price will it bring? What are the laws affecting its pumping and sale?

New developments in the processing of yarns and fabrics must be watched. The effects of synthetics on the financing and distribution of stockings, dresses, and underwear must be followed. The reporter must know the story of silk, cotton, wool, rayon, and nylon, of the synthetics and the plastics, for every new development disturbs the relationships between the industries.

Every trade has characteristics in normal turnover of inventory, of maximum and minimum receivables and liabilities, of typical trade terms, and of seasons. Climate has its influences on the distribution of such items as wearing apparel, foods, medicines, and farm supplies. The fertilizer salesman may obtain his orders from northern distributors in January, while in the Florida and California markets, there may be two seasons in which to call. While overcoats are being sold in Chicago, straw hats are being sold in Palm Beach, and oranges are being harvested in southern California. In all cases, the reporter adds to his special knowledge of a business by his acquired experience which enables him to piece together a more accurate picture of the individual credit risk.

Just as a collector of antique furniture realizes after a careful examination, that a chest of drawers is a fine original colonial piece or apparently has been improved by imitation knobs or a carefully repaired post, so a credit reporter, as he gains in experience, tact, and knowledge in the interpretation of apparently minor, incidental pieces of information, is able to pick up and to fit together facts which to the layman are insignificant and of no importance. That an individual opens a restaurant while his entire previous business life had been spent as a machinist in an automobile factory; that a young man opens a retail store with a capital of $5,000 when a minimum of $10,000 is needed at a particular location; that an owner of a local newspaper purchases a shore front estate, heavily mortgaged, when an intimate knowledge of the financial condition of his business would indicate that he should not be keeping up with the Joneses; that a wholesale business is being started on premises where rents are high; all of these are pieces of driftwood cast upon the beach which must be recognized as valuable, picked up, studied, analyzed, and interpreted.

Chinatown in San Francisco

One of the most interesting in the specialized reporting problems has been provided for many years by the Chinese merchants of San Francisco. It is customary for Chinese merchants to accept the money of their countrymen for investment. There may be from two to eighty-nine partners, or interested parties, in a particular concern one day, and thirty days later, half of these individuals may have withdrawn their money, and as many more, may have become financially interested. Under these circumstances it has been naturally difficult to obtain accurate financial information which would retain its basic value. About 1910, the Chinese Chamber of Commerce was formed in San Francisco to assist in providing that information. Chinatown credit reporters no longer need to carry a calling card on which would be printed in Chinese, the explanation of the mercantile agency business.

The present Chinese settlement in San Francisco numbers twenty thousand persons, the largest oriental group outside of China. It has revealed many concepts of the oriental as a business man. He is not the sinister character so often portrayed in motion picture and story, but a polite, honest, and even fun-loving individual with whom it is a delight to deal, once his confidence has been earned. The exclusion law of 1881 has gradually reduced the proportion of foreign-born merchants, and about thirty-five per cent of the Chinese now in business in the United States are natives of this country. Most of them have been educated in our schools, and many are college graduates with a fluent command of English. All of them, of course, speak Chinese—probably many of them continue to think in Chinese—and some have retained the ancient oriental methods of bookkeeping. This conception, however, is not generally true of the younger generation who now are predominant in business, and as a result, the Chinese quarter yields to the credit reporter a reasonable percentage of financial statements.

The Chinese are reputed to have been the first people to have developed multiple ownership in business organization, and today almost every Chinese business is organized along the peculiar lines of the "Chinese partnership." Very few Chinese business enterprises are incorporated; in most instances, the numerous partners merely subscribe their varying amounts of capital, receive papers corresponding to stock certificates, and select partners to handle the actual management of the business, the remaining partners becoming investors. For example, an investment of $25,000 in a Chinese wholesale firm, might be contributed by seventeen partners in amounts varying from $500 to $10,000. Five of these partners might hold active positions in the business, six might live elsewhere in the United States, and the rest reside in China. Legally each of them would be a general partner. Another complication sometimes found—and which usually adds a few more beads of perspiration to the brow of the reporter—is the custom whereby one Chinese partnership will buy minor interests in other partnerships.

However rapidly the Chinese may have adopted modern business methods, old and entirely oriental customs occasionally appear. Very few Chinese businesses are conducted under the name of the proprietor; they prefer elaborate fictitious styles, many of which are quite poetic. There is, for instance, a restaurant named *Oey Loy Guey,* which translated reads—"This is a lucky place for hungry people to come." *Hang Far Low* often included in a name answers the query, "If you want good food and drink stop here;" *Yat Gaw Min* becomes "One portion of noodles for enjoyment;" and a style including the words *Chong* or *Ling,* used mostly by grocery stores or restaurant supply houses, carries the wish for continued prosperity. Edgar Snow in his recently published volume, *The Battle for Asia,* explained that the name given by the Chinese to Rewi Alley, the energetic New Zealand chief technical advisor of the Chinese Industrial Co-operatives followed this same interesting style. Alley was called *Kao Pi-tzu Kung-Ho Jen*—Tall Nose, the Work-Together Man—a very expressive appellation.

Another strictly Chinese custom which is resurrected on occasions in the colony's business affairs, is that of the "podii." This custom is based upon an ancient convention whereby an evicted tenant is permitted to retaliate against an unjust landlord by placing a price upon the injustice which has been done to him. In the eyes of the Chinese, that particular piece of property is neither rentable, leasable, nor salable, until the claim of the former tenant has been fully satisfied. Should someone rent the property in the meantime, his business would be boycotted by the entire colony, even though he might be in complete ignorance of the existence of the "podii." Thus, it is the responsibility of the purchaser of Chinatown property not only to be sure the title is clear in the eyes of the law, but that the claims of all previous tenants have been satisfied. Strangely enough, a desirable commercial building, standing on the site of one of the most famous deeds in the history of San Francisco, was deserted for several years, a grim reminder that this old Chinese tradition had not lost its power.

The Fishing Industry

In San Diego, California, a credit reporter calls on the fishing fleet. He must ascertain the owner of each boat, its capacity, and the personal standing of the captain and his family. He must be aware of the

current price of sardines at the cannery, the market for fresh fish, and
the luck of the season. At New London, Connecticut, on the opposite
side of the continent, another reporter must be equally alert to the needs
of the market and the prices of cod, halibut, and mackerel at New
York, Boston, and Philadelphia.

Operations in the salmon canning industry are concentrated
principally in the Alaskan waters but the reporter's credit interview
may take place in most any shack, or on any dock or vessel that is convenient. A Seattle credit reporter recently gave a brief description of
those engaged in this very specialized industry:

During his conversation, the reporter must vision a cannery built upon piling in
some small inlet, perhaps two weeks' distant from any population center; he must
vision cannery tenders, and employment conditions. Many times the cannery
owners spend only short seasons in Seattle, and special efforts must be made to see
them at their convenience, which might be at very unusual hours. The average
operator is an honest, hard-working individual who started by pulling a line over
the gunwale of a boat. He is an organizer, able to explain in detail every department of the industry with the exception of the business end, and here he becomes
confused when one talks assets and liabilities. The reporter must, above all, know
the language of the canner and be able to use it fluently and convincingly.

The last sentence in the above quotation emphasizes the need for
the reporter to know "the language of the canner and be able to use
it fluently and convincingly." This same qualification is essential when
interviewing men in every specialized division of industry, as it is the
ability and the knowledge to use the colloquialisms of each trade which
indicate to business men that the reporter has the necessary background
of appropriate knowledge to understand and analyze their activities.

The credit reporter, for example, must know the operations of
labor contractors in the cutting-up divisions of the textile industry, the
assembling processes with the necessity of balanced inventories in the
automotive industry, the size of the packs in the vegetable and fruit
canning industry, the processes of hedging used by cotton mills and
grain elevators, and the technique of being a publisher without having
a printing plant. He must also know every conceivable basis under
which loans might be obtained, secured and unsecured, from commercial banks and trust companies, factors, industrial banks, insurance
companies, savings banks, sales finance companies, specialized finance
companies, personal loan companies, the Reconstruction Finance Corporation, agencies of the Farm Credit Administration, and the Federal
Reserve Banks. He must, indeed, acquire a fundamental but practical
background of wide business knowledge.

The Lumber Industry

In the lumber industry, the situation confronting the reporter in the Pacific Northwest may differ in many respects from problems of the reporter in the South Atlantic lumber district. The differences may be found in the quality and the use of the lumber, transportation methods, storage facilities, marketing methods, and the availability of the market. An experienced reporter has described this industry in the Northwest:

Included in the industry are these separate and distinct operations: logging, log hauling, sawmills, planing mills, shingle mills, pulp mills, box factories, sash and door factories, and the most recent addition, plywood mills. The entire industry is dependent upon the logging trade for its raw material. Therefore, this division of activity is vitally important and the backbone of the entire industry. The actual felling of the timber is done in practically the same manner as it was twenty years ago. The big change has come in the handling of the logs. "Motorization" has rapidly taken place and virtually all log-hauling, except that provided by water, is handled by motor trucks and trailers. This improvement has enabled the loggers to accomplish "selective logging," which is beneficial to the natural sources of the country and at the same time, has a steady influence on the log market. ¶ The profitable operation of a sawmill is dependent upon several facts, probably the most important is its nearness to the supply of timber. It can readily be seen that a concern which must purchase logs in the open market and have them shipped one hundred miles to the mill will have a heavier cost than the sawmill that obtains its logs within a radius of twenty to twenty-five miles. This fact becomes more apparent as the timber supply gradually recedes from the mill. In some cases where a stand of timber has been exhausted, and the owners are unable to acquire additional supplies near enough to the plant so that the cost of transporting the raw material is kept within certain limits, the mill is closed and dismantled. Reporters have found that information concerning the source of supply, the distance that logs must be hauled, and the length of time which the existing supply will last, have revealed, time and again, that a very critical condition will be experienced by the mill owners within a comparatively short time.

Resort Towns

In resort cities, credit reporters have special problems not encountered in centers of manufacturing or in sparsely settled country regions. Reporters operating in such a city as Miami, Florida, for example, are plagued by inquiries on Winter transients, too many of whom are pariahs on normal business. Over two million people visit Miami during the Winter season, and among them are commercial opportunists willing to let any vain creditor pay for his speculative effort in a fancy retail shop, a night club, or a hotel. Here is a typical picture:

There is a solid business element in every resort town, those who have become permanently established and those who have been engaged in business at each season for many years. In addition, however, many people come to Miami during the late Summer months, look around a bit, find a store space which suits them, obtain a lease, and leave. Before they return to open for the season's business, credit inquiries begin to arrive. The banks are unable to help in the majority of cases, landlords usually know nothing more than that they have obtained a rental in advance for six months or one year, and that the money was good because the bank accepted the check for deposit, and it failed to bounce back. ¶ The major industries at Miami are the operation of hotels, apartment houses, and rooming houses. Hotels and apartments are seldom operated by the owners. Leases and sub-leases on such properties change hands so often that it leaves the reporter in a daze. As an example, a hotel under construction on Miami Beach changed owners, according to the records at the court house, seven times before it was completed. Most of the building materials contractors got out and from under, but one dealer stuck to the job and now has only a substantial lien to show for his failure to keep himself informed regarding all changes. The last owner of this particular hotel was a corporation of which the president was a stenographer, twenty years of age.

Qualifications of the Credit Reporter

Credit reporting in the twentieth century is based upon the same principles of impartial but thorough fact finding which inspired the independent credit investigator of a century ago, but reporting in 1941 has been developed into a specialized profession in which the investigation made by the reporter is supported by a steady stream of supplementary facts flowing into the common reservoir of centralized files. Today, every city, town, village, and hamlet in the United States and in the Dominion of Canada is visited on a regular schedule by credit reporters, who watch and report the changing fortunes of every active commercial and industrial business enterprise, large and small.

The skilled credit reporter is in part a business specialist, in part an accountant, in part a detective, in part a student in logic, and in part, a practical analyst of human nature, ever on the alert for information which may indicate which way and with what intensity the wind is blowing and whether it is likely to shift. The man who takes the responsibility of assuming what any individual or group of individuals will do or will be able to do under a given set of business circumstances, must have a broad perspective on American business practices, and a keen understanding of human nature. He holds the tiller of the boat, realizing that there must be hazards if the fishermen are to obtain a full net, but doubly alert to sight the buoys which indicate hidden rocks and shoal water.

X ☆ Work of the Correspondent

AN advertisement which appeared in the 1843 edition of the *New York City Directory*, briefly described the purpose of the recently organized concern known as *The Mercantile Agency*, listed the States and territories which its activities covered, and recited the functions and the calibre of the correspondents who would supply credit information regarding merchants engaged "in the country trade." From this early, concise statement of operations, it is again evident that the great unsolved problem in carrying on trade at this period of our economic life, was to have credit information readily available regarding "country merchants," not the city traders, as information could be obtained more easily on concerns in the important urban centers. This advertisement, which was written two years after the organization of *The Mercantile Agency*, read as follows:

This agency was established in this city, June, 1841, for the purpose of procuring, by resident and special agents, information respecting the standing, responsibility, &c. of country merchants residing in the States of New York, Ohio, Michigan, Indiana, Illinois, the New England States, New Jersey, parts of Missouri and Pennsylvania, and the territories of Iowa and Wisconsin, for the benefit of such merchants in this city as approve the object and become subscribers to the Agency. The principles upon which this business is founded are such as recommend them to every solvent and upright merchant in the community. The information obtained is from attorneys, cashiers of banks, old merchants and other competent persons. . . . The greatest care is taken to have agents of intelligence, good judgment, extensive information and integrity, and the information obtained is imparted to the subscribers confidentially, so as not to injure any one. This Agency has already been instrumental in saving to the subscribers large amounts. . . .

348

In the early years of *The Mercantile Agency,* when the territory west of the immediate Atlantic seaboard and away from the tributary rivers, was sparsely settled, the correspondent was relied upon to keep the credit information on nearby country merchants and traders comprehensive, accurate, and reasonably up to date. He was the first line of information. The great importance of the work of the correspondents, is shown by the detailed instructions sent to them in a letter by Charles F. Clark of *The Bradstreet Company* as late as 1869. These instructions were elaborate and exacting; they called for speed, accuracy, and completeness:

We are now preparing our Reports for Volume Twenty-five, and it will be necessary that we should have this blank returned, filled, within six days from the time of its receipt. We also desire that you shall add to the list, which is on the blank, the names (and give us the full report) of all Merchants, Manufacturers, Bankers, Brokers, Grocers, Saddlers, Millers, Blacksmiths, Wagon-makers, Dentists, Printers and Publishers, etc., etc., doing business in your place, not included in it, in fact, every person who under any circumstances would ask credit away from home. If there are any dealers who have recently come into your midst of whom little is known, please state where they were previously located (after giving us such information as you can), that we may obtain the full particulars from that place. (1) Give length of time in business. (2) Amount of own capital in business. (3) Amount of net worth, after deducting all liabilities of every nature. (4) Of what is estimated wealth composed? (Viz.: Real estate less incumbrances, capital in business, personal property, which includes bonds and mortgages, stocks, notes, etc., etc.) (5) Character? good, fair, poor. (6) Habits? good, medium, poor. (7) Business Qualifications? very good, good, medium, poor. (8) Prospects of success? good, fair, medium, poor. (9) Succeeded whom? if any person or firm, state whom. (10) Give individual names of partners, with age.

This letter is the first extant information indicating what real care and experience was necessary in obtaining the full information needed to analyze the moral and financial responsibility of a seeker of mercantile credit. Many lines of business which were mentioned in these early instructions of 1869, have virtually disappeared over the intervening years, saddlers, blacksmiths, and wagon-makers. Emphasis was placed upon learning where new dealers had previously been located so that "full particulars" could be obtained at that place. That simple admonition is fully as important today.

Up to this time, a correspondent presumably was supposed to know from instinct, from innate reasoning, or from daily experience, the type of information which was desired by prospective creditors. Often, however, he did not know, so clearly shown by many of the early reports which were representative more of personal opinions than of pertinent credit information. In fact, one of the great contributions made by specialized credit organizations in the development of American commerce was the practice which was gradually evolved of obtaining, and then passing on to subscribers, information on which they could base a credit decision, as well as the individual opinion of the credit reporter, himself. It is natural that, at times, there would be different interpretations of the same information.

The ten points outlined in Clark's letter to be covered on "any dealers who have recently come into your midst" give a clear understanding of the essential points of a credit investigation. Today, somewhat more information would be sought when investigating the credit worthiness of a small or moderate size business enterprise, and considerably more when investigating the affairs of a large corporation. The completed investigation would always include the facts which Clark outlined regarding the antecedent record, age, experience, ability, and reputation of the owner or partners in case of a proprietorship or a firm, and of the officers in case of a corporation, the length of time the concern has been in business, the amount and nature of the assets, and the amount and nature of the liabilities.

Well-Known Correspondents

The early correspondents of *The Mercantile Agency* and of *The Bradstreet Company* were cashiers of banks, postmasters, sheriffs, and storekeepers, but the young, active, resident lawyer was the principal source of credit information. He was more inclined to keep fully posted regarding the business ventures and the escapades of neighbors, but, at the same time, he was often unwilling to make the correspondent relationship a lifelong assignment as did so many cashiers of banks, and established merchants.

In 1941, the correspondent continues to be essential and a most dependable arm of the credit patrol, particularly in smaller towns and thinly settled areas. Many correspondents have served from forty to fifty years, and the assignment of reporting the progress of local merchants has, in many cases, become more of a privilege than a task. The calibre of many of the early credit correspondents has been reflected in their achievements in later life. There is, for example, the well-told story of Abraham Lincoln who reported about the grocer and the rat hole that "would bear looking into," a comment which was made in response to a credit inquiry regarding a retail storekeeper located in Springfield, Illinois. Lincoln was a friend of the Tappans, and when President of the United States, he appointed Lewis Tappan's son-in-law, Hiram Barney, Collector of the Port of New York.

Ulysses S. Grant was an early correspondent of *The Mercantile Agency* at Galena, Illinois where he worked in his father's retail hardware and leather store in the years just prior to the opening of the Civil War. Like Lincoln, he had a subtle sense of humor. On one occasion, he reported that a particular young lawyer had nothing but an office chair, a barrel with a board for a desk, and a fine young wife. Grant weighed the risk and threw his evidence on the favorable side with the opinion that the young lawyer had ability and ambition, which were quite as important as capital, and then ventured the cautious suggestion that all small bills would be paid.

William B. McKinley, the twenty-fourth President of the United States, was an active correspondent of *The Mercantile Agency* for many years in his early career while practising law at Canton, Ohio. General Lewis Wallace, soldier, diplomat, and well-known author of *Ben Hur, A Tale of Christ,* was a correspondent over a considerable period of time in the latter years of the nineteenth century at Crawfordsville, Indiana. Thomas Riley Marshall, Vice-President of the United States under President Woodrow Wilson, and the homely philosopher of the "five cent cigar," was a skilled correspondent at Columbus City, Indiana, for many years prior to the time when he was elected Governor of Indiana in 1909. The most recent addition to this distinguished list of correspondents is Wendell L. Willkie, who ran for the Presidency of the United States on the Republican ticket in 1940. Willkie was appointed attorney for *The Bradstreet Company* at Elwood, Indiana, in 1917 shortly after he entered his father's law office. The scroll of the past one hundred years carries the names of scores of correspondents who have become eminent judges, Governors, members of the United States Senate, of the House of Representatives, and of State Legislatures.

John Calvin Coolidge

John Calvin Coolidge was the correspondent of *The Mercantile Agency* at Plymouth Notch, Vermont, a little community 1,420 feet above the sea level, for fifty-two years. He resigned as correspondent on the day when his son was inaugurated as the thirtieth President of the

United States. John Calvin Coolidge ran a country general store and operated an extensive farm; he was telephone, laundry, and news agent; he looked after insurance policies; and he took care of the interests in that section of Vermont of the Ludlow Savings Bank & Trust Co., of which he was one of the trustees. Although he had never studied law for the purpose of admission to the bar, he was never-the-less familiar with the laws of his State and of general legal principals to such an extent that he handled a large amount of semi-legal work such as making out wills and deeds, buying and selling farms and timberlands, until he had built up a wide acquaintance and a substantial estate. Governor William W. Stickney made Coolidge a member of his staff in 1900, and this honor entitled him to the designation of "Colonel" Coolidge by which he was ever afterwards known.

The traveling reporter of *The Mercantile Agency,* who covered northern Vermont, often called on Colonel Coolidge while on his circuit through Plymouth Notch. Colonel Coolidge knew every name well in every nearby village and community. He had drawn most of the deeds and had arranged most of the mortgages. He had accurate, full information regarding titles, encumbrances, values, the state of interest and partial payments, and the same information regarding secured and unsecured loans. He was a perfect mine of information and covered each required item with meticulous exactitude.

Occasionally he would ask the reporter about some nearby or more distant individual to whom he or some one in the village might be considering the shipment of lumber, hay, maple, or farm products. If the individual was reported "good" he would smile approvingly. If the record was not clear, or the financial condition unsatisfactory, he would withhold shipment and "save both the goods and the money," as he would laughingly phrase it.

Other New England Correspondents

Samuel E. Pingree of White River Junction, Vermont, was an "old-time" attorney who for more than one-half of a century was a first class correspondent of *The Mercantile Agency* for the entire town of Hartford. In 1884, and again in 1886, he was elected Governor of Vermont. Governor Pingree took great pride in the accuracy and completeness of his credit reports.

William P. Dillingham was elected Governor of Vermont in 1888, succeeding Samuel E. Pingree. From 1900 until his death in 1923 he sat in the United States Senate. For many years up to the time he went to Washington in 1900, Governor Dillingham was an excellent correspondent of *The Mercantile Agency* for his home town of Water-bury, Vermont. He was a strong, vigorous, dignified character; widely known, honored, and respected.

Carroll S. Page, of Hyde Park, Vermont, was known locally as a politician, and internationally for his green calf skin business. His buyers traveled the north country with their pocket check books, making the best possible trades for cash with farmers and butchers for quality calf skins. Page was elected Governor of Vermont in 1890. Governor Page was such a strong factor that during his life time, by common consent, he set the price for green calf skins in America and was the leading figure in the industry. There was a common saying "as Page goes so goes the market. . . ." He controlled a bank and was interested in an insurance agency. He knew most of the farmers, merchants, and manufacturers of the north country and is said to have had a personal acquaintance with every voter in Lamoille County. They came to him with their difficulties and with their successes. Often he could help with the former and on many occasions his personal advice and financial help were responsible to a marked degree for the latter. Small wonder then that he made an outstanding correspondent for the entire county. *The Mercantile Agency* had correspondents in each town of the county, but when inquiry was made of Carroll Page, his information was infinitely more complete and invariably he covered angles of the situation which could be obtained from no other source.

Reports From Correspondents

Thousands of sturdy, conscientious, observing individuals have maintained the credit patrols in their communities to assist in the normal flow of merchandise on sound credit bases. Some corres-pondents have been more talented than others, some gifted with a more lucid pen, some content to report in staccato telegraphic phrases. Only an occasional correspondent has carried his penchant for details to such a bizarre, if interesting length as the scribe who mailed the following report to his supervising office around 1850:

James Samson is a peddler, aged 30; he comes to Albany to buy his goods, and then peddles them out along the canal from Albany to Buffalo. He is worth $2,000; owns a wooden house at Lockport in his own name; his family reside in it; has a *wife and three children, two boys and one girl; boys named Henry and Charles, aged four and six years; girl named Margaret, two years old; no judgment out or mortgage on property; drinks two glasses cider brandy, plain, morning and evening —never more; drinks water after each; chews fine cut; never smokes; good teeth generally; has lost a large double tooth on lower jaw, back, second from throat on left side; has a scar an inch long on his left leg kneepan; cause, cut himself with a hatchet when only three years old; can be found when in Albany at Pete Mason's, 82 State Street; purchases principally jewelry and fancy articles.*

This picture of James Samson drinking two glasses of cider brandy, plain, morning and evening, never more, drinking water after each; chewing fine cut, never smoking; good teeth generally but with a missing large double tooth on the lower jaw, back, second from throat on left side; might have been lifted bodily from one of the short stories of O. Henry. There is no record of the correspondent who rendered this report but one might wonder if he was not Samson's dentist, or a particularly close friend who might have lifted an elbow with him occasionally when the cider brandy was handy. The correspondent was certainly someone who knew Samson intimately or was able to obtain unusually close information from Samson's associates. Along with these interesting, if somewhat irrelevant details was fundamental credit information; Samson peddled his merchandise along the Erie Canal, he was married, thirty years of age, had three children, was worth $2,000, owned a house in his own name, had no judgment against him, and no mortgage on his property.

The following somewhat more recent report was made by a correspondent in California, regarding Timothy Smith, a trucker. Here imagination and fact follow closely on each other's heels:

This fellow is single and has good sense about getting married in that he won't try it 'til he is at least out of debt and has a home better than the one the girl is living in at the present time; however, he hasn't any girl and is never bothered along that line. Started in with an old clinker of a truck and has built up a very nice business in the trucking line. Has had some hard luck with his old machines at times but has always forged ahead. Has a nice truck at this time and although he tells every-one it is a race between him and "Mr. Green," (bank officer) to see who will have it a year from now, he is doing right well and getting ahead all the time. Of course this is a little country town and quiet at times, but Timothy Smith has done mighty well and has the respect of all who know him.

A fertile imagination and the ability to create atmosphere certainly added a degree of uniqueness to this report. The correspondent, however, was sure to include certain essential credit information; Timothy Smith began business with "an old clinker of a truck" and had made headway. He had used several trucks, and at the time of the report was purchasing a new one, presumably on the typical instalment plan, with a chattel mortgage or a conditional sales contract pledged at the bank to secure the necessary loan. Moreover, Smith was single; he bore a favorable local reputation; had "built up a very nice business in the trucking line;" and was generally known to be "doing right well."

Present-day correspondents take as much pride in their responsibilities to their communities as the early scribes in the remote sections of the country did almost one hundred years ago. Here is a report by a life-long correspondent who might have fulfilled his duty with fifty words but preferred to take four hundred. The seventy-year-old correspondent has created a lively picture of "Bill" and his family. These paragraphs could very easily have come from a current best seller.

William—or Bill—Herbert, has had quite a few occupations during his 40-odd years, but finally he has turned out to be a farmer, and a good one. Bill's younger half-brother, Hugh Frame of Frame & Co., is, according to common gossip here, the money man behind Bill now, and he probably contributes his share of the business brains too; for Hugh is a story-book go-getter who has done well for himself since leaving this small town It's difficult to separate the two of them in the ownership of the properties around here. Hugh may be in on all of them with Bill, although it is generally supposed that Bill owns the filling station, and the White Post Tavern operated by Ivy Sessions who pays Bill $30 a month rent. Hugh may have loaned the money for these properties in the beginning, but Bill no doubt has paid out on them by now. ¶ Bill went on his farm about a mile and a half south of here three or four years ago. There is a big two-story house, other buildings, barns, etc., in pretty good shape on the farm, and a tenant house across the road which is currently rented to Mrs. Wyatt, on whom I reported recently. Bill is going in for watermelons, a good crop on this sandy soil, and has four men working for him at present. He also has hogs and a few cattle. Bill is married to a widow who has a beautiful young daughter (what other reporter gives you all these handsome details?); wife, daughter and all work the farm for all it's worth. ¶ Bill has settled down, is interested in making money, and damned if he won't. He's got a good reputation for paying his debts on the line. Years ago he did a little heavy drinking, got into a few scrapes, but I'll let that go under the general heading of Wild Oats, though he did slightly overstep the young man age limit on that. He's sober now and is never seen in the local hotspots, except possibly to collect the rent at the White Post Tavern here. At the present time his mother is seriously ill; he and she haven't spoken for some years (he's got a lousy temper at times) but it's expected that the family crisis now will restore harmony. So I'll close on the happy note of mother love restored, and leave the rest to you.

Along with the picturesque, if somewhat irrelevant trimmings regarding William Herbert's antecedents and financial responsibilities which appeared in this report, there were included certain pertinent credit facts. "Bill" was in his forties, he had a half-brother Hugh Frame "who had done well for himself since leaving home" and who was reported to have backed him, but now "Bill" apparently owned the gasoline filling station and the White Post Tavern in his own name. "Bill" lived on a farm improved with a large two-story house, a barn, and other buildings all of which were kept in a state of good repairs. He had some hogs, a few cattle, and was cultivating a crop of watermelons with the help of four hired men. "Bill" also owned a tenant house across the way rented to a Mrs. Wyatt. He had established a good reputation for paying his debts "on the line." So, all in all, "Bill" appeared to be responsible for reasonable credit.

During the past eight years, the Federal Government has taken an increasing interest in the farmer, in the crops he would plant and harvest, in the crops he would not plant and would not harvest, in paying for soil preservation, and in making credit available through the variety of specialized governmental agencies described in chapter VI, if not available through established credit channels. The following report, from a correspondent located in the broad State of Texas, indicates the social and economic conundrums which may beset credit judgments under the unusual set of circumstances which are so prevalent today in many agricultural communities:

Raymond G. Nelson is a tenant farmer, some thirty-odd years old—married—I don't know how many children. Is located some 15 miles northwest from here on a farm owned by W. C. Parker, or by W. C. Parker's mother, maybe. Nelson has about five old horses and four cows, and a few farm tools, all of which, including his interest in next year's crop, are mortgaged to the Third National Bank for some four or five hundred dollars, anyway, for more than they are worth. He also owes the bank about $160 more, a note which is also signed by Nelson's brother, M. S. Nelson (former Sheriff of this County) as a surety. This is all Nelson's got, except possibly a few hens and a rooster. ¶ He is just a share cropper, or rather what the agricultural administration designates as a "managing share tenant." He is supposed to pay his landlord one-fourth of his cotton crop, and one-third of all other crops, as rent. But that is a matter of small importance. The income of the managing share tenant consists of, (1) he is now selling his next year's crop by obtaining a government loan thereon, and having his landlord waive his lien in favor of the mortgage given to secure the government loan—and since he is now selling next year's crop, and sold last year's crop in the same way—he probably won't have any next year's crop to amount to anything; and (2) by not raising the crops which he is now mortgaging to the government, and by "retiring" (from cultivation) the land which he has promised his landlord to cultivate, the government will pay him additional benefits, sufficient to keep him from starving. The landlord is supposed to receive a portion of these "benefits," the part which the landlord is to receive being left to the discretion of the agricultural administration.

¶ *Nelson is just the average managing share tenant; harmless, worthless. Such persons were sometimes dependable, and worth something, during the old days when they were just "renters;" but now they have developed into "managing share tenants," who sell their crops one year in advance, and then receive additional benefits for not raising the crop so sold by them. You had better advise subscribers that there is not a chance for anybody to make any money from a "managing share tenant." My reference to them as being "harmless" is not accurate—because they will buy on credit.*

The correspondent who sent in this report regarding Raymond G. Nelson became involved in the problems of a "managing share tenant" in order to explain the background of Nelson's credit standing. The interests of the Federal Government in the marginal producer have become widespread but that interest has hardly helped Nelson to get on his feet. He had some assets, "five old horses and four cows," a few farm tools, possibly a few hens and a rooster, but everything including his next year's crop was pledged to the local bank. Here is a picture of a young farmer in this thirties who was really up against it, a product of poor soil, low prices, and inability to work out his own salvation.

Correspondents in Every Community

Today, *The Mercantile Agency* has approximately 50,000 correspondents in the United States and 8,000 in the Dominion of Canada, upon whom it calls for regular or special reporting assignments. Credit information obtained from these correspondents, no matter how comprehensive, is rarely the sole basis for a credit report. If the information covers a newly established business enterprise, the antecedents of the principals, if they had previously been in business, are investigated from the records of *The Mercantile Agency,* or with the previous employers or associates, wherever located. If the concern is an established enterprise, the current revised information is compared with the report of the traveling reporter, additional information is obtained from the banking depository, from the merchandise suppliers, and from the other sources of enlightenment which have been outlined in chapter VIII. All of this information is then carefully studied, analyzed, arranged, and finally the finished credit report is edited by an experienced report writer. This process is being carried on simultaneously every day of the year with investigations being made on thousands of business establishments by thousands of correspondents in every part of the United States and in every part of the Dominion of Canada.

XI ⚬ *Development*
of the Credit Report

$\mathcal{D}$URING our entire colonial period and during the years of our national life up to the Civil War, two routines were customarily used to place credit information in the hands of actual or potential mercantile creditors. By one method the buyer would forward with his order, letters of reference and recommendation which he had obtained from friends, from his local minister of the gospel, or from local established business men. By the other method, the importer-wholesaler or the wholesale distributor, as the case might be, would write to customers or to friends located in the neighborhood of the buyer, requesting information and personal opinions regarding the honesty and the local reputation of the applicant for credit. Both techniques were widely used. They were used in domestic trade by eastern distributors of merchandise, and in foreign commerce by the English factors, exporters, and merchant-bankers.

In March, 1766, the proprietorship of Jonathan Jackson was succeeded by the firm of Jackson & Bromfield at Newburyport. About four months after its establishment, this firm wrote to Messrs George Kippen & Son of Glasgow, Scotland, forwarding a letter of reference, "Inclosed you have a L^r in our favor from Mr Caleb Blanchard, what he has pleased to say of us, we trust will be amply sufficient to establish our Character & Credit with you, & therefore presume we need say nothing in our own Recommendation." Whatever credit information Caleb Blanchard put in his letter, apparently was of more importance than any information, no matter how detailed and exacting which

Jackson & Bromfield might have given about themselves. Such letters, according to the customs of the time, carried great weight.

Shortly after the end of the Revolutionary War, in April, 1787, Lewis Ogden of New York City wrote similarly to Messrs Daniel Crommelin & Sons, the well known firm of merchant-bankers of Amsterdam, Holland. In addition to enclosing a letter of recommendation from an established New York firm, Ogden also referred to Hope & Co., at this time, probably the strongest banking firm in Europe. "You will observe," he wrote "by the inclosed Letter from Messrs Gouverneur & Kemble that we propose establishing a House in this City under the Firm of Hill & Ogden and as there are many Articles which maybe imported from Amsterdam with more Advantage than from other Parts of Europe We have taken the Liberty to request the Favour of you to execute such orders as we may from time to time transmit to you. As our Mr Hill has not the pleasure of being particularly acquainted with your House and as it is proper whenever a Credit is desired that the party of whom it is requested should be well satisfied on the Subject of substantial Responsibility, our mutual good Friends, Messrs Gouverneur & Kemble have, we trust, in their Letter above adverted to, been sufficiently explicit respecting us; was anything further necessary to insure to us your Confidence we might refer you to Messrs Hope & Co of Amsterdam with whom the late House of Gouverneur Hill & Gouverneur at Curacao, had for many years extensive dealings."*

This method of sending credit recommendations to potential creditors served its purpose in a world of foreign and domestic commerce when business was transacted entirely by proprietorships and partnerships, when capital accumulation was rather modest and transportation relatively slow, when the market was widely scattered and credits were for long periods, and when the buyer, in turn, was compelled to extend long terms to his customers. As proprietorships or firms, the outside means of the owner or owners of a business enterprise, which often was known in a general way to be substantial, were at the risk of creditors.

Rarely was a great deal learned regarding the exact financial responsibility of the buyer although occasionally, as in a letter to Devonsheir & Reeves in 1766, Jonathan Jackson did go so far as to say "... it may not be improper to let you know what Foundation we act upon—we esteem our present joint Capital upwards of £1,000 St^g ..."

---

* *Letter Book of Lewis Ogden, 1787-1798.* (New York Public Library)

General information and more neighborly opinions were obtained regarding the reliability, the honesty, the trustworthiness, and the local reputation of an individual than exact financial information such as balance sheets and profit and loss accounts, which creditors are more accustomed to obtain, today.

Obligations for the payment of merchandise quite generally ran on and on. From the extensive mercantile correspondence which has come down to us, it is quite evident that creditors in the colonial period, and in the early days of our national life were more worried as to how long they might be called upon to wait for payment, than that they would not be paid at all. Eventually, most debts were liquidated with the payment of interest on overdue accounts. One of the most exaggerated examples of this attitude appeared in a letter written by Philip Cuyler from Albany to a Mrs. Catherine Wendell of Schenectady in 1783 regarding a debt of twelve years standing. Cuyler meticulously and quaintly wrote, "I have Repeatedly Inclosed you, your Dec^d Husband's acc^t requesting the payment of it, to which I have had no Answer, so find inclose you the same with my—Ernest Request you would with Speed discharge it as Really think its time after Cred^t of more than Twelve Years.—being much pressed for Cash puts it Out of my power to waite any longer."* Shortly after this unique letter was mailed, the payment was finally made and the account closed.

Pioneer Credit Reports

As the amounts involved in the extension of credit became larger, as the outstanding credits of a particular house covered wider and wider trading areas, and as wholesale distributors went after business more intensively, it became evident that the existing hit and miss manner of obtaining credit information needed basic improvement. This fact apparently was realized by Baring Brothers & Company of London earlier than by anyone else as the greater portion of their extensive capital was being used in financing American trade. The protection of that capital accordingly rested on the ability to obtain more comprehensive, accurate, credit information. As we have seen, arrangements were made by this great firm of merchant-bankers with Thomas Wren Ward in 1829 to act as their resident correspondent in the United States, and to obtain first-hand credit information for their confidential use regarding American houses which might seek credit in London.

* *Letter inserted in the Ledger of Philip Cuyler, 1763-1794.* (New York Public Library)

Typical Credit Reports of Thomas W. Ward

Unusual bits of information occasionally crept into Ward's confidential reports to London, such as, in 1834, "Heckscher is married to Miss Coster—who will have at least 50m£ (£50,000)," or, in 1835 in a letter, Augustus Thorndike was "a man of prudence in his pecuniary concerns, and general good sense, but fond of sporting and fishing, and good living." These reports were the results of the earliest known credit reporter. That the information contained in the voluminous letters and credit reports which Ward conscientiously prepared were extremely valuable, is evidenced by the fact that the system was kept in existence for many years after Ward retired in 1853, and by the success with which Baring Brothers & Company handled their vast American business, through the difficult years following the panic of 1837.

The extensive correspondence which Ward carried on with Baring Brothers & Company reflected a sharp break from the circuitous expressions in business letter-writing which had been typical from the earliest colonial days. The information contained in these letters was direct, outspoken, clear, concise, and to the point. They could very well have been written yesterday by an American business man with wide financial knowledge, understanding, and many influential friends.

The credit reports which Ward prepared for the guidance of the partners in London bore a fascinating touch of candor, clear reasoning, and knowledge of men and affairs. Most of the reports were brief, some revisions bringing earlier information up to date contained only a few words, but they all showed Ward's direct, unmistakable imprint. No-one could read a single credit report without knowing the exact opinion of the writer. Typical of these reports were the following:*

JAMES MEANS—*Is guaranty for Means & Sprague of New York. Mr. James Means*
Boston   *was formerly a large grocer—now rather retired and concerned in manufacturing. Very safe—prudent—and a capital of $70,000 or more. May want to send orders to you for purchases which you may execute with safety.—May 11th, 1833.*

ANDRES DUNLAP—*District Attorney U. S. Court! ! ! A rank radical and high*
Washington   *Jackson man. Has $15,000 and a good income from his profession and other expectations. Safe enough—but I gave him the credit because at the moment he applied there was some talk about the account in London being changed in Washington and he has influence there for good or evil—however I might as well have omitted it.—December 1, 1833.*

* Original correspondence of Thomas Wren Ward with Baring Brothers & Company is filed in the Office of the Public Archives of Canada, Ottawa, Canada.

JAMES H. LEVERICH & CO.—*In the grocery business with a capital of $50,000 or*
New Orleans *$60,000. Mr. L. considered an uncommonly capable and safe sort of man—went from New Jersey and intends to return to New York and live. Oxuard, Remsen, and Howlands and others all say very safe.—October 28, 1835.*

THOMAS D. CURTIS—*Though a personal friend of mine and his business passing*
Boston *before me, I do not know his property. I feel confident that Curtis and Baylies have done a very good business and I have seen no bad business of theirs. I think highly of Curtis as to honor and capacity and conclude he may have $25,000 or $30,000 and Baylies $40,000 or $50,000. I have great confidence that they will always keep safe.—1835.*

LEE & GOODWIN—*Are in order. I am surprised that I have not mentioned Mr.*
Boston *Goodwin's capital. He is a steady, prudent, honorable, popular man worth $80,000. W. Lee has $30,000 or $40,000 and his family have large expectations. The collateral branches all rich and honourable—Lee has failed three times and paid up all each time and I think the chances are in favour of not failing again. They have a handsome India commission business—and do not trade largely on their own account. I see no great hazard unless in selling Rupee bills endorsed by them for Palmer, McKillop & Co. of London but I do not know to what extent their bills are sold. I consider Lee & Goodwin as a good account and they are a very popular house—and you should give them particular advice and trust them with attention and confidence.—1835.*

The five examples quoted above were typical of the somewhat longer reports which Ward made to London. Apparently the information regarding Lee & Goodwin was prepared as a result of a specific request. Many of the reports were more brief, but just as definite and clear-cut. At times it is impossible to tell whether the more condensed reports were the first reports on respective houses going to Baring Brothers & Company, or whether they were revisions which brought the earlier information up to date. Examples of more brief reports made in 1833 show Ward's direct, competent, reporting language, his wide knowledge, and his ability to interpret credit information concisely:

W. & B. F. SALTER—*Ship owners with a brother in Portsmouth—small property—*
New York *not uncovered except through me.*

WM. B. REYNOLDS—*Merchant—owns a packet line to Philadelphia and Real Estate,*
Boston *and owner of the "Duncan" with B. F. Reed and G. D. Carter. Has $70,000. Bold, but supposed safe.*

GRISWOLD & WOOD—*New importers—no capital or only $10,000 under guaranty of*
Boston *Charles Tappan of Gordon & Stoddard and B. Murry—who is very safe.*

JOHN BERTRAM—*Merchant—formerly a High Master—safe—fair man with $40,000*
Salem   *capital.*

EDMUND SWETT—*Ship owner with others—not to be uncovered—has some property,*
Newburyport   *but I do not hear much in favour.*

WALTER BAKER—*Chocolate manufacturer. Probably safe himself—I have guaranty*
Dorchester   *of his father—only credit through me.*

PHINEAS FOSTER—*A retired jobber in dry goods—prudent and said to have $50,000.*
Boston   *I conclude quite safe. Is guaranty for his sons who are super-
               cargos.*

WILLIAM FOSTER—*Supercargo. Has a few thousand dollars. Son of Phineas Foster*
Boston   *who guaranties for him.*

JOHN F. ANDREW—*Merchant—has $8,000 or $10,000 and will receive $20,000 more.*
Salem   *Honest, capable—industrious—does quite enough.*

GEORGE D. CARTER—*Supercargo and part owner of "Duncan." Has $15,000—*
Boston   *Capable—honorable.*

WILLIAM GODDARD—*Safe and handsome property. $60,000 upwards. Very par-*
Boston   *ticular—energetic in business—has influence—apt to like strongly
                and dislike strongly.*

SAMUEL TITCOMB—*Ship owner in part—not to be uncovered.*
Newburyport

NATHANIEL WESTON—*Ship Master—Safe.*
Salem

JOHN H. WAY—*Gentleman—handsome property—no business. Son-in-law of R. D.*
Boston   *Tucker.*

Of the above names, the one which has become the most widely
known over the intervening years is that of Walter Baker of Dorchester,
manufacturers of chocolate. This particular business, when Ward
rendered his brief credit report in 1833, was already seventy-eight years
old. It had been started in 1765 by one John Hannon who, in that
year, ground the first chocolate in North America. In 1772, Dr. James
Baker began to manufacture chocolate also at Dorchester, and eight
years later he acquired full ownership of Hannon's business. In 1791,
a son, Edmund, was taken into partnership and in 1804 Dr. James
Baker, now sixty-five years of age, retired, leaving the business entirely
in the hands of his son. In 1818, Walter Baker, twenty-six years of age,
and the grandson of Dr. James Baker was taken into partnership by his
father. Edmund Baker retired in 1824, leaving the enterprise to Walter
Baker under whose name it became prosperous and widely known.

This was the Walter Baker upon whom Thomas W. Ward rendered his report to Baring Brothers & Company, and Edmund Baker was the father whose guaranty Ward must have held.

By 1835, the correspondence between Ward and Baring Brothers & Company had been organized to the point that code numbers, applied in London, were used wherever possible in referring to particular business enterprises. Reports with code numbers were always revisions of earlier credit information sent to London. Typical reports of this character rendered in 1835 read as follows:

714—Seemed disposed to return to you. May be trusted to any reasonable extent in the way of business. Have more than $300,000 capital.

724—It appears that 724 & 725 are closing their joint concerns and will hereafter do their business separately. This I regret as I relied on 725 to keep 724 safe. He is not however doing much at present and I hope may not. I do not know his property but should think $50,000 and perhaps $70,000 besides expectations. The danger is in his occasional extensions.

1132—The credit for 3,000 pounds to them is all right and may be doubled if wanted.

1187—467 has lately become a limited partner putting in $10,000 so that the capital may now be $25,000. I have kept G & W under the guaranty of 467. It is very possible that this house also may go to 999 in part or in whole. The responsibility of 467 you will perceive is limited.

1302—I have great confidence personally. He appears to be moderate, prudent, and judicious, and I consider him very safe.

1322—Respectable. I know nothing of their means. Mr. Schroeder is said to have some property. Mr. Baker appears to be prudently disposed. He says he is known to some of the members of Messrs. Barings and they either wrote or otherwise expressed a desire that he should do business with them.

After several years of experimentation, Ward finally worked out a somewhat more comprehensive method for giving a general idea of the credit standing of business enterprises. This method represented an early simplified technique of rating which antedated John M. Bradstreet's first rating book by twenty-three years. In this process Ward sent several lithographed copies of a list of business concerns to London at the end of 1834, again in January, 1836, and a third time in January, 1837, with their respective numbers in a column at the left. These numbers were separated into eleven classes. "Foreign Houses" were in category Number 1. American concerns were arranged alphabetically within each group in the other ten classes. Ward described these interesting groupings as of January 27, 1837:

No. 1. Contains the Foreign Houses without regard to character or standing but alphabetically arranged.

2. May be considered as Houses not only entirely safe for what they may do, but likely to continue to under any possible circumstances. They possess, of course, different degrees of wealth, but are placed together in this list on account of wealth, character and habits of business taken together.

3. Is composed also of those whom I consider as quite safe and many wealthy, and many also of your best correspondents, and almost all of the right sort of people, but who from the extent or nature of their business or from circumstances not necessary to enter into, may not be considered as ranking with those whom I suppose are to continue always beyond question.

4. Consists of a class many of whom I should consider safe and some even comparatively rich, but who from the smallness of their transactions, or from their having no abiding place and being abroad as Supercargoes would not seem to belong to a class to be trusted much, or at all unless through me, and it also contains many who from their extension or want of capital might render it unsafe to trust, but contains few or none whose *morals* so far as we know is exceptionable.

5. *No Trust.* This column consists of those who either have not capital or are not of that character to render it desirable to trust them at all.

6. *Houses having various connexions.* Some of whom are safe and even wealthy, but doing with others renders it less important to cultivate and more important to look after.

7. *Houses having other connexions.* Are those contained in our numbers, but doing business wholly with others.

8. *Don't know.* This class contains many whom I have never known and with whom you do not appear to have had any active account or been exposed in any way, and of many others of whom my imperfect knowledge might rather mislead than be useful. They are therefore left to take their chance supposing you will not trust except where you may have certain knowledge of your own.

9. *Failed.*

10. *Dissolved,* and some *failed.*

11. *Dead.*

That the credit information obtained and interpreted by Ward was unusually sound is amply demonstrated by the manner in which Baring Brothers & Company came through the panic of 1837 and the troublesome years which followed, the worst depression up to that time in the United States. In a recapitulation made in 1843, Ward commented upon these lists, "of 250 pronounced undoubted [No. 2] in 1835 —only 16 have failed, & all the rest now undoubted—and of 245 pronounced as likely to continue good [No. 3], 22 have failed—and of 280 of the third class [No. 4], 45 have failed." That record stands as a remarkable tribute to his judgment of men and business enterprises, an individual with a most unusually keen mind, a fundamental understanding of men and their business ventures, and the ability of a really great credit reporter to obtain and skillfully to interpret essential credit information. Thomas Wren Ward set a wonderful example for a long line of men who were to follow in his worthy footsteps.

Typical Credit Reports of Sheldon P. Church

The second specialist in gathering credit information, Sheldon P. Church, was a rugged individualist in the pioneer days of credit reporting. We have seen that he served a circle of New York merchandise distributors, whereas Thomas W. Ward served only one client. Church was the author of the second known volume of printed credit reports which were bound in 1847 without the names of the author or the publisher. This volume contained credit reports on merchants in the West, the South, and the Southwest for the years 1844-1847. It consisted of 434 pages, each page being 13 x 8 inches.

Sheldon P. Church had a very colorful journalistic streak. He was a keen observer and analyst of human nature. Only the initials S.P.C. on two pages of his book of published reports, apparently overlooked when the volume was published, give any inkling of the name of the author. These credit reports were fascinating examples of the free interpretation of information. No words were minced. Unfavorable facts which reflected upon character and honesty were played up with the utmost frankness. Several examples of credit reports from this volume point to Church's characteristic of an acid pen, a colorful vocabulary, and engaging candor:

BINFORD & NIMMO—*A new firm, and doubtless some persons, without analyzing,*
Richmond, Va. *would call it first rate. Mr. Binford has been many years in trade here under different phases, is worth nothing, never made anything, and never will; he is impulsive, restless, uneasy, of no judgment, prudence, or forecast, and the wonder is that Nimmo ever united with him. The latter by himself would be good; he obtained $25,000 by his wife, in part now badly invested. They are men of good character, for ought I learn.—November, 1844.*

THOMAS J. N. BRIDGES—*Will no doubt be doing business in a different name. William*
Memphis, Tenn. *Armour, formerly in Jackson, Tenn., is believed to be proprietor of the establishment, and he has lately come to a settlement of his old liabilities in Baltimore, (a large amount) dictating his own terms, and totally refusing to allow any investigation, or to give any satisfactory explanation of his present condition. He merely surrenders his old unavailable assets, mainly suspended debts, scattered through Tennessee and Mississippi.—January 1st 1845.*

ALFRED THATCHER—*Has lately opened a fresh stock of goods here. The first inti-*
Columbus, Miss. *mation was, that "the New Yorkers have set up a man here lately, and I would not give 10 cents on the dollar for the debts," (no name mentioned). Another authority—"How did your neighbor manage to get a stock of goods?" Answer: "By the art of hocus-pocus, I reckon; I never was more surprised than when I saw the goods turned out here." Another—"Were you in business, would you sell Mr. T. $500 on credit?" Answer: "I wouldn't sell him anything; I wish I could get pay for what he owes me." These are the views of two old merchants, and one lawyer, all of the best standing in Columbus. Mr. Thatcher was formerly in a small business here, and failed; he was a dissipated loafer for the next few years; and for the last year or two, has had a little shop here of meal, onions and bolognas, and has kept sober; but has acquired no standing here. I am told his veracity is questionable; I understand he took with him to New York about $2,500 in drafts on Mobile, and his stock in trade may probably go to pay for them. If such men are safe, who can be called doubtful? I go for "the right of search": suspecting all strange craft.—January 30th, 1845.*

J. S. KIMBALL & CO.——[WRIGHT THE CO.]—*A recent firm, its prospects debateable.*
Burlington, Ia. *Mr. K. is a young Lawyer, in Boston, and may be responsible, but is not known here to be so. His brother had been in trade here, failed, and I believe, took the Bankrupt law. He started again and not long after died. This Attorney then took his place, assumed the debts, and took as a partner, Mr. W. who had before been clerk. Mr. W. is not an efficient, capable business man, and depends a good deal on a Mr. Lamson, who was once in business here and failed. In that process or since he made money, and has loaned this firm some $2,000 or $3,000. The business is a good deal under his control, and debts are incurred, that Wright knows very little about. I get the impression that this Lamson is rather a crafty, equivocal character, and may lead the concern into difficulty, and expect to profit by its downfall.—June, 1846.*

Many of Church's reports, like those of Ward, were staccatic, brief, to the point, but they always carried an unmistakable message. They contained little in the way of ambiguous, side-stepping opinions. Frankly and fearlessly, Church expressed his impressions and convictions without qualifying adjectives. The following examples are typical of his brief, condensed reports:

F. & J. S. JAMES & CO.

HENRY JAMES

KENT, KENDALL & ATWATER

WADSWORTH, TURNER & CO.

BROOKS & HUDSON

LONDON, WILLINGHAM & DREWRY

DANIEL H. LONDON

THOMAS R. PRICE

Richmond, Va.—These are houses concerning which it is hardly proper to institute an enquiry. They are mostly wholesale dealers, and in their different grades as to amount of business, and demands for credit, all are entitled to rank first rate. K. K. & A. are perhaps too sanguine, and have lost largely by bad debts; but still they have made a good deal, and are considered a rich house.—November 15th, 1844.

SEAY & SHEPARD—*Mr. Seay has been a long time in the auction and commission*
Nashville, Tenn. *business—is an industrious, honest man, and has made money. He is regarded as safe for all his engagements.—January 8th, 1845.*

BOND & MURDOCK—*Are going on in their steady, straight, prudent course, and*
Macon, Ga. *making money; are well off and safe.—May, 1845.*

JOHN WATSON—*An old merchant in good standing; owns landed property; is*
Detroit, Mich. *supposed worth $20,000 or more; has had a good share of the Indian trade here, and has made his money in this place. He is safe enough.—July, 1846.*

P. F. VILLIPIGUE—*A large dealer, capable, and generally successful. He now holds*
Camden, S. C. *considerable cotton, and is considered safe: buys in Charleston.—July, 1847.*

Credit Activities of Washington Hite

The first published *Credit Reference Book* was a little volume containing credit information on Kentucky merchants which was collected and printed by Washington Hite, an attorney at Bardstown, Kentucky, in 1846. This publication contained only sixty-four pages, the pages being approximately 6¼x7¼ inches. Both Ward and Church had become experienced travelers and collectors of credit information many years prior to the publication of Hite's local volume.

Unlike other independent credit reporters, Hite was not a resident of a large trading area and he did little or no extensive traveling. He was interested only in making available the credit information on traders in a fairly restricted territory. In the little community of Bardstown, he made a record of Kentucky traders, set the names in type alphabetically with such credit information as he was readily able to obtain, and offered the condensed volume of credit reports to eastern distributors of merchandise. The information was helpful but neither thorough nor elaborate. Hite was a young lawyer who apparently had no national ambitions. His one man credit agency never prospered, although it undoubtedly was helpful to eastern suppliers at the time.

This volume is important, not only because of its origin in the hinterland, but because of its early date. Most of the reports were very brief, rarely over a line or two in length, often they consisted only of a word or two, such as "Good" or "Very Good," and ended with Hite's opinion of the trader from a credit viewpoint. While his reports were not so acid or biting as many of those of Church, there is no indication that he pulled any punches, as many traders were characterized as "unworthy of credit." Here are samples of his concise listings and comments:*

ALLEN, JOHN G.   *Lexington, Fayette Co.—Good and punctual.*

ANDERSON, ELY D.   *Maysville, Mason Co.—Has been in business several years; it is not thought that he can have much capital. He is considered strictly honest.*

BRANNON & DAVIDGE   *Danville, Boyle Co.—Considered good; though nothing is certainly known of them. They came here from Louisville about 4 years since.*

DANIEL, A. G.   *Lancaster, Garrard Co.—Though slow, is considered good now.*

FORTUNE, ELISHA   *Jamestown, Monroe Co.—Not recommended.*

LASHBROOK & WOOD   *Washington, Mason Co.—Good; have cash capital. Wood's father is worth $200,000, and would back him to any reasonable amount.*

MITCHELL, P. L.   *Georgetown, Scott Co.—Very good.*

MORRIS & STRADER   *Lafayette, Barren Co.—Not recommended; they have three stores in different places, and have all their stock vested in them, own neither land nor slaves—are not considered worthy of credit.*

PLATT & WALKER   *Springfield, Washington Co.—Young men, believed to have commenced with about $2,000, 12, or 18 months since— appear to be men of good habits.*

* A copy of this printed *Credit Reference Book* fell into the hands of William T. Dolph, manager of the Louisville office of R. G. Dun & Co. in 1894 and today is in the library of Dun & Bradstreet, Inc. Dolph recorded that Washington Hite died in Jeffersonville, Indiana, penniless, in the early days of the Civil War.

ROGERS & GARRETT *Flat Rock, Bourbon Co.—Very good; men of capital.*

RUSSELL, S. & CO. *Louisville, Jefferson Co.—Very good; have good cash capital.*

SANFORD, J. M. *Lexington, Fayette Co.—A stranger, he hails from New York.*

SCHRADER, A. *Bardstown, Nelson Co.—Grocer; good in a small way.*

SHANKS & SHUMATE *Lancaster, Garrard Co.—Very good; will buy goods for this place in the spring. Shanks resides at Crab Orchard—the firm is a strong one.*

TAYLOR, STEPHEN *Centreville, Fleming Co.—Not good.*

VARMATTA & WILSON *Shelbyville, Shelby Co.—Have some capital, and are well supported, have been in business about one year, are considered good.*

WILLIAMS & EDLER *Albany, Clinton Co.—Very good; firm worth $20,000.*

WHITE & RUSSELL *Richmond, Madison Co.—Undoubted—capitalists.*

WRIGHT, WILLIAM *Russellville, Logan Co.—Very good; old merchant.*

Reports of The Mercantile Agency

The first credit reports which Lewis Tappan collected from his correspondents in 1841 were copied, as already mentioned, in huge ledgers by expert penmen. These early reports were based upon careful appraisals of the local reputations of traders, by investigations at the sources of supply, that is, with the distributors of merchandise in the large wholesale centers, and by investigations with nearby bankers. Information was added at the end of these reports at periodic intervals, bringing them up to date as subsequent investigations were made.

Reports Kept in Ledgers

When a subscriber desired credit information, he called at the office of *The Mercantile Agency,* and the information in a ledger containing the data on that particular account was read to him by one of the clerks. This process was somewhat laborious, but the reports, like those of Ward and Church, were quite condensed and pointed. The subscriber received the information verbally and had nothing tangible to show for his expenditure of money. The information was valuable only so long as he could remember it accurately and fairly completely. He had no credit department, no credit files, no credit reports to which he might like to refer at some future time in his own office. Prior to

Page from an Early Report Ledger
of The Mercantile Agency

1868, however, this routine was modified and reports were copied by pen and ink from the ledger pages and mailed or delivered to subscribers. This process in giving out credit information was followed until 1875 when the original blind typewriter made its initial appearance. Typed reports were then distributed in answer to inquiries. Typical of the hand-written reports kept in these early ledgers were the following:

PETER NAYLOR   Iron   65 Broad St., New York City
June 12/52 Was originally a mftr. of Metal Roofing &c., by wh. he made a great deal of money: is a cautious shrewd gd. bus. man, has always been successful — Is now entirely engaged in the Cali. trade, has, tis said, 100ᵐ/$ invested in the trade, w. 100ᵐ/$ more in R. E. &c. — Owns 3 Stores in Stone St., & one in So. William, besides a ho. in Madison Aven. for wh. he gave 20ᵐ/$ & has since refused 22½ᵐ/$ "Thos. Selby" is his Agt. in Cali. & is a 1st rate bus. man in all respects — "N" has been vy. fortunate in his Cali. bus. — was rich before he went into it, & has made money at it — He is considᵈ gd. for anything he wants.
Jan 24/53 In bus. principally in California Trade, said to have made a great deal of money, some think him extended so much in that trade, that they dispose of his paper immediately, while others from his shrewd bus. capacity & amt of means, have great confidence in him.   April 13' 54 Rich, w. at least 150ᵐ/$ no better man in the trade.   Oct. 28/54 Gd. beyond doubt Is believed to be w. several hundred thousand dolls. Has made, it is sd., a great deal of money in the Calfa. trade.   Mar. 28/55. Has done exceedingly well the last 2 years, & has made consid. money in Calfa.   Oct. 3/55 Is a man of considerab. mes. & in gd. cr. —   Feb. 26/56. Has a house in San Francisco, Califa, under the firm of "T. H. Selby & Co." "S" is an act. bus. man, of fair char., & gd. for his personal engagements, probably, but is not of much pecuniary responsibility, & the cr. of the house — which is gd. here & in Califa. — is dependent upon "N."'s connexion with it.   Oct. 4/56. In good stand'g & cr. & consid. good for his contracts.   Mar. 28/57 Continues in gd stdg. & cr. & regardᵈ reliab. for his contracts.   Oct. 27. Continues to sustain his former gd. stand'g & cr. & tho't gd for his contracts.   Feb. 58. Is supposed to have gone thro' the crisis, without asking any favors. & is now in his usual gᵈ standing & cr. & considᵈ reliable for contracts.   April 14/58, Paid, all thro & nothing has transpired to impair his standing & cr: He keeps his bus. within his means & his paper is regarded favorably. He is tho't sound & reliable for his contracts.   Oct. 58 Standing & Cr. unimpaired, his California bu. is understood to be profitable & well managed by his son in law, Mc Haclon.

The most striking characteristic of these early reports is the degree to which abbreviations were used. In the above report on Peter Naylor of New York City, for example, the two letters "wh." stand for the word "which," "gd." for "good," "Cali." for California," "w." for "worth," "R. E." for "real estate," "ho." for "house," "Agt." for "Agent," "vy." for "very," and so on. Most of these abbreviations were ingenious innovations to save time and space, and they were quite obvious.

This report was opened on June 12, 1852. Naylor was said to have had $100,000 invested in the California trade, and another $100,000 invested in New York real estate. Investigations made from time to time, indicated that the California business was profitable. By February, 1858, he had "gone thro' the crisis" of 1857 "without asking any favors" and his credit standing was unimpaired.

The second typical report is representative of a little later period:

ABRAHAM M. REEVES   Gents Furnishing   104 Nassau St., New York City
Jan. 31/59 He states that he was born in N. Y. aged 26 yrs. marrd̲ that he has been in bus. abt. 2 yrs. that he has abt. 5^m/$ in his bus. wh. is moderately prosps̲ that he buys & sells mostly for Cash, picking up his gds. in a sm. way & that he owes but little at any time. His statement is geny confirmed by outside parties who regard him worthy, prud, capable & gd. for a reasble. Cr.   Mar. 7/60. No change during the past year. Is in good Cr. for his purchases, pays promptly and is regarded an honest man — June 8/60 On the 1st May '60 he associated with him "Eugene D. Perrin," under the firm of "Reeves & Perrin." E. D. P. states, he was born in New York, age 24, was for a time with Bliss, Driggs & Douglass & subsequently in
        the employ of Dingee & Holden until the present
Ab*m* M.   Eugene D.   *firm was fond. he add no cap. to the bus. R. is w.*
REEVES & PERRIN   *abt. 4^m/$ wh. investd̲ in the bus. They design dg. a*
        104 Nassau St.   *mod. Cash bus. Keep within bound & buy oo/.*
on longer time than 2 or 3 mos̲ One Party (Dingee of Holden & D.) states, that he regd̲ R. as an hon. & capable bus. man & wor. of confid. Altho thr. mns. are mod. the firm is in gd. Cr. Buy for Cash on short time
Cr. *& are deemed reliable & entitled to a fair amt. of Cr.   Feb. 20/61 Cont. to have all the cr. they require, pay promptly, & appear to be dg a Small bus.*
        Apl 12/65. ("R" & Cady̲r for) 141 Nassau St.
Abraham M.   Martin Y.   *"R" states that both partners are marrd̲ he (R) is*
REEVES & CADY   *abt 33 Yrs of age and "C" is abt 24: that he (R) has*
        141 Nassau St.   *been in this bus. alone until Octr. 1862 when he entered into partnership with Cady with a joint cap*
of 43^c/$. "R" Contributing 23^c/$ and "C" 2^m/$. He further states that last Octr. the cap was 8^m/$ clear cash and that 5^c/$ will clear all the debts. We learn outside that the firm was fmly "Reeves & Perrin" who dissolved a few years ago that "R & C" are dg. a vy. respectable bus. vy careful active reliab. bus. men, pay promptly, Stand well with the trade and are in gd. cr.   Dec. 5/66 Dg. well, sell all for cash and mostly at retail have about 8 @ 10^m/$ their own money, pay cash, but are in good cr. for bus wants.

Abraham M. Reeves operated a retail "gent's" furnishing shop in New York City. The business started as a modest proprietorship, but over the life of the report, two changes were made in the style; one on June 8, 1860 when the business became a partnership under the name of Reeves & Perrin, and the other in October, 1862 when the style was changed to Reeves & Cady. As changes were made in the name, the new style was inserted in capital letters to the left but below the last comment in the report. Successive comments indicated a moderate size, and a fairly successful business conducted by well regarded principals.

The third report is on the firm of Smith, Campbell & Jolly and covers a much shorter period. The original entry on this report was made in November, 1869 and the last comment on December 20, 1871, about two years and one month later:

J. H.   J. S.   C. H.
SMITH CAMPBELL & JOLLY   FOLSOM, California   GROCERY
Nov. '69. S has been in bus 12 yrs. C has been in the firm 3 yrs. & J 6 months. All are stdy active & shrewd. Capl 15ᵐ/$ Stk insd & equally divided. Pay 30$ per Mo for a gd brick Store. S has a res w 1000$ which is insd. Are careful in giving Cr. Safe in bus. Making money and are in gd Cr. Have gd prospects and are worth clear 15ᵐ to 16ᵐ/$ March '71. Firm compd of "J. H. SMITH" 40 & md "J. S. CAMPBELL" 40 & md & "C. H. JOLLY" 34 & md This house was estabd by "J & J. Spruance." They were succeeded by "J. E. Freeman & Co," they by "Hirstel & Coblentz", they by "Bradley & Seymour", they by "C H Bradley & Co", they by "Smith, Bishop & Jolly" in '68. Late in '69 "Campbell" bot out "Bishop" & the prest conc. was formed. "Smith" was a clk in the house from '56 till he began bus. — "Jolly" also clerked for "Bradley & Seymour" — "Campbell" formy had a store at Salmon Falls nr here — All bear xcellt chars. & are sober, attent. prudt vry fair bus. men. "Smith" began with vy lim. means. He & "Bishop" gave their note for 2ᵐ/$ endorsed by "J. & J. Spruance" wh. was only recently pd.— "Jolly" had 2ᵐ/$ & Campbell not exceedg. 4ᵐ/$. Carry a Stk of 8ᵐ/$ wh. is insd. & rent a gd brick store. Do a sm who. bus. & take the lead in their line — Cr. freely but are vy fair coll. Are est. w. abt their stk clear & have a vy fair prospt. Are consid. reliab. & are understood to be backed by "J & J. Spruance" of S. F. May 16/71. Were burnt out by the great fire May 6/71 wh originated in their basement. They lost on Stk to the amt of $11,000, of wh 6,000$ was covered by insce Will not resume bus as a firm but it is probable Smith will commce again on his own a/c. (Later) "Smith" has gone into same bus on own a/c occupying temporarily a Brick bldg Will remove to old location as soon as present repairs are completed at present has a stk. of abt $3,500 insd for $2,500. Fair Pspcts. Dec. 20 '71 No change

The above report was on a concern located in California. The entries were a little more elaborate than in the first two examples, more than half of the report covering antecedent information regarding the three partners, and the earlier history of the business, which had changed hands several times. Next to the last entry mentioned a loss of $11,000 on stock in "the great fire of May 6/71 wh. originated in their basement" of which $6,000 was covered by insurance. This fire spread and consumed several buildings in the heart of the little town of Folsom with an aggregate loss of $125,000, a very substantial amount at the time.

Each of these three early typical reports contained credit information somewhat similar to that obtained in colonial days on a colonial merchant, opinions regarding the trustworthiness of the individual, his honesty and reliability as judged by those long acquainted with him, how he paid his bills, how much he was worth, the assets which represented his means, and the amount of his liabilities. The reports were quite similar to the more comprehensive examples of Thomas W. Ward and Sheldon P. Church. They were considerably more elaborate than the typical credit reports of Washington Hite.

Where Lewis Tappan made his great economic and social advance over the earlier credit reporters was in the organization and the development of a nation-wide system of collecting credit information which was not restricted to the use of a single client, to a small coterie of business concerns, or to a limited territory, but was available to all wholesale distributors, banks, and insurance companies; and in a more systematic revision of essential credit information. Very rarely was a detailed financial statement obtained, but information was often secured regarding the assets which a trader owned. In the 1870's a financial statement blank was printed for the first time by *The Mercantile Agency,* and the active solicitation of balance sheets was begun.

Developments in Credit Reports

In 1872, the first credit report was reproduced by carbon paper after several years of experimentation to create a duplicating medium by applying shoe blacking to yellow foolscap. These reports were first produced by writing over the carbon paper in pencil. Here was another challenge to the aesthetics of the pen and ink copyists to whom art was far more important than utility.

The first commercial order ever given for typewriters was placed by *The Mercantile Agency* in 1875. This order was for one hundred "machines for writing with type" at a total price of $5,500, and was given to Christopher Latham Sholes who for many years had been trying to interest capitalists and business enterprises in his invention but with no success. Sholes had the machines to fill this first order manufactured by E. Remington & Sons, of Ilion, New York. They became known as the model Remington No. 1. Credit reports now began to take on a new appearance. There were no schools for typists. A circular sent to all branch offices in September, 1875, explained the early results from the use of the new machine, "We know of some operators who can get through fifty to sixty words a minute with ease, while others find difficulty in completing thirty."

The application of the typewriter, carbon paper, and duplicating processes gradually broadened the practicability and the usefulness of credit reports. Over the decades from 1841, credit reports contained about the same type of information and were generally written in one paragraph, except when a rare financial statement was obtained. As succeeding investigations were made, information at successive dates was added to bring the earlier data up to date as shown by the three examples quoted on pages 371 to 373. A report would often contain information spread over two to three years. Then that data would be condensed and another series of paragraphs would be added by subsequent credit investigations during the next two years or so. This practice continued throughout the nineteenth century.

During the early years of the twentieth century, detailed balance sheets were obtained with increased frequency. The base credit report with a financial statement now often ran from one to three typewritten pages in length, instead of a bare paragraph like the earlier examples. The interpretation of credit information began to develop into a recognized science with particular types of information falling into certain well recognized sub-divisions of credit analysis. In 1915, the information in the credit report was divided into six sections, showing a segregation of the collected facts under the captions of Record Data, Financial Statement, General Information, Trade Payments, Fire Record, and Rating, an arrangement which assisted in locating and interpreting specific information in the report.

The gradual development of the credit report from the single opinion of the credit reporter to the present-day elaborate analysis of the business enterprise, represents a continued one-hundred year story in evolution; a story in which the design of the report, its preparation, and its distribution reflects the growth of the machine age, the powerful influences of such servants of travel and communication as railroads and airplanes, telegraph, telephone, teletype, and radio, the spread in the corporation as a unit of business activity, and the rise and development of accounting practice. The constant improvements in methods of communication, the development of national advertising and national distribution, led to the need for more detailed information on the seeker of credit, and greater science in the interpretation of that data. In 1930, the captions which had divided the credit report into six parts for fifteen years were re-arranged, and since that time credit information has appeared in the regular commercial, narrative reports under the headings of History, Method of Operation-Fire Hazard, Financial Statement, Trade Report, Summary, and Rating.

Specialization in Credit Reports

Since 1931, the science of credit investigation and analysis has developed in speed, scope, and technique to meet the increasing needs of our swifter-moving commercial and industrial life. Instead of the colonial selling terms of twelve months, or our early national selling terms of six months, billions of dollars worth of merchandise is sold monthly on terms which range from net seven days in the meat packing industry to instalment terms calling for monthly payments over several years by manufacturers of heavy industrial machinery and durable consumer goods. The vast array of information which is now collected daily from so many divergent sources, reporters' direct calls and investigation, bank and trade investigations, record items of judgments and suits, clippings from daily newspapers and magazines, offering circulars of securities, reports to the Securities and Exchange Commission, and reports filed according to law in certain States, is being constantly sifted, interpreted, and edited into four different types of commercial, narrative credit reports by *The Mercantile Agency* of 1941.

These four different types of credit reports are the Analytical Report, the Registered Supervised Report, the Specialized Industries Report, and the regular Commercial Narrative Report. The Analytical Report is prepared by a reporter who is a highly-trained specialist handling larger complicated cases which often have subsidiary and affiliated companies necessitating a study of consolidated and individual balance sheets, of inter-company loans and inter-company merchandise sales. These concerns generally have a tangible net worth from $75,000 to $500,000,000. Analytical Reports were first edited in 1931.

The Registered Supervised Report, which was first edited in January, 1937, is prepared on business enterprises of an intermediate size, that is, with a tangible net worth between $10,000 and $75,000. Investigations not covered by these two groups, and on concerns in any one of ten divisions of industry in which specialized reporting divisions have been set up, are known as Specialized Industries Reports. These particular ten divisions are the retailers of furniture, coal, household appliances, lumber and building material, women's wear, men's wear, paints and varnishes, shoes, laundries and dry cleaners, and Class 1 motor carriers. They are handled by credit reporters trained in the unusual features and characteristics of these respective divisions of trade.

If an investigation is not handled by one of these three classes of specialized reporters, it is probably on a small retailer, a restaurant, a gasoline service station, a small local proprietorship of which there are several hundred thousand in active operation, and is handled by a reporter who covers all other concerns within a specified geographical district. This specialization in the investigation and the preparation of four different types of commercial credit reports has been developed during the past ten years to produce constantly higher quality reports to serve the expanding requirements of American commerce.

Each report instead of consisting of one paragraph of credit information as was the case fifty years ago, now consists of one or several sheets of 8½ by 11 paper containing concentrated, typed, credit information and the interpretation of that information. In more elaborate complicated cases the report contains ten to twenty pages. Although the kind of information, the vital points which are covered in these different types of reports, is quite similar, the treatment has become increasingly comprehensive and more elaborate due to the specialization, the type of concern under investigation and analysis, and the supervised training of the different classes of credit reporters.

American Economic Institution

This credit report, which has grown in size and complexity with the development of trade, reflects the tremendous industrial and commercial expansion of our country. The credit reporter and the credit report are wholly American in concept. Europe had no pioneers such as Thomas W. Ward, Sheldon P. Church, Washington Hite, or Lewis Tappan, in this field of gathering and reporting basic credit information. Europe had obstacles in national borders, established customs, diverse languages, different currencies, and a decided lack of economic and political freedom. The democratic air of America with its lack of class distinction, its wide horizon, and its innate willingness to put confidence in character enabled this unique but essential system in a broad land to spring up, to take root quickly, and to grow. Nowhere else in the world can a salesman travel by train or motor car and cover a market three thousand miles apart, with people speaking the same language, wearing similar clothes, spending the same kind of money. No custom barriers impede the flow of credits or the delivery of merchandise.

The owner of a department store in Seattle places orders for shoes in Boston, for men's suits in Rochester, for hardware in Chicago, and for women's dresses in New York, and the manufacturers of these products are able to make immediate decisions whether to ship their merchandise to the distant prospective customer, or to refuse the order. The credit reporter keeps the vigil on every active commercial and industrial business enterprise in the country, carefully, thoroughly, almost automatically, so that the essential credit information will be readily available at a moment's notice anywhere in the country. Here is the basic background of dynamic American business.

Growth in Credit Facilities

The need for credit in a young nation became increasingly evident with the stretching of our frontiers, with the development in transportation methods and means of communication. As mercantile terms of trade gradually shortened, business men became increasingly aware of the time factor in the earning power of their working capital and began to offer cash discounts. Freedley, in his manual of 1850, argued for faster turnover by selling at lower prices on shorter terms.

Credit needs were now supplied by a variety of institutions. Commission merchants often accepted a risk for a trader, signing his note from four to eight months at a *del credere* of one to two per cent a month. Pawnbrokers arose and extended credit on ample security, fire and life insurance companies used their reserve funds to extend mortgage loans to individuals, commercial banks were created to serve expanding industry and commerce, mutual savings banks were established by thoughtful humanitarians and more credit became available for mortgage loans. Building and loan associations began to assist wage-earners to acquire homes.

As our population steadily increased, the number of manufacturing, wholesaling, and retailing business enterprises constantly expanded during the second half of the nineteenth century. Old urban centers became greater centers and new cities sprang up at the crossroads of commerce at strategic rail and river junctions. More and more specialization developed in credit institutions. Along came the factor in the textile industry, personal loan companies, title and mortgage guarantee companies, credit unions, industrial banks, sales and discount finance companies, and increased loans by Stock Exchange commission houses to margin buyers of securities. During the first World War, the Federal Government achieved a tremendous power in international credits, and since 1932, a still greater force with its expanding number of lending agencies operating in almost every field of economic endeavor at home. The daily service of these thousands of credit institutions has made our world into the credit economy that it is today.

In a phenomenal century, the States have been knitted into a compact, highly sensitive national economy, but the essential philosophy of American business has remained unchanged. Confidence is freely exchanged in trade and the amount of actual cash used in daily commercial transactions is probably smaller at the present time than in the difficult period of one hundred years ago when the country had plenty of raw materials but no stable currency, nor a definition for it.

Romance of the Credit Report

Both the credit reporter and the newspaper reporter are fact-finders, whose eyes have been sharpened for the rapid identification of essential facts and news. The credit reporter provides the nerve system through which the pulse of active business is recorded. The newspaper reporter's story is finished after he has described the ball game, the train wreck, the court room scene, or after he has interviewed the man of the hour. The credit reporter is a "serial" writer whose story is never finished until the business enterprise withdraws from the commercial or industrial struggle, until it is merged, consolidated, voluntarily liquidated, or until it falls into the chasm of bankruptcy.

Like a "continued story" the credit report increases in interest as the character of the owner, of the partners, or the president of the corporation unfolds, developing strength or weakness as obstacles to progress and profits are encountered. Revisions of the report at periodic intervals are added chapters in the biography of the business enterprise. Suspense is heightened as unforeseen events, a war, a new invention, intense competition from younger more aggressive competitors, threaten the life of the concern. A climax approaches with the future trend of the enterprise uncertain. Then the dénouement. The concern under sound, aggressive management weathers the storm, maintains or improves its credit position, or under weak, unskillful management, joins the daily obituary list of business enterprises. These developments take place every day in our land of commercial and industrial competition, with a freedom to life unknown in any other part of the world. This is our great heritage from James Towne and from Plimoth.

379

APPENDIX

NUMBER AND TOTAL ADMITTED ASSETS (GROSS ASSETS TO 1895) OF
FIRE AND MARINE INSURANCE COMPANIES LICENSED TO
OPERATE IN NEW YORK STATE, 1860-1939

[*Sources: Annual Reports of Superintendent of Insurance, State of New York, 1860-1939.*]

Year	Number	Total Admitted Assets	Year	Number	Total Admitted Assets
1860	153	$44,633,275	1900	182	$329,096,119
1861	155	43,436,075	1901	166	341,004,813
1862	157	46,196,810	1902	165	361,398,011
1863	163	54,003,914	1903	168	386,081,446
1864	183	99,601,980	1904	165	403,071,557
1865	174	97,630,775	1905	179	445,517,342
1866	167	96,269,874	1906	176	418,093,727
1867	144	106,381,805	1907	191	454,370,298
1868	179	120,450,429	1908	185	465,127,824
1869	193	135,897,116	1909	188	515,443,065
1870	197	138,359,321	1910	204	583,650,758
1871	184	125,003,975	1911	213	594,098,862
1872	168	121,391,567	1912	234	641,917,194
1873	210	140,696,522	1913	250	663,888,203
1874	223	160,133,456	1914	264	694,213,078
1875	227	170,902,038	1915	264	783,013,832
1876	226	173,699,730	1916	275	806,939,677
1877	213	165,396,071	1917	280	896,728,088
1878	199	164,714,617	1918	283	1,008,129,553
1879	188	164,160,653	1919	307	1,213,409,109
1880	179	170,774,461	1920	329	1,445,777,657
1881	176	184,865,277	1921	335	1,462,092,452
1882	174	188,408,502	1922	332	1,553,898,766
1883	175	204,578,024	1923	335	1,632,392,468
1884	171	202,550,110	1924	343	1,761,235,543
1885	176	212,841,421	1925	345	1,923,193,149
1886	186	227,848,545	1926	343	2,051,927,395
1887	182	227,702,323	1927	362	2,309,778,875
1888	178	233,473,146	1928	373	2,654,496,211
1889	180	238,779,385	1929	392	2,880,648,913
1890	175	248,792,160	1930	403	2,633,724,081
1891	153	248,420,357	1931	377	2,497,365,242
1892	154	256,535,520	1932	358	2,334,879,721
1893	151	252,095,150	1933	354	2,072,314,409
1894	147	254,402,082	1934	350	2,117,082,179
1895	144	264,080,872	1935	356	2,393,967,465
1896	160	280,170,478	1936	360	2,678,909,556
1897	181	306,913,674	1937	361	2,473,126,199
1898	185	322,044,875	1938	359	2,580,880,538
1899	186	324,024,369	1939	395	2,698,290,380

Note: Marine Insurance Companies were first included in 1865 and Mutual Insurance Companies in 1867.

Table Number Two
Number and Total Admitted Assets of Life Insurance Companies
Licensed to Operate in New York State, 1860-1939

[*Sources: Annual Reports of Superintendent of Insurance, State of New York, 1860-1939.*]

Year	Number	Total Admitted Assets	Year	Number	Total Admitted Assets
1860	17	$24,115,687	1900	40	$1,723,737,723
1861	17	26,670,397	1901	38	1,879,624,564
1862	18	30,123,332	1902	39	2,062,430,804
1863	22	37,838,190	1903	42	2,226,423,202
1864	27	49,027,297	1904	42	2,454,669,486
1865	30	64,232,123	1905	43	2,651,316,714
1866	39	91,587,028	1906	43	2,851,910,924
1867	43	125,548,951	1907	37	2,917,908,918
1868	55	175,262,330	1908	35	3,204,193,351
1869	70	229,097,425	1909	35	3,467,474,821
1870	71	269,520,441	1910	33	3,693,248,328
1871	68	302,558,199	1911	34	3,942,144,356
1872	59	335,168,543	1912	34	4,173,953,579
1873	56	360,140,684	1913	34	4,417,298,211
1874	50	387,281,897	1914	35	4,636,744,620
1875	45	403,142,982	1915	37	4,850,696,881
1876	38	407,406,333	1916	37	5,144,624,477
1877	34	396,420,591	1917	38	5,467,600,437
1878	34	404,079,145	1918	40	5,915,687,963
1879	34	411,353,355	1919	37	6,096,788,789
1880	34	428,332,871	1920	37	6,550,253,577
1881	30	429,534,655	1921	37	7,025,018,706
1882	30	449,602,347	1922	37	7,592,695,566
1883	29	471,805,920	1923	38	8,221,961,332
1884	29	491,487,719	1924	38	9,007,769,626
1885	29	523,664,678	1925	41	10,016,629,309
1886	29	560,125,359	1926	44	11,140,624,404
1887	29	595,679,477	1927	48	12,384,739,493
1888	29	641,747,870	1928	48	13,723,663,099
1889	30	696,943,722	1929	49	15,015,941,517
1890	30	753,228,759	1930	52	16,206,292,642
1891	29	819,402,852	1931	52	17,345,239,518
1892	31	903,734,537	1932	53	17,937,651,871
1893	32	971,857,224	1933	53	18,246,404,342
1894	33	1,056,331,683	1934	53	19,090,827,831
1895	35	1,142,419,927	1935	51	20,328,715,716
1896	36	1,228,324,342	1936	56	21,774,149,831
1897	35	1,334,051,344	1937	57	22,974,476,961
1898	36	1,451,116,914	1938	57	24,292,548,526
1899	37	1,576,334,673	1939	60	25,615,152,335

TABLE NUMBER THREE
NUMBER AND TOTAL ADMITTED ASSETS OF FIDELITY, CASUALTY, SURETY,
CREDIT, AND MISCELLANEOUS INSURANCE COMPANIES LICENSED
TO OPERATE IN NEW YORK STATE, 1864-1939

[*Sources: Annual Reports of Superintendent of Insurance, State of New York, 1864-1939.*]

Year	Number	Total Admitted Assets	Year	Number	Total Admitted Assets
1864	1	$276,789	1902	35	$59,627,656
1865	3	998,835	1903	36	67,354,937
1866	10	2,402,119	1904	38	70,476,877
1867	7	2,222,522	1905	42	78,546,288
1868	3	1,607,013	1906	46	88,446,048
1869	3	1,841,683	1907	49	90,586,309
1870	3	2,119,226	1908	50	105,742,452
1871	3	2,468,664	1909	54	117,818,570
1872	3	2,848,790	1910	54	129,387,972
1873	3	1,584,793	1911	60	145,068,249
1874	5	2,075,810	1912	63	162,406,391
1875	5	2,212,379	1913	62	169,773,657
1876	5	2,115,853	1914	79	186,286,270
1877	5	2,081,993	1915	77	203,303,487
1878	4	1,736,860	1916	71	234,038,470
1879	4	1,849,057	1917	74	282,678,822
1880	5	2,312,662	1918	78	352,613,531
1881	6	3,110,737	1919	81	435,655,717
1882	7	3,617,414	1920	88	529,088,727
1883	8	4,348,662	1921	89	570,901,605
1884	9	4,988,476	1922	96	629,304,966
1885	10	5,453,108	1923	97	685,471,434
1886	11	6,335,034	1924	101	764,836,967
1887	10	7,738,512	1925	103	850,802,053
1888	10	8,646,150	1926	108	967,314,153
1889	10	9,779,577	1927	112	1,107,422,033
1890	11	10,240,254	1928	135	1,284,789,202
1891	14	13,433,714	1929	141	1,372,530,599
1892	13	15,686,690	1930	140	1,338,242,706
1893	18	16,112,607	1931	135	1,305,140,461
1894	20	19,383,822	1932	119	1,224,771,642
1895	24	26,091,860	1933	110	1,067,055,215
1896	25	28,563,940	1934	109	1,087,015,426
1897	25	31,808,633	1935	110	1,217,492,046
1898	26	34,928,788	1936	113	1,393,912,838
1899	30	42,422,788	1937	116	1,466,142,453
1900	31	47,326,359	1938	118	1,619,089,128
1901	33	53,536,824	1939	134	1,744,288,991

TABLE NUMBER FOUR
NUMBER OF STATE AND PRIVATE COMMERCIAL BANKS, AGGREGATE CAPITAL, CIRCULATION, DEPOSITS, AND LOANS, 1782-1862

Sources: Capital and Circulation figures for 1782 and 1783 obtained from a pamphlet "First State-ment of Condition" of the Bank of North America, Historical Society of Pennsylvania; all other figures from Report of Comptroller of the Currency, 1920, Volume II, pages 846-847.

Year	Number of Banks	Capital	Circulation	Deposits	Loans and Discounts
1782	1	$176,000	$672,000	$.........	$.........
1783	1	409,000	456,000		
1784	3	2,100,000	2,000,000		
1785	.	....	....		
1786	.	....	....		
1787	.	....	....		
1788	.	....	....		
1789	.	....	....		
1790	4	2,500,000	2,500,000		
1791	6	12,900,000	9,000,000		
1792	16	17,100,000	11,500,000		
1793	17	18,000,000	11,000,000		
1794	17	18,000,000	11,600,000		
1795	23	19,000,000	11,000,000		
1796	24	19,200,000	10,500,000		
1797	25	19,200,000	10,000,000		
1798	25	19,200,000	9,000,000		
1799	26	21,200,000	10,000,000		
1800	28	21,300,000	10,500,000		
1801	31	22,400,000	11,000,000		
1802	32	22,600,000	10,000,000		
1803	36	26,000,000	11,000,000		
1804	59	39,500,000	14,000,000		
1805	75	40,400,000	....		
1806	..	....	....		
1807	..	....	....		
1808	..	....	....		
1809	..	....	....		
1810	..	....	....		
1811	88	42,609,101	22,700,000		
1812	..	....		....	....
1813	..	65,000,000	66,000,000	....	117,000,000
1814	..	80,300,000		....	....
1815	208	82,200,000	45,500,000	....	150,000,000
1816	246	89,822,297	68,000,000	....	....
1817	...	90,600,000	....	....	....
1818	...			....	....
1819	...	72,300,000	35,700,000	11,100,000	73,600,000
1820	307	102,100,000	40,600,000	31,200,000	....

> Prior to 1863 all com-mercial banks were obliged to report to the Bureau of Internal Rev-enue, and all records of banking operations in the United States were kept by that Bureau. In 1920 the Comptroller of the Currency, and again, in 1933 the Federal Reserve Districts' Banking and In-dustrial Committee au-thorized by Congress to make a report on banking operations, attempted to locate the records missing for certain years in this schedule. That informa-tion was either lost or de-stroyed as neither the Comptroller of the Cur-rency nor the Federal Re-serve Districts' Banking and Industrial Committee were able to locate the missing data.
>
> AUTHOR

Year	Number of Banks	Capital	Circulation	Deposits	Loans and Discounts
1821	...	$.........	$.........	$.........	$.........
1822	...	....	....	....	....
1823	...	....	....	....	....
1824	...	....	....	....	....
1825	...	....	....	....	....
1826	...	....	....	....	....
1827	...	....	....	....	....
1828	...	....	....	....	....
1829	329	110,100,000	48,200,000	40,700,000	....
1830	329	110,186,608	48,400,000	39,500,000	159,800,000
1831	...	....	....	....	....
1832	...	....	....	....	....
1833	...	....	....	....	....
1834	506	200,005,944	94,839,570	75,666,986	324,119,499
1835	704	231,250,337	103,692,495	83,081,365	365,163,834
1836	713	251,875,292	140,301,038	115,104,440	457,506,080
1837	788	290,772,091	149,185,890	127,397,185	525,115,702
1838	829	317,636,778	116,138,910	84,691,184	485,631,687
1839	840	327,132,512	135,170,995	90,240,146	492,278,015
1840	901	358,442,692	106,968,572	75,696,857	462,896,523
1841	784	313,608,959	107,290,214	64,890,101	386,487,662
1842	692	260,171,797	83,734,011	62,408,870	322,957,569
1843	691	228,861,948	58,563,608	56,168,628	254,544,937
1844	696	210,872,056	75,167,646	84,550,785	264,905,814
1845	707	206,045,969	89,608,711	88,020,646	288,617,131
1846	707	196,894,309	105,552,427	96,913,070	312,114,404
1847	715	203,070,622	105,519,766	91,792,533	310,282,945
1848	751	204,838,175	128,506,091	103,226,177	344,476,582
1849	782	207,309,361	114,743,415	91,178,623	332,323,195
1850	824	217,317,211	131,366,526	109,586,595	364,204,078
1851	879	227,807,553	155,165,251	128,957,712	413,756,799
1852	...	....	....	....	....
1853	...	....	....	....	....
1854	1,208	301,376,071	204,689,207	188,188,744	557,397,779
1855	1,307	332,177,288	186,952,223	190,400,342	576,144,758
1856	1,398	343,874,272	195,747,950	212,705,662	634,183,280
1857	1,416	370,834,686	214,778,882	230,351,352	684,456,887
1858	1,422	394,622,799	155,208,344	185,932,049	583,165,242
1859	1,476	401,976,242	193,306,818	259,568,278	657,183,799
1860	1,560	421,880,095	207,102,477	253,802,129	691,945,580
1861	1,601	429,592,713	202,005,767	257,229,562	696,778,421
1862	1,492	418,139,741	183,792,079	296,322,408	646,677,780

Sources: Annual Reports of Comptroller of the Currency. National banks, and State banks and trust companies, 1863 to 1931, in Report for 1931, page 3. National banks, 1932 to 1940, in Report for 1940, page 322. State banks and trust companies, 1932 to 1935, in Report for 1935, pages 127-128; 1936 to 1939 from respective yearly Reports adjusted by deducting number of stock savings banks obtained from office of Comptroller of the Currency; 1940 in Report for 1940, page 223. Private banks, 1924 to 1940 from respective yearly Reports.

Year	National Banks	State Banks and Trust Companies	Private Banks
1863	66	1,466	
1864	467	1,089	....
1865	1,294	349	
1866	1,634	297	
1867	1,636	272	
1868	1,640	247	
1869	1,619	259	
1870	1,612	325	
1871	1,723	452	
1872	1,853	566	
1873	1,968	277	
1874	1,983	368	
1875	2,076	586	
1876	2,091	671	
1877	2,078	631	
1878	2,056	510	
1879	2,048	648	
1880	2,076	650	
1881	2,115	683	
1882	2,239	704	
1883	2,417	788	
1884	2,625	852	
1885	2,689	1,015	
1886	2,809	891	
1887	3,014	1,471	
1888	3,120	1,523	
1889	3,239	1,791	
1890	3,484	2,250	
1891	3,652	2,743	....
1892	3,759	3,359	....
1893	3,807	3,807	....
1894	3,770	3,810	....
1895	3,715	4,016	....
1896	3,689	3,968	....
1897	3,610	4,108	....
1898	3,582	4,211	....
1899	3,583	4,451	....

No authentic information regarding the number of private banks became available until the year 1880 when a law was enacted by Congress requiring returns for taxation purposes. Under that law 2,802 private banks were recorded in 1880, 3,038 in 1881, and 3,391 in 1882. By an Act of March 3, 1883 this law was repealed by Congress and no further reliable figures regarding the number of private banks became available until more recent years.

Number of National, State, and Private Commercial Banks
and Trust Companies, 1863-1940

Year	National Banks	State Banks and Trust Companies	Private Banks
1900	3,732	4,659	...
1901	4,165	5,317	...
1902	4,535	5,814	...
1903	4,939	6,493	...
1904	5,331	7,508	...
1905	5,668	8,477	...
1906	6,053	9,604	...
1907	6,429	10,761	...
1908	6,824	12,062	...
1909	6,926	12,398	...
1910	7,145	13,257	...
1911	7,277	14,115	...
1912	7,372	14,791	...
1913	7,473	15,526	...
1914	7,525	16,076	...
1915	7,605	16,262	...
1916	7,579	17,056	...
1917	7,604	17,576	...
1918	7,705	18,265	...
1919	7,785	18,602	...
1920	8,030	19,603	...
1921	8,154	20,349	...
1922	8,249	19,782	...
1923	8,241	19,686	...
1924	8,085	19,100	560
1925	8,072	18,663	523
1926	7,978	18,149	495
1927	7,796	17,337	467
1928	7,691	16,711	404
1929	7,536	16,045	391
1930	7,252	15,146	361
1931	6,805	13,728	284
1932	6,150	11,690	227
1933	4,902	8,743	181
1934	5,422	9,342	236
1935	5,431	9,467	243
1936	5,374	9,392	131
1937	5,299	9,295	85
1938	5,248	9,126	73
1939	5,209	8,997	64
1940	5,170	9,239	57

Note: Figure of State Banks and Trust Companies for 1940 includes an unknown number of Stock Savings Banks.

Table Number Six
Loans and Discounts of All (National, State, and Private Commercial Banks and Trust Companies, and Mutual and Stock Savings) Reporting Banks, 1835-1940

Sources: 1835 to 1919, Report of Comptroller of the Currency, 1931, pages 1023-1025; 1920 to 1940, Report of Comptroller of the Currency, 1940, page 320.

Year	Total Loans and Discounts	Total Deposits	Year	Total Loans and Discounts	Total Deposits
1835	$365,164,000	$122,054,000	1875	$1,748,009,000	$2,008,620,000
1836	457,506,000	165,507,000	1876	1,727,178,000	1,993,030,000
1837	525,116,000	189,818,000	1877	1,721,038,000	2,006,199,000
1838	485,632,000	145,707,000	1878	1,561,219,000	1,920,898,000
1839	492,278,000	143,376,000	1879	1,507,354,000	2,149,192,000
1840	462,897,000	119,856,000	1880	1,662,256,000	2,222,106,000
1841	386,488,000	107,752,000	1881	1,902,037,000	2,649,062,000
1842	323,958,000	88,273,000	1882	2,050,453,000	2,777,421,000
1843	254,545,000	77,625,000	1883	2,233,539,000	2,883,977,000
1844	264,906,000	116,549,000	1884	2,260,704,000	2,848,554,000
1845	288,617,000	114,358,000	1885	2,272,236,000	3,078,153,000
1846	312,114,000	125,132,000	1886	2,433,784,000	3,186,179,000
1847	310,283,000	120,332,000	1887	2,943,309,000	3,718,639,000
1848	344,477,000	142,641,000	1888	3,161,216,000	3,891,096,000
1849	332,323,000	121,274,000	1889	3,477,596,000	4,310,516,000
1850	364,204,000	146,304,000	1890	3,853,533,000	4,576,433,000
1851	413,757,000	175,375,000	1891	4,031,024,000	4,682,695,000
1852	429,761,000	182,158,000	1892	4,336,889,000	5,297,460,000
1853	408,944,000	195,179,000	1893	4,368,677,000	5,065,422,000
1854	557,398,000	238,511,000	1894	4,085,069,000	5,267,669,000
1855	576,145,000	235,557,000	1895	4,268,923,000	5,538,634,000
1856	634,183,000	265,426,000	1896	4,251,157,000	5,486,182,000
1857	684,457,000	288,026,000	1897	4,215,978,000	5,787,188,000
1858	583,165,000	237,102,000	1898	4,652,279,000	6,554,165,000
1859	657,184,000	327,784,000	1899	5,177,594,000	7,900,303,000
1860	691,946,000	309,735,000	1900	5,657,687,000	8,513,030,000
1861	696,778,000	318,505,000	1901	6,425,431,000	9,896,122,000
1862	646,678,000	357,466,000	1902	7,189,110,000	10,625,592,000
1863	654,068,000	503,692,000	1903	7,738,981,000	11,179,144,000
1864	554,653,000	379,951,000	1904	7,982,023,000	11,864,925,000
1865	517,524,000	688,963,000	1905	9,027,298,000	13,332,801,000
1866	682,327,000	758,480,000	1906	9,893,757,000	14,207,429,000
1867	709,316,000	743,619,000	1907	10,763,912,000	15,358,215,000
1868	765,487,000	797,490,000	1908	10,437,992,000	15,116,863,000
1869	801,437,000	771,496,000	1909	11,446,722,000	16,668,219,000
1870	863,757,000	775,100,000	1910	12,521,809,000	17,584,175,000
1871	990,267,000	887,839,000	1911	13,046,390,000	18,581,475,000
1872	1,123,038,000	926,577,000	1912	13,953,607,000	19,719,288,000
1873	1,439,877,000	1,625,183,000	1913	14,626,772,000	20,138,553,000
1874	1,564,383,000	1,740,049,000	1914	15,339,478,000	21,359,842,000

LOANS AND DISCOUNTS OF ALL (NATIONAL, STATE, AND PRIVATE
COMMERCIAL BANKS AND TRUST COMPANIES, AND MUTUAL
AND STOCK SAVINGS) REPORTING BANKS, 1835-1940

Year	Total Loans and Discounts	Total Deposits	Year	Total Loans and Discounts	Total Deposits
1915	$15,758,673,000	$22,031,669,000	1928	$39,155,988,000	$58,431,061,000
1916	17,933,577,000	26,462,501,000	1929	41,433,126,000	57,910,641,000
1917	20,665,939,000	30,470,159,000	1930	40,510,108,000	59,847,195,000
1918	22,591,221,000	32,615,468,000	1931	35,210,500,000	56,864,744,000
1919	25,088,978,000	37,685,972,000	1932	28,089,853,000	45,390,269,000
1920	30,650,050,000	41,725,224,000	1933	22,387,818,000	41,533,470,000
1921	28,688,971,000	38,664,987,000	1934	21,431,153,000	46,625,041,000
1922	27,628,331,000	41,128,352,000	1935	20,419,260,000	51,586,123,000
1923	30,157,810,000	44,249,524,000	1936	20,839,159,000	58,339,815,000
1924	31,288,318,000	47,709,028,000	1937	22,698,176,000	59,822,370,000
1925	33,598,506,000	51,995,059,000	1938	21,311,161,000	59,379,550,000
1926	35,843,208,000	54,069,257,000	1939	21,516,279,000	64,576,694,000
1927	37,103,309,000	56,751,307,000	1940	22,557,670,000	71,153,458,000

TABLE NUMBER SEVEN
NUMBER OF MUTUAL SAVINGS BANKS, NUMBER OF DEPOSITORS, TOTAL
DEPOSITS, AND AVERAGE PER DEPOSITOR, 1816-1940

Sources: 1816 to 1819, "Modern Story of Mutual Savings Banks" by Franklin J. Sherman, page 57, (New York, 1934); 1820 to 1834, and 1841 to 1845, compilation made from Directory of Mutual Savings Banks (January, 1940); 1835, 1840, 1846 to 1851, and all figures through 1851 giving Number of Depositors, Deposits, and Average per Depositor from Report of Comptroller of the Currency, 1920, Volume I, page 241; 1888 to 1940, from Reports of Comptroller of the Currency, 1888 to 1913, 1939 and 1940 from respective Annual Reports, 1914 to 1938 from Report of 1938, page 150.

Year	Number of Banks	Number of Depositors	Deposits	Average Per Depositor
1816	1	......	$........	$......
1817	2	......	....	......
1818	4	......	....	......
1819	8	......	....	......
1820	10	8,635	1,138,576	131.86
1821	10	......	....	......
1822	10	......	....	......
1823	13	......	....	......
1824	14	......	....	......
1825	17	16,931	2,537,082	149.84
1826	18	......	....	......
1827	22	......	....	......
1828	27	......	....	......
1829	30	......	....	......
1830	31	38,035	6,973,304	183.09
1831	36	......	....	......
1832	38	......	....	......
1833	41	......	....	......
1834	50	......	....	......
1835	52	60,058	10,613,726	176.72
1836	..	......	....	......
1837	..	......	....	......
1838	..	......	....	......
1839	..	......	....	......
1840	61	78,701	14,051,520	178.54
1841	61	......	....	......
1842	65	......	....	......
1843	65	......	....	......
1844	66	......	....	......
1845	70	145,206	21,506,677	168.77
1846	74	158,709	27,374,325	172.48
1847	76	187,739	31,627,479	168.46
1848	83	199,764	33,087,488	165.63
1849	90	217,318	36,073,924	165.99
1850	108	251,354	43,431,130	172.78
1851	128	277,148	50,457,913	182.06
1852	..	....	....	......
1853	..	....	....	......
1854	..	....	....	......

Year	Number of Banks	Number of Depositors	Deposits	Average Per Depositor
1855	...	....	$...........	$......
1856	...	....	....	......
1857	...	....	....	......
1858	...	....		
1859	...	....		
1860	...	....		
1861	...	....		
1862	...	....		
1863	...	....		
1864	...	....		
1865	...	....		
1866	...	....		
1867	...	....		
1868	...	....		
1869	...	....		
1870	...	....		
1871	...	....		
1872	...	....		
1873	...	....		
1874	...	....		
1875	...	....		
1876	...	....		
1877	...	....		
1878	...	....		
1879	...	....		
1880	...	....		
1881	...	....		
1882	...	....		
1883	...	....		
1884	...	....		
1885	...	....	....	.....
1886	...	....	....	.....
1887	...	....	....	.....
1888	628	3,506,936	1,216,100,471	346.76
1889	637	3,519,139	1,270,269,218	360.84
1890	637	3,765,218	1,336,001,150	354.88
1891	647	3,948,528	1,402,332,665	355.15
1892	643	4,091,385	1,459,221,779	356.65
1893	649	4,290,712	1,550,820,403	361.43
1894	646	4,276,697	1,538,305,070	359.69
1895	664	4,393,519	1,597,343,160	363.12
1896	677	4,584,503	1,688,190,603	368.20
1897	666	4,691,444	1,737,099,370	370.12

> Records of savings banks
> which the Comptroller of the
> Currency compiled prior to
> 1888 included both mutual
> savings banks and stock sav-
> ings banks. The first com-
> mercial banking institution to
> include the word "savings" in
> its title was the State Trust &
> Savings Bank of Buffalo, or-
> ganized in 1852 ("The De-
> velopment of Trust Com-
> panies in the United States"
> by James G. Smith, page 328,
> 1928), so records of savings
> institutions compiled prior to
> that date were strictly mutual
> savings banks. Reports for
> 1937 and prior years include
> one bank in the State of Cali-
> fornia reported as a mutual
> savings bank but since that
> date considered a State com-
> mercial bank.

Year	Number of Banks	Number of Depositors	Deposits	Average Per Depositor
1898	659	4,835,138	$1,824,963,410	$377.44
1899	655	5,079,732	1,960,709,131	385.99
1900	652	5,370,109	2,134,471,130	397.47
1901	660	5,612,434	2,260,273,524	402.73
1902	657	5,870,859	2,380,200,804	405.42
1903	657	6,116,594	2,512,468,458	410.76
1904	668	6,286,375	2,602,040,775	413.92
1905	668	6,463,677	2,736,533,039	423.37
1906	678	6,753,037	2,908,710,654	430.73
1907	678	7,071,219	3,055,287,322	432.07
1908	676	7,137,481	3,065,686,012	429.52
1909	642	....	3,143,498,348	......
1910	638	7,481,649	3,360,563,842	449.21
1911	635	7,690,973	3,460,551,646	449.95
1912	630	7,850,889	3,608,534,400	459.63
1913	623	8,098,967	3,769,334,550	465.40
1914	634	8,274,418	3,915,143,000	473.16
1915	630	8,305,562	3,946,069,000	475.11
1916	622	8,590,746	4,135,552,000	481.40
1917	622	8,935,055	4,340,805,000	485.82
1918	625	9,011,464	4,344,166,000	482.07
1919	622	8,948,808	4,723,629,000	527.85
1920	620	9,455,327	5,172,348,000	547.61
1921	623	9,619,260	5,395,552,000	560.91
1922	619	9,665,861	5,686,720,000	588.94
1923	618	10,057,436	6,282,618,000	624.67
1924	613	10,409,776	6,686,366,000	642.32
1925	611	10,616,215	7,139,510,000	672.51
1926	620	11,053,886	7,558,668,000	683.80
1927	618	11,337,398	8,054,868,000	710.47
1928	616	11,732,143	8,665,592,000	738.62
1929	611	11,748,085	8,981,020,000	764.47
1930	606	11,895,000	9,191,000,000	772.00
1931	600	12,356,114	10,017,225,000	810.71
1932	594	12,521,750	10,021,852,000	800.36
1933	576	12,683,788	9,699,509,000	764.72
1934	578	13,077,111	9,764,596,000	746.69
1935	571	13,213,211	9,902,107,000	749.41
1936	566	13,165,045	10,037,169,000	762.41
1937	564	13,265,605	10,185,738,000	767.83
1938	562	12,505,071	10,146,230,000	811.37
1939	552	....	10,432,803,000	......
1940	551	....	10,631,438,000	......

394

NUMBER OF BUILDING AND LOAN ASSOCIATIONS, MEMBERSHIP, AND TOTAL ASSETS,

1898-1939

Sources: 1898 to 1930, "History of Building and Loan in the United States," H. Morton Bodfish, Editor-in-Chief, page 136, (Chicago, 1931); 1931 to 1939, compilation made by United States Savings and Loan League, Chicago, Illinois.

Year	Number	Membership	Total Assets
1898	5,576	1,617,837	$600,135,739
1899	5,485	1,512,685	581,866,170
1900	5,356	1,495,136	571,366,628
1901	5,302	1,539,593	565,387,966
1902	5,299	1,530,707	577,228,014
1903	5,308	1,566,700	579,556,112
1904	5,265	1,631,046	600,342,386
1905	5,264	1,642,127	629,344,257
1906	5,316	1,699,714	673,129,198
1907	5,424	1,839,119	731,508,446
1908	5,599	1,920,257	784,175,753
1909	5,713	2,016,651	856,332,719
1910	5,869	2,169,893	931,867,175
1911	6,099	2,332,829	1,030,687,031
1912	6,273	2,516,936	1,137,600,648
1913	6,429	2,836,433	1,248,479,139
1914	6,616	3,103,935	1,357,707,900
1915	6,806	3,334,899	1,484,205,875
1916	7,072	3,568,432	1,598,628,136
1917	7,269	3,838,612	1,769,142,175
1918	7,484	4,011,401	1,898,344,346
1919	7,788	4,289,326	2,126,620,390
1920	8,633	4,962,919	2,519,914,971
1921	9,255	5,809,888	2,890,764,621
1922	10,009	6,364,144	3,342,530,953
1923	10,744	7,202,880	3,942,939,880
1924	11,844	8,554,352	4,765,937,197
1925	12,403	9,886,997	5,509,176,154
1926	12,626	10,665,705	6,334,103,807
1927	12,804	11,326,261	7,178,562,451
1928	12,666	11,995,905	8,016,034,327
1929	12,342	12,111,209	8,695,154,220
1930	11,777	12,343,254	8,828,611,925
1931	11,442	11,338,701	8,417,375,605
1932	10,997	10,114,792	7,750,491,084
1933	10,727	9,224,105	6,977,531,676
1934	10,920	8,370,146	6,450,424,392
1935	10,534	7,049,567	5,888,710,326
1936	10,256	6,125,971	5,741,935,430
1937	9,762	6,233,019	5,711,658,410
1938	8,951	6,829,167	5,629,564,869
1939	8,328	6,499,511	5,674,262,030

TABLE NUMBER NINE
NUMBER OF REMEDIAL LOAN SOCIETIES, NUMBER OF LICENSED OFFICES
OF PERSONAL LOAN COMPANIES, AND OUTSTANDING LOANS
OF PERSONAL LOAN COMPANIES, 1910-1940

Sources: Number of Remedial Loan Societies, 1910 to 1933, "Regulation of the Small Loan Business," Louis N. Robinson and Rolf Nugent, page 147, (New York, 1935); 1934 to 1940 from The National Federation of Remedial Loan Associations, Detroit, Michigan. Number of Licensed Offices of Personal Loan Companies, 1929 to 1939, from the American Association of Personal Finance Companies, Washington, D. C. Estimated outstanding loans, 1912 to 1937, "Consumer Credit and Economic Stability," Rolf Nugent, pages 388-389, (New York, 1939); 1938 to 1940, from Russell Sage Foundation, New York.

Year	Number of Remedial Loan Societies	Regulated Personal Loan Companies	
		Number of Licensed Offices	Estimated Outstanding Loans
1910	16	.....	$..........
1911	21	.....	....
1912	25	.....	195,000
1913	34	.....	269,000
1914	37	.....	2,762,000
1915	40	.....	9,249,000
1916	36	.....	9,260,000
1917	35	.....	15,771,000
1918	34	.....	17,748,000
1919	34	.....	20,142,000
1920	32	.....	24,345,000
1921	31	.....	30,000,000
1922	30	.....	35,716,000
1923	29	.....	44,709,000
1924	29	.....	55,936,000
1925	28	.....	74,821,000
1926	28	.....	98,277,000
1927	28	.....	137,191,000
1928	27	.....	193,191,000
1929	27	3,766	263,205,000
1930	26	3,619	287,121,000
1931	26	3,620	288,816,000
1932	26	3,510	256,555,000
1933	25	3,423	232,004,000
1934	25	3,347	245,464,000
1935	25	3,355	267,085,000
1936	25	3,426	301,001,000
1937	22	3,553	351,071,000
1938	22	3,619	351,000,000
1939	22	4,036	409,000,000
1940	19	.....	495,000,000

TABLE NUMBER TEN
NUMBER OF CREDIT UNIONS, MEMBERSHIP, OUTSTANDING LOANS,
AND AMOUNT OF TOTAL ASSETS, 1909-1940

Sources: Number of Credit Unions, 1909 to 1911, 1915, 1920, 1930, 1934, membership and total assets, 1915, 1920, 1925, 1930, "Regulation of the Small Loan Business," Louis N. Robinson and Rolf Nugent, pages 89-93, 153, (New York, 1935); number, 1921, "Cuna Emerges," Roy F. Bergengren, page 19, (Madison, Wisconsin, 1939); number, 1925, 1929, 1932, and 1933, "Consumers' Credit and Production Cooperation in 1933," Florence E. Parker, page 52, (U. S. Department of Labor, Bulletin 612, 1935); number, 1923 and estimated outstanding loans, 1910 to 1937, "Consumer Credit and Economic Stability," Rolf Nugent, pages 100, 360, 361, (New York, 1939); number, membership, and total assets, 1936, "Consumer Cooperation in the United States," Florence E. Parker, pages 120-129, (U.S. Department of Labor, Bulletin 659, 1936); number, 1938 to 1940, membership and total assets, 1940, Credit Union National Association, Madison, Wisconsin; estimated outstanding loans, 1938 to 1940, from Russell Sage Foundation, New York.

Year	Number	Membership	Estimated Outstanding Loans	Total Assets
1909	1	....	$	$ ....
1910	2	....	14,000	....
1911	18	....	35,000	....
1912	.....	....	95,000	....
1913	.....	....	191,000	....
1914	.....	....	314,000	....
1915	48	7,600	540,000	471,000
1916	.....	....	1,009,000	....
1917	.....	....	1,627,000	....
1918	.....	....	2,500,000	....
1919	.....	....	3,988,000	....
1920	142	39,800	6,248,000	3,568,000
1921	190	....	8,274,000	....
1922	.....	....	11,229,000	....
1923	200	....	14,175,000	....
1924	.....	....	17,339,000	....
1925	419	130,700	19,811,000	21,165,000
1926	.....	....	23,315,000	....
1927	.....	....	26,543,000	....
1928	.....	....	29,437,000	....
1929	974	....	31,972,000	....
1930	1,017	292,800	30,968,000	40,910,000
1931	.....	....	29,125,000	....
1932	1,612	....	26,930,000	....
1933	2,016	....	27,371,000	....
1934	2,400	....	32,155,000	....
1935	.....	....	44,332,000	....
1936	5,440	1,209,902	66,024,000	88,012,706
1937	.....	....	92,808,000	....
1938	7,000	....	114,000,000	....
1939	8,291	....	150,000,000	....
1940	8,700	2,514,000	200,000,000	214,000,000

INDEX

Index

A

414

415

ROADS:
Colonial, 328
Lotteries for construction of, 61-62
ROBINSON-PATMAN ACT, 326
ROSS, WILLIAM P. M., *The Accountants' Own Book and Business Man's Manual,* 289-290
ROYAL AFRICAN COMPANY, 72
RUBBER:
British-American treaty for barter of, 56
Price maintenance of, 26-27
RUM:
Colonial trade in, 22-23, 54-55, 82
Credit transactions in, 70
West Indian trade in, 54-55
RURAL ELECTRIFICATION ACT OF 1936 . . . 263
Rural Electrification Administration, 217, 222, 262-263
RUSSELL SAGE FOUNDATION, 200-201, 207
RUSSIAN BUREAU, INC., 218

S

ST. BARTHOLOMEW'S LOAN ASSOCIATION, 199
SALMON CANNING INDUSTRY, Credit reports on, 345
Sanborn Map Company, Inc., 164
Savings and Loan Associations, Federal, 183-184, 233, 239-240
Savings and Loan Insurance Corporation, Federal, 184, 214-215, 220, 239, 242-244
Savings Bank of Newport, 143
SAVINGS BANKS:
Mutual, 59-60, 88, 139-146, 152, 178-181, 223, 227, 237, 244, 345, 378, 390-394
Stock, 390-391
SAVINGS BANKS ASSOCIATION, Loan fund of New Hampshire, 179
Savings Banks Trust Company, Loans and investments of, 179
SCHOOL DISTRICTS:
Credit reports on, 322
R F C loans to, 222, 225
SCHUYLKILL NAVIGATION CO., 123
SEAMEN, Credit restrictions on, 63-64
SECOND-HAND CLOTHING BUSINESS, Pawnbroking from, 115-116
SECRETARY OF AGRICULTURE, 256-257
SECURITIES AND EXCHANGE COMMISSION, 171-172, 376
SELLER'S MARKETS, Nineteenth century, 157
SEVILLE PIECES OF EIGHT, Colonial use of, 32
SHARECROPPERS, Rehabilitation loans to, 260-262
SHERLEY, JAMES, 13-14, 185

SHILLINGS, Colonial pine-tree, 32, 35
SHIPS:
Barter in sale of colonial, 49-52, 72
Description of seventeenth century, 3-4, 72
SHOLES, CHRISTOPHER LATHAM, Invention of typewriter by, 374
SHOPS, Colonial store *versus,* 73
SILVER, 4, 7, 18, 22-23, 27, 30-35, 82, 275
Singer Sewing Machine Company, 195
SIX-PENNY PIECES, 32
SLAVE TRADE, Colonial, 55, 83
SLAVES, Number in 1840 of, 284
SLOW ACCOUNTS, Collection of, 70-72
SMALL LOAN COMPANIES, Growth of, 88, 151-152, 199-202, 345, 378, 396
SMITH, ADAM, *Wealth of Nations,* 8
SMITH, JOHN, 19-20
SMITH, SIR THOMAS, 9, 57-58, 68
Society for establishing useful manufactures, 134, 211-212
SOCIETY OF NATIONAL HISTORY OF PARIS, 107
SOLE PROPRIETORSHIPS, Colonial, 72-73
SPANISH COINS, Colonial use of, 32-35, 40, 82
SPECIALIZED FINANCE COMPANIES, 52, 345
SPECIALIZED INDUSTRIES REPORTS, *Mercantile Agency,* 376
SPECIALIZED MERCANTILE AGENCIES, 299
"SPECIE CIRCULAR," Speculation curbed by, 280-281
SPECIE PAYMENTS:
Resumption in 1879 of, 158
Suspension in 1837 of, 151, 275-276, 284
SPECULATION, 45-46, 62, 73, 90-91, 141, 151-152, 277-281, 284
SPRINKLER LEAKAGE INSURANCE, Automatic, 172
SPRUCE PRODUCTION CORPORATION, 218
STAGECOACH, Travel by, 327-328
STAMP ACT, 83, 89
STANDISH, MILES, 13
STATE BANKS (*see also* Commercial Banks), 151, 176, 236-238, 244, 275-276, 278-279, 281, 386-391
STATE BONDS, Brokers in sale of, 329
STATE CAPITALISM, Trends toward, 214
State Title and Mortgage Company, 194
STATES (*see also* United States):
Complexity of financial transactions of, 321-322
Financing of public utilities by, 211-212
Individual *Reference Books* of, 316
Interest-bearing treasury notes of, 46
Lotteries under laws of, 62
Maps of, 314
Paper money issues of, 44, 46
Tax levies in, 46

THE SINEWS OF AMERICAN COMMERCE
is set in Linotype Granjon with hand set headings in
Typo-script. The paper stock is Laid China White
Vellum. The bronze medallion on the face of the
cover was reproduced from the original plaque by
Georg Lober, N.A. The composition and press work
was done by the Printing Division of Dun & Bradstreet,
Inc., at Brooklyn, N. Y.